The Konstantinos Karamanlis Institute for Democracy Series on European and International Affairs

Series Editor

Konstantinos Karamanlis Institute for Democracy
18, Rigillis Str.
10674 Athens
Greece

For further volumes:
http://www.springer.com/series/8346

The Konstantinos Karamanlis Institute for Democracy Series on European and International Affairs consists of edited multi-author works dealing with contemporary political and socio-economic issues of European and international concern. It attempts to offer comprehensive and up-to-date accounts of the relevant debates currently taking place within the discipline of International Relations. The series is addressed to a wide audience: undergraduate and postgraduate students, scholars, think tanks and decision-makers.

Pantelis Sklias • Nikolaos Tzifakis
Editors

Greece's Horizons

Reflecting on the Country's Assets and Capabilities

Springer

KONSTANTINOS KARAMANLIS
INSTITUTE FOR DEMOCRACY

CES
CENTRE FOR EUROPEAN STUDIES

Editors
Pantelis Sklias – Nikolaos Tzifakis
Department of Political Science and International Relations
University of Peloponnese
Corinth, Greece

This is a joint publication of the Centre for European Studies and the Konstantinos Karamanlis Institute for Democracy. This publication receives funding from the European Parliament.

ISSN 1866-1270 ISSN 1867-4488 (electronic)
ISBN 978-3-642-34533-3 ISBN 978-3-642-34534-0 (eBook)
DOI 10.1007/978-3-642-34534-0
Springer Heidelberg New York Dordrecht London

Library of Congress Control Number: 2013931215

Printed on acid-free paper

Springer is part of Springer Science+Business Media (www.springer.com)

Acknowledgements

We are indebted to several people for their support in preparing this collective volume. First, we would like to thank Mariana Pirgioti, Director General of the Konstantinos Karamanlis Institute for Democracy, and Tomi Huhtanen, Director General of the Centre for European Studies, who enthusiastically embraced this project and made it part of the joint activity of their institutes. We are also grateful to *Springer* for consenting to publish this book. Katharina Wetzel-Vandai and Irene Barrios-Kežić have once again provided us the necessary support during the production phase. Furthermore, we wish to express our gratitude to the Editage team for their meticulous work in copy-editing the manuscript. Special thanks are also extended to Antonis Klapsis and Antigoni Kouvidi, our colleagues in the Konstantinos Karamanlis Institute for Democracy, who have tirelessly assisted us at different stages of this venture. Last, but not least, we are hugely indebted to the contributors of this volume, who entrusted us with their original research and inspiring ideas.

August 2012

Pantelis Sklias
Nikolaos Tzifakis

The Editors

Pantelis Sklias (1969) is a professor of International Political Economy (IPE) at the Department of Political Science and International Relations of the University of Peloponnese. He was also a visiting lecturer at the Department of International and European Studies of the University of Macedonia and visiting lecturer and assistant professor from 2002 to 2007 at the Department of International Economic Relations and Development of the Democritus University of Thrace. Since 2002, he has taught at the Hellenic Open University. He graduated in 1990 from the Department of International Studies at the Panteion University in Athens. He was awarded an MA in international relations in 1991 and a PhD in IPE in 1998 from the University of Sussex. The title of his PhD thesis was 'Non Governmental Organizations and the IPE, with special reference to the European Union's Development Policy'. In 2000, he completed his postdoctoral thesis at the Hellenic Centre of Political Research of Panteion University with a fellowship from the State Fellowship Foundation. His postdoctoral research topic was 'The IPE of the relations between the EU and the countries of Central and Eastern Europe and the ex-Soviet Union'. From 1999 to 2002, he was a visiting research fellow at the Postgraduate Centre for Culture, Development and the Environment (CDE) of the University of Sussex. His research interests include institutions, states and markets, global governance, global political and economic relations, international development, and civil society.

Nikolaos Tzifakis is an assistant professor of international relations at the Department of Political Science and International Relations of the University of Peloponnese and research associate at the Centre for European Studies in Brussels. He graduated in 1996 from the Department of Political Science and International Studies of the Panteion University in Athens. He was awarded an MA with distinction in international relations and strategic studies in 1997 and a PhD in international relations in 2002 from Lancaster University. He has been a visiting lecturer at the Department of Political Science of the University of Crete, the Department of Geography of the Harokopion University of Athens, and the School of Humanities of the Hellenic Open University. His research interests include contemporary developments in the Balkans, EU external relations, and international relations theory. His recent publications include articles in peer-reviewed journals such as *Cambridge Review of International Affairs*, *Ethnopolitics*, *European Foreign Affairs Review*, *Global Society*, *International Journal*, *Journal of Political and Military Sociology*,

Journal of Southern Europe and the Balkans, *Perspectives on European Politics and Society*, and *Southeast European and Black Sea Studies*. In 2008, he was awarded the Marcel Cadieux Distinguished Writing Award for his co-authored article with Professor Asteris Huliaras in *International Journal*.

Abbreviations

ADB	Asian Development Bank
ASEP	Supreme Council for Civil Personnel Selection
ASO	Autonomous Currant Organisation
BAP	Burgas–Alexandroupolis pipeline
BEP	Break-even point
BSEC	Organization of the Black Sea Economic Cooperation
BTC	Baku–Tbilisi–Ceyhan
CAREC	Central Asia Regional Economic Cooperation
CCS	Carbon capture and storage
CEE	Central and Eastern Europe
CHP	Combined heat and power
CSU	Christlich-Soziale Union in Bayern, Christian Social Union of Bavaria
DEPA	Public Gas Corporation
EATL	Joint Study on Developing Euro-Asian Linkages
EBRD	European Bank for Reconstruction and Development
EC	European Communities
ECB	European Central Bank
ECO	Economic Cooperation Organization
ECOFIN	Economic and Financial Affairs Council
EEC	European Economic Community
EFSF	European Financial Stability Facility
EFSM	European Financial Stabilization Mechanism
EGS	Enhanced Geothermal System
EGEC	European Geothermal Energy Consortium
EIB	European Investment Bank
EL.STAT.	Hellenic Statistical Authority
EMR	Eastern Mediterranean Region
EMU	Economic and Monetary Union
EPIA	European Photovoltaic Industry Association
ERE	Ethniki Rizospastiki Enosi, National Radical Union
ESCB	European System of Central Banks
ESM	European Stability Mechanism

ESPO	European Sea Ports Organisation
ESTIF	European Solar Thermal Industry Federation
EU	European Union
EurAsEc	Eurasian Economic Community
EUROS	European Registry
EWEA	European Wind Energy Association
FDI	Foreign direct investment
FYROM	Former Yugoslav Republic of Macedonia
GDP	Gross domestic product
GHG	Greenhouse gas
GRT	Gross registered tons
HELMEPA	Greek Marine Environment Protection Association
ICJ	International Court of Justice
IDB	Islamic Development Bank
IGB	Interconnector Greece–Bulgaria
IKA	Social Insurance Institute
ILO	International Labour Organization
IMF	International Monetary Fund
IMO	Intergovernmental Maritime Organization
INSEE	French National Institute of Statistics
IO	Implementing Organisation
IOBE	Foundation of Economic and Industrial Research
IRR	Internal rate of return
ISPFS	International Ship and Port Facility Security
ITGI	Interconnector Turkey–Greece–Italy
JPTS	Joint Permanent Technical Secretariat
LED	Light emitting diode
LTROs	Longer-term refinancing operations
MARPOL	Marine pollution
MNCs	Multinational corporations
MNEs	Multinational enterprises
MoS	Motorways of the sea
MoU	Memorandum of understanding
NATO	North Atlantic Treaty Organization
ND	New democracy
NPV	Net present value
OECD	Organization for Economic Cooperation and Development
PASOK	Pan-Hellenic Socialist Movement
PDI	Percentage difference index
PEPs	Politically exposed persons
PERS	Port environmental review system
PIDA	Programme for Infrastructure Development in Africa
PMs	Photosynthetic microbes
PPP	Public–private partnership
PSOE	Partido Socialista Obrero Español, Spanish Socialist Workers' Party

PV	Photovoltaic
SAFEMED	EuroMed Cooperation on Maritime Safety and Prevention of Pollution from Ships
SEE	South East Europe
SEEP	South East Europe Pipeline
SEZ	Special Economic Zone
SGP	Stability and growth pact
SHP	Small hydropower plants
S&P	Standard and Poor's
SOLAS	Safety of life at seas
STE	Solar thermal electricity
SYRIZA	Synaspismos Rizospastikis Aristeras, Coalition of the Radical Left
TAP	Trans Adriatic Pipeline
TEM	Trans-European North-South Motorway
TER	Trans-European Railway
TEN	Trans-European Networks
TEN-T	Trans-European Transport Networks
TMN-T	Trans-Mediterranean Transport Network
TRACECA	Transport Corridor Europe–Caucasus–Asia
UK	United Kingdom
UN	United Nations Organization
UNESCAP	United Nations Economic and Social Commission for Asia and the Pacific
UNECE	United Nations Economic Commission for Europe
UNEP	United Nations Environment Programme
USA	United States of America
WTTC	World Travel and Tourism Council
WTO	World Tourism Organization
WW II	World War II

Contents

Part III Microeconomic Sectors

List of Figures

The Greek Tourism Industry and the Challenge of the Economic Crisis

Prospects for Local Development Based on Cultural Assets/Heritage: The Residents' Perspective

Energy Resources and Their Use in Greece: Possible Paths to Future Economic Development and Sustainability

The Burgas–Alexandroupolis Pipeline: Macroeconomic Impact for Greece

List of Maps

List of Tables

Energy Resources and Their Use in Greece: Possible Paths to Future Economic Development and Sustainability

The Burgas–Alexandroupolis Pipeline: Macroeconomic Impact for Greece

The Role of Greece as a Transport Node in the South Eastern Europe

The Greek Agro-Food Industry: Regional Competitiveness in a Globalised Market

Greece's Outward FDI: A Window for Growth?

Contributors

Andreas Antoniades Department of International and European Studies, Panteion University, Athens, Greece

Aristidis P. Bitzenis Department of International and European Studies, University of Macedonia, Thessaloniki, Greece

George Galanos Department of International Economic Relations and Development, Democritus University of Thrace, Komotini, Greece

Evangelia Georgitsoyanni Department of Home Economics and Ecology, Harokopio University, Athens, Greece

Periklis Gogas Department of International Economic Relations and Development, Democritus University of Thrace, Komotini, Greece

Gregory J. Grigoropoulos Department of Naval Architecture and Marine Engineering, National Technical University of Athens, Zografou, Greece

Konstantinos J. Hazakis Department of International Economic Relations and Development, Democritus University of Thrace, Komotini, Greece

Costas Kiparissides Department of Chemical Engineering, Aristotle University of Thessaloniki, Thessaloniki, Greece

Angelos Kotios Department of International and European Studies, University of Piraeus, Piraeus, Greece

Stella Ladi Department of Political Science and History, Panteion University, Athens, Greece

Alexandra Lappa Department of Home Economics and Ecology, Harokopio University, Athens, Greece

Kostas A. Lavdas Department of Political Science, University of Crete, Rethymno, Greece

Panagiotis Liargovas Department of Economics, University of Peloponnese, Tripoli, Greece

Maria M. Mendrinou Department of International and European Studies, University of Piraeus, Piraeus, Greece

John C. Mourmouris Department of International Economic Relations and Development, Democritus University of Thrace, Komotini, Greece

Evangelia Mylona Department of Home Economics and Ecology, Harokopio University, Athens, Greece

Pyrros Papadimitriou Department of Political Science and International Relations, University of Peloponnese, Corinth, Greece

Theophilos Papadimitriou Department of International Economic Relations and Development, Democritus University of Thrace, Komotini, Greece

Manos G. Papazoglou Department of Political Science and International Relations, University of Peloponnese, Corinth, Greece

Spyridon Repousis Department of Economics, University of Peloponnese, Tripoli, Greece

Spyridon Roukanas Department of International and European Studies, University of Piraeus, Piraeus, Greece

Anna Saiti Department of Home Economics and Ecology, Harokopio University, Athens, Greece

Eleni Sardianou Department of Home Economics and Ecology, Harokopio University, Athens, Greece

Pantelis Sklias Department of Political Science and International Relations, University of Peloponnese, Corinth, Greece

Dimitrios A. Tsamboulas Department of Transportation Planning and Engineering, National Technical University of Athens, Zografou, Greece

Maria Tsampra Department of Business Administration of Food and Agricultural Enterprises, University of Western Greece, Agrinio, Greece

Aristotle Tziampiris Department of International and European Studies, University of Piraeus, Piraeus, Greece

Nikolaos Tzifakis Department of Political Science and International Relations, University of Peloponnese, Corinth, Greece

Vasileios A. Vlachos Department of International and European Studies, University of Macedonia, Thessaloniki, Greece

Beyond Nemesis and Salvation: A Reorientation of the Debate on the Greek Economic Crisis

Pantelis Sklias and Nikolaos Tzifakis

The Greek economic crisis has imperilled the stability of the eurozone, generating much global anxiety. Policymakers, analysts, and the media have daily debated the course of the Greek economy, prescribing ways to move forward. While many European decision makers have expressed faith in the country's recovery on the basis of the Second Economic Adjustment Programme and its merits, an increasing number of commentators have questioned the programme's fundamental assumption—the indispensability of austerity measures amidst the economic recession (Krugman, 2012a; Stiglitz, quoted in Moore, 2012). Some economists have insisted on the need for a European-wide approach to the crisis, with greater institutional steps towards a fiscal union (e.g. Varoufakis, in an interview, Sales, 2012). Others (predominantly German analysts and decision makers) have suggested that, at present, each country should assume primary responsibility for its own problems, so as not to encourage or reward fiscal imprudence and profligacy (e.g. Dieter, 2012). Another strand of the debate concerns Greece's future in the eurozone. Although most European decision makers tirelessly affirm that the country's membership in the European Monetary Union is not in question,[1] some analysts have predicted (and recommended) Greece's exit from the European common currency (Rogoff, in an interview, Böll & Sauga, 2012; Sinn, in an interview, Kaiser, 2012; Roubini, 2012). A few commentators even assert that the country is a 'lost cause' or 'beyond repair' (Krugman, 2012b; Feldstein, quoted in Michelson, 2012). Apparently, most pessimistic economic analyses refer to the main deficiencies of the Greek economy, namely, low competitiveness and productivity, red tape, large-scale corruption, an extensive shadow economy, and a bloated

[1] For an opposite view, see Alexander Dobrindt, General Secretary of the Christian Social Union (CSU) in Germany, quoted in Jones and Hudson (2012).

P. Sklias • N. Tzifakis (✉)
Department of Political Science and International Relations, University of Peloponnese, 47 Dervenakion St and Adimantou, Corinth 20100, Greece
e-mail: psklias@hotmail.com; tzifakis@uop.gr

P. Sklias and N. Tzifakis (eds.), *Greece's Horizons*, The Konstantinos Karamanlis Institute for Democracy Series on European and International Affairs,
DOI 10.1007/978-3-642-34534-0_1,

and inefficient public sector. More importantly, they direct attention towards the country's insufficient progress in implementing certain structural reforms.

Notwithstanding the merits of the above criticism of the Greek economy and its performance, one should not underestimate the efforts that the country and its citizens have made. Contrary to conventional wisdom, Greece ranks first among all OECD countries in terms of its responsiveness to reforms from 2008 to 2011 (OECD, 2012, 24–30). In addition, we should not lose sight of the fact that the country's authorities have taken unprecedented austerity measures and very unpopular decisions to manage the crisis. Successive cuts in salaries and pensions and recurrent increases in taxes have contributed to the reduction in fiscal deficit. According to a report of European Commission officials, Greece has, in the last 2 years, achieved a fiscal adjustment that is 'much larger than most other fiscal consolidation episodes in EU countries observed in the past' (Mors et al., 2012, 1). Indeed, a J.P. Morgan brief remarks that the limited success of the country's fiscal adjustment is because of the extreme magnitude of the Greek fiscal effort—a task further complicated by its occurrence in the context of a monetary union (Panigirtzoglou, Mac Gorain, Lehmann, & Evans, 2012, 2–3). In 2012, the Greek economy is in its fifth consecutive year of recession and has shrunk by around 15 % in the previous 4 years. Unemployment has risen from 8.3 % in 2008 to 22.6 % in the first quarter of 2012 (EL.STAT, 2008, 2012). Tens of thousands of small and medium enterprises have closed down and poverty is widespread and endemic. Goldman Sachs (2012) reports a 23 % reduction in the average labour cost since mid-2010 and concludes that the 'Greek economy has adjusted more than the market has given it credit for'.

Many criticisms of the Greek economic performance have been fair and to some extent well deserved. The main causes of the crisis are indeed domestic, and Greece itself is primarily responsible for its macroeconomic problems. However, the constant reproduction of negative discourses has, in time, led to their transformation into negative stereotypes and, in the words of Andreas Antoniades (see next chapter), into 'negative signifiers'. The Greek people have been commonly presented as corrupted, lazy, unreliable, and feckless. A few very pejorative analyses have gone so far as to depict Greece as a 'junkie' (Geert Wilders quoted in *DutchNews.nl,* 2011). As a Romanian commentator explains, 'According to the myth that accompanies these portrayals, national vices are at the origin of the crisis that has engulfed the European project' (Stoiciu, 2012). In other words, searching for simplistic monocausal explanations is frequently more attractive than striving to unravel a far more complex picture involving several factors (both domestic and international). In this context, a few very interesting grassroots public diplomacy campaigns, such as 'Give Greece a Chance', 'Repo(we)r Greece', and 'We are all Greeks', have been launched with the aim of challenging the misperceptions about the country.

This book analyses the main causes of the crisis and assesses the efficiency of the fiscal consolidation policies followed so far. However, it proceeds further. It attempts to stimulate discussion on the country's development model and long-term prospects. It goes beyond the immediate management of the crisis and it debates on Greece's assets and capabilities which may propel the return to sustainable growth and prosperity. It endeavours to raise those issues that will preoccupy the country once the austerity-first policies come full circle. This is all the more important as the success of these policies will most likely depend on the extent to which they are embedded within a broader strategic vision for the country. Hence, this collection of essays seeks to provide motivation and inspiration for change by indicating some of the economic sectors where Greece maintains a comparative advantage.

The book is loosely divided into three parts. The first part discusses the political dimensions of the crisis. It explores the impact of the financial crisis on Greece's image and influence in the international system and it analyses various aspects of the country's political-administrative outlook. While taking note of the international consolidation of a negative image of the country, it highlights Greece's persistent Europeanisation and unchanged foreign policy orientation and prescribes new directions and initiatives for the country's external relations. Moreover, it discusses the political factors that caused the crisis and presents some ideas on the reform of Greece's leadership and policymaking models. The second part focuses on the macroeconomic framework of the crisis and analyses the policies followed so far at both the national and eurozone levels. It discusses the major deficiencies in the management of the crisis and offers some ideas for increasing the efficiency of Greek policies and improving the governance of the eurozone. The third and final part focuses on microeconomic concerns. It explores the potential for revival offered by sectors such as shipping, tourism, and agriculture and presents the advantages of certain economic policies, such as investments in renewable energy, the construction of the Burgas-Alexandroupolis Pipeline, and the creation of a special economic zone (SEZ) in Thrace.

The first chapter examines how the international press has portrayed the Greek economic crisis. Andreas Antoniades undertakes a systematic study of the reporting of the crisis by daily newspapers in eleven countries from September 2009 to October 2010. The author observes the gradual consolidation of a very negative portrayal of the country at the international level. He analyses these negative discourses on Greece and concludes that only time and considerable effort on the part of the country can reverse this negative representation.

In the next chapter, Aristotle Tziampiris assesses how the economic crisis has affected Greece's foreign policy priorities. The author demonstrates that the country's geographical position and its participation in Euro-Atlantic institutions have contributed to preserving much of its influence on crucial external relations issues. The chapter claims that Greece's foreign policy might even prove to have been an underutilised asset in the country's return to growth strategies, if opportunities are exploited in the construction of regional networks for the transportation of energy resources and in bilateral relations with countries such as Israel, Russia, and China.

Kostas Lavdas and Maria Mendrinou investigate whether Greece's Europeanisation is a failed project. The authors observe that although Greece's European orientation commenced as an elite-driven mission, it has in time evolved into a widespread and enduring process. This is best manifested in the attitudes of the Greeks towards the Union and in the country's extent of compliance with the

EU legislation. The chapter suggests that Greece's Europeanisation is a persistent and interactive process whose prospects will be eventually determined by the complex interplay of domestic and European developments.

The chapter by Manos Papazoglou examines the responsibility of the country's leadership for the many dysfunctions of the state and economy since the restoration of democracy in 1974. It notes the prevalence in the 1980s of the model of transactional leadership, based on populism, clientelism, and polarisation. Although subsequent governments initiated some reforms, their results were modest at best and did not affect the clientelistic and populist networks. The author argues that adherence to a model of transforming leadership, revolving around sustainability, Europeanisation, and political stability, will facilitate the country's return to prosperity.

Stella Ladi focuses on policymaking in Greece. She shows that these processes are best explained, both theoretically and empirically, by the incremental and garbage can models. A central feature of the country's policymaking is the predominance of patronage and legalism at the expense of expertise and best practices. Ladi contends that the introduction of the evidence-based model of policymaking in the Greek political-administrative system might be beneficial—given the country's high level of human capital—if it is done carefully and with the full support of the government.

In the next chapter, Panagiotis Liargovas and Spyridon Repousis argue that Greece's current policy mix, based on austerity, generates recession and renders fiscal targets elusive. The authors assert that Greece should follow a different set of policies, focusing on the attainment of growth and stimulation of supply. They advocate a series of structural reforms, emphasising the need to combat corruption and fraud in both the public and private sectors, through the implementation of certain measures.

Angelos Kotios and Spyridon Roukanas discuss the continuing mismanagement of the Greek economic crisis, pointing to both the ineffectiveness of domestic policies and the deficiencies in the eurozone's governance. The authors claim that overcoming the crisis requires the adoption of different policies at two levels. For Greece, its economy and political system require a broad set of structural reforms. At the eurozone level, the authors advocate a more centralised crisis management, through the establishment of permanent transfer mechanisms of funds and the creation of a European Banking Union.

Pyrros Papadimitriou observes that policies in the eurozone have so far fought the symptoms of the crisis but not its root causes. In particular, these policies have not effectively addressed the problems of unsustainable debt burdens and the deteriorating competitiveness of some eurozone members. The European approach to the crisis has hitherto been in terms of south Europe making adjustments rather than in terms of a common convergence endeavour by the north and south. The author thinks that overcoming the crisis will require creditor countries to assume a much larger share of its cost.

The contribution of Gregory Grigoropoulos explains the role of the shipping sector in the Greek economy. It notes that this sector constitutes the largest source, after exports, of foreign currency for the country and provides employment to thousands of people. However, although Greek ship owners control around 15 % of the world transport capacity, the country does not take advantage of shipping's full potential contribution towards economic development. Grigoropoulos recommends that Greece should improve its ship management and operations infrastructure and provide incentives to ship owners to increase investment in the country's shipping sector.

The next chapter, by George Galanos, deals with the contribution of tourism to the Greek economy. This sector generates more than 15 % of the country's GDP and employs more than 18 % of its workforce. The author analyses the development of tourism in Greece and highlights the fact that the expansion of this sector has been unorganised and un-co-ordinated and has progressed with little regard for the environment. The chapter explains the negative impact of the crisis on tourism and recommends its re-organisation, on the basis of a new model of sustainable development that will emphasise the improvement of infrastructure and establishment of a new investment framework.

Evangelia Georgitsoyanni, Eleni Sardianou, Alexandra Lappa, and Evangelia Mylona investigate how Greece's rich cultural heritage can contribute to its development. They study the theme of cultural tourism and demonstrate its potential for generating sustainable economic activity for the benefit of local communities in different regions of the country. The authors use the municipality of Sikyon as their case study and highlight the critical role of local residents in developing cultural tourism. If the local community has a positive perception of tourism, it will invest in associated activities and will support Greece's overall efforts to take advantage of its cultural heritage.

The chapter by Anna Saiti explains the relationship between education and economic development and notes the benefits to society from substantial investments in higher education. Saiti asserts that the Greek education system is suffering from a chronic crisis, not remedied by the state's ceaseless corrective interventions. The chapter argues the need to introduce long-term strategic planning in the country's education system to increase its efficiency and improve the quality of human capital.

Costas Kiparissides advocates the need of embedding the Greek development model into energy-conservation policies; he includes higher energy conversion efficiency, recycling, and increased use of renewable energy technologies. The author expresses concern about the country's high dependence on energy imports and its reliance on coal-fired power plants, which generate large quantities of greenhouse gas emissions. Kiparissides suggests that Greece should exploit more of its renewable energy potential (especially wind and solar power), in order to benefit in terms of growth, competitiveness, and job creation.

The contribution of Periklis Gogas and Theophilos Papadimitriou focuses on a specific investment project in the energy sector that has not materialised so far, namely, the construction of the Burgas-Alexandroupolis Pipeline. According to plans, this proposed pipeline will transport crude oil from the Black and Caspian Seas to the international markets. The authors analytically demonstrate the financial viability of the project and its positive macroeconomic impact at both the national and the local levels, predominantly in terms of employment and government revenues.

In the next chapter, John Mourmouris investigates the impact of investments in transportation infrastructure on the stimulation of growth. The chapter challenges the widely held view that there is a straightforward causal relationship between these two factors. Mourmouris explains that transport investments do not necessarily trigger new productive activities and discusses some examples of failures and deficiencies in recent investments in Greek transportation infrastructure. Overall, the chapter contends that Greece should adopt a regional development plan which considers its economic needs.

The chapter by Dimitrios Tsamboulas discusses Greece's role in the regional transportation networks from a geopolitical perspective. Tsamboulas presents the planning of different projects in which Greece participates, for example, the trans-European transport network (TEN-T), the so-called Motorways of the Sea; Trans-Mediterranean Transport Network (TMN-T); Black Sea Ring Highway, Trans African Network, and a series of Euro-Asia links. The author concludes that if Greece takes advantage of the opportunities provided in the creation and extension of these networks, it can evolve into a regional transport node.

Maria Tsampra examines the prospects for the Greek agricultural sector in the contemporary globalised market, in which there is a rising demand for traditional region-specific food products characterised by high safety, quality, and diversity. The author outlines the main characteristics of the Greek agro-food sector, indicating its fragmented entrepreneurship, the prevalence of independently owned small-scale production units, and its orientation towards the domestic market. Tsampra suggests that some Greek agro-food firms could exploit opportunities in the international market for niche or specialty production, if they received more institutional support and access to marketing expertise and financing.

The contribution from Konstantinos Hazakis observes the growing influence of SEZs worldwide and proposes the creation of such a zone in Thrace. The chapter draws on the experience of similar zones elsewhere to identify the possible key obstacles in their creation in Greece. Hazakis asserts that an SEZ can act as 'a catalyst of structural shift' in Thrace and articulates a set of guidelines which might increase the zone's creation spillover effects over the regional economy.

Finally, Aristidis Bitzenis and Vasileios Vlachos examine the prospects for the Greek outward foreign direct investments (FDIs) in the Balkans. The two authors provide a theoretical analysis of the benefits a country acquires from its outward FDIs, including, among others, the repatriation of profits and the growth of employment and the enhancement of human capital in the regions of origin of investments. The authors argue that though the sovereign debt crisis at home has seriously weakened the resources of most Greek multinationals in the Balkans, yet preserving most outward FDIs is crucial for stimulating economic growth in the country.

Taken as a whole, this collection of essays progressively moves from an analysis of the causes of the crisis and the policy responses so far to a debate on some of the country's advantages and capabilities that should underpin its new development model and propel the return to growth. Therefore, the book challenges the picture of Greece as a country doomed to failure, where everything falls apart.

References

Böll, S., & Sauga, M. (2012, February 20). US economist Kenneth Rogoff 'Germany has been the winner in the globalization process'. *Der Spiegel*. http://www.spiegel.de/international/business/us-economist-kenneth-rogoff-germany-has-been-the-winner-in-the-globalization-process-a-816071.html. Accessed 10 July 2012.

Dieter, H. (2012). Why Merkel won't bail out the profligate. *The World Today, 68*(5), 27–29.

DutchNews.nl. (2011, May 19). *Liberal MP and Wilders clash over support for Greece*. http://www.dutchnews.nl/news/archives/2011/05/vvd_leader_and_wilders_clash_o.php. Accessed 10 July 2012.

EL.STAT. (2008, June 19). Labour force survey (1st quarter 2008). *Press Release*. National Statistical Service of Greece. http://www.statistics.gr/portal/page/portal/ESYE/BUCKET/A0101/PressReleases/A0101_SJO01_DT_QQ_01_2008_01_F_EN.pdf. Accessed 10 July 2012.

EL.STAT. (2012, June 14). Labour force survey (1st quarter 2012). *Press Release*. Hellenic Statistical Authority. http://www.statistics.gr/portal/page/portal/ESYE/BUCKET/A0101/PressReleases/A0101_SJO01_DT_QQ_01_2012_01_F_EN.pdf. Accessed 10 July 2012.

Goldman Sachs. (2012, June 11). Greek economy has adjusted more than the market has given it credit for. *Global Markets Daily*.

Jones, G., & Hudson, A. (2012, July 23). Greece should pay wages in Drachmas: German MP. *Reuters*. http://www.reuters.com/article/2012/07/23/us-germany-greece-idUSBRE86M07J20120723. Accessed 23 July 2012.

Kaiser, S. (2012, February 20). Top German economist 'restructuring Greece within the Euro is illusory'. *Spiegel Online*. http://www.spiegel.de/international/europe/top-german-economist-restructuring-greece-within-the-euro-is-illusory-a-816410.html. Accessed 10 July 2012.

Krugman, P. (2012a, March 11). What Greece means. *The New York Times*. http://www.nytimes.com/2012/03/12/opinion/krugman-what-greece-means.html. Accessed 10 July 2012.

Krugman, P. (2012b, June 24). The great abdication. *The New York Times*. http://www.nytimes.com/2012/06/25/opinion/krugman-the-great-abdication.html. Accessed 10 July 2012.

Michelson, R. (2012, June 8). 'Greece is beyond repair': Harvard professor. *CNBC News*. http://www.cnbc.com/id/47722040. Accessed 10 July 2012.

Moore, M. (2012, January 17). Stiglitz says European austerity plans are a 'suicide pact'. *The Telegraph*. http://www.telegraph.co.uk/finance/financialcrisis/9019819/Stiglitz-says-European-austerity-plans-are-a-suicide-pact.html. Accessed 10 July 2012.

Mors, M., Astra, Z., Cardoso, P., Carone, G., Christensen, J. E., Dionyssopoulou, F., et al. (2012, March). *The second economic adjustment programme for Greece, March 2012* (Occasional Papers, 94). Brussels: Directorate-General for Economic and Financial Affairs, European Commission.

OECD. (2012). *Economic policy reforms 2012: Going for growth*. Paris: OECD Publishing.

Panigirtzoglou, N., Mac Gorain, S., Lehmann, M., & Evans, L. (2012). *Global asset allocation: Flows & liquidity*. London: J.P. Morgan Securities Ltd.

Roubini, N. (2012, May 17). Greece must exit. *Project Syndicate*. http://www.project-syndicate.org/commentary/greece-must-exit. Accessed 10 July 2012.

Sales, L. (2012, June 18). Greek election holds questions for economy and eurozone. *ABC News* (Australia). http://www.abc.net.au/7.30/content/2012/s3527981.htm. Accessed 10 July 2012.

Stoiciu, V. (2012, February 13). Lazy Greeks, a neo-liberal cliché. *Presseurop*. http://www.presseurop.eu/en/content/article/1506361-lazy-greeks-neo-liberal-cliche. Accessed 10 July 2012.

Part I

Political Dimensions of the Crisis

At the Eye of the Cyclone: The Greek Crisis in Global Media

Andreas Antoniades

This chapter aims to assess the impact that the Greek economic crisis has had on the image of Greece at the international level. With this aim in view, it analyses the nature and evolution of, and the dominant themes in, the European and international media discourses on the Greek crisis. I examine the defining elements of the current international image of Greece, the rationales underlying these elements, and how widespread these elements are. Through this analysis, I trace and analyse the similarities and differences in the manner in which the different national and regional public discourses portrayed the Greek economic crisis. Thereby, I hope to contribute to a systematic analysis of how Greece is viewed *from the outside* as a result of its economic crisis.

This chapter focuses on 11 countries: the UK, Germany, France, Spain, Poland, the USA, China, India, Japan, Korea, and Singapore. In each of these countries, we use the national political newspaper (broadsheet) with the highest circulation as a representation (if partial) of public discourse. For France, we have analysed the newspaper *Le Figaro*; for Spain, the newspaper *El Pais*; for Poland, the *Gazeta Wyborcza*; for India, *The Times of India*; and for Singapore, *The Straits Times*. In the case of Germany we have analysed the newspaper *Die Zeit*, which, although is the highest in circulation among broadsheets, is published on a weekly rather than daily, basis. For thc UK and the USA, we have used *The Times* and *The New York Times* respectively. These have the second highest

---

This chapter draws from a large research project that was conducted by the Athens Centre for International Political Economy at the Institute of International Relations in Athens. The complete results are available in Greek at the following electronic address: http://www.idis.gr/acipe/#5. The author would like to thank all the trainee researchers involved in the project. Thanks are also due to the Centre for Global Political Economy at the University of Sussex and the Hellenic Observatory at the London School of Economics for their valuable research support.

A. Antoniades (✉)
Department of International and European Studies, Panteion University, 136 Syngrou Avenue, Athens 17671, Greece, and Department of International Relations, University of Sussex, UK
e-mail: A.A.Antoniades@sussex.ac.uk

P. Sklias and N. Tzifakis (eds.), *Greece's Horizons*, The Konstantinos Karamanlis Institute for Democracy Series on European and International Affairs,
DOI 10.1007/978-3-642-34534-0_2,

circulations in their respective countries. However, according to most analysts, they provide a better representation of the public discourse of their countries as compared to the *Daily Telegraph* and the *USA Today*, which are the highest circulating dailies in the UK and USA respectively. For China, we have used the 'official' party newspaper that is published in English, the *Daily China*. For Japan, we have analysed the English edition of the Japanese newspaper with the highest circulation, *The Daily Yomiuri*. For Korea, we have used *The Korea Times*, the highest circulating English daily in the country.

Of course, no single newspaper (even one with the highest circulation) can offer an accurate and complete reflection of the public discourse in a country. This is more so, if we consider the fact that a newspaper not only reflects, but also attempts to shape/construct the domestic public agenda and public discourse. Yet, a systematic analysis of the manner in which the highest circulating newspaper of any country covers and frames the emergence of any given issue, is able to offer us important information regarding a significant part of the public discourse of that country. Thus, although partial, the information gained from the analysis of high-circulation newspapers is important in its own right, especially in a comparative cross-national research framework, as the one employed here.

Finally, the analysis of this chapter focuses broadly on the first year of the Greek economic crisis, and in particular on the period between September 2009 and October 2010. Broadly speaking, this period covers the six months before and after the decision of the Greek government to officially request financial support from the European Union (EU) and the International Monetary Fund (IMF) (the official Greek request for the activation of an EU/IMF rescue package was made on 23 April 2010). The aim of this chapter is to examine how the international press viewed and covered the build-up towards the official Greek request for financial support, how it reacted to the decision of the EU/IMF to offer a rescue package to Greece, and the impact that these developments had on the international image of Greece.

1 Greece Moves to Centre Stage in the Brave New Debt World

This part of the chapter presents and analyses the aggregate quantitative data on the emergence, evolution, and characteristics of the discourse on the Greek crisis in the eleven international newspapers examined (hereafter referred to as the 'press sample').

Figure 1 presents a time series of the total number of articles/references to the Greek crisis. It is clear that Greece came on the radar of the global media in December 2010. A number of interesting observations were made about this initial stage of the Greek crisis.

As expected, 85 % of articles from December are from the European press. There is, however, a difference in emphasis on the Greek issue between Western Europe on the one hand, and Central and Eastern Europe (CEE) on the other.

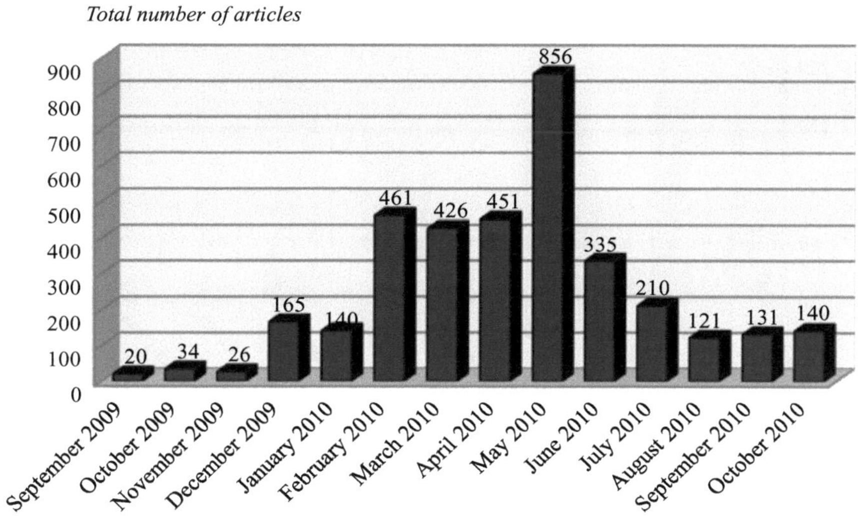

Fig. 1 Number of articles with reference to Greek politico-economic developments. Articles from the following newspapers have been included: *Gazeta Wyborcza, Daily China, Die Zeit, El Pais, Le Figaro, The Daily Yomiuri, The Times of India, The New York Times, The Korea Times, The Straits Times, and The Times*

The latter is seen to be less concerned with the developments in Greece. Figure 2 demonstrates that the relevant references in the Polish *Gazeta Wyborcza* in December add up to only about two-thirds of those occurring in any of the West European dailies in our press sample. There is also a considerable discourse on Greece in *The New York Times* (lower in intensity but close to that of the Polish newspaper), as well as in the *China Daily* (one-fourth of the West European average). Yet, in the period before the agreement for the bailout, the attention of the international press reaches its peak in February 2010, when, with the exception of the Japanese newspaper, there is a substantial number of references to Greece in all the examined newspapers.

Why do December 2009 and February 2010 appear as turning points for the international press' discourse on the Greek crisis? Why is the number of references to Greece in February 2010 greater than in March or April, when we have the build-up towards and the request for a rescue package? It is indeed very difficult to establish firm causal links with regard to the above questions, especially taking into consideration the cross-national approach of the present research. Yet, on 30 November, 2009, the EU's Economic and Financial Affairs Council (ECOFIN) expressed concerns with respect to the Greek debt, and the Greek prime minister stated that the 'Greek economy is in intensive care'. On December 8, the rating agency Fitch downgraded Greece's credit rating from an A− to a BBB+. On December 14, the government announced measures that aimed to cut the budget deficit by 4 % within a year, and this triggered massive strikes and demonstrations. On December 16, the rating agency Standard and Poor's (S&P) downgraded Greece

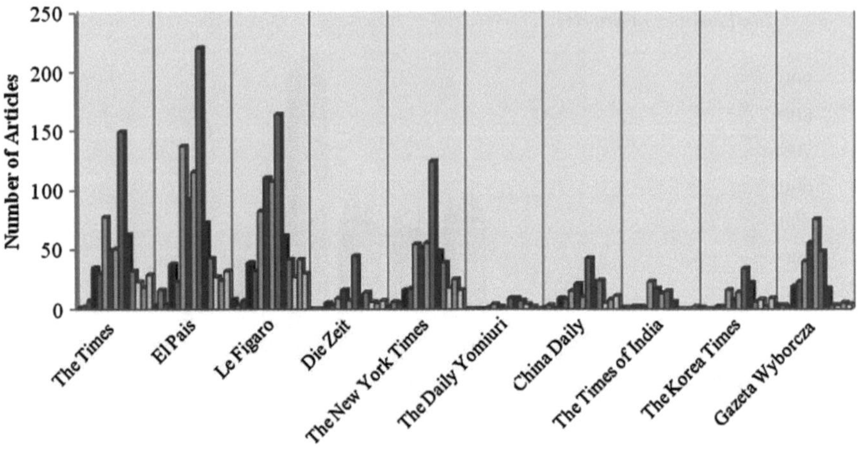

Fig. 2 Number of articles per month that refer to Greek politico-economic developments, during the period September 2009 to October 2010. *Die Zeit* is a weekly newspaper (i.e. the above numbers refer to one paper per week, not seven, as in all other newspapers in this sample). *The Straits Times* is excluded from the above Figure because we have no systematic data for the period May–October 2010

from an A− to a BBB−. Shortly thereafter, on December 19, the spread between the Greek and German 10-year bonds rose to an eight-month high, at 2.72 %. Following Fitch and S&P, on December 22, the rating agency Moody's downgraded Greece from A1 to A2. Thus, it is clear that in December, the Greek economy and its debt came increasingly under the spotlight at the European level. It is also in this month that the Greek prime minister described the Greek economic situation in dramatic terms. Moreover, the three dominant credit rating agencies downgraded Greece's creditworthiness, pushing Greece further towards the centre stage of the global economic crisis. Finally, the economic measures and cuts announced by the Greek government triggered domestic reactions that attracted serious international attention. These dynamics account for the shift in the international press discourse on the Greek crisis that we observe in this month.

The second peak in the pre-rescue package period is February 2010. It can be argued that the key issue in understanding the 'eruption' of the international interest in Greece in February is not what happened in that month, but rather, what had not happened. February seems to represent the peak of uncertainty with regard to what was going to happen in Greece. On February 3, the European Commission approved the Greek Stability Programme, but the caveats linked to its approval increased the uncertainty regarding whether this programme was going to deliver on its aims. On February 11, the German Chancellor opposed a Greek bailout and stated that Greece must deal with its own problems itself. In essence, during this month, Greece failed to receive any credible (re)assurances at the European level that the EU or Eurozone member-states would step in to support Greece, should there be a problem with its debt refinancing. Rather, the opposite happened. The European leaders at all levels (both EU and domestic), through their public statements and pronouncements, increased the uncertainty about what was going on and what could happen regarding the 'Greek issue'. That is why this month functioned as both a turning point and as a peak in the first phase of the Greek crisis. Once this uncertainty started gradually dissolving at the European level and the idea and modalities of the 'rescue mechanism' started being negotiated, the intensity of the international discourse on the Greek crisis lessened. This does not mean that the Greek issue left centre stage. Rather, the opposite. From February onwards, and at least up to June, Greece continued to be at the centre of global interest.

May 2010 represents an absolute peak in the international discourse on the Greek crisis, during the period under examination (see Fig. 1). The degree of European and international attention on Greece in this month is indeed astonishing. With the exception of *The Times of India* and *The Daily Yomiuri* (Japan), all newspapers in our press sample published more than one article with reference to Greece per day (at least on average). For example, *El Pais* published 221 articles, *Le Figaro* 165 articles, *The New York Times* 125 articles, the *Gazeta Wyborcza* 49 articles, and *The Korea Times* 34 articles. The events that took place in May 2010 are equally telling. Among others, the Eurogroup and the IMF approved €80 billion and €30 billion loans respectively for Greece; the European Central Bank stated that Greek bonds would be accepted as collaterals regardless of their low credit rating (May 3); the S&P, and later Fitch, downgraded Greece's creditworthiness. There were massive anti-austerity demonstrations in Greece during which three people died (May 5), the Greek parliament approved new austerity measures (May 6), and the EU reached an agreement for the creation of European financial stability mechanisms with a firepower of €500 billion.

After May, the number of references to Greece in the international press decline significantly. Yet, the discourse on the Greek crisis remains vividly present in the international media. Interestingly, a qualitative change in the content of this discourse seems to have taken place after May 2010. In particular, the spotlight seems to move gradually from Greece onto the EU. That is, the focus at that point was not on what was happening in Greece, but what the EU was doing to deal with it, as well as what it was doing to deal with the European debt crisis in general. Yet, towards the end of this period, there again seems to have been a slight but gradual increase in the references to Greece, which signifies that Greece was moving anew to the centre of the global media radar.

2 From Iris to Eris: The Media's Stance Towards Greece

Having discussed how the number of references changed with time, we should now focus on the stance taken by the international newspapers towards Greece. In what follows, I attempt to assess the various attitudes (positive, negative, neutral) that are evident in the discourse on Greece in our press sample. For instance, an article that focuses on the British economy in *The Times* may present Greece

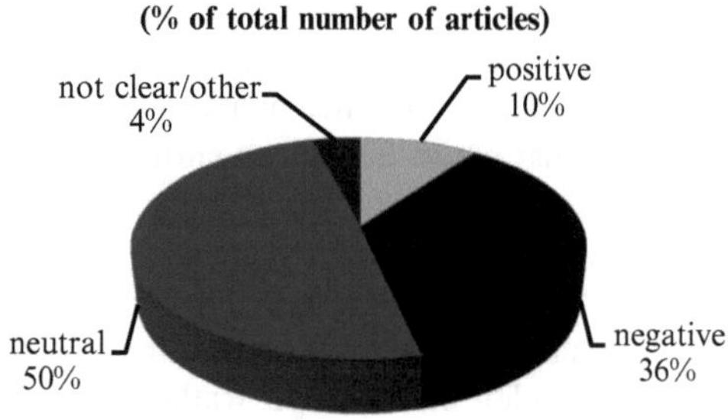

Fig. 3 The stance of the international press towards Greece

as an 'example to avoid'. I take this to be part of the discourse of that particular newspaper on the Greek crisis. Moreover, I consider such less explicit instances of the discourse on Greece to be sine qua non for understanding and deciphering the actual characteristics of the international discourse on the Greek crisis and its implications for the international image of Greece.

Figure 3 displays the percentage figures for the different attitudes to Greece in all the articles that have been examined. It is clear that the majority of articles/references refer to the Greek crisis in a rather descriptive manner, without making any explicit or implicit value judgements (at least those that are easily discernible). These constitute 54 % of the total number of articles. Yet, besides these descriptive (i.e. purely informative) references, a large number of articles produce or reproduce negative/adverse comments, opinions, or analyses on Greece. These constitute 36 % of the total number of references, a figure that clearly surpasses the figure for positive references, which amount to only 10 % of the total. In order to place these numbers in context, we should remember that in the framework of public diplomacy, countries hire specialised public relations companies that attempt to get a few positive/negative articles published in the major media outlets. In this case, we discern substantial (in terms of high numbers, consistency, and duration) negative reporting on Greece in most international media over most of the 14-month period under examination. Clearly, this negative media blitz cannot but have had a substantially damaging effect on the international image of Greece. In other words, this negative media blitz not only reflected but also generated entrenched negative attitudes and connotations, not only among political elites outside Greece but also among the general public across the globe.

Besides these aggregate figures, it is also interesting to examine how the stance of the international press towards Greece evolved over time. In this regard, Fig. 4 suggests that the decision of the EU and the IMF to offer financial support to Greece had a moderating impact on the value judgements on Greece. Thus, after the bailout agreement we observe a decline in the amount of both negative and positive references and an increase in 'neutral coverage' with regard to the Greek crisis. Noticeably, the reduction of 'negative reporting' is more significant than that of 'positive reporting', even though the negative reporting continued to remain at a rather high level.

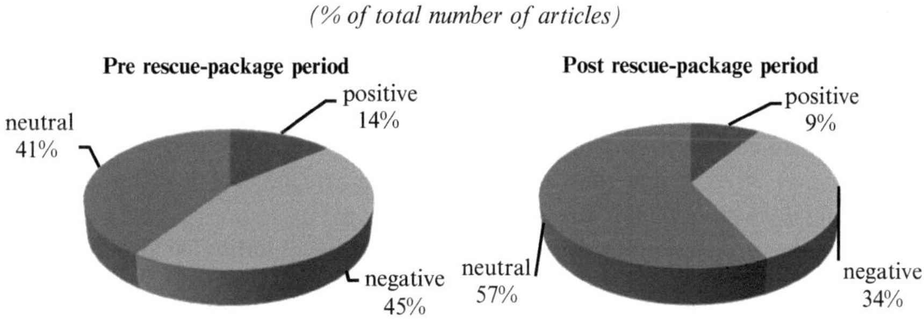

Fig. 4 Stance towards Greece before and after the EU/IMF rescue package

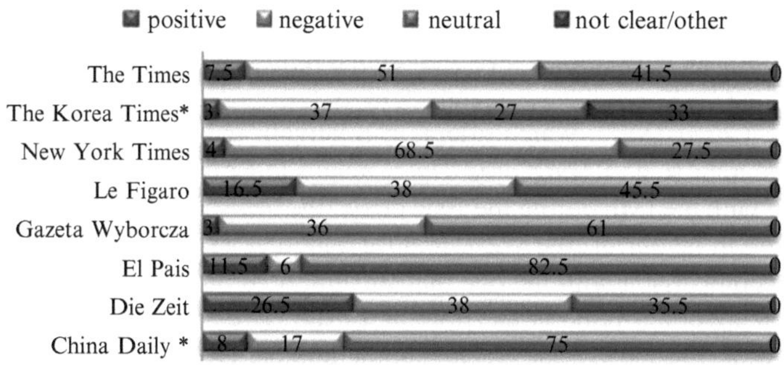

Fig. 5 Stance towards Greece in each newspaper. In the cases of *The Korea Times and China Daily*, the results refer only to the period May–October 2010

Figure 5 disaggregates the above findings, providing data on the attitude to Greece for each newspaper.[1] Interestingly, the most negative discourse was generated in the Anglo-Saxon newspapers, the *New York Times* and *The Times*, where the negative references constitute more than half of their respective total number of references. This is rather unexpected given the fact that the two newspapers occupy different ends in the political spectrum (*The Times* centre-right; *the New York Times* centre-left). It is also worth underscoring, however, that the percentage of negative references found in the *New York Times* is significantly higher than those found in *The Times*. This fact may point to a difference in view between the two sides of the Atlantic, which surpasses the broader Anglo-Saxon/Continental dichotomy.

In the continental European press, the negative reporting approaches 40 %. Moreover, there is no considerable difference in the articulation of the discourse

[1] In each of these newspapers, different authors have adopted different stances towards Greece. The term 'newspaper stance' is used for convenience and signifies only whether the majority of the references to Greece in each newspaper are positive, negative, or neutral.

on Greece between the West European press on the one hand and the Central and East European press on the other. The only exception is the Spanish *El Pais*, which adopts an overwhelmingly neutral approach. Indeed, *El Pais* is the only newspaper in our sample in which the positive references exceed the negative ones; a 'deviation' that may be partly explained by the ideological stance of the newspaper. Yet, the deviation is so strong that it should be taken to indicate a different South European perspective on the Greek crisis.

The picture is different if one focuses on the positive reporting on Greece. In this regard the highest percentage of positive references is found in the German *Die Zeit* (26.5 %), followed by the French *Le Figaro* (16.5 %) and the Spanish *El Pais* (11.5 %). Arguably, *Die Zeit*, following its tradition that favours moderation and an in-depth analysis of contested issues, was consciously attempting to construct a more balanced approach to the German public discourse, which was dominated by an excessively negative reporting on Greece.

The difference between the two East Asian newspapers is also interesting. The discourse in *The Korea Times* is considerably more negative in comparison with that in the *China Daily*, which adopts a relatively more neutral approach. The opinionated approach of *The Korea Times* relates to Korea's own experience of its interaction with the IMF during the Asia crisis (the newspaper criticises the IMF for being biased in favour of 'the West' and for adopting a much softer programme in Greece, in comparison with the one that was imposed on Korea).

Another important issue is the framing of the Greek crisis. Is the Greek crisis discussed as a 'European issue' related to the broader issues of European concern? Is the Greek crisis discussed as an international issue related to the global economic crisis? Alternatively, is the Greek crisis used to discuss domestic issues or problems? Based on these three questions, one can discern three different framings in the discourse on the Greek crisis. First, the 'European' framing, where the Greek crisis is discussed as a European issue that is related to broader issues of European (economic) governance. Second, there is the 'global' framing, where the Greek crisis is used as a means to discuss the global economic crisis and issues of global governance. Third, there is the 'domestic' framing, where the Greek crisis is used as a means to discuss domestic affairs (in each country). Figure 6 presents the respective findings.

Analysing the different framings of the Greek crisis is important in order to understand the diverse nature and characteristics of the discourse on the Greek crisis across different countries and regions. In general, the European and the US press adopt a 'European frame' in their analysis. The Greek crisis is approached as a European issue that needs to be dealt with by Europe, and which has repercussions on Europe itself. This frame is particularly strong in the case of the Polish newspaper *Gazeta Wyborcza* (69 % of the articles). This may point to a distinctive CEE perspective on the role of the EU in the economic crisis (of course to the degree to which the Polish newspaper can be viewed as representative of CEE attitudes). Particularly, the 'deviation' of the Polish newspaper from the European average may be explained by the different experience of the CEE countries from the current international financial crisis, as well as their very different experience during their

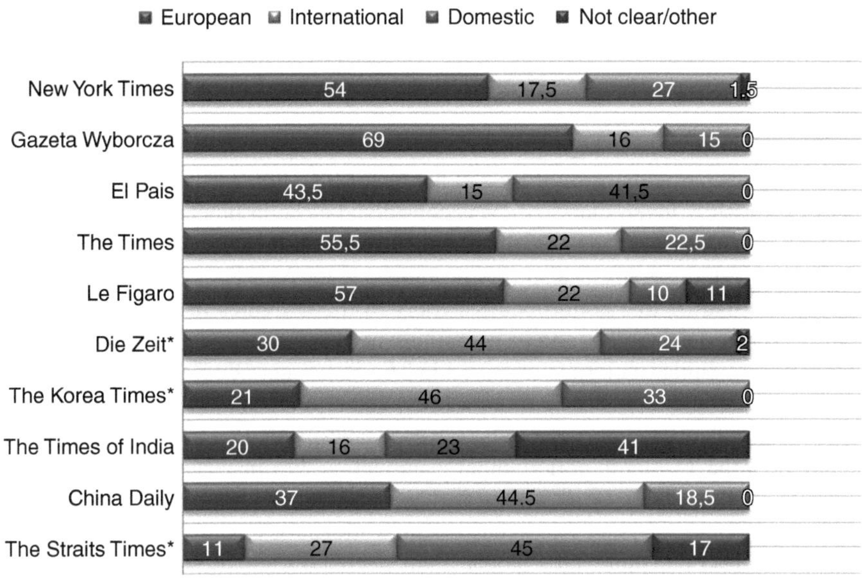

Fig. 6 The framing of the Greek crisis in each newspaper. In the case of The Times of India, The Korea Times, and Die Zeit the results refer only to the period May–October 2010. In the case of The Straits Times, the results refer only to the period September 2009–April 2010

'transition to capitalism' and their perception of the role that the EU (member states and institutions) played in these processes.

The same frame also dominates the reporting in the *Le Figaro*, *The Times*, *The New York Times*, and the *El Pais*. They all approach the Greek crisis as a 'European news item' and criticise the inability of the EU, its institutions and its member states, to take effective and resolute action that would solve the crisis (also see below). The only 'western' newspaper that takes a different stance is *Die Zeit*. Despite its balanced approach towards Greece, the German newspaper seems to approach the Greek crisis not so much through a 'European' but through a 'global' frame. Indeed, in this regard, the approach taken by *Die Zeit* seems to be closer to the approach taken by the *China Daily* and *The Korea Times*, rather than that of the other European newspapers.

With regard to Asia, there seems to be a divergence in the perspectives from China and India. Indeed, *The Times of India* is the only Asian newspaper in our sample that favours a 'European' frame, whereas the *China Daily*, *The Korea Times*, and *The Strait Times* (Singapore) favour a 'global' frame in their analysis of the Greek crisis. Equally interesting is the fact that in all Asian newspapers in our sample there is also a very strong 'domestic' frame. In these, the context and main concern of the many articles that refer to the Greek crisis is the possible main repercussions of the Greek crisis in their countries (i.e. how these countries are and will be affected by the crisis), and how their countries resemble or differ from Greece. As analysed below, a great part of the negative discourse on Greece is developed in this context, where Greece is presented as an 'example to avoid'. It is also worth noticing that in *The Times of India* and *The Strait Times* (Singapore), this domestic frame is stronger in comparison to both the European and the global frame.

The domestic frame holds, indeed, an important place in all the newspapers examined. Its particular prominence in the Spanish *El Pais* (41.5 % of the articles) is not surprising, given that Spain was considered close in line, after Greece, for a bailout, and the issue 'why Spain is not Greece' dominated the Spanish public discourse. Yet, this frame is also very prominent in the *New York Times* (27 % of the articles), a finding that confirms the anxiety of the US elites regarding the Greek (and European) debt crisis, and its potentially negative impact on the US and global economy. A similar pattern is observed in *The Times* and *Die Zeit*. In contrast, the view from Poland seems to be more relaxed and removed.

Yet, the balance between the frames in each newspaper does not remain the same throughout the 14-month period under examination. For instance, after the bailout agreement, the *China Daily* seems to have changed its approach considerably, putting more emphasis on the domestic implications for China. Thus, the percentage of articles that employed a global frame declined from 56 % in the first period (September 2009–April 2010) to 33 % in the second period (May–October 2010), while those employing a domestic frame increased from 6 % to 33 % in the second period. A similar pattern is observed in *El Pais* and *Gazeta Wyborcza*. In the former, the articles employing a domestic frame increased from 36 % in the first period to 47 % in the second period, and in the latter, the increase was from 10 % to 20 %. Interestingly, the *New York Times* seems to have been moving in the opposite direction. The percentage of articles adopting a domestic frame fell from 35 % to 19 % in the second period, while those adopting a global frame increased from 9 % to 26 % in the same period. This signifies a shift in the domestic US discourse, from an instrumental use of the Greek example for domestic politics purposes, and discussions on the strengths and vulnerabilities of the US economy, to the potentially global and systemic implications of the Greek and European debt crisis. Finally, in some newspapers, such as *The Times*, there seems to be no significant change in terms of the frames used during the period under examination.

3 Deconstructing the Greeks: Corrupt, Lazy, and Morally Offside

This last section aims to sketch the qualitative characteristics that define the nature and the parameters of the negative discourse on Greece in the international press. There are at least three dominant themes that give shape to this negative discourse: 'corruption', 'lack of credibility', and 'irresponsibility'. The repetitive, extensive, and intensive mobilisation of these themes in relation to Greece, in the entire media sample and throughout the period under examination, points to a very serious damage to the image of Greece at the international level. In this context, what we observe happening is the following. During the period under examination, 'Greece' evolved rapidly from an object of critique, that is, something that is being criticised, to a negative reference point and to something that conveys a negative meaning. In this way, the implications of the negative discourse on Greece exceeded the sphere of the overt and the conscious and started to operate also at unconscious, subliminal levels. The latter are very difficult, if not impossible, to influence, let alone reverse or even control. However, let us see how these dominant themes and dynamics played out on the ground.

First, let us consider the theme of corruption. 'Corruption' is omnipresent in most analyses on Greece. It emerges as the definite characteristic and a distinctive quality of Greek politics and society. For instance, *The Times* and the *Gazeta Wyborcza* speak of an 'endemic culture of tax evasion' and of tax evasion as a 'Greek habit' (see, for example, Gazeta Wyborcza, 2010; Wighton, 2010); the *Die Zeit*, the *New York Times*, and the *El Pais* refer to the system of the 'fakelaki' (see, for example, Sanchez-Vallejo, 2010; Suzanne, 2010; Thumann, 2009); the *Le Figaro* discusses the 'familles clientélistes au pouvoir' (Hauter, 2010); and the multiple references to the phenomenon of 'cooking the books' (see, for example, Campbell & Goldfarb, 2009; Robin, 2010; *The Straits Times*, 2010). These are only a few examples from an entire array of references where Greece is portrayed as a political system and a society that is permeated and defined by corruption. Thus, in a sense, 'Greece' emerges and is consolidated as the (corrupted) *other* of the (rational) western society (especially in the western media). In some respects, this shift resembles the rapid rise of the discourse on 'crony capitalism' that emerged during the Asian crisis of the 1990s, both as an explanation of the crisis and a re-affirmation of the superiority of 'western capitalism'.

Second, there is the issue of 'lack of credibility'. The most destabilising deficit for Greece, during the period under examination, was not its fiscal deficit but its credibility deficit. The acknowledgement of the manipulation of its economic statistics was the last nail in a years-old coffin. Although, the acknowledgement of data falsification by the Greek government referred to the fiscal deficit for 2009, very soon doubt was cast on the statistical data on which Greece's entry into the Eurozone was based. As a result, Greece's very membership of the Eurozone fell open to question. 'Greek statistics' became a global joke. The repercussions for Greece's image and credibility in the European and international arena can hardly be underestimated. References to Greece as an 'unreliable' and 'untrustworthy' state acquired a 'common sense' quality in the European (north and south) and international press (see, for example, Bielecki, 2010; Cano, 2010; Class, 2010; Heuser, 2010a, 2010b; Missi, 2010; The Korea Times, 2010). The same applies for the view that Greece did not 'deserve' to be, and should have never been, admitted' in the Eurozone (ibid., see also, Pinzler & Tatje, 2010; *The Times*, 2010).

Third, there is the issue of 'irresponsibility'. This theme is not separate from the themes of 'corruption' and 'credibility'. Yet, what makes it distinct from the latter two is its emphasis on morality and ethics. What underlies this aspect of the discourse on Greece is the notion of an *excess* in Greek behaviour and style of life—an excess in which the roots of the Greek crisis are to be found. The lexicon of this moralising discourse is not of course new. For instance, Greece is referred to as a 'black sheep' (Arnaud, 2009), a 'free-rider' (Lachevre, 2009), a 'profligate' state (Kulish & Kitsantonis, 2010; Kulish & Pauly, 2010; see also, Heuser, 2010a, 2010b). The Aesop's fable of 'the cricket and the ant' also prevails, either to describe Greece, or to juxtapose the Greek (or the south) and German (or the north) way of life. *The Strait Times* writes that 'Greece was often Europe's problem child', and that '[m]ore than half of Greece's population are state employees, and many just shuffle papers' (Eyal, 2010), while *The New York Times* refers to the Greeks' inclination for 'volema': '[In Greece] alongside a strong desire for reform lies a deep sense of resignation. Many Greeks find the status quo, however problematic, more convenient than a new order; they aspire to finding what is known as "volema", a comfortable setup within the prevailing system' (Donadio & Carassava, 2009).

The issue of culture was not exempted from this discourse. Expectedly, the German press has been the most outspoken in stressing this dimension. The characteristics of the Greek society put Greece in a different category in comparison to the other European societies: 'Greeks are not Europeans' (Thumann, 2009). Yet, this rationale was many times extended to the 'European south' as a whole: 'The mentality in the South is well-known; they don't respect laws and regulations! They operate with their own laws—for the rest, they are "Europeans"!' (Brost, 2010; *The Korea Times,* 2010).

Thus, from the beginning of 2010 Greece has widely been used in the international press (and the national and international debates and politics reflected therein) as an 'example to avoid' and a 'justification means' for policy reform. For instance, as the *Daily Yomiuri* reports, Naoto Kan, the Japanese prime minister, '[r]eferencing Greece's fiscal crisis. . .asked those present at the meeting to commit to raising the consumption tax' (Shuhei et al., 2010; see also, *The Daily Yomiuri,* 2010a, 2010b). Naoto Kan has also stated that 'Japan must take action "before it becomes like Greece"' (Naohisa, 2010; see also, *The Daily Yomiuri,* 2010c; *The Korea Times,* 2010). This latter warning statement, that is, 'not to become like Greece', is indeed present in all the media samples that we analysed. The same applies to the related reassuring statement, 'we are not Greece' (or, for instance, 'Spain is not Greece') (see, for example, Abellan, 2010; *El Pais,* 2010; Krugman, 2010). The frequency of the usage of these two phrases is a testament of how Greece had evolved from an object of critique to a negative signifier at the international level. This is clear also in the many different negative ways in which the name of the country is used. For instance, in the run up to the Polish 2010 presidential elections, the Prime Minister Donald Tusk stated: 'We would have now become the Greece of Central Europe, if we had followed the advices of Jarosław Kaczyński' (Wroński, 2010; see also, Grochal, 2010). Such statements are indeed indicative of the way in which Greece figured in the international press from 2010 onwards. The following Table complements this picture by presenting some more indicative negative adjectives and phrases referring to Greece from the newspapers *El Pais* and the *New York Times* (Table 1).

Last but not least, it should be noted that the analysis of the press sample reveals a significant qualitative difference between the period before and after May 2010,

Table 1 Indicative negative references to Greece

El Pais	New York Times
Threat, indiscipline, poor relative, unreliable, epitome of irresponsibility, weak, weakest link, systematic liar, instability, Greek virus, fragile, gangrene, sick, beggar, vicious circle, abyss, Spain is not Greece	Greek style financial crisis, profligacy, precarious economy, Greece of the North, Athenian affinity for deficits and debt, Greece as the world's worst performer, tax evasion as a national pastime, The transit system in New York has turned into Greece: dead broke, we are not Greece

when the deal for the rescue package was concluded. In particular, whereas before April/May it was Greece that was under the spotlight of the global media and at the heart of the critique in the international press, after April/May the spotlight seems gradually to have been moving away from Greece and onto Germany and the European institutions, and their inability to deal effectively and timely with the crisis in Greece in particular and in Europe in general. At that time, there appears to have emerged a unique window of opportunity for Greece. So long as Greece made headline news and was at the gunpoint of the international media, any attempt to restore a sense of stability in its economy was immediately neutralised. Now, for the first time, the spotlight was gradually moving away from Greece. Furthermore, the shift of the focus and interest of the global media from Greece onto Germany and the European institutions, and their failure to deal effectively with the crisis, produced some sympathy for Greece and deflected some criticism from Greece to Germany and the European institutions. Yet, soon the situation in Greece became worse rather than better, and after October 2010, Greece started to attract the global media spotlight again. An opportunity seems to have been lost.

Conclusion

Our aim in this chapter was neither to analyse the veracity of the international press discourse on Greece and the Greek crisis, nor to systematically analyse its origins and mode of diffusion. Reports and articles from international news agencies, such as the Reuters and Bloomberg, were reproduced in several of the newspapers under examination. Furthermore, at least to some degree, the negative discourse on Greece from the outside (i.e. how others viewed Greece) was a reflection of the negative discourse on Greece from the inside (i.e. the debates taking place in Greece). Therefore, the origins and channels of international dissemination of the discourse on Greece were multiple and interlinked.

The main aim of this paper was to present a cartography of this negative discourse on Greece. When did it emerge? How did it evolve and why? What were its nature and characteristics? What were its defining themes? The conclusion from this analysis is not optimistic for Greece. Our research findings point to the consolidation of a very negative image for Greece at the international level. Even more worrying is the fact that Greece, during the period under examination, was transformed into a 'negative signifier' and used as such by political, economic, and media elites in all the eleven countries examined. For Greece, to reverse this negative image will take time, systematic effort, resources, and imagination.

References

Abellan, L. (2010, May 2). No hay comparacicσn posible entre Espaρa y Grecia. *El Pais.*

Arnaud, R. (2009, December 14). Le gouvernement grec cherche à reconstruire l'union nationale; Le premier ministre présente son programme d'économies pour sauver le pays. *Le Figaro.*

Bielecki, T. (2010, May 3). Grecja dostanie 110 mld euro pomocy od krajσw euro i MFW. *Gazeta Wyborcza.*

Brost, M. (2010, February 18). Griechische Tragoedie. *Die Zeit.*

Campbell, I., & Goldfarb, J. (2009, December 9). Lesser lights in the Euro Zone. *The New York Times.*

Cano, F. (2010, August 15). Bulgaria, ajuste sin fin. *El Pais.*

Class, T. (2010, April 22). Europa soll es richten? *Die Zeit.*

Donadio, R., & Carassava, A. (2009, October 3). Greek socialists hope for comeback; but even supporters of party fear the vote Sunday can't solve crisis. *The New York Times.*

El Pais. (2010, February 10). El viejo navνo; Hay un sector de la industria patria que permanece inmune a la crisis.

Eyal, J. (2010, February 5). Relief for EU as Greece acts on mounting debt; But doubts remain over whether govt pledges to cut spending can be kept. *The Straits Times.*

Gazeta Wyborcza. (2010, May 26). *Grecja: 234 urzędnikσw z resortu finansσw kantowało na podatkach.*

Grochal, R. (2010, May 28). Tusk uderza w Kaczyńskiego. *Gazeta Wyborcza.*

Hauter, F. (2010, February 11). La Grèce prise au piège de ses incohérences. *Le Figaro.*

Heuser, U.-J. (2010, March 4). Nicht schon wieder! *Die Zeit.*

Heuser, U.-J. (2010, April 29). Der letzte Sirtaki. *Die Zeit.*

Krugman, P. (2010, May 16). No somos Grecia. *El Pais.*

Kulish, N., & Kitsantonis, N. (2010, March 6). Germany offers no financial help to ailing Greece. *The New York Times.*

Kulish, N., & Pauly, S. (2010, February 16). Germans upset over helping Greece. *The New York Times.*

Lachevre, C. (2009, December 10). La Grèce, épreuve de vérité pour l'euro. *Le Figaro.*

Missi, A. (2010, February 16). Bruselas vigilarα a los Estados para evitar falsificaciones en las cuentas. *El Pais.*

Naohisa, I. (2010, July 14). Quirky poll result could be watershed. *The Daily Yomiuri.*

Pinzler, P., & Tatje, C. (2010, May 12). Warum sollte ich Fehler gestehen? Der Währungskommissar der Europäischen Union, Olli Rehn, will den Euro retten–und dafür sündige Mitgliedsländer maßregeln. Zur Not auch Deutschland. *Die Zeit.*

Robin, J.-P. (2010, January 14). Le défi de la BCE, réunifier la zone euro. *Le Figaro.*

Sanchez-Vallejo, M. A. (2010, May 16). Odisea 2.0: Grecia busca cσmo salir de la crisis. *El Pais.*

Shuhei, K., et al. (2010, June 19). Upper House Election 2010; Parties claim same ground on tax reform. *The Daily Yomiuri.*

Suzanne, D. (2010, May 2). Greeks' wealth is found in many places, just not on tax returns. *The New York Times.*

The Daily Yomiuri. (2010a, May 9). Prevent Greek crisis from spreading further [Editorial].

The Daily Yomiuri. (2010b, July 20). Drawing up next year's budget a touchstone [Editorial].

The Daily Yomiuri. (2010c, June 12). What Kan Cabinet should do to revitalize Japan.

The Korea Times. (2010, July 27). Euro design lacks cultural diversity.

The Straits Times. (2010, March 8). Greek crisis: hedge funds not to blame.

The Times. (2010, February 10). Greek tragedy; the indebted economies of Southern Europe threaten the financial stability of the eurozone. The need for a bailout illustrates the flaws in monetary union.

Thumann, M. (2009, December 17). Griechenland. *Die Zeit*.

Wighton, D. (2010, September 13). Dodgy moves and illegal evasion that cost Britain £95bn a year. *The Times*.

Wroński, P. (2010, June 27). Kaczyński kontra Komorowski. Pierwsze starcie. *Gazeta Wyborcza*.

Greek Foreign Policy in the Shadow of the Debt Crisis: Continuity and New Directions

Aristotle Tziampiris

1 Weakness of Greek Foreign Policy

Greece's foreign policy has been defined to a considerable degree by the relative weakness of the modern Greek state:

> Weakness is the most common, natural and pervasive view of self in the small state and it afflicts its leaders and influences their behavior in many ways . . . It is the dominant fact of the state's international existence. It is unpleasant to be aware of it, either in strategic or human terms, and it often leads to a search of compensation or for an attitude which, when struck, reduces its significance (Vital, 1967, 33).[1]

The management of this relative weakness has been compounded by a decision-making system that has too often been devoid of institutional substance, while being influenced by personal, populist, and partisan considerations (Lagakos, 1996; Tziampiris, 2000; Yianoulopoulos, 1999). It has even been concluded that 'Greek foreign policy can properly be accounted for . . . by seriously taking into consideration three factors: public opinion, the role of personality and the interplay between personalities and society/public opinion' (Ioakimidis, 1999, 142).

In other words, Greece's diplomacy has historically displayed a number of problematic aspects and even elements of dysfunction. Ultimately, any country's external relations derive legitimacy, resources, influence, and power from its domestic political and economic arrangements. The recent and acute economic crisis facing Greece has exposed a series of structural weaknesses and internal contradictions. It has essentially emerged that 'the modern Greek society and economy . . . is a monster,

[1] For a revealing comparison of high-level US and Greek official visits that demonstrates the public and practical diplomatic realities and consequences of this relative Greek weakness, see Kiesling (2006, 83–84).

A. Tziampiris (✉)
Department of International and European Studies, University of Piraeus, 150 Androutsou Str, Piraeus 18534, Greece
e-mail: atziampiris@gmail.com

P. Sklias and N. Tzifakis (eds.), *Greece's Horizons*, The Konstantinos Karamanlis Institute for Democracy Series on European and International Affairs,
DOI 10.1007/978-3-642-34534-0_3,

a modern day hydra, with seven heads: cronyism, statism, nepotism, clientelism, corruption, closed shops and waste' (Manolopoulos, 2011, 81). The result has been a mountain of debt that before the March 2012 'haircut' arrangements—worth about 105 billion euros and representing 'the largest ever sovereign debt restructuring' (Birnbaum, 2012)—was estimated to be as high as '$1.2 trillion, or more than a quarter-million dollars for every working Greek' (Lewis, 2011, 43).[2]

The challenges to the Greek economy seem enormous, especially when taking into account that 'by the end of 2012 [it] will have shrunk by close to 20% in 4 years' (Landon, 2012). Furthermore, countless reports about the falsification of data, inability to fully collect taxes, and various other negative idiosyncrasies and practices prevalent in Greek society have undoubtedly damaged the country's credibility, prestige, and reputation. This is no idle matter since, as Gilpin (1981, 31) points out, 'prestige, rather than power, is the everyday currency of international relations'. Keohane (1984, 116) further cautions that for governments 'reputation is a crucial resource'.

It can thus be concluded that Greek foreign policy is facing adverse political and economic circumstances. However, this chapter argues that the diplomatic situation is not as dire as it may first seem.[3] Furthermore, operating under conditions of turmoil has historically been more of the norm, since conditions of unprecedented stability and 'normality' have only been displayed over the past few decades. Today, as a member of the United Nations, NATO, the EU, and the eurozone, Greece retains several institutional tools to pursue a more dynamic and proactive foreign policy within a framework characterised primarily by a steady orientation and goals. In this sense, Greece's diplomacy can emerge as an underexplored and integral part of the country's return to growth strategies.

This chapter first presents the areas where Greek diplomacy has primarily displayed continuity since the beginning of the debt crisis (relations with the EU, NATO, the US, Turkey, and the Balkans). Next, it focuses on the entirely new directions pursued more recently that have included close ties with Russia and Israel. Finally, the chapter concludes with observations about the principles that guide Greek foreign policy and suggestions for future policy preferences.

2 Continuity in Greek Foreign Policy

The primary orientation of Greek foreign policy remains Euro-Atlantic. Athens is determined to remain as close as possible to the core of European integration, including staying a member of the eurozone—a policy preference actually

[2] As of late January 2012, most references to Greece's debt made use of an amount of approximately 350 billion euros.

[3] It is noteworthy that in his comprehensive account of current Greek foreign policy, Professor (Kouskouvelis, 2012, 47) stresses that 'the difficulties created by the economic crisis are smaller than what can someone assess initially and in a rather shallow manner'.

supported by 70 % of Greek citizens (see Chaffin, 2012). This strategy enjoys broad bipartisan backing and in many ways it has come to define Greek diplomacy (and to a considerable degree its domestic policies) over the past two decades, particularly since the eruption of the debt crisis in 2009–2010. Despite recriminations and popular feelings of bitterness, disappointment, and suspicion between certain key EU states, such as between Germany and Greece, the fact remains that the latter views itself and its future as an integral part of the Union. This resolve and essential ideological preference should not be underestimated by the international community.[4]

Moreover, Greek decision makers consider the continuation of active NATO membership as being of paramount importance. At the same time, bilateral relations with the US have probably reached, during the debt crisis, the best level since the fall of the Greek military junta in 1974. It is of significance that for the first time in living memory, the numerous (and at times daily) mass demonstrations in Athens have had no anti-American content, nor have they concluded in front of the US Embassy according to a long-established 'protocol'. Targets have rather included the German Chancellor Angela Merkel, corrupt local politicians, and (particularly) the troika of the International Monetary Fund, European Central Bank, and European Commission) but never the Barack Obama administration. Although it may be premature to declare anti-Americanism a thing of the past in Greece (Botsiou, 2007; Kotzias, 2010, 110–114), the fact remains that Greek society is currently concentrating on much more pressing issues. At the same time, the US has been willing to donate to Athens, for free, several hundred Abrams tanks and M133 armoured personnel carriers that were previously employed in Iraq.[5] Furthermore, Washington DC has refused to create any diplomatic trouble after Greece's condemnation by the International Court of Justice (ICJ) (discussed later in this section). Thus, it is possible to conclude that the already strong Greek–American relations will continue along an excellent path.[6]

Concerning relations with Turkey, there is also substantial continuity.[7] Since the 1999 Helsinki European Council, Athens has supported Ankara's European prospects. Greece officially recognises only the continental shelf issue as a bilateral dispute and continues to support a bi-zonal, bi-communal solution for the Cyprus issue (Liakouras, 2007). The hope and strategy has been that the path towards

---

[4] Greece's European orientation has been in operation long enough that a discussion of the degree and ways in which Greek foreign policy might have been Europeanised has emerged, although complicated by disagreements about definitions (Economides, 2005; Stavridis, 2003; Tsardanidis & Stavridis, 2011; Tziampiris, 2009).

[5] It seems that the Greek government will be responsible for the transportation of the tanks and personnel carriers to Greece. At the time of writing, this deal had yet to be concluded.

[6] For a somewhat more sceptical approach towards Greece's relations with the US within a bold and comprehensive approach towards Greek foreign policy, see Markezinis (2010).

[7] Greek–Turkish relations have commanded considerable academic attention from Greek scholars. Indicative of the scholarship involved and the range of arguments in what constitutes a lively and consequential debate are Ifantis (2005), Yallourides and Tsakonas (1999), and Heraclides (2001).

eventual Union accession would contribute to the resolution of all bilateral problems including Cyprus. However, this has not turned out to be the case.

Based on numerous interviews and discussions with Greek decision makers, substantial doubt has now emerged about whether Turkey will ever complete its European journey. In addition, because of the debt crisis, it is an open question whether Greece can continue to keep defence spending at the same levels as before, a development that may require the rethinking of national deterrence strategy (Ifestos & Platias, 1992). These realisations, in conjunction with the impressive rise of Turkish economic and geopolitical power and ambitions, almost necessitate a new strategy towards the neighbouring state. However, it has yet to materialise in any comprehensive or entirely satisfactory manner. To a certain degree, the new directions in Greek foreign policy presented in the next section could also be viewed as a response to relations with a rising Turkey.

Turning to the Balkans, Athens continues to actively support the Euro-Atlantic prospects of all regional states. Consensus has emerged according to which the national interest is best served by having stable, prosperous, and democratic neighbouring countries in what constitutes an area with obvious strategic importance for Greek political and economic interests. However, Greece is now in a much weaker position to successfully lead any major pro-accession efforts such as the one that culminated with the 2003 Thessaloniki declaration that made clear that the future of the western Balkans firmly belongs in the Union. Nevertheless, Greek diplomacy, already preparing for the upcoming Greek Presidency in 2014, is pushing for the so-called Agenda 2014. The aim is to see all western Balkan states accede to the EU by that date, symbolically one century after the beginning of the First World War. Although this is unrealistic, setting and pursuing such a goal remains a worthwhile endeavour because it helps focus Union efforts on unfinished business in the region.

The economic crisis means that Greek businesses will not be able to continue to play the same positive role of investing, trading, and creating jobs in South East European countries (Greek investments in the region had reached 11.8 billion euros by the beginning of 2010) (Kathimerini, 2010). Although this will have a somewhat negative impact, Greek firms and banks will not vanish from the picture but rather remain active, albeit at a reduced level.

On Kosovo, Athens continues to withhold official recognition for the new state. This issue is viewed as a fundamentally regional one with potential international ramifications and not simply as a dispute involving the Albanian and Serb communities. Unlike Cyprus, Greek officials have never categorically denied recognition at some future point, leaving somewhat open the possibility that such an outcome could be part of other and perhaps broader regional understandings (Tziampiris, 2008). The recent deal struck between Serbia and Kosovo on how the latter can be represented at an international level and the subsequent decision to grant Serbia EU candidate status represent significant developments that have the potential of eventually resolving the Kosovo issue in a manner satisfying Greek concerns (see Brunwasser, 2012; Castle, 2012).

As regards Albania, economic and political relations should remain at an overall positive level.[8] A major unresolved bilateral issue involves the maritime borders and continental shelf delimitation agreement of 2009. This became subject to populist criticism by Albania's Socialist opposition party and it was eventually reversed by the country's Constitutional Court. Reaching a final deal on this issue would help create a solid and trustworthy framework for co-operation that could prove of significance, especially if certain energy projects (e.g. the Trans Adriatic Pipeline) that traverse both countries are built.

Concerning the name dispute with the former Yugoslav Republic of Macedonia (FYROM), the debt crisis will not lead to the abandonment of Greece's official (since 2007) position: a name with a geographic connotation of the term Macedonia (e.g. Northern Macedonia) *erga omnes*. Considerations of regional stability, pressure emanating from Brussels and Washington, and a more flexible attitude from Skopje may produce a settlement on a more restricted scope or lead to certain interim scenarios. However, there is no political space or willingness to further alter the fundamentals of the new name position, which the majority of the Greek people actually oppose. In all likelihood, it will remain unchanged and unrelated to developments on the economic front.

This assessment is also unlikely to be influenced by the decision (5 December 2011) of the ICJ that represents the most significant development on the name dispute since the eruption of the debt crisis. Specifically, Greece was condemned for having violated the 1995 Interim Accord: '[the ICJ] ... concludes that the Respondent [Greece] objected to the Applicant's [FYROM's] admission to NATO within the meaning of the first clause of Article 11, paragraph 1, of the Interim accord' (ICJ, 2011, 28). FYROM had also 'request[ed] relief in the form of an order of the Court that the Respondent henceforth refrain from any action that violates its obligations under Article 11, paragraph 1, of the Interim Accord'. However, on this issue, '[t]he Court ... determines that its finding that the Respondent has violated its obligation to the Applicant under ... the Interim Accord, *constitutes appropriate satisfaction*' (ICJ, 2011, 47; emphasis added).

The interpretation of the ICJ ruling that emerged in Athens (with one important qualification to be discussed in the next section) was that Greece was condemned only in the narrow, legal question and that the judgment does not limit Athens' future actions on this issue. At the same time, no immediate pressure towards Athens was registered by NATO, the EU, or the US (see Tziampiris, 2012, 125).

[8] On Greek–Albanian relations, see also Kouskouvelis (2012, 48–49).

Based on the above, it emerges that the debt crisis has not caused any discontinuities in Greek diplomacy towards the EU, the US, Turkey, Cyprus, and the Balkans. However, it is not surprising that diminishing resources and the rise of Turkey have also required the search for new directions in Greek foreign policy, to which we turn next.

3 New Directions in Greek Foreign Policy

As the fundamentals of the Greek economy were apparently fast deteriorating (a fact that was not made public and was perhaps not appreciated in its full magnitude until 2009–2010), Athens pursued a significant shift and reorientation in its relations with Russia. During his tenure (2004–2009), Greece's Prime Minister Kostas Karamanlis had seven meetings with Russian President Vladimir Putin (as opposed to only two with George W. Bush and one with Barack Obama). They resulted in the pursuit of multidimensional co-operative schemes in a number of areas.

In September 2006, it was announced that Russia, Bulgaria, and Greece would sign a deal to construct the Burgas–Alexandroupolis pipeline that was supposed to carry oil from the Caspian region. Furthermore, in June 2007, Karamanlis and Putin announced their intention to co-operate in the construction of the South Stream gas pipeline. This project was correctly viewed as directly competitive to the Nabucco pipeline project, long favoured by the US. A relevant memorandum was signed in April 2009 and the Greek Parliament endorsed the agreement with overwhelming multi-partisan support in August 2009. Finally, Athens announced in December 2007 its intention to buy some 420 BMP-3M armoured personnel Russian tanks worth approximately 1.2 billion euros, thus becoming the only NATO member state to directly purchase military material from Moscow.

These somewhat spectacular moves cannot be explained based on any civilisational affinity with Eastern Orthodox Russia but rather by national interest calculations (Tziampiris, 2010).[9] The aim was to use the Burgas–Alexandroupolis and South Stream pipelines—in conjunction with the construction of the Interconnector Turkey–Greece–Italy (ITGI) and Interconnector Greece–Bulgaria (IGB) projects—to make Greece into a regional energy transportation hub while somewhat reducing energy dependence on pipelines crossing through Turkey. Athens also intended to benefit from Russia's international influence, especially at the level of the United Nations Security Council.

This ambitious program did not survive international reactions and budgetary concerns. Objections from the Bulgarian government have meant that the Burgas–Alexandroupolis pipeline has entered a stage where the prospects of

[9] According to Bakoyannis (2012, 4), who as Foreign Minister oversaw the strengthening of bilateral ties with Russia, Athens had 'one and only goal: the exploitation of the strategic geographical position of Greece and the strengthening of its role in the international energy stage'.

eventual construction are extremely doubtful. There is also some uncertainty about South Stream, especially the Greek part of the project, while it is likely that the ITGI will not be completed. As a result, it is now probable that the 'pipeline energy planning that took place during the 2006–2009 period [will be] completely nullified' (Bakoyannis, 2012, 37). Finally, the decision to buy Russian tanks was rescinded by the subsequent Greek administration, citing constraints because of the debt crisis. In fact, during roughly the period between 2009 and 2012 (largely coinciding with the premiership of George Papandreou), relations between Moscow and Athens were neither close nor significant.

By contrast, the same period witnessed a transformation of Greek relations with Israel.[10] Since 1948, affairs between the two states had been ambivalent, detached, and characterised by suspicion, mutual recriminations, and even enmity (Abadi, 2000; Nachmani, 1987). Only gradually and grudgingly did they begin to somewhat slowly improve (Athanassopoulou, 2003). However, following Israeli Prime Minister Benjamin Netanyahu's historic visit to Greece in August 2010 (the first by a sitting Israeli Prime Minister), co-operation between the two countries emerged as broad and multifaceted. It now covers the realms of defence (including joint air force and naval military exercises), culture, tourism, (400,000 Israelis visited Greece in the past year), and economics (several projects are being discussed in fields such as agro-technology and desalination).

The avowed political determination for closer ties has been successfully tested at least twice. Specifically, in early December 2010, Israel was hit by a serious natural disaster: wildfires that left more than 40 people dead while several thousand had to be evacuated. Greece almost immediately underwrote a 70-member 4-day rescue operation team comprising crewmembers, pilots, firefighters, and several planes. Both President Simon Peres and Prime Minister Netanyahu conferred awards of honour to the Greek firefighters who received wide and positive press coverage in Israel, contributing to popular pro-Greek feelings.[11]

The second test involved the so-called 'Freedom Flotilla II' comprising 10 ships and some 400 activists, 50 of which were Greek citizens. Only two ships contained humanitarian aid that totalled less than 4,000 tons and included some 600 footballs. After being effectively discouraged to embark on such a mission from Turkey and Cyprus, the activists and their fleet congregated in the Greek port of Piraeus where they clearly expected nothing but encouragement. However, their cardinal error was their inability to understand that Israeli–Greek relations had undergone a sea change during the previous 12 months.

Problems for the flotilla soon materialised. In suspicious circumstances, the propeller of one ship was damaged. Greek inspectors, possibly following official instructions, adopted a strict interpretation of the law and found various technical

[10] The discussion of Israeli–Greek relations is based on the author's forthcoming study of these developments.

[11] In his visit to Athens in January 2012, Israel's Defence Minister Ehud Barak stressed this point publicly on a number of occasions.

and legal violations in the ships. Eventually, citing safety concerns, Greece banned outright the vessels from leaving Piraeus. One ship decided to ignore the ban and headed for Gaza. Greek officials quickly boarded speedboats and forced it to return in an operation that contained various still unacknowledged risks.

The Greek government, broadly supported in its actions by the UN, the EU, the US, and Israel, subsequently announced that it was willing to ferry the humanitarian aid to Gaza under UN supervision. This option was endorsed by the President of the Palestinian Authority Mahmoud Abbas but was rejected by the activists. Particularly critical of Athens was Hamas, which explained developments based on pressure exerted by 'Zionist conquerors'. Greece's various far left parties also criticised the Greek government.

The most significant consequence of the specific actions pursued by Athens is that in all probability lives were saved. This should not be underestimated, especially since nine people were killed at the previous Gaza flotilla. By not allowing the vessels to disembark, Greece publicly demonstrated to the international community its new relationship with Israel, while Athens contributed to stability in the eastern Mediterranean during a time of uncertainty and transition.

Positive regional ramifications may also ensue from the significant recently discovered offshore natural gas fields in the eastern Mediterranean, which are at the very heart of closer Israeli–Greek relations. In Israel,

> proven gas reserves [have been found amounting] to 300 bcm [billion cubic meters], most of it in the offshore Tamar field ... The reserves figure is expected to rise by a further 453 bcm after production tests are completed at Leviathan field ... An additional 550 bcm of gas [are expected] to be discovered in Israeli economic waters which eventually will bring the country's total reserves to 1,300 bcm (Gordon, 2011).

At the same time in Cyprus, the so-called Lot 12 named 'Aphrodite' (one out of 13 such lots) was initially estimated to hold seven trillion cubic feet of natural gas, worth as much as 70 billion euros and enough to cover the island's needs for more than 200 years (Fileleftheros, 2011). Subsequent estimates brought the size of the find down to a still significant 5.1 trillion cubic feet (To Vima, 2012).

The development and export of these gas finds could represent a potential regional 'game changer'. It would certainly alter Israel's position compared with Europe and lessen the continent's energy dependence on Russia (especially significant now that the prospects of the Nabucco gas pipeline project seem problematic).

In addition, it is not necessarily far-fetched to envision one day the creation of an energy network of gas pipelines that can bring together and produce incentives for co-operation and substantial profits for Israel, Greece, Cyprus, Egypt (if it stabilises in a responsible fashion), a future Palestinian state (if there is gas in its putative territorial waters), and Iran (if there is ever a regime change).

However, the consequential export of natural gas from Israel and Cyprus (by far the most likely scenario even if certain amounts are diverted to cover domestic needs) ultimately involves Greece. One of the options being discussed is the construction of an undersea pipeline possibly following the route from Leviathan to Cyprus to Crete to mainland Greece. Perhaps more feasible is to liquefy natural gas in a specially constructed platform that is to be built in Cyprus and then de-liquefy it in Greece where it can enter a system of pipelines in order to reach other European markets. In both cases, Greece manages to become an important energy transportation hub, securing energy supplies and becoming an indispensable part in an ambitious and potentially immensely profitable strategic plan that can bring Israel closer to Europe and be conducive to stability in the eastern Mediterranean and the Middle East.

Unlike the case with Russia, closer relations with Israel enjoy staunch support from Washington and broad bipartisan support in Greece (they are essentially administration-proof). Crucially, no discernible backlash or negative public reactions have taken place in the Arab world.[12] This presents an opportunity for Greek diplomacy to play a positive regional role. By being close to the Arab, Muslim, and Jewish peoples of the Middle East, Athens can offer good offices and contribute to the maximum degree possible towards facilitating various peace efforts. Finally, co-operation with Israel has the great virtue of including Cyprus as part of a triangular strategic and energy-related endeavour in the eastern Mediterranean that could even help resolve some long-standing disputes. Co-operation with Israel represents the most exciting, significant, and consequential new direction in Greek foreign policy.

4 Conclusions: The Way Forward

Despite the grave debt crisis, Greece continues to enjoy several advantages and assets. It occupies a key geographical position in South East Europe and the eastern Mediterranean. Relations with the US, the world's predominant power for the foreseeable future (Kagan, 2012, 101–140; Nye, 2011, 153–204) are stronger than ever, while those with the Arab world have been (and continue to be) excellent. Athens can now be a credible interlocutor with Israel as well, thus making possible the undertaking of initiatives that contribute towards stability in the Middle East. In addition, Greece still plays a significant role in supporting the Euro-Atlantic prospects of all western Balkan states. Continued membership in NATO, the EU, and the eurozone bestow significant institutional advantages and act as an (admittedly imperfect) form of 'insurance' against potentially aggressive behaviour by neighbouring states.

Greek foreign policy remains staunchly Euro-Atlanticist. More recently (and after the various populist and partisan-driven failures of the 1980s and 1990s), it has striven to operate (often imperfectly) according to the principles of political realism (Carr, 1964, 20; Morgenthau, 1985, 3–17). The emphasis has clearly been on the pursuit of national interests, viewed through the prism of power relations. In an era

[12] The sole exception was Syria's recognition of FYROM with its constitutional name in the aftermath of Netanyahu's visit to Greece. According to interviews with Greek decision makers, Syrian diplomats linked their action to Greece's new relationship with Israel.

characterised by the regional rise of Turkey and reduced military and diplomatic budgets because of domestic economic challenges, Athens has attempted to adapt accordingly, emphasising diplomacy and seeking new co-operative ventures. It is precisely in this light that the efforts to revitalise relations, first with Russia and then with Israel, have to be interpreted.

In the future, Greek diplomacy can opt for additional policies both proactively and confidently, thus assisting the country's return to growth. First, particular emphasis should continue to be placed on energy-related projects in the eastern Mediterranean and South East Europe. The goal must be to make the country a significant regional energy transportation hub (Stournaras, Danchev, & Paratsiokas, 2011). Athens must actively pursue the exploration and exploitation of oil and natural gas within its own territorial waters. Recent developments on this front have been encouraging: some of the world's largest energy corporations have declared an interest in conducting seismic tests in the Ionian Sea and off southern Crete with the aim of finding oil deposits. According to Greek experts, 'the possibility [exists] of [finding] deposits that could produce 200,000 barrels [of oil] per day' (Liagkou, 2012). Additional finds could create a situation where in '15–20 years at least 350–500,000 barrels [of oil could be produced daily] which with a conservative estimate of 100 USD per barrel, could bring total revenues at 40 billion euros and for the Greek state [at] 10–15 billion euros' (Liagkou, 2012).[13]

Within this context, Athens should weigh up moving towards declaring its own Exclusive Economic Zone. This is its sovereign right and it will eventually require delimitation agreements with neighbouring states. However, regardless of the legal debate currently raging in Greece, the fact remains that it was the companies exploring natural resources in Cyprus and Israel that requested such agreements between those two states (based on the author's interviews with the relevant decision makers). This fact strongly suggests that an Exclusive Economic Zone declaration would further assist Greece's energy-related explorations and plans.

Athens should also act to secure a role in the EU's plans for the creation of a southern gas corridor to transport natural gas primarily (and at least initially) from the Shah-Deniz field in Azerbaijan. Greek experts have already cautioned that

> despite Greece's initial preference for ITGI, once Sha[h]-Deniz decided in favour of TAP [the Trans Adriatic Pipeline] the Greek government must immediately embrace the project and facilitate its completion at the earliest possible time . . . Otherwise, the final decision . . . will be in favour of either Nabucco or SEEP [South East Europe Pipeline]. To prevent such a development, an active diplomatic effort . . . should be undertaken by Greece (Dokos & Tsakiris, 2012, 6).

Second, relations with Russia must be more balanced within a prudent framework that does not challenge Greece's Euro-Atlantic position. Co-operative actions in the realms of trade, tourism, and culture, as well as perhaps on certain energy-related

---

[13] The Greek government has also declared its intention to invite international energy companies to conduct oil and natural gas exploration tests on 10–12 lots on Greece's land territory (Ethnos, 2012).

plans, have to be pursued.[14] A situation of discontinued relations with Moscow is not particularly helpful to national interest considerations, although the existence of certain clear limits ought to be taken into account.

Third, Athens has to seriously weigh up withdrawing from the 1995 Interim Accord with FYROM. Such a move would have to consider various international parameters, would require intense prior diplomatic talks with key states, and would almost certainly be followed by a serious negotiating push to resolve the name dispute. Although for the short-term the ICJ decision is not creating diplomatic problems for Greece, this could change if a more lengthy timeframe is taken into account, especially given a close analysis of the various Court arguments (Mallias, 2012). Prudence also dictates a more proactive approach on this issue, which would probably further boost bilateral economic relations.

Finally, Greece has to continue to deepen economic, political, and cultural ties with China (Cosco already plays a key role in the port of Piraeus having competed a long-term deal worth some $5 billion), while pursuing mutually beneficial ventures with states such as India and Brazil. In this manner, it will be both in tune with the twenty-first century global power shifts that seem to be slowly underway (Brzezinski, 2012; Tzifakis, 2012) and also help strengthen the national economy.

The current debt crisis clearly represents a serious challenge for Greek diplomacy. However, the Greek state has a proven historical track record of overcoming much more serious crises. Consider that in the twentieth century alone, Greece confronted two Balkan Wars, two World Wars, the 1922 Asia Minor Catastrophe, a mass population exchange with Turkey, Fascist and Nazi occupations that included a deadly famine and the annihilation of its Jewish communities, a disastrous Civil War, mass immigration abroad, numerous *coup d'etats*, several major dictatorships, the 1974 Cyprus events, and near military confrontations with Turkey in 1976, 1987, and 1995.[15] On the economic front alone, Greece went bankrupt in 1932 (and also in 1827, 1843, and 1893 during the nineteenth century) and faced acute economic problems during several periods, including the 1940s and early 1950s.

From an historical viewpoint, the current crisis is neither unprecedented nor even close to being the worst, and it is worth keeping in mind that after every catastrophic phase, after every setback, Greece managed to survive, recover, and even prosper. The resilience and adaptability of the Greek people, as well as that of Greek diplomacy, are not to be underestimated. After all, Athens was on the winning side of all major international confrontations of the past 100 years,

[14] For example, in Spring 2012, there were reports that Gazprom might be interested in buying a stake in Greece's DEPA gas monopoly (The National Herald, 2012). It is also worth noting that the argument has been made that 'a 30- or 50-year deal that provides Russia's navy with basing rights at Piraeus might one day make sense for both sides. Over time, the deal could bring Greece's cash-starved government as much as $200 billion' (Bremmer, 2012). However, such a deal would in effect require Athens to relinquish its Euro-Atlantic orientation and organisational membership and thus face potentially tremendous political and economic complications. Hence, it is highly unlikely that this scenario will ever come to fruition.

[15] See also Veremis and Couloumbis (1994, 64).

remained the only non-communist Balkan state, and became the first in the region to join NATO and the then-European Economic Community. Despite the debt crisis, Athens can still play a positive role contributing to a multiplicity of international stabilising efforts. It would simply constitute a mistake to exclude Greece from any future regional developments.

References

Abadi, J. (2000). Constraints and adjustments in Greece's policy toward Israel. *Mediterranean Quarterly, 11*(4), 40–70.

Athanassopoulou, E. (2003). Responding to a challenge: Greece's new policy towards Israel. *Southeast European and Black Sea Studies, 3*(1), 108–125.

Bakoyannis, D. (2012). Greece's energy planning is being overturned: Greek-Russian relations and contemporary dangers. *Foreign Affairs [Hellenic Edition], 1*(3), 33–37 (in Greek).

Birnbaum, M. (2012, March 9). Greece secures needed backing for credit swap. *Washington Post.* http://www.washingtonpost.com/business/economy/greece-secures-needed-backing-for-credit-swap/2012/03/09/gIQA3MTd0R_story.html. Accessed 30 July 2012.

Botsiou, K. (2007). Anti-Americanism in Greece. In B. O'Connor (Ed.), *Anti-Americanism: History, causes, themes. Vol. 3: Comparative perspectives* (pp. 213–234). Oxford: Greenwood World Publishing.

Bremmer, I. (2012, March 21). Greece could replace Syria as Russia's mediterranean friend. *Financial Times.* http://blogs.ft.com/the-a-list/2012/03/21/greece-could-replace-syria-as-russias-mediterranean-friend/. Accessed July 2012.

Brunwasser, M. (2012, February 24). Kosovo and Serbia reach key deal. *The New York Times.* http://www.nytimes.com/2012/02/25/world/europe/25iht-kosovo25.html. Accessed 30 July 2012.

Brzezinski, Z. (2012). *Strategic vision. America and the crisis of global power.* New York: Basic Books.

Carr, H. E. (1964). *The twenty years' crisis 1919–1939: An introduction to the study of international relations.* London: Macmillan Palgrave.

Castle, S. (2012, March 1). Serbia, once outcast, is candidate to join EU. *The New York Times.* http://www.nytimes.com/2012/03/02/world/europe/serbia-is-candidate-for-european-union.html. Accessed 30 July 2012.

Chaffin, J. (2012, February 18/19). Athens rehearses the nightmare of a default. *Financial Times.* http://www.ft.com/intl/cms/s/0/76d064c6-5992-11e1-8d36-00144feabdc0.html. Accessed 30 July 2012.

Dokos, T., & Tsakiris, T. (2012). *A strategic challenge: the role of Greece in Europe's southern gas corridor strategy* (Policy Paper 17). Athens: Hellenic Foundation for European and Foreign Policy.

Economides, S. (2005). The Europeanisation of Greek foreign policy. *West European Politics, 28*(2), 471–491.

Ethnos. (2012, March 6). New lots for research. http://www.ethnos.gr/article.asp?catid=22770&subid=2&pubid=63626133. Accessed 30 July 2012 (in Greek).

Fileleftheros. (2011, December 29). Natural gas for 200 years in the hip of 'Aphrodite'. http://www.philenews.com/el-gr/New-Homepage-With-Slider/4995/90488/fysiko-aerio-gia-200-chronia. Accessed 30 July 2012 (in Greek).

Gilpin, R. (1981). *War and change in world politics.* Cambridge: Cambridge University Press.

Gordon, J. (2011, December). Will Israel win the energy prize in the Levant Basin? *New English Review.* http://www.newenglishreview.org/custpage.cfm/frm/7937/sec_id/102952. Accessed 30 July 2012.

Heraclides, A. (2001). *Greece and the 'threat from the east'.* Athens: Polis (in Greek).

ICJ. (2011, December 5). *Judgment. Application of the interim accord of 13 September 1995 (The Former Yugoslav Republic of Macedonia v. Greece)*. http://www.pdfdownload.org/pdf2html/view_online.php?url=http%3A%2F%2Fwww.kouskouvelis.gr%2Fsite%2Fimages%2Fstories%2FJudgment_5.12.2011.pdf. Accessed 30 July 2012.

Ifantis, K. (2005). Greece's Turkish dilemmas. *Southeast European and Black Sea Studies, 5*(3), 379–394.

Ifestos, P., & Platias, A. (1992). *Greek deterrence strategy*. Athens: Papazisis Publishers (in Greek).

Ioakimidis, P. C. (1999). The model of foreign policy-making in Greece: personalities versus institutions. In S. Stavridis, T. Couloumbis, T. Veremis, & N. Waites (Eds.), *The foreign policies of the European Union's Mediterranean states and applicant countries in the 1990's* (pp. 140–159). London: Macmillan.

Kagan, R. (2012). *The world America made*. New York: Knopf.

Kathimerini. (2010, January 21). At 11.88 billion: Greek investments in the Balkans. http://news.kathimerini.gr/4dcgi/_w_articles_economyepix_1_29/01/2010_388624. Accessed 30 July 2012 (in Greek).

Keohane, R. (1984). *After hegemony: Cooperation and discord in the world political economy*. Princeton: Princeton University Press.

Kiesling, B. J. (2006). *Diplomacy lessons: Realism for an unloved superpower*. Washington, DC: Potomac Books.

Kotzias, N. (2010). *The foreign policy of Greece in the 21st century: For a new, energetic, democratic, patriotic strategy in the era of globalization*. Athens: Kastaniotis (in Greek).

Kouskouvelis, I. (2012). Greek foreign policy in the crisis. *Foreign Affairs Hellenic Edition, 1*(1), 46–56 (in Greek).

Lagakos, E. (1996). *Populism in our national issues*. Athens: I. Sideris Publishers (in Greek).

Landon T. (2012, February 21). New bailout is a reprieve for Greece, but doubts persist. *The New York Times*. http://www.nytimes.com/2012/02/22/business/global/greece-dodges-bullet-with-new-bailout-but-doubts-remain.html. Accessed 30 July 2012.

Lewis, M. (2011). *Boomerang: Travels in the new third world*. New York: W. W. Norton.

Liagkou, C. (2012, March 3). Within 2012 the first drill, revenues in seven years. *Kathimerini*. http://www.kathimerini.gr/4dcgi/_w_articles_politics_2_03/03/2012_474595. Accessed 30 July 2012 (in Greek).

Liakouras, P. (2007). *The Cyprus issue from Zurich to Lucerne: In search of a federal resolution*. Athens: I. Sideris Publishers (in Greek).

Mallias, A. (2012). *Analysis of the Decision of the International Court at the Hague. Application of the Former Yugoslav Republic of Macedonia Against Greece* (Working Paper 25/2012). Athens: Eliamep (in Greek).

Manolopoulos, J. (2011). *Greece's 'odious' debt: The looting of the Hellenic Republic by the euro, the political elite and the investment community*. London: Anthem.

Markezinis, V. (2010). *A New foreign policy for Greece: In the framework of the gradual independence of Europe from the US*. Athens: A. A. Livani (in Greek).

Morgenthau, H. (1985). *Politics among nations The struggle for power and peace* (6th ed.). New York: Knopf.

Nachmani, A. (1987). *Israel, Turkey and Greece: Uneasy relations in the East Mediterranean*. London: Routledge.

Nye, S. J. (2011). *The future of power*. New York: Public Affairs.

Stavridis, S. (2003). *The Europeanisation of Greek foreign policy: A literature review* (European Institute Occasional Paper). London: LSE.

Stournaras, Y., Danchev, S., & Paratsiokas, N. (2011). *Greece as Europe's energy highway: Natural gas pipeline projects going through Greece*. Athens: Foundation for Economic and Industrial Research.

The National Herald. (2012, March 16). *Gazprom may bid for Greek gas monopoly*. http://www.thenationalherald.com/article/54268. Accessed 30 July 2012.

To Vima. (2012, March 7). At 5.1 trillion cubic feet the find at the Cypriot EEZ. http://www.tovima.gr/world/article/?aid=447226. Accessed 30 July 2012 (in Greek).

Tsardanidis, C., & Stavridis, S. (2011). Greece: from special case to limited Europeanisation. In R. Wong & C. Hill (Eds.), *National and European foreign policies: towards Europeanisation* (pp. 111–130). London: Routledge.

Tziampiris, A. (2000). *Greece, European political cooperation and the Macedonian question*. Aldershot: Ashgate.

Tziampiris, A. (2008). Greek foreign policy towards Kosovo's independence. *Südosteuropa, 56*(3), 403–406.

Tziampiris, A. (2009). Greek foreign policy and the macedonian name dispute: from confrontation to europeanisation? In O. Anastasakis, D. Bechev & N. Vrousalis (Eds.), *Greece and the Balkans: Memory, Conflict and Exchange* (pp. 138–156). Newcastle upon Thyme: Cambridge Scholars Publishing.

Tziampiris, A. (2010). Greek foreign policy and Russia: political realignment, civilizational aspects and realism. *Mediterranean Quarterly, 21*(2), 78–89.

Tziampiris, A. (2012). The Macedonian name dispute and European Union accession. *Southeast European and Black Sea Studies, 12*(1), 115–133.

Tzifakis, N. (2012). Change in international politics: an introduction to the contemporary debate. In N. Tzifakis (Ed.), *International politics in times of change* (pp. 1–14). Heidelberg: Springer.

Veremis, T., & Couloumbis, T. (1994). *Greek foreign policy: prospects and problems*. Athens: I. Sideris Publishers (in Greek).

Vital, D. (1967). *The inequality of states*. Oxford: Clarendon.

Yallourides, C., & Tsakonas, P. (Eds.). (1999). *Greece and Turkey after the end of the cold war*. Athens: I. Sideris Publishers (in Greek).

Yianoulopoulos, Y. (1999). *Our noble blindness' foreign policy and 'national issues' from the 1897 defeat to the Asia Minor catastrophe*. Athens: Vivliorama (in Greek).

Contentious Europeanisation and the Public Mind: Greece in Comparative Perspective

Kostas A. Lavdas and Maria M. Mendrinou

1 Introduction

Much has been said in literature and the media about the awkward aspects of Greece's EU membership, trajectory, and accomplishment. Is Greece an unworthy and rather ungrateful beneficiary of the EU's political and economic development? Or is Greece's place in Europe undergoing evolution, in response to particular domestic, transnational, European, and global challenges, as has been the case with practically every member state throughout the post-1980s period of the EU's existence? The latter line of argument is put forward in this essay, which aims to situate the case of Greece's contentious Europeanisation in a comparative perspective. It focuses, in particular, on Greek perceptions of European institutions and the country's changing relations with a changing EU. The chapter concludes that there is strong evidence to suggest that Greece's Europeanisation has been an impressively persistent project, while the extent to which future generations will view it as a tenacious project or as an obstinate one, will depend on the complex interactions between domestic, European, and international developments.

K.A. Lavdas (✉)
Department of Political Science, University of Crete, Rethymno 74100, Greece
e-mail: klavdas@alum.mit.edu

M.M. Mendrinou (✉)
Department of International and European Studies, University of Piraeus, 150 Androutsou Street, Piraeus 18534, Greece
e-mail: mendrinou@unipi.gr

P. Sklias and N. Tzifakis (eds.), *Greece's Horizons*, The Konstantinos Karamanlis Institute for Democracy Series on European and International Affairs,
DOI 10.1007/978-3-642-34534-0_4,

2 The Political Aspects of Greek Membership

The chequered formation of Europe's composite polity (Lavdas & Chryssochoou, 2011) has resulted in a series of complex, far-reaching, and in part, rather unpredictable implications for the member states. In fact, despite twists and oscillations, it is the EU—more than any other formation beyond the nation state—that has been able to assume properties that increasingly make us think of it as a 'state' (Stoker, 2006, 153–154). This is because the EU has become a complex set of institutions affecting our lives and, consequently, forces us to think that we need ways of influencing institutions that take decisions for us at not only the national, regional, local, and neighbourhood levels, but also at the supranational level.

In other words, it is increasingly becoming evident that the EU also offers a politically relevant terrain for citizens is also to be found on the EU level. Furthermore, in its workings, the EU has institutionalised a complex learning process of change and adaptation. Both dimensions—the increasing relevance of the EU level for the everyday lives of the people and the enduring learning processes of institutional workings at the EU level—testify to the need for an approach that would capture the dynamics of change 'from a diplomatic to a political arena', 'from policy to polity', or 'from democracies to democracy', in a difficult and discontinuous process of establishing a novel institutional matrix (see Lavdas & Chryssochoou, 2011).

In this context, even before formal accession to the EU, candidate states undergo processes of Europeanisation, influenced by conditionality (when it comes to relations with the European institutions) as well as domestic shifts and transformations. The process and outcome of accession politics depend on (a) the formation of a European strategy, (b) the consolidation of that strategy within the ruling bloc, (c) the effective handling of opposition to the basic features of the European strategy, (d) the degree of commitment on the part of consensus-makers and consensus-enforcers, and (e) the structural features of the political system (opportunities, veto points, etc.) which affect the ways in which actors engage in politics (see Lavdas, 1997). In most cases, the formation and subsequent consolidation of a European strategy involves considering a number of parameters, including the pre-established economic and trading patterns of the state in question, the major geostrategic concerns of the political elites, and the perceived interests of business elites.

The real-life, everyday workings of the EU went through an intricate web of EU-states interaction, captured (since the 1990s) under the various approaches to Europeanisation. In this perspective, interactions work in the context of more general Europeanisation processes, which concern adaptation, adjustment, impact, interactions, and feedback, beginning in anticipation of membership and expanding to more synchronised developments during the later stages of full membership. However, in order to grasp the complex implications of Europeanisation, we have to take into account not just the obvious, top-down dimension of the EU's impact (on domestic policies, actors, and institutions) but also the various interactive dimensions. Some of the recent over-conceptualisations of Europeanisation have not been able to move beyond a simple top-down framework. Indeed, as Císař rightly argues,

> in order to get a more complete picture of Europeanisation, one needs to focus on interactions among the three principal actors–states, supranational (European) institutions, and nonstate actors. If this is done, it will soon be clear that there is no simple logic behind Europeanisation that could be modelled on the basis of the top-down adaptation pressure from the EU. This pressure presents only one mechanism of Europeanisation among several (Císař, 2007, 26).

During earlier phases of Europeanisation, both its dimensions—impact and interaction—were so closely intertwined with economic modernisation that the distinction became blurred: 'economic liberalization and Europeanisation have been the twin processes gradually reshaping the political economies of the European South since the 1980s' (Lavdas, 1996, 254).

Greece's policy tradition of 'disjointed corporatism' (Lavdas, 1997) entails a matrix of asymmetric linkages between the state and organised interests, resulting in a markedly reform-resistant articulation. In spite of this, Europeanisation has been a tenacious, if asymmetric and chequered process. We suggest that Greece's tenacious Europeanisation is the combined outcome of a particular domestic and European constellation: the long-term co-existence of an elite-formed and sustained European strategy since the 1960s (bracketing the authoritarian parenthesis in 1967–1974) and considerable structural impediments to economic liberalisation and modernisation (Lavdas, 1997). As we will see, this has resulted in a widespread and enduring pattern of support for the Europeanisation project, despite oscillations. In Greece, Europeanisation was, and still is, an interactive course through challenges, problems, constraints, and opportunities in a reform-resistant context. However, the processes of Europeanisation reached a critical turning point when interest politics and the structural power of key domestic actors led to the manifestations of a limited reform capacity (Featherstone & Papadimitriou, 2008).

The political system has recently acknowledged the need to effectively transform the public administration system so that it can adapt to contemporary challenges. Many efforts have been made for towards reaching this goal; however, the results are not yet fully visible. Undoubtedly, the EC/EU's contributions to Greece's economic development and political-administrative modernisation have been considerable. From the Integrated Mediterranean Programmes of the 1980s, through the Structural Funds, to the more recent combination of loans and assistance, the European dimension has served both as an anchor for the democratic regime and as a source of policy transfer, policy learning, and financial assistance. Indeed, Greece's political, economic, and social developments since the regime change in 1974 were initially able to produce both political stability and impressive growth rates. Culminating in the exemplary Olympics of 2004, which were able to boost Greece's international image as a modern, European nation,[1] the period since

[1] On the short-lived impact of the Olympic Games as a successful international 'mega event' see Fola (2011).

1974 appeared to confirm the consolidation of a successful political economy. Perversely, against this background, with the adoption of the euro, the ability of weaker eurozone members to borrow was drastically improved. Relatively cheap credit became a possibility in every corner of the eurozone. A result of this, combined with the effects of the 2008 international financial crisis and inadequate political leadership, was the intensification of borrowing in an attempt to counter the early and somewhat misleading symptoms of the crisis. In Greece, the devastating implications of the deflationary efforts of successive austerity programs led to sharp increases in unemployment and the shrinking of the economy. In this context, the mobilisation of networks of social support and the activities of diverse groups (such as the Medical Association of Athens) and institutions (such as the Greek Orthodox Church) provided noteworthy auxiliary structures to public efforts to combat the effects of poverty.

At the same time, at the EU level, the jury is still out on the future policy mix necessary to tackle the spreading fiscal and financial crisis. In the current juncture, it may well be that a new 'EU Consensus' may eventually open the door to a more coherent European approach to European political economy and economic governance, irrespective of the structure of membership, which is a distinct but obviously connected and crucial issue (Lavdas & Chryssochoou, 2011).

3 From Frustrated Republicanism to Bureaucratic Populism?

Reputedly, Greeks know a thing or two about politics. However, the reasons why they do—the conditions that help nurture a political culture prone to intense politicisation—are diverse and, at least some of them, divergent. And they form a crucial background for an understanding of the position of contemporary issues of governance in the public mind.

In fact, as we have suggested elsewhere, political development in modern Greece can be best approached with the help of three different conceptions of politics: civic commitment in a free polity, guardianship, and voluntarism in a populist or (alternatively) a republican version. These have been embedded in three distinct discursive contexts formed in the course of political development: frustrated early republicanism, conservative authoritarianism, and voluntarist anti-necessitarianism (see Lavdas, 1997, 2000).

Indeed, the years preceding and immediately following the establishment of the Greek state were associated with a frustrated republican impulse. *Vide* the declarations of the Epidaurus, Astros, and Troizina assemblies in 1822–1827. By contrast, the Kingdom of Greece led to the articulation and final predominance of a concept of politics as guardianship with a strong underlying exclusionary thrust. The exclusionary dimension was later reinforced with the bloc mentality associated with the civil war of the 1940s and its aftermath. The culmination of this period, that is, the introduction of explicit authoritarianism with the coup in 1967, can be seen as taking the view of politics as guardianship to its extreme conclusion, thereby changing the parameters of the debate.

The third conception of politics emerges in the context of the break with conservative-authoritarian rule in 1974. The break in 1974 also represented a certain departure from routine politics: for a crucial albeit brief historical moment, a number of different political outcomes appeared possible. This transitory emphasis on political possibilities left an unmistakable mark on the Third Republic: a sense of political possibilities combined with the defiance of inherited structures, and of the traits and constraints that shaped them, tends to characterise the dominant post-1974 conceptions of politics and citizenship.

This particular form of anti-necessitarianism constructs its conception of politics in terms of a seemingly expanding horizon of political possibilities. The conception of politics in this context retains elements of the civic emphasis that the previous two concepts had endorsed in markedly different ways, but registers a heightened state of anticipation of new forms of substantive popular participation in the polity. Some aspects of this conception led to valuable searches for the remarkable potential inherent in Greek republican sensibilities; other aspects simply provided ammunition for the populist digression of the 1980s.[2] Yet it is also true that active citizenship, for many Greeks, acquired a substantive dimension after 1974.

As the international financial crisis that exploded in September 2008 became a major issue within the EU, developments led to a reopening of discussions over key issues and dilemmas of the eurozone and economic governance. Questions of economic governance and issues of democratic accountability became equally crucial in this context. After all,

> historically, political orders have been the result of contention and only rarely, if ever, of social contracting. Hence, they are partial solutions that tend to reflect prevailing interests [...] Democracy sometimes followed the state-making exercise. As such, it has been tied to the particular order of the state. Even contemporary cross-border social movements remain focused on the traditional institutions of the state [...] in light of the difficulties of finding publicly agreeable justifications for the European project, this is perhaps the issue that needs addressing: How useful is democracy, as a historically contingent paradigm, for ordering relations outside the state? (Sissenich, 2007, 353).

In today's Greece, the *financial-cum-economic* crisis reshaped the parameters of the debate. From a longer-term perspective, it may seem as if the crisis simultaneously wreaked havoc on the social fabric and forced open a window of opportunity. In view of the latter, a new pragmatism may become part of the changing conception of politics. However, to achieve this, we will need to curb some of the structural constraints on large-scale reform while at the same time reassuring Greek citizens that national democratic accountability is not a thing of the past. Both aspects are crucial: it is the combination that matters. What do the behaviour of the Greek state and the trends in Greek public opinion tell us about the chances to achieve the desired combination?

[2] See the analysis in Lyrintzis (1987).

4 Back to Viewing Non-compliance as Weakness

A certain ambiguity regarding compliance has marked Greece's record of EC/EU membership. From a partial recourse to strategic non-compliance in the 1980s, when perceived setbacks for Greek interests at the stage of European policy formation were addressed at the stage of policy implementation, we have come to a renewed interest in the administrative problems and the related weaknesses which underlie non-compliance.

At present, Greece has been at the spotlight for its weak implementation record and, even more so, for its shabby compliance record with respect to the *acquis communautaire*. However, Greece's difficulties with compliance are not a country-specific feature; rather, they represent a systemic condition that concerns all EU member states and is linked to the particular qualities of the present stage of European integration (see Mendrinou, 1996). Although Greece's compliance record has only slightly improved in quantitative terms, an examination of the legal basis of the different cases of infringement procedures initiated by the Commission against Greece suggests a more pronounced qualitative improvement. Table 1 compiles the percentage distribution of cases of infringement procedures by legal base and compares two successive periods.

As the table shows, during the last decade there has been a considerable decrease in the percentage of breaches under the legal base of rules and regulations for Greece, reaching a percentage which is in fact lower than the EU average. In addition, particularly improved are the percentages concerning directives even when compared to the EU total, with the exception of the case of 'not properly applied' directives. This legal base of alleged infringements suggests serious weaknesses on the part of Greece's administration and legal system—which has been marked by overregulation and a multiplicity of often-contradictory legal provisions—that apparently fail to properly apply well-implemented directives.[3]

5 Trust and the Emerging Euro-Wide Scepticism

The prospect of participating in the organisational developments that took shape among European states following WW II had become predominant in Greek politics, not only in the early 1960s but also in the late 1970s and the early 1980s. The Association Agreement with the EEC, signed in 1961, ended abruptly as a result of the military coup of 1967. It was the restoration of democratic rule in 1974 that renewed the interest for enhancing the European prospects of the country. The 1976 application for full membership, the signing of the Accession Treaty in 1979, and the joining of the EC in 1981, had been supported by the great majority of Greek people, though at the time there were major political forces, such as the

[3] On non-compliance and monitoring and enforcement in the EU, see inter alia Mendrinou (1996), Kohler-Koch (2005), and Falkner, Treib, Hartlapp, and Leiber (2005).

Table 1 The distribution of cases of infringement procedures by legal step and legal base for Greece and the EU (in percentage)

	No communication of directives	Not properly implemented directives	Not properly applied	Rules, regulations, decisions	Total
Letter of formal notice					
1983–2000					
Greece	66.33	4.05	11.97	17.64	100.00
EU	65.45	5.59	14.06	14.91	100.00
2001–2010					
Greece	61.02	6.59	21.02	11.36	100.00
EU	66.38	7.32	14.75	11.56	100.00
Reasoned opinion					
1983–2000					
Greece	61.00	3.90	11.08	24.02	100.00
EU	56.46	8.03	16.09	19.43	100.00
2001–2010					
Greece	62.21	5.64	20.46	11.69	100.00
EU	55.57	11.11	18.29	15.03	100.00
Reference to the court					
1983–2000					
Greece	53.54	4.04	12.63	29.80	100.00
EU	47.83	10.41	17.72	24.04	100.00
2001–2010					
Greece	58.79	6.04	20.88	14.29	100.00
EU	50.45	12.58	20.97	16.00	100.00

Source: European Commission (2012a)

PASOK (Pan-Hellenic Socialist Movement), that were ostensibly against EC membership.[4] Since then, Greek public opinion has displayed an overwhelmingly positive stance towards the EU.

As Fig. 1 shows, in the period 1981–2011, the majority of the Greek public consider EU membership as 'a good thing'.[5] Overall, the positive responses of the Greek public on EU membership were well above the EU average while at the same time the negative responses were well below the corresponding EU average. There are only two periods in which the Greek public's attitudes diverge from this pattern. The first was during the initial years of the country's membership, 1981–1988,

[4] The Greek public opinion on European integration had been polled by the *Eurobarometer* as early as the autumn of 1980, before the country's actual accession. According to these polls, an impressive 59 % of the respondents were in favour of European unification, and a few months later, that percentage increased to 60 % (*Eurobarometer* 15, 1981, 17).

[5] The question's wording in the *Eurobarometer* is as follows: 'Generally speaking do you think that (our country)'s membership of the EU is a "good thing"'?

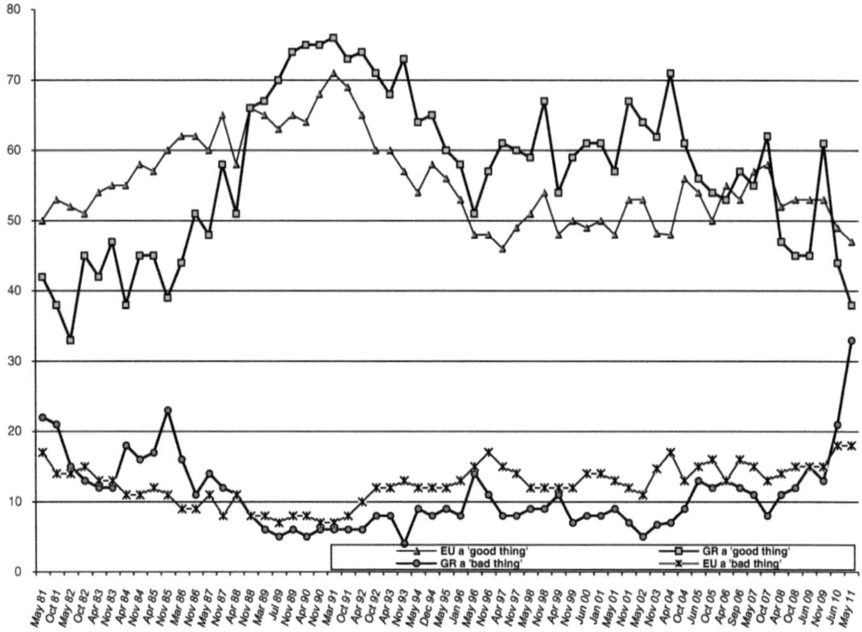

Fig. 1 EU Membership is ‘a good or a bad thing’, Greece and EU average. *Source*: European Commission (2012b)

when the governmental party, PASOK, was expressing reservations at the time on the conditions of the country’s accession. The reservations in question had led to considerable uncertainty in Greek public opinion on the prospects of the country’s membership. The second period of divergence consists of the most recent years, during the acute economic crisis. The current data display a noteworthy decline in positive attitudes of the Greek public towards EU membership while equally pronounced is the rise of those who consider that EU membership is ‘a bad thing’. However, Fig. 1 also shows that, although in less marked terms, the general trend of the EU average is in the same direction as that of Greece, since a drop in the positive responses has been registered in the 2011 *Eurobarometer* in other member states hit by the crisis (Italy, Portugal, and most of the new member states of the 2004 enlargement of the EU).

The above findings are further confirmed by the stance of the Greek public on the benefits accrued from EU membership.[6] The Greek public, in overwhelming numbers, considers that the Greek accession to the EU was particularly beneficial. Figure 2 compiles the relevant data for Greece in comparison with the EU average for the same period. It is apparent that the Greek public has been viewing EU

[6] The question’s wording is as follows: ‘taking everything into account, would you say that GREECE has on balance benefited or not from being a member of the EU’?

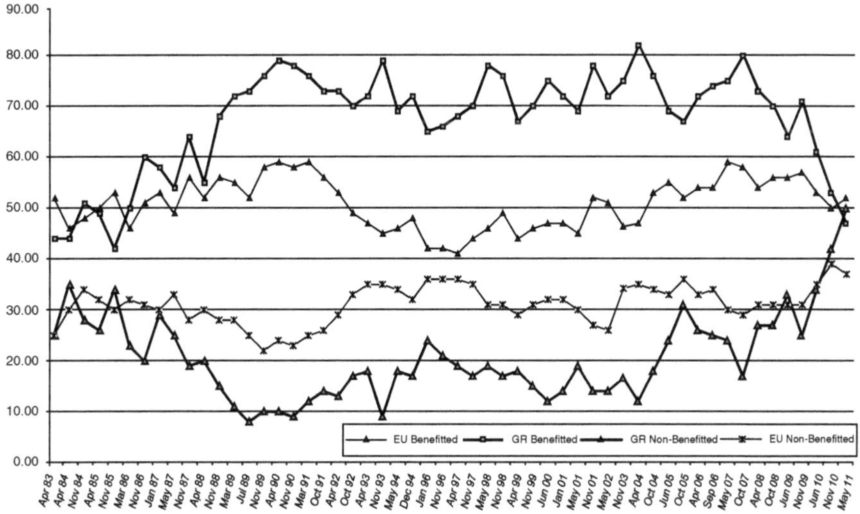

Fig. 2 'Benefited' and 'non benefited from EU membership', Greece and EU total. *Source*: European Commission (2012b)

membership as particularly beneficial for Greece. In particular, during the period 1983–2010 the average of those who responded that Greece has benefited from EU membership was 68 %, compared to 51 %, which is the corresponding EU average. However, the most recent *Eurobarometer* surveys displayed a considerable drop in the percentage of positive responses, apparently a result of the economic crisis and the particular conditions set by the EU (and the IMF) on Greece's bailout. The impact of the intensity of the economic situation developed in Greece is confirmed by the pronounced rise in the percentage of those who considered that the country has not benefited by EU membership that in 2011 rose to 50 %, which is the second highest in the EU27 (the UK occupies the first position).

The recent shift in Greek public opinion on the EU appears to be directly linked to the current economic conditions in Greece. As Fig. 3 shows, during 2003–2011, the Greek public overwhelmingly expressed its trust in the EU with percentages well above the ones for the national government.[7] Moreover, the Greek public displayed considerably more trust in the EU than the average European does, a feature that declined only after 2010. This decline, however, is not unique to Greece: as the EU average demonstrates, it is indicative of a more widespread tendency that appears in the data of other member states as well. It is in fact even more marked as a tendency in the old and older member states, such as France, Germany, but also Portugal, and Spain.

[7] The wording of the question is as follows: 'I would like to ask you a question about how much trust you have in certain institutions. For each of the following institutions, please tell me if you tend to trust it or tend not to trust it'? 'The European Union' 'The (NATIONALITY) government'. European Commission, *Eurobarometer*.

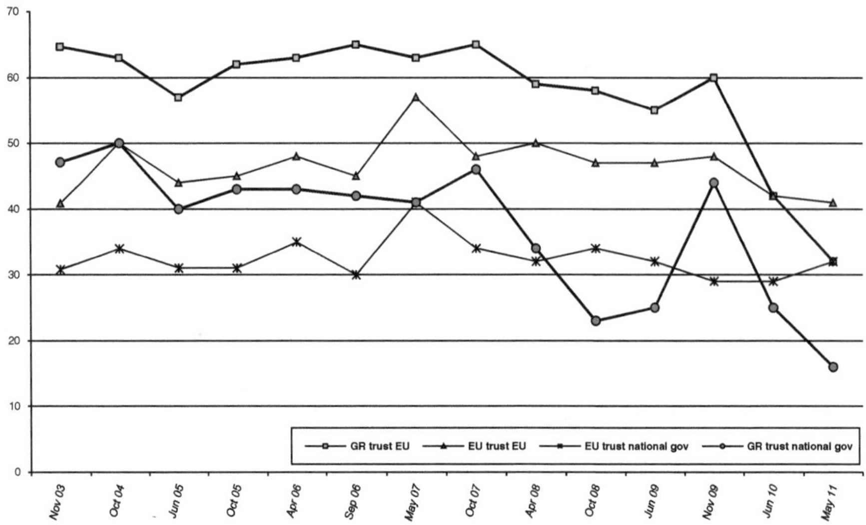

Fig. 3 Percentage trust in the EU and in the national government. *Source*: European Commission (2012b)

These findings suggest less a tendency towards political cynicism than an increase in *scepticism* among the EU publics.[8] The importance of this distinction cannot be overestimated. The emergence of scepticism is closely linked to questions of trust and accountability, not apathy and alienation. In other words, while cynicism tends to imply alienation vis-à-vis the institutions and/or arrangements concerned, scepticism tends to reflect various forms of criticism on the part of public vis-à-vis the institutions and/or arrangements, and may also involve issues of accountability which may relate to criticism of a pattern or, in some cases, the experience of failed expectations.

Questions of trust and accountability influence the public's approach to different levels of European governance, but they also possess an unmistakably interactive quality. For example, an influential analysis of the US political business cycle has shown that the percentage of the public predicting an economic upturn increases before a presidential election (Suzuki, 1992, 989–996). Figures 4 and 5 present a crucial if indicative—pending further analysis—test for the comparative shifts in the perceptions of trust in the EU and in national governments. Based on data provided by Eurobarometer, our analysis compiles the Percentage Difference Index (PDI) attempting to construct a model on trust in national governments and in the EU. Our figures suggest a dynamic influence of policy outcomes and the policy responses of EU and national institutions in the context of an evolving crisis.

[8] On the relation between 'cynicism' and 'scepticism' with respect to the questions of trust and accountability see Cook and Gronke (2005, 785 and 799–801) and Mishler and Rose (1997).

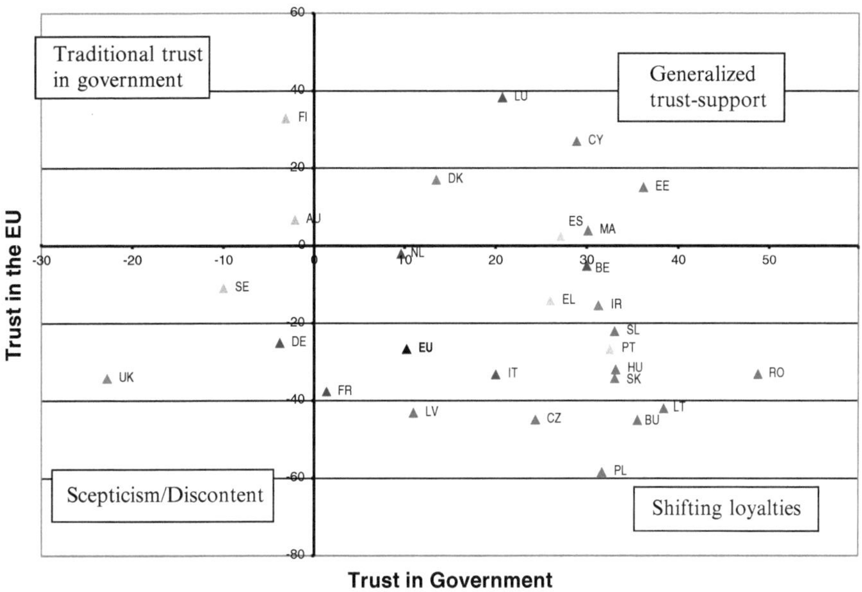

Fig. 4 Plot of PDI of trust for the national government and the EU for the period October 2005–April 2008

The figures plot the PDI between those who 'tend to trust' and those who 'tend not to trust' their national government (*Y*-axis) and the EU (*X*-axis) for the average of two successive periods. The first period is from October 2004 to April 2008 (based on data from eight *Eurobarometer* surveys) and the second from October 2008 to May 2011 (based on data from five *Eurobarometer* surveys). The plotting of the PDI helps us form four main groupings on the basis of the degree of trust in relation to both the EU and the national governments. In the first grouping (upper right), the public opinion of the member states express trust in both the EU and the national governments, suggesting a generalised trust towards both categories of institutions. The lower right grouping concerns publics that mainly tend to trust the EU but have negative trust with respect to their governments, tentatively suggesting a shift in loyalties. The third grouping (upper left) displays the opposite features, mainly trust for the national government but not for the EU, suggesting a traditional perception of trust in government. Finally, the fourth grouping (lower left) refers to publics with negative PDI for both their national government and the EU, indicating the development of scepticism and possible discontent vis-à-vis both levels of governance.

The shifts are remarkable. For example, the positioning of the member states of the 2004 enlargement may lead to diverse approaches to the impact of accession and post-accession politics and policy on the public of Central and Eastern Europe. In the particular context of the present paper, the impact of the current crisis on the changing attitudes in the member states (such as Greece, Spain, Portugal, Latvia,

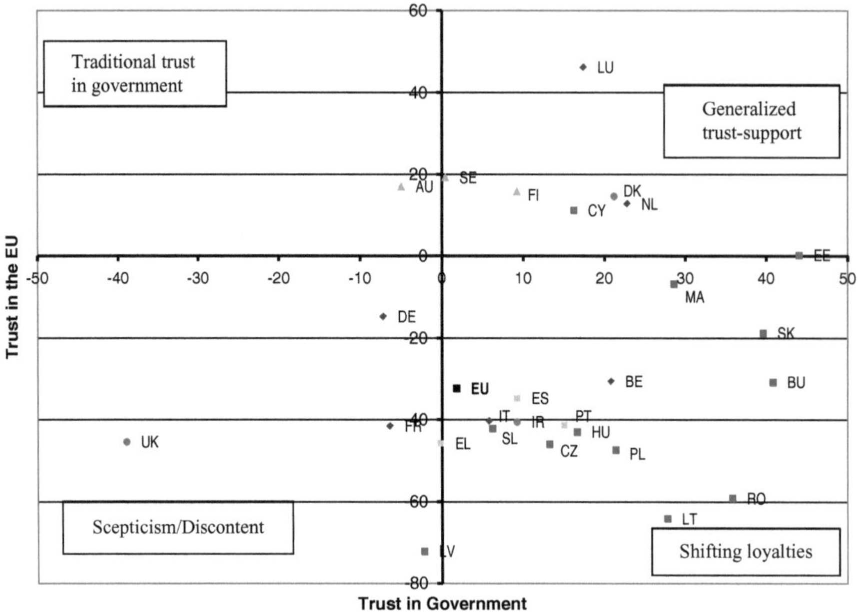

Fig. 5 Plot of PDI of trust for the national government and the EU for the period October 2008–May 2011

and even France) that have been affected—in various ways—by the crisis is of particular interest. Further analysis will explicate the patterns that appear to have formed since 2008.

6 Conclusion: Tenacious or Obstinate?

We have argued that Greece's tenacious Europeanisation has been the combined outcome of a particular domestic and European constellation: the long-term co-existence of an elite-formed and sustained European strategy since the 1960s (bracketing the authoritarian parenthesis of 1967–1974) and considerable structural impediments to economic liberalisation and modernisation (Lavdas, 1997). We have shown that a widespread and enduring pattern of support for the European project has emerged, despite oscillations, and the changes in this pattern have been generally in line with developments in other member states, as far as an increase in scepticism is discernible.

Of course, there are also signs of a decrease in the dynamic of the domestic European thrust, largely as a result of the acute financial, fiscal, and economic crisis after 2008 and especially since 2010. Is Greece's Europeanisation better defined as tenacious or as obstinate? Merriam-Webster defines 'obstinate' as 'perversely adhering to a [. . .] course, in spite of reason, arguments, or persuasion', as in the sentence 'obstinate resistance to change'. In Greece, Europeanisation was, and still is, an interactive course through challenges, problems, constraints, and opportunities in a reform-resistant context. Whether the persistence in its course on the part of certain groups, strata, and elites, projects the image of obstinacy rather than tenacity will depend on factors that include not only domestic changes and transformations—including economic and administrative reform and shifts in public opinion—but also EU-level developments. We have demonstrated the force of the comparative impact of the current crisis on the changing attitudes in member states (such as Greece, Spain, Portugal, Latvia, and even France) that have been affected in various ways by the crisis.

On paper, at least, a pluralism of views with regard to the current crisis and the most appropriate strategies to tackle it may be a good thing. It may also be an antidote to the emerging hegemony of a particular parochialism, that is, of the current worldview advocated by those favouring an exclusively austerity-geared approach. At the same time, however, the dangers of populism are always present in the Greek context. The new government that took office as a result of the national elections on 17 June 2012, based on three-party support spearheaded by ND, is a government which expresses the choice for Europe. Whether that choice, which confirms a deep-rooted European strategy of the Greek state, will prove successful is a matter that will depend on a truly interactive (hence largely unpredictable) combination of domestic, European, and international developments.

References

Císař, O. (2007). Between the national and supranational? Transnational political activism, conflict, and cooperation in the integrated Europe. *Contemporary European Studies, 1*, 21–36.

Cook, T. E., & Gronke, P. (2005). The skeptical American: Revisiting the meaning of trust in government and confidence in institutions. *Journal of Politics, 67*(3), 784–803.

European Commission. (1981). Eurobarometer 15. http://ec.europa.eu/public_opinion/archives/eb/eb15/eb15_en.pdf. Accessed 4 June 2012.

European Commission. (2012a). Annual reports on monitoring the application of EU law. http://ec.europa.eu/eu_law/infringements/infringements_annual_report_en.htm. Accessed 3 June 2012.

European Commission. (2012b). Eurobarometer. http://ec.europa.eu/public_opinion/archives/eb/. Accessed 3 June 2012.

Falkner, G., Treib, O., Hartlapp, M., & Leiber, S. (Eds.). (2005). *Complying with Europe: EU harmonisation and soft law in the member states*. Cambridge: Cambridge University Press.

Featherstone, K., & Papadimitriou, D. (2008). *The limits of Europeanisation: Reform capacity and policy conflict in Greece*. London: Palgrave Macmillan.

Fola, M. (2011). Athens City branding and the 2004 Olympic Games. In K. Dinnie (Ed.), *City branding: Theory and cases* (pp. 37–47). London: Palgrave Macmillan.

Kohler-Koch, B. (Ed.). (2005). *Linking EU and national governance*. Oxford: Oxford University Press.

Lavdas, K. A. (1996). The political economy of privatization in Southern Europe. In D. Braddon & D. Foster (Eds.), *Privatization: Social science themes and perspectives* (pp. 155–187). Aldershot: Dartmouth.

Lavdas, K. A. (1997). *The Europeanisation of Greece: Interest politics and the crises of integration*. London: Macmillan.

Lavdas, K. A. (2000). Concepts of politics in modern Greek political culture: An essay on the history of political concepts. Paper presented at the ECPR workshop on *'The history of political concepts: A new perspective on European political culture'*, ECPR Joint Sessions of Workshops 2000, University of Copenhagen, May 24–28.
Lavdas, K. A., & Chryssochoou, D. N. (2011). *A Republic of Europeans: Civic potential in a Liberal milieu*. Cheltenham: Edward Elgar.
Lyrintzis, C. (1987). The power of populism: The Greek case. *European Journal of Political Research, 15*(6), 667–686.
Mendrinou, M. (1996). Non-compliance and European Commission's role in integration. *Journal of European Public Policy, 3*(1), 1–22.
Mishler, W., & Rose, R. (1997). Trust, distrust and skepticism: Popular evaluations of civil and political institutions in post-communist societies. *Journal of Politics, 59*(2), 418–451.
Sissenich, B. (2007). Justification and identity in European integration: Comments on Morgan and Ferrara. *Constellations, 14*(3), 347–354.
Stoker, G. (2006). *Why politics matters: Making democracy work*. London: Palgrave Macmillan.
Suzuki, M. (1992). Political business cycles in the public mind. *American Political Science Review, 86*(4), 989–996.

The Reform Leadership: Strategy and Resources for Post-crisis Greece

Manos G. Papazoglou

Greece's multifaceted crisis has attracted international media attention as a result of its domestic, European, and even worldwide consequences. What is the share of responsibility attributed to politics and government? Notwithstanding the urgent changes required in the economy and public finances, what sort of changes are under way as regards the political system? Which negative aspects of the government and party organisation should be revised in order to restore trust in the political system? What lessons can we draw from the (failed) prevailing paradigm of leadership in Greek politics?

The present paper draws on recent research on leadership in Greek politics (Papazoglou, 2012). It examines the crisis from the perspective of the political system and places emphasis on the government and party leadership. It assesses the governmental achievements and shortcomings since the restoration of democracy (1974) and seeks explanations with reference to the literature on Greek politics. It is argued that transactional leadership, one that rests on populism, clientelism, and polarisation, came at the cost of a low governmental record, as was the case with governments in the 1980s. Moreover, external factors, such as convergence with the EMU criteria, acted as catalysts for policy reforms. Yet, governments in the 1990s largely failed to pursue full-scale changes by which to lay more efficient foundations for the functioning of the state and economy. Finally, the paper offers a forward-looking perspective with regard to three specific issues, namely sustainability, Europeanisation, and political stability, which may be useful guides for a concept and practice of leadership that matches efficient and democratic governance.

M.G. Papazoglou (✉)
Department of Political Science and International Relations, University of Peloponnese,
47 Dervenakion St and Adimantou, 20100 Corinth, Greece
e-mail: epapaz@yahoo.gr

P. Sklias and N. Tzifakis (eds.), *Greece's Horizons*, The Konstantinos Karamanlis Institute for Democracy Series on European and International Affairs,
DOI 10.1007/978-3-642-34534-0_5,

1 Leadership

According to a classic definition, 'Leadership over human beings is exercised when persons with certain motives and purposes mobilize, in competition or conflict with others, institutional, political, psychological, and other resources so as to arouse, engage and satisfy the motives of followers' (Burns, 1978, 18).

The study of leadership involves first three overarching factors, namely political context, power, and supporters. Successful leaders make a good assessment of the political context and of the opportunities and limits for action. They manage their legitimate power and attract supporters for the causes they pursue.

Power is indispensable for the achievement of political tasks, for it enables the activation of essential resources. Leadership is normally attached to formal positions (*ex officio*), such as those of the government, parties, public authorities, or international organisations. However, other forms of leadership do not presuppose holding positions of formal authority. This is the case with leadership exercised over ideas and opinions, and the influence exerted by expert advisers upon great policy projects (e.g. the Economic Monetary Union).

Holding power and exerting leadership are quite different things. US Presidents have generally held similar powers, but have had a very different record as regards their policy achievements. In other words, holding a driving license does not make you Michael Schumacher, if you do not also possess his talent, experience, his Ferrari F1 vehicle, and support-team.

Winston Churchill and Tony Blair performed their political duties in entirely different political contexts. The former made an excellent diagnosis of the international political context and shaped effective strategies. The latter had a good grasp of political trends in Britain according to which he repositioned the main aims of his party and government, thereby achieving electoral hegemony for nearly a decade.

Supporters constitute one of the most crucial factors in exercising leadership in a representative political system, for they legitimise (most notably through elections) political tasks and facilitate the implementation of policy tasks (e.g. complying with anti-smoking legislation) (Kellerman, 2008).

One useful distinction in the concept of leadership is that between 'transactional' and 'transforming' (Burns, 1978, 19–20). Transactional leadership involves the exchange of valued things between bargaining parties (leaders and supporters) having related purposes, but it does not forge an enduring bond between the two. On the other hand, transforming leadership means that leaders and supporters provide mutual support in the advancement of a common purpose that has a transforming effect on both.

2 The Politics of Leadership in Greece

The election results of May and June 2012, the first general elections after the country's bail-out, caused seismic effects on the party system by making evident the lack of trust in the political system. This was evinced by the dramatic fall in the share of votes of the governing parties, especially of the PASOK, the large share of votes gained by anti-systemic parties and the emergence of the leftist SYRIZA as the main opposition party, which projected a mixed agenda of pro-EU stance and Euroscepticism, populism and progressiveness, contestation and alternative governance.

Konstantinos Karamanlis (1974–1981) achieved transforming changes in the political system and improved the country's position on the international arena, but was less successful in restructuring the economy. Andreas Papandreou followed a transactional model of leadership (i.e. populism, clientelism, and polarisation) and prioritised short-term party electoral results at the expense of the medium-term performance of the government. Successive leaders [K. Mitsotakis (1990–1993), Andreas Papandreou (1993–1996), K. Simitis (1996–2004), Kostas Karamanlis (2004–2009, nephew of the late Konstantinos Karamanlis), and George Papandreou (2009–2011, son of the late Andreas Papandreou)] were able to generate only a modest amount of reform, mainly because they failed to direct the party and government functions effectively towards far-reaching policy change. In the following, I shall examine in more detail the forms of leadership that prevailed in Greek politics in the last few decades.

2.1 Transforming Leadership of Polity Change

The fall of dictatorship in 1974 marked the foundation of a political system that dropped many of the prevailing features of the old establishment. A referendum legitimised, with a clear and indisputable majority (69.18 %), the abolition of monarchy, and a multi-party system emerged as the result of removing constitutional and other restrictions on the communist party. Moreover, the holding of free elections encouraged the re-formation of the main party groupings. It also led to an overwhelming majority for the centre-right New Democracy (ND) party and the formation of a stable government. A new constitution recognised the fundamental rights and guarantees of political liberalism.

Many of the above issues were indeed thorny in the past decades and caused significant political instability and tensions, as for instance the century-old rivalry between royalists and anti-royalists or the civil war between the right and communists. Therefore, the wide ranging changes of 1974–1975 are rightly termed 'Metapolitefsi' (polity changeover) to the extent that they gave rise to a very new political context, entailing new rules of political competition and exercise of power, and new party identifications.

The Metapolitefsi involved two other considerable political developments: the accession of Greece to the EEC in 1981—seen as a way of consolidating liberal democracy and increasing national security (Valinakis, 1989, 189)—and the smooth transfer of executive power from the conservatives (ND) to the socialists (PASOK).

The changes in polity from 1974 onwards may rightly be seen as a case of transforming leadership, that is, a type of relationship between leadership and supporters where both uphold common causes that have a mutual transforming effect on both. The PM Konstantinos Karamanlis had a clear diagnosis of the political situation in the aftermath of the *Colonels' Junta* regime. Seizing the opportunity, he pushed forward new democratic arrangements with admirable determination and a consensual approach. The new arrangements modernised the political system and proved durable in the coming decades, while they also facilitated political reconciliation, especially between the right and the left, who were hitherto divided by old animosities and the legacy of the civil war (Siani-Davies & Katsikas, 2009).

In this regard, 'transforming leadership' suitably describes the role of almost all party leaders in the consolidation of the new democratic regime (Karakatsanis, 2001), but especially of Konstantinos Karamanlis (the conservative ERE party and subsequently the conservative New Democracy Party leader) and Andreas Papandreou (the leader of the socialist party PASOK, which represented considerable radical trends in the society but channelled their expression through parliamentary channels).

Konstantinos Karamanlis was a political leader. He was a former prime minister (1955–1963) who had considerable experience and domestic and international prestige, which made him capable of facing the challenge of substantial constitutional changes.

Konstantinos Karamanlis acted as a national, rather than a party, leader and dealt with the major reform issues with a view towards lawfulness and legitimacy. He exerted a transforming and moderating influence within the conservative party and on its supporters by encouraging tolerance for choices such as the legalisation of the communist party and the abolition of monarchy, and led the party's ideological re-orientation towards the democratic centre-right, thereby guiding the party away from extreme right-wing positions.

One of the most important features of Karamanlis' leadership has been the balanced approach to the duties of government and party leadership. In other words, under his leadership the party's electoral priorities did not curtail the implementation of governmental programmes.

As regards national defence and security issues, the New Democracy Party (ND) governments had to deal with conflicting relationship with Turkey, following the latter's military invasion of Cyprus (1974). Karamanlis insisted on diplomatic means for resolving these issues (through the UN and the international judiciary) (Svolopoulos, 2008, 325).

Compared with the great polity changes, policy outcomes were rather poor, especially as regards changing the paradigm of national economy in order to catch up with the competition from and productivity levels of the other EEC countries. Instead, state intervention was still seen as the catalyst (but acted in fact as the obstacle) for economic activity. Indeed, considerable segments of the industry, the banks, or even the major airline carrier Olympic Airways, were nationalised. Moreover, high levels of military spending combined with the consequences of the oil crises in the 1970s hindered economic growth (Antonakis, 1999).

Konstantinos Karamanlis led his government by dominating the decision-making process at the expense of a collective function of the cabinet (Loverdos, 1991). He had been the indisputable leader of the conservative party (since he succeeded Papagos and founded the ERE) until 1963, when he had to depart following his conflict with the Palace and his defeat by the Centre Union Party. His departure left the party with an inconclusive political strategy, internal conflicts, and poor electoral results. A similar situation emerged for the ND following Karamanlis' choice to stand for Presidency in 1980.

It is true that Karamanlis foresaw the electoral downturn of ND (from 54.4 % votes in 1974 to 41.84 % in 1977) and made the wise choice of relinquishing the duties of government leadership. More importantly, however, the Presidency of Karamanlis acted as a form of checks and balances to the Premiership of A. Papandreou from 1981 onwards. The radical rhetoric of PASOK had spread fears regarding the fundamentals of the political apparatus of the state and the position of the country within the EEC or the NATO.

2.2 Transactional Leadership of Populism and Polarisation

The radical elements in PASOK's physiognomy did not come as a surprise. Meynaud (2002, 378–379) fittingly pointed out that in the 1960s the rightists and the centrists moved closer to each other, so that the left needed a clear line of demarcation between itself and the right. A similar understanding of the political situation seems to have driven the political strategy of PASOK, the founding declaration of which (1974) voiced some radical ideas regarding national independence, popular sovereignty, and the economy.

The choice of radicalism and polarisation against the right was facilitated by the fact that, in contrast with the case of Spain, the short period of dictatorship allowed for both a relatively smooth return to the democratic rule and for the continuity of the major party groupings and voters' identification (Hamann & Sgouraki-Kinsey, 1999).

The shift of the conservatives to moderate ideology left PASOK with the only choice of following a more radical agenda in order to sharpen its distinctiveness vis-à vis the opponent party (Pappas, 2009, 77–87). The electoral gains of PASOK rose from 13.6 % in 1974 to 25.3 % in 1977. In 1981, the increase was even more dramatic, 48.1 % of the votes, thereby enabling it to form a majority government. It attracted voters from other parties of the centre-left, and even from the ND (Nicolacopoulos, 2005, 263).

The PASOK leadership did not deliver substantial 'transforming' effects. Undoubtedly, it contributed to bringing groups holding extreme anti-establishment views to parliamentary politics, thereby ending their direct or indirect exclusion from the state. PASOK articulated these radical views and endorsed ways of political mobilisation that did not threaten the democratic establishment per se, while gaining fresh political recruitment (Couloumbis, 1992; Karakatsanis, 2001, 177–178; Nicolacopoulos, 2005, 263–264).

The case of PASOK is best described as transactional leadership, given the populist and clientelistic methods it used for attracting voters. Populism guided PASOK's electoral and governmental practice (Lyrintzis, 1987, 1993), which, in combination with polarisation, sharpened party identities (Pappas, 2009, 219–225).

Before 1981, PASOK's electoral tactic entailed polarisation against the right, against Konstantinos Karamanlis himself, and against the economic and state elites. It also entailed opposition to the international powers and assertions that national sovereignty had been compromised. It projected a set of radical, and over-simplistic, ideas about the economy and society. In a way familiar to populists, it claimed to represent the ordinary 'non-privileged' citizens, a category with which the vast majority of citizens could identify themselves, and promised 'change' (Pappas, 2009, 148–150).

Once in power, PASOK's leadership did not exert a transforming influence on its supporters but, instead, found itself fettered by its own electoral promises and, therefore, subject to its voters' demands for immediate and privileged access to state's resources—given the citizens' high expectations for higher incomes and improved standards of living (Voulgaris, 2008, 121–128).

PASOK has been a 'charismatic party' (Pappas, 2009, 113–125) led by an indisputable leader, who accumulated organisational powers that he exercised through a small group of die-hard presidentialists. Some of the main features were the lack of specific party rules and of a stable party hierarchy, the limited use of collective bodies, and ideological ambiguity. Andreas Papandreou himself dominated the functions of the party and exerted ideological hegemony through a combination of 'hard' power (i.e. marginalising the dissidents) and 'soft'/persuasive power.

In fact, the dominant position of the leader made PASOK no different from the old conservative parties ruled by Papagos and Konstantinos Karamanlis (Spourdalakis, 1988, 280–284). PASOK passed through many different phases of party development—a cadre party in 1974, a mass party and movement in 1974–1977, a government and catchall party in 1974–1985, and a cartel party 1985 onwards (Spourdalakis, 1998, 15–74).

Papandreou as prime minister acted as *primus solus*, rather than as a *primus inter pares,* at the expense of the collective functioning of the cabinet (Loverdos, 1991). This is evident from the very frequent cabinet reshuffles and the replacement of the ministers of Economics (Pappas, 2009, 188–193).

Notwithstanding the record of governmental policies in the field of social protection, education, the agricultural sector, and the health system, PASOK generally failed to implement a consistent and coherent programme of reforms. On the contrary, many of the choices made by the government in the 1980s seem to have been detrimental to public finances and the modus operandi of the state apparatus.

The welfare state was seen as instrumental to economic growth, but actually the growing public debt, low productivity, and high unemployment hindered growth and the long-term sustainability of welfare policies (Gravaris, 1998). Indeed, the sharp increase of public spending, the rising cost of public debt, and the inefficient tax-collection mechanism had debilitating effects on the fiscal situation of the country (Thomadakis & Seremetis, 1992).

In many respects, Papandreou's approach to leadership prioritised the party's short-term electoral gains at the expense of medium-term achievements of the government. Certainly, electoral concerns were hardly a secondary issue for a party with a vast increase in electoral gains 7 years after its foundation.

Nevertheless, the choice of transactional leadership was not the only option for PASOK. In contrast with PASOK, the Spanish socialists (PSOE) under González, once in government in the 1980s, revisited their radical ideology, promoted moderation and consensus, and implemented economic reforms with a view to pursuing development, which, in turn, allowed the redistribution of surplus to the least advantaged groups (Pappas, 2010).

2.3 Leadership of Limited Reform

In the 1990s, the model of populist leadership gradually lost ground in favour of a more reformist model of government leadership. This was clearly a consequence of the effects of the first, namely of the decay of public finances and the national economy, as much as of the phenomena of political corruption, for which many members of the government were accused and sentenced. Moreover, the treaty of Maastricht created a major policy project, the Economic and Monetary Union (EMU), which acted as an external catalyst for domestic policy change.

As a result, Europeanisation, understood as a means for converging with the EU standards of living, income, education, and so on, guided much of the policy content of governmental programmes in the 1990s. The centre-right Mitsotakis government (1990–1993) initiated a programme of structural reforms and privatisation. Andreas Papandreou's government (1993–1996), despite his fierce opposition to Mitsotakis' policies, made a considerable shift towards endorsing the tasks of converging with the EMU criteria regarding sound public finances, inflation, and exchange rates. Hence, economic reforms and inter-party consensus gathered momentum, thereby enabling governments to implement policy changes that were unthinkable in the past. The two governments led by Simitis (1996–2004) had a generally favourable political context and accomplished the task of EMU entry.

The Mitsotakis government was the first to attempt the shift to the governance paradigm—from a populist to a reformist trend—seen as a means of tackling all those hurdles that used to hinder the proper functioning of the state and the economy. As Pelagidis (2005) describes it, a few well-organised groups, taking advantage of the state's inability to control their activity, distributed state revenues among their members.

The Prime Minister Mitsotakis also initiated privatisations in the banking, energy, industry, and telecommunication sectors and established free competition in sectors in which state-controlled companies used to have monopoly (Pagoulatos, 2007).

However, the government faced fierce opposition from the public sector interest groups. Moreover, a nationalist-populist movement that emerged regarding the issue of FYROM quickly destabilised the government, which finally stepped down. One of the problems of the Mitsotakis government was inadequate political and social capital or concrete support for the reforms it pushed through. Despite the clear mandate it received in 1990 (46.89 %), its parliamentary group did not have sufficient seats to allow the party to form a government on its own strength.

The return of A. Papandreou in government in 1993 with an unquestionably clear mandate (46.88 %) and a considerable parliamentary majority marked a decisive turn because it permitted fully endorsing many of the economic policy tasks put forward by the previous government. This marked the shift from the practices of populism and clientelism of the PASOK leadership and followers. One of the major reforms that it passed was the establishment in 1994 (Law 2190 on ASEP) of an independent agency for selecting personnel for public administration, by means of objective criteria.

In many respects, A. Papandreou's government acted by taking full stock of the economic and political situation. The Greek economy was lagging behind that of even the newer members of the EU and the public finances were still problematic. However, the opposition party (ND) consented to reforms, while the public sector interest groups were left with no serious political support. A. Papandreou, utilising all his political capital, legitimised the shift to EMU-guided reforms and set the grounds for their accomplishment, thereby leaving behind fertile grounds for his successor K. Simitis, who led the government and the party from 1996 to 2004.

The EMU acted as the external catalyst for domestic reform (Featherstone, 2005). Simitis proclaimed a project of modernisation, a rather vague idea which was mainly conceived as Europeanisation, and formed a group of supporters in the government and the party in order to attain his aims.

One of the major achievements of Prime Minister Simitis was the infrastructure programme, which was further accelerated by the Olympics of 2004. Furthermore, new institutions were created, such as the Ombudsman, the Data Protection Authority, one-stop services, and the Economic and Social Committee, in order to lay better foundations for the state-society relationship (Diamantouros, 2002, 42–45; Mouzelis & Pagoulatos, 2003).

The Simitis government's record did not come up to its potential and expectations. 'Modernisation' remained a rather vague concept, subjective in nature, which did not constitute a cohesive programme of reforms (Lyrintzis, 1998, 2005).

As regards public administration, very few steps were taken for a complete state reform. The Greek administrative system was still far from approaching the European administrative standards. Corruption and clientelism, to the extent that they served party interests, were still evident in the public administration (Papadoulis, 2006).

The constitutional amendment in 2001 failed to create the necessary political checks and balances, so as to reduce the impact of economic and social interests and further consolidate the rule of law (Eleftheriadis, 2005).

Greece also had a low record of compliance with EC law, thereby provoking the European Commission to 'yellow card' the country and even to refer the case to the Court of Justice of the European Union. The modernisers' government kept an ambivalent position, using the EC legislation only as far as it served its policies, and delaying its implementation when that tended to be politically costly (Christianos, 2008).

It is true that the EMU was the essential external impetus for reforms. However, the government acted only as a 'policy-receiver' and thus, lacked a capacity to act more actively in co-forming the aims of reforms beyond the scope of nominal convergence criteria (Featherstone, 2003).

Moreover, it failed to reduce the close connection of employees' interest groups with parties. Nor did it reduce the efforts of these groups to exhibit an oppositional stance and exert pressure on party and government members. Nor did it raise the costs of non-agreement, so as to make a veto-position expensive (Zambarloukou, 2006).

This was essentially made evident by the labour market reforms between 1997 and 2000, when improper preparation and the government's inability to deal with the interest groups resulted in inadequate policy results (Papadimitriou, 2007).

In its attempt towards reducing public spending in the health system the government failed to confront the professional and entrepreneurial groups with vested interests in the existing system (Mosialos, 2007).

As regards welfare, the intention of Europeanisation did not bring about tangible outcomes in the sustainability of the pensions system or in the quality of welfare services, compared with those delivered to the citizens of other member states (Sotiropoulos, 2004).

The liberalisation of the visual media market took place without specific rules. Therefore, monopolies prevailed in the media market and private television became the leading medium of political communication, consequently becoming the object of competition between parties and political personnel (Daremas & Terzis, 2000).

Simitis managed to become dominant in the party, thereby creating a new PASOK managed by administrative elite, which manned the decision-making positions in the government and state institutions. Yet, the old clientelistic and populist networks survived (Kazamias, 2005). Simitis did not really bring about 'transforming' changes in the way the party was functioning. The latter was seen primarily as a mechanism for electoral mobilisation and political support for the government, and offered very few real participatory opportunities for its members (Georgiadou, 2002).

The Kostas Karamanlis (nephew of Konstantinos Karamanlis) government (2004–2009) quickly lost pace in implementing reforms. Public spending sharply increased, partly because of the 2004 Olympics, but also because of the lack of a coherent strategy for reducing the unnecessary costs burdening the public budget. The new government's choice to hold elections in 2007 in order to get a fresh mandate boomeranged, as it brought only a thin parliamentary majority, thereby further hindering the capacity to pass important bills and take hard decisions.

Most importantly, the limited reforms of the 1990s left the economy and the public finances vulnerable to the world crisis in 2008, when increased financial assistance was required for the survival of the Greek banking system (Pagoulatos & Triantopoulos, 2009).

To sum up, the model of transactional leadership prevailed in Greek politics. Leaders accumulated powers at the expense of intra-party democracy and of a more deliberative and inclusive decision-making process. Even when populism and polarisation were dropped to a certain extent, leaders largely failed to balance the duties of directing the government and the party by prioritising electoral success over policy effectiveness, thereby delaying—or implementing in a fragmentary way—all those necessary reforms that were viewed as having political costs.

3 A Challenge: Leadership for a Sustainable Government

The crisis of the Greek state and economy may be considered a symptom of a problematic match between leadership and governance, that is, of postponing many far-reaching decisions regarding the fundamentals of the state and economy that ought to have been made in a timely manner, following a close inspection of European and international trends. The crisis results from the effects of globalisation on productivity, competition, and internationalisation of the national economy, of a growing public debt on state budget efficiency, of demographic trends on pension systems, of climate change on natural resources, of tax evasion on public finances, and of delayed Europeanisation reforms on the process of modernisation.

All of the above render urgent a reconfiguration of the standard of leadership, if the country has to return to economic growth and protect the most vulnerable citizens, and if the political system is to restore trust and respond to citizens' claims for accountable and efficient governance.

In the following, I shall put forward a few proposals, which I feel would contribute to maximising the assets and resources of Greece, by combining democratic and effective leadership with sustainable governance.

3.1 Sustainability

The concept of sustainability is found at the core of modern governance. The United Nations (1987) classic definition reads: 'sustainable development is development that meets the needs of the present without compromising the ability of future generations to meet their own needs'.

Within the EU, sustainable development includes three distinctive elements: *efficient economic development* that meets the criteria of social justice and is environmentally sustainable.

Therefore, decision making should take into account the medium and long-term impact of current policies on the social, economic, and natural resources, in order to ensure prosperity and equal opportunities for present and future generations.

Two examples stand out in my view for the politics of sustainability. First, education is one of the most significant fields contributing towards equal opportunities for every citizen, and, in the meantime, for embedding a sense of responsibility and allegiance—indispensable features of a democratic citizenship. Second, tourism, one of the most dynamic sectors of the Greek economy, should be guided by the principles of sustainability in order to safeguard the most significant asset, namely, natural resources.

3.2 Europeanisation

The term is conceived in different ways. However, it refers to a complex two-layered process in which integration into Europe shapes politics and policies at the national level and leads to divergent results within member states (Schmidt, 2006; Schmidt & Radaelli, 2004).

Greece is certainly a beneficiary of European integration, if we take into account convergence with the EMU criteria on many significant economic and social indices. Nevertheless, non-compliance with certain important aspects of governance, most notably the deficit levels under the EMU, the liberalisation of services or structural reforms, seems to hinder Greece's full adaptation to the EU economy and accordingly, the maximisation of the economic benefits that it may derive.

The challenge for leadership is to move from a practice of enforced Europeanisation to that of participatory Europeanisation. The former refers to the cases of nominal (but not substantial) convergence with the EMU criteria (and the problems of collecting and reporting fiscal data) and the fragmentary way of implementing directives, regarding, for example, waste management.

On the other hand, participatory Europeanisation allows for a more dynamic involvement of national and regional decision-making centres with the multi-level forms of governance in the EU, so that, in accordance with the principle of subsidiarity, decisions are made at the level more appropriate to the issue under consideration. In that way, good practices are diffused, specific local requirements are matched with the national and European priorities, and resources are allocated to the executive units that can achieve more efficient outcomes.

One example of participatory Europeanisation is the 'Europe 2020' project regarding a strategy for smart, sustainable, and non-discriminatory development (European Commission, 2010). Certainly, a multilevel *sui generis* polity, such as the EU, generates its own democratic deficits (Papazoglou, 2005) and legitimacy crises (Papazoglou, 2010) that have to be dealt with. Citizens acquire new competences for having a say in the process of European integration (Papazoglou, 2010).

The role of the state is changing towards the mobilisation of economic and social agencies for promoting economic development. The relational state (Mendoza &

Vernis, 2008) aims at advancing co-operation between state and social agencies in order to establish a sense of 'co-responsibility' in problem solving. For instance, it may promote public–private partnerships and forms of 'public entrepreneurship' or 'corporate social responsibility'.

Another meaningful term is that of 'partnered governance' (Midttun, 2008) according to which governments try to involve societal actors in order to deal with social and environmental issues that could not have been tackled by the government alone (e.g. in the fields of waste-recycling or energy saving).

3.3 Political Stability

One of the factors that destabilise the government is what I call the 'republican tension' in Greek politics, that is, forms of collective action against political domination and in favour of societal issues. However, the republican tension often has a negative impact on democracy to the extent that it exceeds the democratic boundaries within which contestation is a legitimate option for citizens. In the field of societal culture, the issues and cleavages, under certain circumstances, become politicised and reinforce nationalist sentiments in ways that are discriminating against minorities. In the field of governance, civil disobedience is often thought to be a legitimate (and unconditional) option for criticising the government.

Against these shortcomings of the republican tension, I shall briefly explain the significance of liberal nationalism and republican contestation. First, liberal nationalism (Dagger, 1997; Kymlicka, 2001; Miller, 1995, 2000; Tamir, 1993) suggests that nation states are the ideal contexts for democracy but also points out the functional significance of political community and national identity for conceptualising the public interest and democratic participation. In this view, claims of societal culture should come to terms with the fundamentals of liberal constitutionalism, and abstain from forms of activity that jeopardise the equal standing of every citizen and one's own right to self-determination.

Second, contestation is certainly in line with the republican concern for eliminating conditions of political domination and manipulation (Pettit, 2001, 143–150). Yet, republicanism insists that liberties are safeguarded by the law (and are not against it) and presupposes a continuous supervision of the political process and the duties of participation (Skinner, 1992, 219, 1998, 7). Laws fundamental to liberties should not be subject to an easy amendment in accordance with the preferences of majority (Pettit, 1997, 181).

Civil disobedience is not an unconditional right of citizens. Rawls (1971, 73–78, 312–336) defines civil disobedience as a public and non-violent political act addressed to the majority in order to change legislation or policies but cannot be seen as a general right to disobey the law. Disobedience should be justified with reference to the violation of freedoms or a threat to social justice (Dworkin, 1977, 192–199).

In a liberal polity, respect to the liberal rules is a universal duty (Macedo, 1990) and is essential for the public evaluation of laws and public policies through an exchange of reasonable arguments. Loyalty to the law is seen as a fair-play commitment of citizens to the extent that they benefit from the public goods of political society (Dagger, 1997, 46–79). Political society constitutes a fair system of co-operation, organised around publicly recognised rules and procedures acceptable by all (Rawls, 1993, 2001, 16, 5–6).

A 'well-ordered' society is founded on a political concept of justice supported by the citizens, notwithstanding the different concepts of 'the good' they uphold (Rawls, 1993, 2001, 35, 9).

To conclude, the challenge for Greek politics is to clearly rewrite its political narrative along the lines of strong adherence to democracy and Europeanisation. The time is ripe for the leadership to lay new foundations for exercising power, to become responsive to urgent societal needs, and to balance the interests of their electoral base with the pursuit of sustainable development, especially with a view to the least advantaged and future generations (Papazoglou, 2012). Democratic deliberation should be a meaningful option within parties as well as within the procedures of law-making (Papazoglou, 2009).

The new coalition government (June 2012) may establish a new paradigm: for a consensual mode of decision making, strong accountability, and policy effectiveness. The opposition party SYRIZA may establish itself as an alternative governing party by securing its electoral stability and creating a cohesive programme of policy tasks that would receive strong political support.

References

Antonakis, N. (1999). Guns versus butter. A multisectoral approach to military expenditure and growth with evidence from Greece, 1960–1993. *Journal of Conflict Resolution, 43*(4), 501–520.

Burns, J. (1978). *Leadership*. New York: Harper Perennial.

Christianos, V. (2008). Greece and the acquis communautaire in front of the European Court of Justice. In N. Maravegias (Ed.) *Greece in the European Union* (pp. 62–68). Athens: Themelio (in Greek).

Couloumbis, T. (1992). Andreas Papandreou: The style and substance of leadership. In T. Kariotis (Ed.), *The Greek socialist experiment: Papandreou's Greece 1981–1989* (pp. 85–95). New York: Pella.

Dagger, R. (1997). *Civic virtues: Rights, citizenship and republican liberalism*. Oxford: Oxford University Press.

Daremas, G., & Terzis, G. (2000). Televisualization of politics in Greece. *International Communication Gazette, 62*, 117–131.

Diamantouros, N. (2002). State-citizenship relationship, institutions and civil society in the beginning of the 21st century. In Y. Voulgaris et al. (Eds.), *The prospects of modernization in Greece* (pp. 42–45). Athens: Kastaniotis (in Greek).

Dworkin, R. (1977). *Taking rights seriously*. London: Duckworth.

Eleftheriadis, P. (2005). Constitutional reform and the rule of law in Greece. *West European Politics, 28*(2), 317–334.

European Commission. (2010). *Communication, Europe 2020*. Strategy for smart, sustainable and inclusive development. COM (2010) 2020 final, 3.3.2010. Commission of the European Communities. Luxembourg.

Featherstone, K. (2003). Greece and EMU: Between external empowerment and domestic vulnerability. *Journal of Common Market Studies, 41*(5), 923–940.

Featherstone, K. (2005). Introduction: 'Modernisation' and the structural constraints of Greek politics. *West European Politics, 28*(2), 222–241.

Georgiadou, V. (2002). Labour Party, SPD and PASOK. Systems of party direction and organizational restructuring. In E. Katsoulis (Ed.), *New social democracy. Politics, institutions, organizational structures* (pp. 325–411). Athens: Sideris (in Greek).

Gravaris, D. (1998). Building the welfare state: From party discourse to state policies. In M. Spourdalakis (Ed.), *PASOK. Party, state, society* (pp. 91–120). Athens: Patakis (in Greek).

Hamann, K., & Sgouraki-Kinsey, B. (1999). Re-entering electoral politics: Reputation and party system change in Spain and Greece. *Party Politics, 5*, 55–77.

Karakatsanis, N. (2001). *The politics of elite transformation. The consolidation of Greek democracy in theoretical perspective*. London: Praeger.

Kazamias, P. (2005). The rise and fall of a state party. In T. Pelagidis (Ed.), *Blocking reforms in Greece. An evaluation of modernization* (pp. 59–82). Athens: Papazisi (in Greek).

Kellerman, B. (2008). *Followership: How followers are creating change and changing leaders*. Boston: Harvard Business Press.

Kymlicka, W. (2001). *Politics in the vernacular: Nationalism, multiculturalism and citizenship*. Oxford: Oxford University Press.

Loverdos, A. (1991). *Government, collective functioning and political responsibility*. Athens: Sakkoulas (in Greek).

Lyrintzis, C. (1987). The power of populism: The Greek case. *European Journal of Political Research, 15*(6), 667–686.

Lyrintzis, C. (1993). PASOK in power: From 'change' to disenchantment. In R. Clogg (Ed.), *Greece, 1981–89: The populist decade* (pp. 26–46). London: Macmillan.

Lyrintzis, C. (1998). Political crisis? New political trends and the potential of 'modernization'. In M. Spourdalakis (Ed.), *PASOK. Party, state, society* (pp. 78–88). Athens: Patakis (in Greek).

Lyrintzis, C. (2005). The changing party system: Stable democracy, contested 'modernisation'. *West European Politics, 28*(2), 242–259.

Macedo, S. (1990). *Liberal virtues: Citizenship, virtue and community in liberal constitutionalism*. Oxford: Clarendon.

Mendoza, M. X., & Vernis, A. (2008). The changing role of governments and the emergence of the relational state. *Corporate Governance, 8*(4), 389–396.

Meynaud, J. (2002). *Political powers in Greece 1946–1965*. Athens: Savvalas (in Greek).

Midttun, A. (2008). Global governance and the interface with business: New institutions, processes and partnerships. Partnered governance: Aligning corporate responsibility and public policy in the global economy. *Corporate Governance, 8*(4), 406–418.

Miller, D. (1995). *On nationality*. Oxford: Clarendon.

Miller, D. (2000). *Citizenship and national identity*. Cambridge: Polity.

Mosialos, E. (2007). Interest groups and the reform of the health system in Greece. In K. Featherstone (Ed.), *Politics in Greece. The challenge of modernization* (pp. 302–333). Athens: Okto (in Greek).

Mouzelis, N., & Pagoulatos, G. (2003). Civil society and citizenship in postwar Greece. *Greek Political Science Review, 22*, 5–29 (in Greek).

Nicolacopoulos, I. (2005). Elections and voters, 1974–2004: Old cleavages and new issues. *West European Politics, 28*(2), 260–278.

Pagoulatos, G. (2007). The politics of privatizations: Re-defining the boundaries between public and private. In K. Featherstone (Ed.), *Politics in Greece. The challenge of modernization* (pp. 211–242). Athens: Okto (in Greek).

Pagoulatos, G., & Triantopoulos, C. (2009). The return of the Greek Patient: Greece and the 2008 global financial crisis. *South European Society and Politics, 14*(1), 35–54.

Papadimitriou, D. (2007). In search of a collective escape: The 2000 reform of the Greek labour market. In K. Featherstone (Ed.), *Politics in Greece. The challenge of modernization* (pp. 243–269). Athens: Okto (in Greek).

Papadoulis, K. (2006). Clientelism, corruption and patronage in Greece: A public administration approach. *Teaching Public Administration, 26*, 13–24.
Papazoglou, M. G. (2005). *Citizenship and democratic legitimacy in the European Union: Euro-republicanism and the concept of responsive citizenship* (PhD Thesis). Essex University.
Papazoglou, M. G. (2009). *The challenges of Europeanisation and deliberation for the Greek political system. Euro-republicanism and the democratic management of consensus and contestation.* Athens: Papazisis (in Greek).
Papazoglou, M. G. (2010). Assessing models of citizenship in the EU. The idea of responsive citizenship. *Citizenship Studies, 14*(2), 221–236.
Papazoglou, M. G. (2012). *Modern political leadership. Crisis and new foundations of governance.* Athens: Papazisis (in Greek).
Pappas, T. (2009). *The charismatic party. PASOK, Papandreou, power.* Athens: Patakis (in Greek).
Pappas, T. (2010). Macroeconomic policy, strategic leadership, and voter behaviour: The disparate tales of socialist reformism in Greece and Spain during the 1980s. *West European Politics, 33*(6), 1241–1260.
Pelagidis, T. (2005). Vikings in Greece. Revenue-hunters against the collective interest. In T. Pelagidis (Ed.), *Blocking reforms in Greece. An evaluation of modernization* (pp. 109–164). Athens: Papazisi (in Greek).
Pettit, P. (1997). *Republicanism.* Oxford: Oxford University Press.
Pettit, P. (2001). *A theory of freedom: From the psychology to the politics of agency.* Cambridge: Polity.
Rawls, J. (1971). *A theory of justice.* Revised edition 1999. Oxford: Oxford University Press.
Rawls, J. (1993). *Political liberalism.* New York: Columbia University Press.
Rawls, J. (2001). *Justice as fairness: A restatement.* Cambridge: Belknap.
Schmidt, V. A. (2006). Procedural democracy in the EU: The Europeanisation of national and sectoral policy-making processes. *Journal of European Public Policy, 13*(5), 670–691.
Schmidt, V. A., & Radaelli, C. (2004). Policy change and discourse in Europe: Conceptual and methodological issues. *West European Politics, 27*(2), 183–210.
Siani-Davies, P., & Katsikas, S. (2009). National reconciliation after Civil War: The case of Greece. *Journal of Peace Research, 46*(4), 559–575.
Skinner, Q. (1992). On justice, the common good and the priority of liberty. In C. Mouffe (Ed.), *Dimensions of radical democracy: Pluralism, citizenship, community* (pp. 211–224). London: Verso.
Skinner, Q. (1998). *Liberty before liberalism.* Cambridge: Cambridge University Press.
Sotiropoulos, D. (2004). The EU's impact on the Greek welfare state: Europeanisation on paper? *Journal of European Social Policy, 14*, 267.
Spourdalakis, M. (1988). *The rise of the Greek socialist party.* London: Routledge.
Spourdalakis, M. (Ed.), (1998). *PASOK. Party, state, society.* Athens: Patakis (in Greek).
Svolopoulos, K. (2008). The Greek foreign policy 1945–1981. In K. Svolopoulos, K. Botsiou, & E. Chatzivasileiou (Eds.), *Konstantinos Karamanlis in the 21st century* (pp. 310–330). Athens: K. Karamanlis Foundation (in Greek).
Tamir, Y. (1993). *Liberal nationalism.* Princeton: Princeton University Press.
The United Nations. (1987). Report of the world commission on environment and development: Our common future. Transmitted to the General Assembly as an Annex to document A/42/427–Development and International Co-operation: Environment.
Thomadakis, S., & Seremetis, D. (1992). Fiscal management, social agenda and structural deficits. In T. Kariotis (Ed.), *The Greek socialist experiment, Papandreou's Greece 1981–1989* (pp. 203–255). New York: Pella.
Valinakis, J. (1989). *Introduction to Greek foreign policy 1949–1988.* Athens: Paratiritis (in Greek).
Voulgaris, J. (2008). *Greece of Metapolitefsi 1974–1990: Stable democracy marked by postwar history.* Athens: Themelio (in Greek).
Zambarloukou, S. (2006). Collective bargaining and social pacts: Greece in comparative perspective. *European Journal of Industrial Relations, 12*, 211–229.

Evidence-Based Policy Making in Greece

Stella Ladi

1 Introduction

The ongoing politico-economic crisis in Greece has intensified the discussion about the capabilities and failures of the Greek state, both inside the country and abroad. It became apparent soon enough that the austerity measures aimed at restoring Greece's public finance were not enough. Both the first (2010) and the second (2012) Memorandum outlined a number of structural reforms that needed to be combined with the austerity measures in order to yield long term results. One of the most important structural reforms was the downsizing of the public sector and the modernisation of public administration. Not surprisingly, the structural reforms and especially those that involved restructuring of the public sector, proved to be the most difficult to implement. Even the reforms that started being implemented, needed time to mature and to show their results. As a consequence, the politico-economic crisis has deepened and the lack of trust towards the political elites has grown (Ladi, 2012a, 2012b).

This chapter focuses on policy making in Greece and the possibility of improving it through the adoption of evidence-based policy-making practices. Rather than discussing the weaknesses of Greek public administration and the possible avenues for its improvement, which have been successfully analysed up to now (e.g. Sotiropoulos, 2007; Spanou & Sotiropoulos, 2011), this chapter builds upon these findings and attends to the dominant policy-making style in Greece. Policy making in Greece is compared with some of the most significant policy-making models in the literature, namely the *rational*, the *incremental*, and the *garbage can* models, in order to conclude which one better explains the current policy-making style. The incremental and the garbage can models appear more convincing from both

S. Ladi (✉)
Department of Political Science and History, Panteion University, 136 Syngrou Avenue, Athens 17671, Greece
e-mail: stellaladi@gmail.com

P. Sklias and N. Tzifakis (eds.), *Greece's Horizons*, The Konstantinos Karamanlis Institute for Democracy Series on European and International Affairs,
DOI 10.1007/978-3-642-34534-0_6,

a theoretical and an empirical point of view. Nevertheless, the purpose of this exercise is to propose the introduction of evidence-based policy making, which derives from the rational model (Sanderson, 2002) as a possible avenue for improving policy making, and, therefore, policy decisions and implementation in Greece. It is no wonder that, given the limited rationality of the policy process, such an attempt would not be without problems.

The chapter is divided into two sections. The first section discusses policy making in Greece, taking as its starting point the literature on Greek public administration and some recent policy reform attempts. The second section focuses on evidence-based policy making and outlines its advantages and limitations in order to provide some thoughts on its possible application to Greece. The concluding section discusses the possible role of experts in policy making for Greece and outlines avenues for further research.

2 Policy Making in Greece

One of the key problems for Greece's development and for its economic recovery is the function of the public administration and, more generally, the predominant policy-making style. The contemporary administrative model in Greece was established in the 1970s, in the context of Greece's transition to democracy and the economic stringency of the period. Although during the last 30 years, the key democratic institutions have been fully established and embedded within the political system, public administration remains weak, and to a large extent, dependent on political parties. The Greek public administration has traditionally been hierarchical and centralised as far as its institutions and control mechanisms are concerned. Its administrative system is dominated by the party in government, which means that continuity in governance is more often the exception than the rule (Spanou, 2008). Two of the most common allegations against public administration in Greece are lack of effectiveness and widespread corruption (Sotiropoulos, 2007). Patronage, which is caused by the dominance of the party in office, is claimed to be the most important reason for the failure of Greek public administration. It undermines the technical and personnel capacity of public administration by violating the principle of meritocracy in the selection, assignment, and development of personnel. Patronage also has a great impact on public procurement and the choice of contractors. In a way, patronage is often the cause of both corruption and of inefficiency (Ladi, 2012a, 2012b). Another aspect of the dominant model in Greece, which directly affects its policy-making style, is legalism and formalism, devoid of effective controls and strict sanctions against law-breakers. Quite the opposite, respect for formal rule is fragmented and informal practices often oppose and ignore formal rules (Spanou, 1996). The large number of often-conflicting regulations is frequently the result of patron-client relations and of attempts to deviate from the general rule in order to provide benefits to specific social groups (Sotiropoulos, 2007).

The drawbacks of Greek public administration have an immediate bearing on public policy making. In this chapter, the focus is on policy formulation and decision making in order to describe the dominant policy-making style in Greece. Since 1974, the key characteristic of policy making in Greece has remained unchallenged. This characteristic can be summarised as the legalism of the policy process. The policy tool that has been mainly used for the solution of social problems is the preparation of laws, followed by administrative-legal documents such as presidential decrees, ministerial decisions, and administrative circulars (Christofilopoulou, 1992). In reality, public policy is conceived as the simple passing of legislation, as if there were no need for follow-up and implementation measures, and the evaluation of results. The interests, values, and political goals of the dominant political party, and of the interest groups that support it, dominate the legislation. It goes without saying that the rational-comprehensive policy/decision-making model can be easily falsified by the Greek case in a manner similar to many other instances (e.g. Edwards, 1954), given that it does not take into account values, interests, and political goals.

Policy making in Greece is much closer to two other well-known policy-making models, which are the incremental model (Lindblom, 1959) and the garbage can model (March & Olsen, 1989), depending on the specific case and on the timing of the policy/decision. In the incremental model, the main assumption is that policy decisions are not taken according to what is rational or desirable, but according to what is possible. Thus, policy making is better described as a process of muddling through and of incremental changes that builds upon already existing institutions and policies. It is easier to continue with the status quo, rather than to proceed with radical transformations. First, because the various interests persist and it is difficult to take from them what they have previously acquired, and second, because bureaucratic procedures favour continuity rather than change (Howlett & Ramesh, 1995). Many of the policy changes in Greece can be described as incremental. Even in the cases where more radical legislation is put forward, the actual implementation remains incremental and this is why we often talk about inertia or lack of implementation. For example, the latest legislation on Higher Education (Law Gazette no. 195, 6/9/11) introduces radical reforms such as a new higher education management system and the abolishment of the university asylum. In practice, and as of today, only a fraction of the legislation has been applied and this concerns the most incremental clauses of the legislation that do not cause conflict. The garbage can model rejects all kinds of rationality in the policy/decision-making process and claims that it is a very complex and unpredictable process that has little to do with the choice of the best means in order to accomplish specific policy goals (March & Olsen, 1989). For them, policy makers rarely set specific policy goals and their decisions are taken in a random way based on their preferences, which are also changeable. It would not be surprising if some of the policy decisions of the last decades in Greece confirmed the garbage can model. However, the aim of this section is not to provide an in-depth discussion of the various policy-making models, but to show that policy-making is not necessarily rational.

An interesting question concerns how crisis and exogenous pressures affect policy/decision-making processes. In the case of the current Greek economic crisis, it has been shown that exogenous pressure, via the two Memoranda, has been pointing towards radical reforms (Ladi, 2012a, 2012b). For example, in the area of public sector employment, personnel evaluation and the linkage of wages to productivity and tasks have been promoted (Memorandum of Economic and Financial Policies, 2010). This is a reform which, if implemented, would be rather radical in terms of Greek public administration standards. Nonetheless, the primary aim of most of the reforms was to reduce public sector cost and that was the logic that prevailed in all legislation. It is not surprising that that even in cases where the legislation was more advanced, the reforms that have been implemented, have been either incremental or cost cutting. For example, the relatively successful 'Cl@rity' programme via which all public entities' decisions should be published on-line in order to be implemented can be best described as an incremental reform (http://diavgeia.gov.gr/en, accessed on 22 June 2011). To the contrary, the infamous labour reserve policy for the public sector was a cost-cutting change that aimed to reduce spending and to avoid more radical reforms such as the dismissal of public servants. Additionally, it can be claimed that the Greek policy-making style did not change because of the crisis, given that dealing with intensified public problems remains legalistic. The continuous evaluation rounds from the troika and their recommendations that ask for much more than the passing of legislation, is not without importance (e.g. European Commission, 2011). It remains to be seen whether the idea that public policy is not only about legislation will be embedded in the Greek politico-administrative system. In the next section, we turn to the advantages and problems of evidence-based policy making and its usefulness for Greece.

3 Evidence-Based Policy-Making: Advantages and Criticisms

There is a common desire for more informed public policies, in the belief that this would reduce policy failure and policy inertia. In this section, we turn to a discussion of knowledge and policy making, in order to define evidence-based policy and discuss its advantages and limitations, both in general and for Greece in particular. There are four key approaches in the literature describing the relationship between knowledge, policy making, and consequently policy reforms (Ladi & Dalakou, 2010, 93–94). The first approach has its roots in Weber (1978) and sees the relationship between knowledge and public policy as part of a rational paradigm where the state, in need for information and in order to achieve better policy making, turns to experts. Evidence-based policy making derives precisely from this tradition. The second approach understands the relationship between power and knowledge as indirect, in the sense that knowledge is diffused in society and it influences the power centres by default (Weiss, 1986). The third approach builds upon the idea of an organic relationship between knowledge and power and the emergence of new power centres, which try to influence policy making such as policy institutes and think tanks (Foucault, 1972). Finally, the most recent approach emphasises the symbolic importance of knowledge for the legitimisation of political decisions and for gaining support from various groups and organisations (Boswell, 2009). It is already possible to argue that a more tight relationship between knowledge and policy making does not directly lead to better policies.

Evidence-based policy making was first developed in the United States. However, soon other countries, such as the UK under the Blair government, adopted the belief that evidence could improve policies. Plewis (2000, 96) provides one of the few definitions and says that, 'policy initiatives are to be supported by research evidence and that policies introduced on a trial basis are to be evaluated in as rigorous a way as possible'. This means that evidence can and should inform both the development and the implementation of policies. It should inform the decision-making process during the designing of policies and also during evaluation, and it should be able to direct policy makers on whether they should continue with a particular policy or whether they should amend it. Sanderson (2002) calls for evidence-based policy to pay more attention to two more aspects of the policy process. The first is evidence of problems that should be dealt by public policy interventions and the second concerns the process of setting the objective in order to help policy makers to prioritise their goals. His argument is that quantitative evidence is not enough and that qualitative data and emphasis on theoretical explanation of policy problems are also important. Similarly, according to Davies, Nutley, and Smith (1999), one of the first questions that need to be answered is what constitutes evidence for effectiveness of public service. It is already apparent that although evidence-based policy making in the first instance sounds ideal, its application is not without problems and criticisms.

It has already been shown that evidence-based policy making is closely linked with a rational policy-making model. One of the key assumptions is that the instrumental use of research and evaluation can improve public policies. All the criticisms that apply to the rational model, also apply to evidence-based policy making. The key set of criticisms has its roots in the constructivist and interpretivist position, which emphasises that the knowledge of the social world is socially constructed. This means that informing policy making based on 'objective' evidence becomes complex and this is especially the case for evidence that derives from quantitative data (Sanderson, 2002). Weiss (1986) argues that social science research is used most of the time in a conceptual rather than instrumental way, which means that beliefs and principles play a much more important role than raw data. Parsons (2002) offers an even harsher critique of evidence-based policy making with direct reference to its use by the Blair government. He claims that evidence-based policy making excludes some important elements of policy making, which are people, power, and politics. He distinguishes between 'evidence' and 'ideas' in order to show that policy making is not an ideology/value-free zone where professionals are informed by objective evidence. In the same vein with Sanderson (2002), he reminds us that the task of policy analysis is to clarify values and contexts and not to produce evidence in order to drive policy making. Does this mean that there is no place for evidence in policy making? Evidence based policy making 'is remarkable for the extent to which it frames "evidence" around the concepts of knowledge as *episteme* and *techne*, whereas the Lasswellian orientation would stress the vital role of another kinds of knowledge identified by Aristotle: *phronesis*, or practical wisdom' (Parsons, 2002, 56). Taking this observation as a starting point, we argue that evidence does have a place in policy making, when defined broadly and when the timing is right.

The next question to be addressed is whether the evidence-based approach could improve policy making in Greece. As was discussed in the previous section, policy making in Greece does not function according to the rational-comprehensive model. All criticisms that apply to the model for its lack of attention to power and values in policy making are fully confirmed by the Greek case. A reason for this is the dominance of the patron-client relationship in policy making. This means that many of the policy decisions only make sense for specific groups that are favoured by the political system in return for their political support (Sotiropoulos, 2007). This, in turn, signifies that policy making and policy decisions are quite often neither comprehensive nor rational for the majority of the citizens. It also means that public administration is often dragged into decisions and practices that are not based on any type of evidence or common sense and are difficult to implement. Nevertheless, in the last few decades, public administration in Greece has been commissioning numerous studies to private consultants and public research centres in order to get evidence for better policy making in areas such as public administration reform, social policy, health policy, etc. (http://resources.ekdd.gr/knowledge/, accessed on 10 June 2012). Given the policy-making style described above, a lot of these studies were just filed, rarely used, and often lost over time. In March 2012, the Ministry of Public Administrative Reform and e-Government (2012) announced the creation of a database for all public sector studies, whether commissioned or in-house. Responsible for assembling, diffusing, and providing proposals for its utilisation, is the Documentation and Innovation Unit of the National Centre for Public Administration and Local Government. This decision was made in light of the public administration reforms taking place in response to the troika's evaluation of the two Memoranda. It is still early days for deciding whether this attempt to gather and make better use of already existing evidence will be successful.

Another aspect of the same discussion is whether the timing is right for introducing evidence-based policy making in Greece. The politico-economic crisis in which Greece has found itself since 2009 has created an environment that rhetorically favours reforms but is, in actual terms, very sceptical about them. It has increased the lack of trust towards the political elites that have not taken ownership of the reforms and prefer to regard them as stemming from exogenous pressures and governments. These observations lead us to the conclusion that although Greek public administration could benefit from evidence-based policy making, given all its limitations, the timing is not perhaps ideal. Any such attempt should be made with caution and with the full support of the government.

Conclusion

Evidence-based policy making is an attractive idea for a country such as Greece, which needs and is in the process of making multiple public policy reforms. It could also be argued that Greece has the necessary human capital for producing the required evidence for such reforms. There are indeed many instances when experts have informed the policy process, although this has never happened in a politically neutral environment (e.g. Ladi, 2005, 2007; Lekakis, 2000). The Papadimos' government (November 2011–May 2012) constitutes the latest example of trust placed on a technocrat by the political system, although the decision was taken reluctantly and there was no political will to extend his service for a longer time. More comparative research on the role of experts in the policy reform processes and of the relationship between academics and politicians would be useful. More specifically, it would be interesting to analyse the advance of academics to political positions and vice versa, and the way these have influenced policy decision making and implementation.

In this chapter, it was shown that policy making in Greece can be best explained by the incremental and garbage can models. The implication of this is that evidence-based policy making, which derives from the rational model, cannot be easily introduced into Greek policy making. The reason for this is the predominance of legalism and patronage as the key factors that inform policy making, rather than expertise and best practices. Additionally, it was claimed that introducing important changes in policy making, such as more focus on evidence in times of crisis, has to take place very carefully because of the increased lack of trust in the political system. For evidence-based policy making to work, evidence has to be defined in broad terms and to endorse not only quantitative and qualitative data, but also theoretical explanations. The aim should be not only to reinforce the *episteme* and *techne* but also the *phronesis*, which could prove to be more important for an in-depth reform of the Greek politico-administrative system.

References

Boswell, C. (2009). *The political uses of expert knowledge*. Cambridge: Cambridge University Press.

Christofilopoulou, P. (1992). Professionalism and public policy making in Greece: The influence of engineers in the local government reforms. *Public Administration, 70*(1), 99–118.

Davies, H., Nutley, S., & Smith, P. (1999). Viewpoint: Editorial: What works? The role of evidence in public sector policy and practice. *Public Money & Management, 19*(1), 3–5.

Edwards, W. (1954). The theory of decision making. *Psychological Bulletin, 51*(4), 380–417.

European Commission. (2011). *The economic adjustment programme for Greece, fourth review* (Occasional Papers, 82). Brussels: Economic and Financial Affairs, European Economy.

Foucault, M. (1972). *The archaeology of knowledge*. Oxford: Routledge.

Howlett, M., & Ramesh, M. (1995). *Studying public policy: Policy cycles and policy subsystems*. Oxford: Oxford University Press.

Ladi, S. (2005). Policy learning and the role of expertise in the reform process in Greece. *West European Politics, 28*(2), 279–296.
Ladi, S. (2007). The role of experts in Greek foreign policy. *Hellenic Studies/Etudes Helleniques, 15*(1), 67–84.
Ladi, S. (2012a). The Greek economic crisis: A trigger for public administration reforms? In P. Liargovas (Ed.), *Greece: Economics, political and social issues* (197–207). New York: Nova Science Publishers, Inc.
Ladi, S. (2012b). *The Eurozone crisis and austerity politics: a trigger for administrative reform in Greece?* (GreeSE Paper, 57). LSE: Hellenic Observatory.
Ladi, S., & Dalakou, V. (2010). *Public policy analysis.* Athens: Papazisis (in Greek).
Law Gazette no. 195. (2011, September 6). Hellenic Republic.
Lekakis, J. (2000). Environmental policy-making in Greece: Examining the interaction of bureaucratic and academic cultures. *Journal of Environmental Policy & Planning, 2*, 69–86.
Lindblom, C. (1959). The science of muddling through. *Public Administration Review, 19*(2), 79–88.
March, J., & Olsen, J. (1989). *Rediscovering institutions.* New York: The Free Press.
Memorandum of Economic and Financial Policies. (2010, May 3). Greece.
Memorandum of Economic and Financial Policies. (2012, March 11). Greece.
Ministry of Public Administrative Reform and e-Government. (2012, March 8). *Press Release.* http://www.ydmed.gov.gr/?p=1574. Accessed 20 August 2012.
Parsons, W. (2002). From muddling through to muddling up—evidence based policy making and the modernisation of British government. *Public Policy and Administration, 17*(3), 43–60.
Plewis, I. (2000). Educational inequalities and education action zones. In C. Pantazis & D. Gordon (Eds.), *Tackling inequalities: Where are we now and what can be done* (pp. 87–100). Bristol: Policy.
Sanderson, I. (2002). Evaluation, policy learning and evidence-based policy making. *Public Administration, 80*(1), 1–22.
Sotiropoulos, D. (2007). *State and reform in contemporary south Europe.* Athens: Potamos (in Greek).
Spanou, C. (1996). On the regulatory capacity of the Greek state. A tentative approach based on a case-study. *International Review of Administrative Sciences, 62*(2), 219–37.
Spanou, C. (2008). State reform in Greece: Responding to old and new challenges. *International Journal of Public Sector Management, 21*(2), 150–73.
Spanou, C., & Sotiropoulos, D. (2011). The odyssey of administrative reforms in Greece, 1981–2009: A tale of two reform paths. *Public Administration, 89*(3), 723–37.
Weber, M. (1978). Economy and society: An outline of interpretive sociology. In: G. Roth & C. Wittich. Berkeley: University of California Press.
Weiss, C. (1986). Research and policy-making: A limited partnership. In F. Heller (Ed.), *The use and abuse of social science* (pp. 214–35). London: Sage.

Part II

The Macroeconomic Framework

Greece's Way Out of the Crisis: A Call for Massive Structural Reforms

Panagiotis Liargovas and Spyridon Repousis

1 Introduction

Since May 2010, Greece has been operating under an agreement put forward by the so-called troika of the European Central Bank, the European Commission, and the International Monetary Fund (IMF). The main purposes of this agreement have been (a) to reduce Greece's fiscal deficits and debt to a sustainable level, (b) to implement structural reforms to make the economy more efficient and competitive, and (c) to allow government finances to recover to the point where Greece can return to borrowing from private financial markets at sustained interest rates (IMF, 2012). Although more than 2 years have passed since this agreement was approved, the economic situation in Greece, which entered its fifth year of recession in 2012, remains dire. According to the IMF (2012), Greece will lose more than 20 % of GDP in 2012 compared with its peak in 2007.[1] This vast loss of income is comparable with some of the worst financial crises in the twentieth and twenty-first centuries.[2]

Although the focus of the governments' policy mix was based on austerity, mainly associated with wage cuts and new taxes, this chapter argues that Greece should address the root cause of its indebtedness rather than the subsequent symptoms. We suggest rather shifting focus onto massive structural reforms, which will be designed to lead to substantial improvements in the level of Greek competitiveness and to the reconstruction of the deeply problematic public sector in the country.

[1] Specifically, the percentage change in GDP was −0.2 % in 2008, −3.25 % in 2009, −3.5 % in 2010, and −6.9 % in 2011. It is projected to be −6.2 % in 2012.

[2] For an extensive analysis of previous economic crises, see Reinhart and Rogoff (2009).

P. Liargovas (✉) • S. Repousis
Department of Economics, School of Management and Economics, University of Peloponnese, Tripolis Campus, Tripoli 22100, Greece
e-mail: liargova@uop.gr; spyrep@otenet.gr

P. Sklias and N. Tzifakis (eds.), *Greece's Horizons*, The Konstantinos Karamanlis Institute for Democracy Series on European and International Affairs,
DOI 10.1007/978-3-642-34534-0_7,

The remainder of this chapter is thus organised as follows. The next section discusses the main problems with pro-cyclical and counter-cyclical policies in Greece. The chapter then considers alternatives to the policies being implemented, while the following section focuses on the example of corruption as a major structural problem. Finally, the last section offers some conclusions.

2 Debt, Deficits, and Austerity

The relation between debt and deficit is bidirectional. It is also known as the 'snowball effect'. Debt is a snowball that grows as it rolls. Interest payments on the accumulated debt represent an expenditure that is also added to the current deficit. Further, when a country borrows from abroad to cover its deficits it consumes more than it produces. This additional consumption is brought about from the imports purchased by the country from foreign banks and foreign financial institutions using the money that it borrows from them.

In light of the foregoing, managing a country's debt repayment requires first reducing the deficit and then eliminating it altogether in order to avoid adding new debt to pre-existing levels. In the next stage, a primary surplus in excess of the debt interest rate payments is formed in order to reduce the debt further. However, overall debt can be reduced even if the deficit is zero or slightly positive because what is important is not the debt itself, but rather the debt-to-GDP ratio. If GDP increases significantly and debt remains stable, then the debt-to-GDP ratio reduces. This demonstrates that primary surpluses are not a panacea, because even a small deficit combined with a high growth rate is beneficial at reducing the percentage of debt in relation to GDP. The growth rate of the real economy is thus important for maximising prosperity and happiness in society. Therefore, austerity programs create a vicious circle: austerity leads to recession and reduces GDP even if the deficit remains unchanged.

In summary, the troika-inspired fiscal adjustment measures are pro-cyclical. Fiscal tightening reduces aggregate demand in the economy, causing it to shrink further. As a result, government revenues reduce (tax payments fall as income declines) and government spending increases automatically because of the higher demand of unemployment insurances. This makes fiscal targets even more difficult to achieve.

The only way in which Greece can recover from this vicious circle of debt and recession is through growth. Growth can theoretically be achieved through an increase in either aggregate demand or aggregate supply. An increase in aggregate demand (i.e. a counter-cyclical policy) is what Keynes suggested in 1929 to overcome the Great Depression. However, whether Keynesian policies are a suitable alternative to managing the current economic crisis in Greece remains open to debate. Advocates of such an alternative ignore the structural problems of the Greek economy. Specifically, they ignore the preconditions under which a Keynesian policy of increased spending could be carried out. One such precondition is that the country must have a strong production base, which is currently latent because of weak demand, but is able to produce competitive goods and services. Therefore, demand can stimulate existing, but weak, supply, as seen in the US during the 1930s and 1950s.

However, the current problem in Greece is the production base itself. Incidentally, the same problem was apparent in the case of the failed socialist experiment of Mitterrand in France in the beginning of the 1980s as well as the expansionary policies in Greece during the 1980s. The supply side is more important today because all economies (including that in Greece) are open. A boost in demand would at best only breathe temporary life into the fragile production structures in Greece, which is not a sustainable solution.

Greece has found itself in an unfavourable situation since joining the eurozone, namely fiscal and external deficits and low competitiveness. Under this scenario, expansionary policies may well deliver political votes but they also lead to chaotic bankruptcy. Thus, the Greek economy is suffering from a supply problem rather than a demand problem, which requires a thorough, realistic, and credible plan of economic reconstruction; in short, Greece needs a supply-side revolution (Arghyrou & Kontonikas, 2012, 6).

3 Why Carry Out Structural Reforms?

A number of comparative studies and surveys have shown that Greece ranks last as regards state efficiency or the introduction of competitive forces into the economy. For example, according to the World Bank's latest annual 'Doing Business' survey, published in 2012 (World Bank, 2012), Greece is ranked 100th of the 183 participating countries, behind Vietnam and Yemen. Opening a new business in Greece is almost impossible; sadly, closing one is somewhat easier. Further, Greek companies are constrained by a raft of disincentives, such as laws and bureaucratic obstacles that make it hard to do business. In a recent survey, IOBE (2010) counts 250 of them. In the same survey, IOBE (2010, 8) estimates that freeing up all the closed professions could boost Greece's GDP by up to 17 %. Other studies, such as those carried out by the Centre for Planning and Economic Research (2005) and OECD (2012), have reached similar conclusions.

The above-described rankings reflect the fact that Greece has suffered from a long period of structural weakness and systemic delays that were not tackled when the economic environment in Greece and internationally was supportive and the adjustment costs were substantially lower. Structural reforms now represent the only path to recovery, under the given conditions of the debt crisis that deprive the government from implementing expansionary fiscal policy.

Such reforms aim primarily (although not exclusively) at improving economic efficiency, namely making better use of the available resources and thereby increasing domestic wealth and broadening Greece's production capacities by attracting new investment and reallocating resources from non-tradable to tradable areas. Through these proposed reforms, the government can change the prevailing incentives and disincentives as well as the rules and institutions that enforce them. In other words, structural reforms aim at the reconstruction of the deeply problematic state sector and a substantial improvement in Greek competitiveness. For this to be achieved, the following four conditions need to be met:

- Abolishing all bureaucratic obstacles and other protectionist policies.
- Dismantling rigidities in the labour market.
- Improving confidence and liquidity in the banking sector.
- Cultivating institutional stability and confidence in the political system.

First, by abolishing bureaucracy and eradicating all barriers to trade and obstacles to economic activity, the government could establish a policy framework that favours the reallocation of capital from non-tradable to tradable areas, since it will become far simpler, faster, and cheaper to exploit the available resources in order to set up an enterprise. Second, dismantling rigidities in the labour market would address structural unemployment at its source, thus facilitating the repositioning of workers to the export sector. Third, by ensuring stability and liquidity in the banking system, capital flight would be reduced, silent bank runs minimised, and the looming financial panic would disappear, allowing for renewed economic activity. Finally, and perhaps most importantly, policymakers need to ensure that institutional stability is preserved. This means two things: (a) not changing the political order every few months and (b) ensuring that economic policies have long-term horizons instead of being altered every few weeks. By meeting these four conditions, the country would establish the necessary framework to expand production capacities, ultimately reversing the current deficit and bringing about recovery in the long run.

4 Systemic Corruption as a Major Structural Imbalance

Transparency International-Greece's 'National Integrity System assessment' found that 98 % of Greeks believe corruption is a major problem in their country and that 88 % think bribery is part of the business culture. This study also uncovered corruption in all segments of the Greek economy. It stated that 'buildings built illegally can be approved later, accounts can be validated without being seen by a tax inspector, and, most worryingly given the role of budget opacity in the debt crisis, many Ministries have 'special accounts' to which normal rules of budgetary transparency do not apply' (Transparency International, 2012). In 2011, Transparency International ranked Greece 80th out of 183 countries in its corruption perception index, ahead of only one EU country, Bulgaria, indicating that it has a medium to high degree of public sector corruption as perceived by businesspeople and country analysts. This ranking was on par with El Salvador, Morocco, Peru, and Thailand.

Hundreds of cases have shown the scale of the problem. According to a 2012 audit carried out by the Ministry of Labour, 200,000 main and supplementary pensions were found to be fraudulent and their cancellation has resulted in a net benefit to the long-suffering state-owned pension funds of 750 million euros per annum. The audit found that many people were illegally receiving pensions for over two decades, while interestingly, after their cancellation, only seven or eight people turned up to reclaim them (Kathimerini, 24 April 2012).

Another audit conducted by the Ministry of Health showed that on the island of Zakynthos, of the 700 people receiving the 'blindness benefit' (2 % of the island's population compared with 0.6 % on a global basis according to the World Health Organization), only 100 turned up to claim the benefit as part of the audit, of which 60 were found not to be blind (Wall Street Journal, 3 April 2012).

In the municipality of Elefsina, Attika, 107 files concerning apparently fraudulent cases of welfare benefits have been sent to the public prosecutor's office. On the island of Kalymnos, during July and August 2011, 595 cases of people with severe disabilities were registered. On this basis, with a population of 8 % of the entire Dodecanese, Kalymnos officially boasts 31 % of the cases of severe disability of the entire prefecture. Moreover, in the Dodecanese, 68 people receive the 'heating fuel benefit' of which 59 live on Kalymnos (87 % of the total).[3]

In March 2012, seven employees of the Kallithea branch of IKA (the largest social security organisation in Greece) were arrested and charged over a massive fraud involving millions of euros that were stolen via a primitive but effective scheme made possible through the active participation and collaboration of the public.

According to the General Inspector of the Greek public administration, only 1 % of corruption in the Greek public sector is detected and Greek state fraud losses from corrupted public servants are estimated to amount to 20 billion euros annually (Kathimerini, 29 May 2010). Meanwhile, a 2010 study by the Washington-based Brookings Institution estimated that corruption costs Greece the equivalent of 8 % of GDP a year (Kaufmann, 2010). Indeed, Greece's inability to tackle corruption in both the public and private sectors threatens to undermine its very efforts to turn around the domestic economy. A number of studies have also shown that corrupt countries are less successful at consolidating their budgets (Arin, Chmelarova, Feess, & Wohlschlegel, 2011; Kaufmann, 2010). Therefore, there is an urgent need to fight this problem. Below we offer some ideas in this regard.

4.1 Corruption and Fraud in the Public Sector

The Greek public administration could develop several methods for proving a person has an illegal income and/or illegal assets. First, common hiding places should be investigated, as illegal gains can be hidden, for example, through currency hoards or precious metals at home. In addition, cashier and travellers cheques can be used for hiding assets: making wire transfers and cash transactions in banks below 15,000 euros in Greece are a way of avoiding a Currency Transaction Report.

[3] For more details, see Reform Watch Greece (2012).

In order to recover the proceeds of fraud and corruption, tax authorities should also investigate private banking departments. Private banking provides highly personalised and confidential products to wealthy clients and politically exposed persons (PEPs). Greek legislation could cope with offshore companies' problems by implementing Controlled Foreign Corporation Legislation, a feature of the income tax system designed to limit the artificial deferral of tax using lower taxed offshore entities. Taxpayers must include in their income statements the amounts earned by foreign entities they or related persons control.

Further, so-called indirect methods of establishing income, such as 'net worth', 'bank deposit analysis', and 'expenditures', should be investigated. The net worth method adapts readily to nontax investigations of illegal income, and thus it can be used when a person has accumulated wealth and acquired assets with illicit proceeds. This causes the subject's net worth to increase from 1 year to the next. A net worth investigation has several stages, the first of which is the identification of the subject's assets, liabilities, and living expenses. The formula for calculating net worth is described below:

Assets
Less: Liabilities
Equals: Net worth
Less: Prior year's net worth
Equals: Net worth increase (decrease)
Plus: Living expenses
Equals: Income (or expenditures)
Less: Funds from known sources
Equals: Funds from unknown sources.

Another established indirect method is the bank deposit analysis method. As with the net worth method, the aim is to search for funds from known and unknown sources (i.e. to analyse a subject's banking activity rather than his/her assets and expenditures). The objective is to take all the subject's bank deposits for a given period, subtract any transfers between accounts, and then add any expenditure made in cash to calculate total income during this period, as follows:

Total deposits to all accounts
Less: Transfers and re-deposits
Equals: Net deposits to all accounts
Plus: Cash expenditures
Equals: Total receipts from all sources
Less: Funds from known sources
Equals: Funds from unknown sources

Transfers between accounts and removals/re-deposits are subtracted because this type of fund does not represent income. Further, only expenditures made in cash are considered, because this money was spent instead of deposited, while those made by cheque are ignored.

Third, the expenditures method compares the subject's known sources of funds, with any excess expenditure thus representing income from unknown sources. This method is simpler than the net worth analysis because it can be carried out using only one period, whereas the latter must start from a base year. The formula used to compute net worth using the expenditures method is shown below:

Known expenditures

Less: Known source of funds

Equals: Funds from unknown sources.

When illegal income and/or assets are found using any of these methods, then asset recovery and repatriating wealth are important factors to reduce corruption and improve the economy, especially in countries that have high levels of external debt such as Greece.

Bribery represents another corruption scheme in the Greek public sector, namely the use of payments to influence an employee to send business to the vendor making the payments. Examples of bribery include kickbacks (return of a proportion of a monetary sum received, especially because of coercion or a secret agreement) and bid rigging (pre-arrangement of a bid to a particular vendor instead of to the lowest bidder). A change in the lifestyle of an employee, discovery of a relationship between an employee and a vendor, or the weak segregation of duties in approving vendors and invoices can all be features of bribery. The behaviour profiles of employees involved in bribery schemes may include drug and/or alcohol addiction, financial problems, gambling habits, private debts, high number of dependents, extraordinary medical expenses, and significant and regular expenses for entertainment and/or travel. Further, bribes can be disguised as 'consultant fees' in which consultants act as conduits for channelling the funds, less a nominal commission, back to the company official. Prevention methods include (a) rotating duties of approving contracts and/or vendors and bid responsibilities and (b) segregating duties of approving vendors, awarding contracts, and approving invoices.

Whistleblowing can also help contain fraud by encouraging employees to report the Greek public sector department they work for when they uncover illegal activities taking place. Employees are usually unwilling to engage in whistleblowing because they are afraid of being dismissed or forced out. Therefore, it is important to have suitable legislation in place to encourage whistleblowing where existing systems are not working. Restoring trust in the public sector must involve greater access to information to promote transparency, perhaps the most important weapon against fraud.

4.2 Social Security Fraud

Another common type of fraud in Greece is so-called 'death fraud', according to which family members avoid declaring the death of a person in order to continue receiving his/her pension and social security benefits. Three main tools can be used to combat this type of corruption. First, Greek legislation must take account of the many legislative deterrents to identity theft in the US, such as the Identity Theft and Assumption Deterrence Act of 1998, the Gramm Leach Bliley Act of 1999, and the Identity Theft Penalty Enhancement Act of 2004. In addition, cross-referencing financial databases, tax refund files, healthcare claims files, vendor or contract files, and accounting files can uncover many cases of death fraud. Finally, investigators and auditors could be trained to become certified fraud examiners or anti-money laundering specialists.

4.3 Capital Flight, Import Duty Fraud, and Underground Banking

Capital flight is a major problem in many countries, including Greece, and has serious economic, political, and social ramifications, such as eroding the country's tax base and increasing the public deficit and public debt. Abnormal prices in international trade may also indicate capital flight, import duty fraud, income tax evasion, or money laundering. The economic impact of over-invoiced imports to Greece from the US and under-invoiced exports from Greece to the US shifts as much as $400 million in income annually out of Greece to the US and over $5.5 billion out of Greece to all other countries (Pak, Zanakis, & Zdanowica, 2003). Further, the Treasury of Greece loses an estimated $1.4–2 billion revenue annually from worldwide trade-shifted income (Pak et al., 2003, 54). By auditing only the top 25 income-shifting items with the US, the Greek treasury could capture about three-quarters of the income shifted from all exports and over half of the income shifted from all imports.

Although foreign direct investment (FDI) is crucial for the Greek economy, the authorities must be able to cope with transfer pricing, profit repatriation, and, especially, money laundering. According to Brada, Drabek, and Perez (2012), 10 % of total FDI flows and over half of FDI to money laundering countries are intended to facilitate illicit money flows, thus causing costs and reputational risk for the host country. The adoption of the new anti-money laundering law in Greece has, however, resulted in significant progress with regard to fighting illegal capital flight.

Another useful approach to restoring transparency in international transactions would be to regulate the Greece–Albania remittance corridor. Remittances are mostly sent by the kinds of customers Greek commercial banks do not consider to be 'prime' customers. As such, remittances are often sent to rural areas, where large banks tend not to be present. Remittances in Albania—which are estimated to be approximately 9–10 % of GDP—represent an important inflow to both households and to the entire economy. The ratio of remittances to GDP is higher than that of FDI, acting as an incentive towards the economic and financial development of the country.

Several factors support the preference of migrant workers to transfer funds through the carriage of cash or underground banking (*hawala*). Albanians have long placed limited trust in Albanian banks because depositor confidence was undermined and many people lost their savings following the collapse of pyramid schemes in 1997. However, confidence is gradually being restored and deposits in banks have grown over recent years.

A policy recommendation could be to implement bilateral initiatives between Greece and Albania that foster the development of transfer mechanisms for remittances, thereby promoting economic activity. Moreover, programs that aim to increase transparency and offer insurance for remittances would help decrease cash carrying. In addition, policymakers should raise the awareness of migrants of the benefits of financial institutions through ethnic newspapers, advertisements, and brochures at customs points when leaving Greece (Liargovas & Repousis, 2011, 323).

Further, employers should be encouraged or even mandated to pay Albanian workers through migrant bank accounts, thereby increasing migrant trust in the banking system. Explaining the risks and lowering the costs of remittance commissions in the Greek Postal Office for small remittances would also help, while supporting the integration of legal and documented Albanians to Greece and advising them how to develop legal businesses would be another solution. Finally, Albania could support the growth of ATM networks and increase banking access to rural households.

4.4 Corporate and Political Corruption

The final type of corruption discussed in this chapter includes corporate fraud, stock manipulation, corporate and political corruption, and presenting false financial statements, especially for companies listed on the Athens Stock Exchange. To combat such corruption Greece must fully implement the 'Business Principles for Countering Bribery' released by Transparency International, which aims to engage the private sector in anti-corruption efforts. An anti-corruption program should also target areas such as political contributions, PEPs, charitable contributions and sponsorships, gifts, hospitality, and expenses. Moreover, Greece has to update its anti-corruption laws, perhaps by considering implementing a regulation like the UK Bribery Act. Such legislation must (a) criminalise direct and indirect acts of general bribery (including commercial bribery) and the bribery of foreign officials and (b) exercise broad jurisdiction over all individuals and corporate entities in Greece.

Conclusions

In the wake of the current economic climate in Greece, the Greek government has only one approach, namely to recover and return to growth and prosperity in the eurozone. However, there are no easy solutions or measures for implementing this plan. An action plan for growth is thus necessary in order to reorient the production model, increase competition in product and labour markets, improve the business environment, encourage the efficient utilisation of EU funds, promote 'green' growth and reduce oil dependency, and upgrade the education system as well as tourism and overseas maritime transport. In this regard, specific reform measures should be taken in terms of taxation, bank credits, international commercial relations (exports, imports), public sector and corporate sector fraud and corruption, and the securitisation and privatisation of public companies and assets.

References

Arghyrou, M., & Kontonikas, A. (2012). The EMU sovereign debt crisis: A call and an opportunity for a Greek supply-side revolution. Available at: http://www.greekeconomistsforreform.com. Accessed 23 Aug 2012.

Arin, P. K., Chmelarova, V., Feess, E., & Wohlschlegel, A. (2011). Why are corrupt countries less successful in consolidating their budgets? *Journal of Public Economics, 95*(7–8), 521–530.

Brada, J. C., Drabek, Z., & Perez, F. (2012). Illicit money flows as motives for FDI. *Journal of Comparative Economics, 40*(1), 108–126.

Centre for Planning and Economic Research. (2005). *Economic and social effects of the opening of closed professions in Greece*. Athens: Centre for Planning and Economic Research (in Greek).

IMF. (2012, March). *Greece: Request for extended arrangement under the extended fund facility* (Country Report No. 12/57).

IOBE. (2010). *The Greek economy*. Athens: IOBE (in Greek).

Kaufmann, D. (2010). *Can corruption adversely affect public finances in industrialized countries?* The Brookings Institution. http://www.brookings.edu/research/opinions/2010/04/19-corruption-kaufmann. Accessed 23 August 2012.

Liargovas, P., & Repousis, S. (2011). Underground banking or hawala and Greece-Albania remittance corridor. *Journal of Money Laundering Control, 14*(4), 313–323.

OECD. (2012). *Economic policy reforms: Going for growth 2012*. Paris: Organisation for Economic Co-operation and Development.

Pak, S., Zanakis, S., & Zdanowica, J. (2003). Detecting abnormal pricing in international trade: The Greece-USA case. *Interfaces, 33*(2), 54–64.

Reform Watch Greece. (2012, March 17). Corruption Blues Underscore the Need for Deep Systemic Reform in Hellas. http://reformwatchgreece.wordpress.com/2012/03/17/corruption-blues-underscore-the-need-for-deep-systemic-reform-in-hellas/. Accessed 23 Aug 2012.

Reinhart, C. M., & Rogoff, K. S. (2009). *This time is different: Eight centuries of financial folly*. Princeton: Princeton University Press.

Transparency International. (2012). National Integrity System Assessment Greece. http://media.transparency.org/nis/cogs/?Country=ge. Accessed 23 Aug 2012.

World Bank. (2012). *Doing business survey*. Washington: World Bank.

The Greek Crisis and the Crisis in Eurozone's Governance

Angelos Kotios and Spyridon Roukanas

1 Introduction

After the global financial crisis of 2008–2009, the EMU governance system faced the challenge of having to address the serious implications of the crisis for the countries of the Eurozone. It should be noted that the international financial crisis did not cause strong internal tensions in the EMU system. However, the debt and competitiveness crisis of the Greek economy revealed the structural and functional weaknesses of the EMU governance and caused a series of institutional and managerial changes. As a result, the system of governance has been reformed and, with the crisis continuing, is still undergoing reconstruction. The nature of the Eurozone crisis has been dynamically transformed and the initial crisis has evolved into multiple crises. Due to the global financial crisis, it began as a crisis of the European financial system, evolved into a recession and liquidity crisis, then became a debt crisis and solvency crisis and, today, it is a systemic crisis with international dimensions (Schambaugh, 2012). There is no doubt that the crisis came early to the Eurozone mainly due to the collapse of the global financial system and the recession that followed. However, the member states and the institutions of governance and procedures of the Eurozone are responsible for the development, expansion, and continuous worsening of the crisis (Wolf, 2012). The central questions posed in the analysis that follows are:

- Why were the original structures of governance of the Eurozone system unable to deal with the crisis in an effective way?
- What changes did the crisis in Greece and in the other countries of the Eurozone bring about in the institutions and political governance of the Eurozone?

A. Kotios • S. Roukanas (✉)
Department of International and European Studies, University of Piraeus, 126 Grigoriou Lambraki St., 18534, Greece
e-mail: akotios@gmail.com; sroukana@webmail.unipi.gr

P. Sklias and N. Tzifakis (eds.), *Greece's Horizons*, The Konstantinos Karamanlis Institute for Democracy Series on European and International Affairs,
DOI 10.1007/978-3-642-34534-0_8,

- How effective were the new governance mechanisms in coping with the crisis?
- What is the system of governance that can be expected to safeguard consistency and sustainability of the European economic and monetary union?

2 Eurozone's Governance: Original Structure and Functions

2.1 Structure and Responsibilities

The original system of governance of the Eurozone, as reflected in the European Union Treaty (Maastricht Treaty), and in some other institutional interventions before the establishment of EMU in 1999, was initially characterised by a division of political responsibilities and by diversification in the process of integration (Thygesen, 2011).

Thus, the monetary policy is supranationalised and is implemented by the European System of Central Banks (ESCB), which does not constitute a new body of the EU, but is a system of decision making that the new institution of the European Central Bank (ECB) and national central banks undertake jointly. In essence, this is not a new joint central bank like the USA's Federal Reserve, but an intergovernmental body responsible for a common monetary policy (Seidel, 2011). The common monetary policy is independent of political interference and its sole objective is price stability. The direct financing of the EU institutions and of the public sector in the member states of the Eurozone is prohibited. The member states retain their national operational and supervisory systems for banks and other financial institutions. The Council is responsible for the exchange rate policy, while the Commission and the ECB participate indirectly in the decision making. The member states are responsible for the fiscal policy. However, the policy must conform to the principles and procedures of fiscal discipline, as mentioned in the Maastricht Treaty and enhanced by the Stability and Growth Pact of 1997. In order to strengthen the budgetary discipline, the principle of 'no bailout' was institutionalised. The ECB is prohibited from being a 'lender of last resort'. Thus, it cannot directly lend funds to the governments of member states or directly purchase bonds. The fiscal discipline is supervised and exercised by the Commission and the Council, through recommendations, warnings, and sanctions that seek to lead a state deviating from the fiscal criteria back into track. The member states enjoy autonomy in the implementation of the general economic policy. There is no supranationalisation in this field. Member states are only committed to follow the jointly agreed Broad Economic Policy Guidelines. In case of deviation from these Guidelines, the Council may make recommendations. The Commission is involved in this process because it has the right to monitor, evaluate, inform, warn, and submit recommendations to the Council. All other specific economic policies, such as income policy, social policy, regional policy, structural policy, industrial policy, etc., remain the responsibility of the member states.

2.2 Structural and Functional Deficiencies

Right from the beginning, the EMU system of governance displayed multiple structural weaknesses, which analysts have identified (Kotios, Galanos, & Pavlidis, 2011; Papastamkos & Kotios, 2011). These structural weaknesses and systemic deficits include the following:

First, there is the basic limitation of the common monetary policy. Unlike other countries such as the US (Schelkle, 2012), the Eurozone's monetary policy has monetary stability as its sole aim, with a prescribed (arbitrary) maximum average annual inflation rate of 2 %. This has the effect of excluding other objectives, such as economic growth and employment, thereby depriving the member states of an important tool of countercyclical policy.

Second, the supranationalisation and de-politicisation of the monetary policy was not accompanied by corresponding supranationalisation of other areas of economic policy. Despite certain restrictions, the fiscal, income, and social policy remain the responsibility of the member states. Thus, monetary union has not been associated with union in other economic fields.

Third, there is the limitation in the ability of the member states to pursue countercyclical macroeconomic policies. The supranationalisation of the monetary policy, the institutional and the real constraints on fiscal policy, and the disappearance of national exchange rate policy within the euro area have weakened the ability of the member states to manage their economies. Therefore, in times when the external deficits rise, or during recessions, the member states are asked to implement measures, particularly in the fields of income and structural policy, resulting in social reactions.

Fourth, there is the absence of mechanisms to prevent and manage crises. This deficit can be attributed to the naive expectations of the political leadership of the member states of that time; that monetary stability and fiscal discipline, combined with the loose co-ordination of economic policy, would either prevent the occurrence of shocks or crises within the Eurozone or isolate them in individual states—this while preventing transmission to other members of the monetary union. The warning about the potential occurrence of asymmetric shocks within the member states was ignored (Eichengreen, 2009).

Fifth, there is the lack of solidarity mechanisms, that is, the transfer of income from the countries that benefit more from the monetary union to countries facing problems in internal competition with other Eurozone countries and exhibiting deficits in current account. In contrast, all federal states, such as the US or Germany, have established a compensatory payment to the poorest regions (Cottarelli, 2012; Hallerberg, Strauch, & von Hagen, 2009; Rogoff, 2012). Obviously, the importance of balance of payments within the euro area was ignored and it was considered that the burden of adjustment required ought to be borne only by the states with deficit (Höpner & Rödl, 2012; Wolf, 2012).

Sixth, there is the dependence of the member states on the private financial markets and the absence of a 'lender of the last resort', in times of liquidity crisis or insolvency. The member states, unlike almost all other nations of the world, have no direct access to the central banks' funds in times of crisis. Thus, borrowing in euro is essentially proportional to borrowing in foreign currency. If the markets stopped lending, then the only options left are external public financing or bankruptcy (De Grauwe, 2011, 2012).

The system of governance of the Eurozone, in addition to its structural weaknesses and deficits, failed to work effectively to some extent (Papastamkos & Kotios, 2011; Wolf, 2012). For instance, the notorious budgetary discipline was abolished in practice, especially when Germany and France refused to reduce budget deficits. The 'solidarity' among finance ministers introduced a highly flexible application of the procedures and sanctions (Eichengreen, 2012). The revision of the Stability and Growth Pact in 2005 introduced exceptions to the fiscal criteria.

The question that arises is whether and how the deficits and dysfunctions of the Eurozone's governance have encouraged or caused the emergence of the Greek crisis.

3 The Effect of the Eurozone's Governance on the Emergence of the Greek Crisis

The crisis of the Greek economy began as a heavy liquidity crisis, became a sovereign debt crisis and subsequently a generalised economic, social, and political crisis, and ended up being a discussion on 'drachmaization'. It is to be noted that the crisis is mainly homemade (Kotios et al., 2011).

However, the question that comes up is whether the EMU's governance has contributed to the genesis of Greek crisis. The answer is affirmative if one takes into consideration the following arguments (Papastamkos & Kotios, 2011):

First, the EMU has allowed the accession of countries with excessive debt, well above the 60 % of the GDP, and budget deficits close to (or actually above, because of the creative accounting) the limit of 3 %. Therefore, countries that were highly vulnerable to debt crises were included into the Eurozone.

Second, because of competitive risks, the EMU membership should also have depended on convergence criteria of the real economy (e.g. productivity, innovation, economic environment, administrative performance, and competitiveness). In this way, premature inclusion in the competitive environment of the EMU of unprepared national economic systems could have been avoided. Unfortunately, however, Greece joined the EMU only on the basis of nominal economic criteria.

Third, following its accession in the Eurozone, Greece in each year had a deficit above 3 % of GDP, while debt remained well above the 60 % of GDP. The fiscal discipline was not applied effectively, allowing the derailment of public finances in Greece.

Fourth, the issue of financing public deficits and rising current account deficits was systematically neglected, as was, in general, the issue of internal macroeconomic imbalances in the EMU (De Grauwe, 2011; Wolf, 2012). There was also no provision in the treaty to address the private external debt that caused the mounting deficits in the current account.

Fifth, the co-ordination of economic policies and the implementation of the National Reform Programmes were ineffective, in the context of the Lisbon Strategy.

In conclusion, it was not the original system of the EMU governance that caused the Greek crisis. However, it did fail to prevent it. Moreover, the country's membership in the Eurozone has allowed and encouraged excessive public borrowing and private capital inflows for financing the huge Greek current account deficits.

4 The Management of the Greek Crisis in the Eurozone

The Greek crisis management, both on the part of the Greek government and of the EU, is an example to be avoided (Featherstone, 2011; Kotios et al., 2011). Certainly, the causes of the Greek crisis are many and the problem of excessive debt was caused mainly by errors of internal economic policy. Nevertheless, the situation before 2008 was largely manageable. The international financial crisis, though it has not caused the Greek debt crisis, has aggravated and accelerated the crisis. It is significant that in 2007, even before the crisis, the country showed a debt equal to 107.4 % of GDP and fiscal deficit of 6.5 %. The situation worsened dramatically in 2009, when Greece followed an expansionary fiscal policy. As a result, the budget deficit soared to 15.6 % of the GDP and debt to 129.4 % (European Commission, 2012a). However, the country continued to borrow on favourable terms. For example, in November 2009 and, despite correcting the fiscal deficit figure (from 6 % to 12.7 % of GDP), the spread of 10-year Greek government bonds remained at 139 basis points (EEAG, 2011).

The new deficit figures and Fitch's degradation of the country's credit rating from A to A− in October 2009 should have led to immediate measures for consolidating the public finances. In contrast, the new government proceeded to social payments and filed a dull budget. In December 2009, the three major rating agencies downgraded the creditworthiness of the country, leading to a continuous increase in the spread of the Greek 10-year bond, which in January 2010 exceeded 300 units. The spread rally began, which in turn increased the difficulties of financing the Greek government.

The first package of fiscal adjustment in February 2010 was not enough to convince the markets. Therefore, in less than a month (March 2010), the Greek government announced more restrictive measures, which, like the measures in the first package, focused on horizontal cuts in wages and benefits and increases in indirect taxes. These measures caused massive strikes, increased prices, and aggravation of the recession. Since it was tackling the symptoms rather than the causes of the crisis, rating agencies continued to downgrade the country, while in the Greek market the bond spread increased and in April 2010 to exceeded 1,000 units, making borrowing from the markets almost prohibitive (Kotios et al., 2011).

Finally, on April 23, 2010, the country submitted to the IMF and the Council of the EMU a request for public funding. On the 2 May, the EU, the ECB, and the IMF decided to grant Greece a loan of 110 billion euros (80 billion from the 15 EMU countries and 30 billion from the IMF). The loan was associated with Greece's signing of the first Memorandum, which included the adjustment measures to be taken (European Commission, 2010). In order to monitor the measures, a tripartite committee (troika) was created with representatives from the European Commission, the ECB, and the IMF. The loan for Greece had an intergovernmental character and was based on the provisions of aid to a country in an emergency. It was the first time that the Eurozone was asked to manage such a crisis. In the absence of institutionalised mechanisms for crisis management and because of the 'no bailout' clause, the member states were late in addressing the Greek issue. However, fears about the transmission of the crisis (domino effect) to other heavily indebted countries, fears about the consequences of bankruptcy in the banking systems, and concerns about the image of the euro area and about the overall European integration led the EMU countries, apparently without enthusiasm, to consent to the funding scheme for Greece. Thus, in response to the Greek crisis, the EMU has created a precedent for financial support, without the need for institutional changes. Subsequently, and due to fears of collapse in other countries of the Community region, the Eurozone developed other means of dealing with crises, such as the European Financial Stabilization Mechanism (EFSM) and the European Financial Stability Facility (EFSF). Subsequently, in order to establish a permanent mechanism for the euro area member states that would ensure, in course of time, the financial stability of the whole Eurozone, the European Council adopted the European Stability Mechanism (ESM), to be activated by mid-2012.

It should be pointed out that the loan deal in Greece followed the tradition of the IMF's commitments towards implementing a programme of fiscal and structural adjustment. This programme took the form of a Memorandum, which would be evaluated and adjusted periodically. This was a binding program, with clear obligations, time-bound actions, consultations, and monitoring processes. A year after the adoption of the first Memorandum, due to divergence in the programme objectives, Greece adopted in June 2011 a Medium Term Stabilization Programme (2012–2015), in order to speed up fiscal and structural reforms and privatisations (Hellenic Republic, 2011a, 2011b). The new measures provoked unprecedented social and political reactions.

The pronounced deviations from the stated objectives, the risks that the bankruptcy of Greece posed for the cohesion of the Eurozone, and the gradual realisation that this was not just a country's debt crisis but a systemic crisis of the Eurozone, lead to the decisions of the Summit of 21 July 2011 (Council of the European Union, 2011a).

These decisions included granting new public loans to Greece, cutting the private debt, buying back bonds, increasing the debt-duration by 15–30 years, and strengthening the country's development through a Marshall Plan-type programme. However, the decisions that were not associated with a strict timetable for implementation have not brought expected results. Variations from the agreed adjustment plan forced the country to take additional measures in October 2011. The failure to implement the decisions of the Summit of July and the liquidity problems in other Eurozone countries have strengthened their uncertainty for the future. This resulted in the convening of a new Summit on 26 October 2011 to establish a definitive plan to tackle the crisis. This meeting reached the following decisions (Council of the European Union, 2011b): granting a new loan to Greece of 130 billion euros, 'voluntary' haircut of private debt by 50 %, recapitalisation of Greek banks by the state via EFSF funds, and signing a new memorandum. This new memorandum was signed in March 2012 (European Commission, 2012b).

With the current crisis management policies at the national and the European level, the country has not only failed to recover, but instead, faces a widespread crisis, a continuous deterioration of all economic and social indicators, and political instability and uncertainty. The Greek problem of dealing with the debt has now become an issue of maintaining its membership in the euro area and is, thus, a question of continuing with the project of monetary integration of Europe (Deutsche Bank, 2012; HSBC, 2012; UBS, 2012). At this point, a series of questions arises: Why did the Greek crisis management fail? To what extent is this due to the system of governance of the Eurozone? What were the new changes to the system and what are the features that can ensure the sustainability of the Eurozone? The following analysis can provide some answers to these questions.

5 The Crisis of Eurozone's Governance

5.1 The Greek Crisis as a Process of Uncovering Weaknesses in the Governance System

The debt and liquidity crisis in Greece has initially worked as a process of uncovering a series of arrhythmias, problems, and deficits in the system and governance of the EMU. In particular, the Eurozone crisis revealed (Papastamkos & Kotios, 2011) the following.

6 Structural and Functional Deficiencies of the Eurosystem

It was found that all the weaknesses and shortcomings in the architecture of the EMU have played an important role both in causing the crisis and in its inefficient management.

7 Weaknesses of the European Decision-Making Mechanism

The Greek crisis has shown that the EMU system results in huge problems in decision making (Hughes, 2011). It did not develop a joint strategy to tackle the effects of the financial crisis and reacted with a significant delay in tackling the Greek debt crisis and the liquidity problems of other countries in the EU periphery. In the absence of a centralised system of crisis management and allocation of roles, different actors have emerged in all the EU institutions—member states of the

Eurozone, international institutions, and powerful countries. All these actors have expressed and often express diverging views, without a single instance of effective co-ordination, thereby destabilising the markets. The Eurozone Summit was highlighted as a top decision making body, but without restraining the destabilising actions of other actors within and outside the Eurozone. The IMF's involvement in the management of the European crisis and in the adoption of methods of and in the supervision of lending illustrates the weakness of the EMU countries in managing their own problems (Kyriakopoulos, 2011; Matthes, 2010). Finally, questions have been raised about the democratic status of the crisis management decisions (Hughes, 2011). This is because the decisions were taken by national governments and institutions without prior involvement of either the national parliaments or the European Parliament.

8 The Huge Deficit of European Leadership and the Emergence of Economic Nationalism and Chauvinism in Some Member States

The lack of an effective EU leadership was expressed in many ways. First, it did not function as effectively as it did in the past in the traditional Franco–German axis. On the contrary, the crisis has highlighted the dominant role of Germany (Bohn & de Jong, 2011; Hughes, 2011; The Economist, 2011). Many governments in the EMU countries determined their attitude towards the crisis based on their internal politics and not the public interest (Aslund, 2011; Dullien & Guerot, 2012). In an environment of economic nationalism and populism, it is often difficult for governments to extend effective support to partner countries in crisis.

9 The Risks of Transmission of the Crisis to the Entire Eurozone

The Greek crisis has shown that a serious national disorder is risky for all the EMU countries and puts the entire Eurozone to the test. The debt crisis in one country can spread to another through a series of channels (Arghyrou & Kontonikas, 2010; Darvas, Pisani-Ferry, & Sapir, 2011). Due to the strong interdependencies, the Eurozone countries have a direct interest in stabilising the unbalanced economies. The deeper the crisis, the greater are the costs for all. Consequently, the EMU countries are destined to a co-operative game, so there are benefits for all (win–win game). If a country in crisis is not supported by the others and left to go bankrupt, then there are losses for all (lose–lose game) (Schilirò & Carfi, 2012).

10 Excessive Reactions of the Financial Markets and Rating Agencies

In times of crisis, there is generally an overreaction in the money and capital markets. The same was the case with the Greek crisis (De Grauwe, 2011). There was a large increase in interest rates and a sharp decrease in prices of Greek bonds in the secondary markets. Moreover, bank credits decreased drastically, thereby exacerbating the liquidity problem and recession. The role of the rating agencies proved to be particularly negative; their ratings and forecasts influenced the behaviour of markets and risk premiums.

10.1 Reasons for the Failure of Crisis Management

There is no doubt that the Greek crisis management has failed. Since the beginning of the crisis, the total public debt increased in absolute terms and as a percentage of the GDP (from 129.4 % of the GDP in 2009 to 160.2 % in 2012). Despite the unprecedented haircut of private debt, the remaining Greek public debt cannot be considered as sustainable. The fiscal deficit was reduced substantially (e.g. from 15.6 % of the GDP in 2009 to 9.1 % in 2011), but continues to remain high, given the existence of primary deficits and high interest payments (about 7 % of the GDP). After 5 years of shrinking GDP, Greece has lost more than 15 % of its national income. Due to the recession, unemployment rose from 7.7 % in 2008 to over 20 % in 2012. The haircut of private debt, reduction in deposits, and capital outflow caused many problems for the Greek banks and led to a drastic reduction of liquidity in the economy, as reflected by the reduction in monetary aggregates and the continuing decline in banking credit growth (Bank of Greece, 2012; Heller, 2012). In consequence, the Greek economy is characterised by strong imbalances and multiple vicious circles.

In conclusion, the performance of the Greek crisis management has been disappointing. The failure of the Greek crisis management has many causes. The most important is the internal reluctance to adjustment, due to structural weaknesses in the Greek political system. However, there also causes related to the deficits or malfunctions in the Eurozone's governance system. The following could be considered as some of the causes.

The failure to address the crisis at its initial stage: As mentioned, negligence and timidity on the part of the Greek government and constant revisions of public deficit data caused devaluation of the country's credibility and destabilised the financial markets, which in turn exacerbated the financial crisis (Kotios et al., 2011). For their part, the institutions of the Eurozone and the other member states, continued for long with complaints and recommendations, instead of intervening effectively. At the beginning of the crisis, they considered that the problem was national and had to be solved by national measures. The likelihood of the contagion spreading to other countries of the EMU, or the probability of the existence of a systemic crisis, was ignored completely. In addition, the ability of a country to face the crisis from its own resources was overrated, given the context of a monetary union permitting free movement of capital. Thus, both the national governance system and the European one, instead of a direct intervention, allowed the crisis to snowball. The decision to support Greece was too timid and came too late, and as it turned out, was not a definitive solution to the problem. This also was the case with subsequent decisions of the Eurozone for Greece. All the decisions came too late. The European crisis management was more a reaction to real market developments and less a preventive intervention. Additionally, it was obvious that the packages towards Greece did not provide a definitive solution to the problems. Essentially, these were interim measures based on unrealistic scenarios, and contained the minimum that would allow the economy to survive at the lowest possible level, but not to recover. The philosophy of these packages was 'support and punishment'.

The economic policy of the Memoranda: The agreed policy, as expressed through the two Memoranda and the interim operations of the troika, proved ineffective, and rather than solving the problem, made it worse. The question that comes up is whether this negative development was due to the policy recipe or to the lack of application. First, it seems that the problem with the Memoranda is twofold: On the one hand, it is roughly about programmes of fiscal and structural adjustment, without internal cohesion, without a goal hierarchy, and without *ex ante* evaluation of concrete outputs and results. The initial applied policy of fiscal adjustment has given more emphasis on revenue growth and less on reducing costs of the state, and has not included measures to ensure social cohesion. The necessary structural adjustments for strengthening the development process require time for improving the supply side of the economy. The economy of the country needs some short-term development interventions with immediate results, in order to put the country on the path of growth. In other words, the emphasis of the adjustment programme was on reducing deficits through austerity measures, and not through economic growth. Consequently, the recession and the failure to ensure the sustainability of Greek debt can be viewed as normal results of the implemented programme. On the other hand, the implementation by the Greek governments of many of the agreed measures and reforms has been poor, with long lags, timidity, and inconsistency. From the beginning, political, economic, and social distributional interest groups created a bloc that resisted adjustment.

Some political forces in Greece caused a new division in Greek society on the basis of a static, but dangerous conflict—between those who were pro memorandum and those who were anti-memorandum. The result is what we experience: generalised crisis, insecurity, uncertainty, flight of capital and investment, vicious circles of debt and recession, and political and social conflict.

The dispute over sharing the cost of Greek crisis: The management of Greek crisis is also a management of distributing the costs of the crisis. For instance, while it became clear that the Greek government debt was not sustainable and should be reduced through a haircut, this raised the question whether the private lenders or public lenders would bear the cost. Each of these two groups has tried to avoid taking a loss. Eventually, after political pressure, the private sector (banks and insurance funds) accepted a 50 % haircut. This caused liquidity problems for the banking and insurance systems of Greece and some other countries, thus increasing the demands for loans through the EFSF for re-capitalising banks or supporting insurance funds. By contrast, the governments of the Eurozone have so far avoided a partial deletion of their loans to Greece or the transfer of resources in favour of Greece, fearing the reaction of their constituents and the exit from markets of other countries of the EU periphery.

The provocative and aggressive rhetoric of the crisis: The management of the Greek debt crisis was not supported by a serious European diplomacy. Derogatory statements, euro exit threats, and political interventions damaged the image of Greece and led to internal political and social reactions. Instead of creating a climate of confidence, this diplomacy has produced insecurity and uncertainty in the markets.

The inefficacy of the new Eurozone governance: The policy of creating a new governance for the Eurozone dealt mostly with the creation of new institutions of governance with limited effectiveness regarding the current solvency and liquidity crisis (Gros, 2011; Oesterreichische National Bank, 2011; Schilirò, 2011). This refers to the 'six pack' proposed by the decisions of the Commission and the Council entitled 'Euro plus' and the 'fiscal pact'. These initiatives aimed to improve fiscal discipline and the harmonisation of national economic policies to address macroeconomic imbalances, and promote policies to reduce fiscal deficits. In contrast, there was no growth initiative. The agreed financial support mechanisms, the resources for which come from funds and securities of the euro area member states, thereby burdening their creditworthiness, have limited resources. Moreover, their delayed interventions are discounted by the markets or lead to their being perceived as not competent to solve problems. This could explain the fact that after each intervention, the position of the supported country in international markets deteriorates.

The inadequate involvement of the ECB: In the crisis of the Eurozone, the ECB tried to react with various means such as reducing its key interest rates, providing liquidity to the banking system (through the Main Refinancing Operations and Long Term Refinancing Operations), halving the minimum reserve ratio, broadening the collateral eligibility rules, and purchasing government bonds in secondary markets (Cottarelli, 2012; De Grauwe, 2012; Welfens, 2012). The ECB's interventions in support of Greece came too late, thereby reducing their effectiveness (Hughes, 2011). Furthermore, the ECB, although it purchased Greek bonds in secondary markets at a price far below the nominal value (ca 70 % of nominal value), denied not only to cut them, but also ordered the repayment of the nominal value, making significant gains (Slater & Georgiopoulos, 2012).

The political management of the crisis: The conditions for the granting of loans included in the Memoranda led to a reduction of the sovereignty of Greece and provoked strong reactions (Hughes, 2011). In an independent country, the imposition of adjustment policies from abroad is hardly accepted by the population, because the latter do not consider such policies to be driven by internal political and social forces.

What is more, in periods of intense and lasting recession, it is difficult to implement necessary reforms if one does not provide political measures for mitigating adjustment costs. Moreover, the loan agreements had been seen as an external intervention in the functioning of Greek democracy, in the political system, and in the internal legal order (Gros, 2012).

Conclusion

The foregoing analysis points to the conclusion that in the case of the Greek crisis, the governance system of the Eurozone has failed. Although not directly causing the current debt crisis, the structural and administrative shortcomings and gaps in the governance of Eurozone allowed the crisis to occur and, to an extent, aggravated it. Consequently, it is above all a Greek crisis, but is also a crisis of the Eurozone's governance. The new support programme and the haircut of private debt improved the terms of serving the Greek debt, but it was not a proper solution to the problem. The debt of Greece will continue to be very high and the interest payments per year will be an important part of the Greek GDP. In any case, without support for real economic growth and competitiveness, the long-term sustainability of Greece's debt is doubtful. Despite the progress that has been made in the structure and mechanism of the Eurozone governance, there is no doubt that the systemic Euro crisis has not lost its dynamics. The crisis of a monetary union, which is far from being an optimal currency area, is inherent (Rogoff, 2012). It could only be solved by creating institutions and intervention mechanism similar with those applicable to federal states, namely, a common growth policy, interstate income distribution, common fiscal and social policy, harmonisation of the political cycle, stable democratic institutions, and the centralisation of crisis management. Historical experience shows that monetary union requires political union as well. The new tools of governance of the EMU are difficult to operate effectively and permanently without causing new political tensions. The operating conditions of the Eurozone could be improved by the establishment of an automatic mechanism for the transfer of income from competitive economies to those less competitive, creating a single institution for crisis prevention and management (e.g. an European Monetary, Social, and Development Fund), increasing the possibility of the ECB and ESM to provide liquidity to the Member States and European banks in a more direct way (Buiter & Rahbari, 2011; Daianu, 2012; De Grauwe, 2012). Furthermore, significant improvements could result in the creation of a European Banking Union (Financial Times, 2012; Fuest, 2012). However, a supranationalisation of all economic policies would not prove fruitful, because of the different structures prevailing in each country, and because of the asymmetric shocks, the treatment of which requires differentiated interventions based on the principle of subsidiary (Ahrens, 2012). The final solution of the Greek crisis in the Eurozone requires more efforts from both sides. As far as Greece is concerned, what is needed is a serious effort to rebuild the country through a broad set of reforms at almost all levels of economy, politics, and society. The country will never overcome the crisis unless it cures the structural causes that led to the collapse. On the part of the Eurozone, the crisis management needs to be changed. The new support philosophy must evolve from 'help and punishment' to 'help without punishment'. Greece needs more of supportive actions and less of destabilising and degrading statements.

References

Ahrens, J. (2012, April). Bessere Governance durchmehrFlexibilisierung. *Wirtschaftsdienst*, 225–230.

Arghyrou, M. G., & Kontonikas, A. (2010). *The EMU sovereign-debt crisis: Fundamentals, expectations and contagion*. Seminar at the Hellenic Observatory, The European Institute, LSE.

Aslund, A. (2011, May 20). *The failed political economy of the Euro crisis*. http://www.case-research.eu/sites/default/files/publications/Ebrief_2011_10_Aslund.pdf. Accessed 25 June 2012.

Bank of Greece. (2012, June 18). *Greek contribution to the euro area monetary aggregates*. http://www.bankofgreece.gr/BogDocumentEn/Greek_contribution_to_euro_area_monetary_aggregates.xls. Accessed 25 June 2012.

Bohn, F., & de Jong, E. (2011). The 2010 euro crisis stand-off between France and Germany: Leadership styles and political culture. *International and Economic Policy, 8*, 7–14.

Buiter, W., Rahbari, E. (2011). *The future of the euro area: Fiscal union, break-up or blundering towards a 'you break it you own it Europe'*. 15 April 2012. http://www.willembuiter.com/3scenarios.pdf. Accessed 25 June 2012.

Cottarelli, C. (2012). Sovereign debt crisis: Why in Europe and not elsewhere? *Intereconomics, 47*(2), 74–75.

Council of the European Union. (2011a, July 21). *Statement by the heads of state or government of the Euro area and institutions*. Brussels: Council of the European Union. http://www.consilium.europa.eu/uedocs/cms_data/docs/pressdata/en/ec/123978.pdf. Accessed 25 June 2012.

Council of the European Union. (2011b, October 26). *Euro summit statement*. Brussels: Council of the European Union. http://www.consilium.europa.eu/uedocs/cms_data/docs/pressdata/en/ec/125644.pdf. Accessed 25 June 2012.

Daianu, D. (2012). *Euro Zone crisis and EU governance: Tackling a flawed design and inadequate policy arrangements*. Warsaw: Center for Social and Economic Research.

Darvas, Z., Pisani-Ferry, J., & Sapir, A. (2011). A comprehensive approach to the Euro-area debt crisis: Background calculations. *Bruegel Policy Brief, 2* (Brussels).

De Grauwe, P. (2011). The Governance of a Fragile Eurozone. *CEPS, Working Document No. 346*, May.

De Grauwe, P. (2012, May 31). A self-inflicted crisis. *CEPS Commentary*.

Deutsche Bank. (2012, May). The geuro: A parallel currency for Greece? *Global Market Research*. http://www.scribd.com/doc/94526659/G-euro-DB. Accessed 25 June 2012.

Dullien, S., & Guerot, U. (2012). The long shadow of ordoliberalism: Germany's approach to the Euro crisis. *European Council on Foreign Relations, Brief, 49*. http://www.ecfr.eu/page/-/ECFR49_GERMANY_BRIEF_AW.pdf. Accessed 25 June 2012.

EEAG. (2011). *The EEAG report on the European economy, "Greece"* (pp. 97–125). Munich: CESifo, European Economic Advisory Group.

Eichengreen, B. (2009, January 20). Was the euro a mistake? *Voxeu.org*. http://voxeu.org/index.php?q=node/2815. Accessed 25 June 2012.

Eichengreen, B. (2012). European monetary integration with benefit of hindsight. *Journal of Common Market Studies, 50*(1), 123–136.
European Commission. (2010, May). *The economic adjustment programme for Greece* (Occasional Paper, 61). Brussels: Economic and Financial Affairs, European Economy.
European Commission. (2012a, January, Spring). European economic forecast. Brussels: Economic and Financial Affairs, European Economy.
European Commission. (2012b, March). *The second economic adjustment programme for Greece* (Occasional Paper, 94). Brussels: Economic and Financial Affairs, European Economy.
Featherstone, K. (2011). The Greek sovereign debt crisis and EMU: A failing state in a skewed regime. *Journal of Common Market Studies, 49*(2), 193–217.
Financial Times. (2012, June 5). *Banking union and the euro's future*. http://www.ft.com/cms/s/0/f7485428-ac0e-11e1-923a-00144feabdc0.html#axzz1xI68JceD. Accessed 25 June 2012.
Fuest, C. (2012, June 7). Wir brauchen eine Bankenunion. *Frankfurter Allgemeine*. http://www.faz.net/aktuell/wirtschaft/europas-schuldenkrise/schuldenkrise-wir-brauchen-eine-bankenunion-11776758.html. Accessed 25 June 2012.
Gros, D. (2011, March 14). Pact for the euro: Tough talk, soft conditions? *Voxeu.org*. http://voxeu.org/index.php?q=node/6206. Accessed 25 June 2012.
Gros, D. (2012, June 1). Democracy vs. Eurozone. *Project Syndicate*. http://www.project-syndicate.org/commentary/democracy-versus-the-eurozone. Accessed 25 June 2012.
Hallerberg, M., Strauch, R., & von Hagen, J. (2009). *Fiscal governance in Europe*. Cambridge: Cambridge University Press.
Hellenic Republic, Ministry of Finance. (2011a, June). *Medium term fiscal strategy 2012–15*. Athens: Hellenic Republic, Ministry of Finance. http://www.minfin.gr/content-api/f/binaryChannel/minfin/datastore/8d/78/0e/8d780e3337a1e1cb20d1a1707686d7399be4913a/application/pdf/MTFS.pdf. Accessed 25 June 2012.
Hellenic Republic, Ministry of Finance. (2011b, April). *Hellenic national reform programme 2011–2014*. Athens: Hellenic Republic, Ministry of Finance. http://ec.europa.eu/europe2020/pdf/nrp/nrp_greece_en.pdf. Accessed 25 June 2012.
Heller, G. (2012, February 15). ECB ready to forego Greece bond profit. *Reuters*. http://www.reuters.com/article/2012/02/15/us-eurozone-greece-asmussen-idUSTRE81E0FU20120215. Accessed 25 June 2012.
Höpner, M., & Rödl, F. (2012). Illegitim und rechtswidrig: Das neuemakroökonomische Regime im Euroraum. *Wirtschaftsdienst, 92*(4), 219–222.
HSBC. (2012, May 23). *Greek crisis-four scenarios for the Eurozone*. https://www.research.hsbc.com/midas/Res/RDV?p=pdf&key=Hf8yVE0JWE&n=331018.PDF. Accessed 25 June 2012.
Hughes, K. (2011, November). *European politics and the Euro crisis: Ten failures* (Policy Paper). Brussels: Friends of Europe.
Kotios, A., Galanos, G., & Pavlidis, G. (2011). Greece and the Euro: The chronicle of anexpected collapse. *Intereconomics, 46*(5), 263–269.
Kyriakopoulos, I. (2011). Economic and monetary governance: A post-crisis assessment. *World Economics, 12*(4), 93–108.
Matthes, J. (2010, February 27). Why the IMF should be involved in solving imminent fiscal debt crises in Eurozone countries. *Voxeu.org*. http://www.voxeu.org/index.php?q=node/4683. Accessed 25 June 2012.
Oesterreichische National bank (Eds.) (2011). *EU Governance Reformed*, Monetary Policy & The Economy, Quarterly Review of Economic Policy 4/11, Vienna.
Papastamkos, G., & Kotios, A. (2011, November 16). *Krise der Eurozone: Krise des Systems oder der Politik?* (Online Papers). Berlin: Institut für Europäische Politik. http://www.iep-berlin.de/fileadmin/website/09_Publikationen/Sonstige/2011-11-15_Eurozone__Papastamkos_Kotios.pdf. Accessed 25 June 2012.
Rogoff, K. (2012, April 4). A centerless Euro cannot hold. *Project Syndicate*. http://www.project-syndicate.org/commentary/a-centerless-euro-cannot-hold. Accessed 25 June 2012.

Schambaugh, J. (2012, March 12). *The Euro's three crises* (Brookings Papers on Economic Activity Spring 2012). http://www.brookings.edu/~/media/Files/Programs/ES/BPEA/2012_spring_bpea_papers/2012_spring_BPEA_shambaugh.pdf. Accessed 25 June 2012.
Schelkle, W (2012). Good Governance in crisis or a good crisis for governance? A comparison of the EU and the US. *Review of International Political Economy, 19*(1), 34–58.
Schilirò, D. (2011, April 13). *A new governance for the EMU and the economic policy framework* (MPRA Paper, 30237). http://mpra.ub.uni-muenchen.de/30237/. Accessed 25 June 2012.
Schilirò, D., & Carfì, D. (2012, April 5). *A framework of coopetitive games: Applications to the Greek crisis* (MPRA Paper, 37855). http://mpra.ub.uni-muenchen.de/37855/. Accessed 25 June 2012.
Seidel, M. (2011), Die Europäische Zentralbank, Zentrum für Europäische Integrationsforschung, Rheinische Friedrich-Wilhelms-Universität Bonn, Working Paper B 01/2011, http://www.zei.uni-bonn.de/dateien/working-papaer/b01-2011. Accessed 25 June 2012.
Slater, S., & Georgiopoulos, G. (2012, May 17). Greeks not alone in bank savings exodus. *Reuters*. http://www.reuters.com/article/2012/05/17/us-banks-deposits-idUSBRE84G0MG20120517. Accessed 25 June 2012.
The Economist. (2011, November 12). *Europe's big two—the Nico and Angela show*. http://www.economist.com/node/21536868. Accessed 25 June 2012.
Thygesen, N. (2011, April 10). *Governance in the Euro area—approaching an optimum currency area?* Paper presented in Institute for New Economic Thinking Conference, Bretton Woods. http://ineteconomics.org/bretton-woods/paper-presented-bretton-woods-conference-niels-thygesen. Accessed 25 June 2012.
UBS. (2012, May 18). Greek exit: The cost for Europe. *USB Investment Research, European Weekly Economic Focus*. http://www.instutrade.com/media/10923/ubs-greece.pdf. Accessed 25 June 2012.
Welfens, P. J. J. (2012, June 1). *Overcoming the Euro crisis*. Johns Hopkins University, American Institute for Contemporary German Studies, Transatlantic Perspectives. http://www.aicgs.org/publication/overcoming-the-euro-crisis/. Accessed 25 June 2012.
Wolf, M. (2012, May 3). *Why the Eurozone crisis is not over*. Paper delivered in National Economists Club and Peterson Institute for International Economics, Peterson Institute, Washington DC. http://www.iie.com/publications/papers/wolf20120503ppt.pdf. Accessed 25 June 2012.

The Eurozone Rebalancing Challenge: Lessons from the Past and Dilemmas for the Future

Pyrros Papadimitriou

1 Introduction

In March 2011, the European governments decided to create a permanent European Stability Mechanism (ESM). In December 2011, the European Central Bank (ECB) decided to lower its refinancing rate to 1 % and to offer two new longer-term Refinancing Operations (LTROs).[1] In March 2012, a haircut was imposed on private holders of Greek debt. These decisions have led many policy makers and analysts to conclude that the Eurozone is finally on the right track towards solving its debt problems.

The experience of the last few months, however, does not support this conclusion. Rather, a series of facts has shown that these measures do not suffice to solve the Eurozone's problems and act, at the most, as buying—time mechanisms. They appear to fight the symptoms but do not cure the disease or, more appropriately, they buy time until the fundamental issues are addressed. The fundamental problems that the Eurozone faces are dealing with unsustainable levels of debt, significant deterioration in the competitiveness of some member countries, and that the unification process of the European Union has almost remained stagnant since the inception of the single currency.

Against this background, this paper shows that the architecture of the Eurozone, established at the end of the 1990s, was bound to lead the whole project into trouble and, today, saving the euro is a difficult task with significant policy dilemmas. I have structured the paper as follows. Section 1 provides a brief overview of how the architecture of the Eurozone has contributed to fiscal unruliness by creating a

[1] In response to the LTROs offerings, European banks borrowed 489 billion euros in December 2011 and 530 billion euros in February 2012.

P. Papadimitriou (✉)
Department of Political Science and International Relations, University of Peloponnese,
47 Dervenakion St and Adimantou, Corinth 20100, Greece
e-mail: papdimit@gmail.com

P. Sklias and N. Tzifakis (eds.), *Greece's Horizons*, The Konstantinos Karamanlis Institute for Democracy Series on European and International Affairs,
DOI 10.1007/978-3-642-34534-0_9,

framework of perverse incentives. Section 2 discusses the present situation in the countries of the Eurozone and the dilemmas that policy makers face, while Sect. 3 provides an analysis of the alternative ways of saving the euro and the cost entailed. Section 4 develops policy recommendations.

2 The Architecture of the Eurozone

If one wants to understand the causes of the present crisis in the EU, she has to study the dynamics and the context in which the single currency has been introduced. At the end of the 1990s, there was an evident tendency to include as many countries as possible in the monetary union. The decreasing competitiveness of the European Union (see Papadimitriou, 2008) and the fear that the prosperity in Europe was at risk contributed to the perception that it was necessary to complete the internal market through a single currency and to provide the European Union with the characteristics of a continental economy. In this context, the Maastricht Treaty's criteria started being interpreted with greater flexibility. More emphasis was given to the tendency of the countries to fulfil the fiscal criteria, and, explicitly or implicitly, countries were allowed to use techniques of creative accounting in order to meet the criteria. 'Innovative' one-off transactions—such as securitisation, financial derivatives, and one-off- payments by state related entities—that allowed spending without increasing the recorded deficit, are examples of creative accounting techniques.[2]

On the other hand, the monetary unification established in 1999 was regarded by the member countries as a big step towards unification, and no country was actually prepared to accept other restrictions on its autonomy. Fiscal policy remained in the hands of the national governments and the Eurozone became a monetary union without fiscal backups. Consequently, almost all the pressure of adjustment has fallen on the labour markets.

The big troubles[3] that could ensue from the establishment of a monetary union of members, with divergent ethics and capabilities in the management of public finances and with uneven economic strength, led to the establishment of the Stability and Growth Pact (SGP).[4] The SGP (of 1997 and its reform in 2005) imposed the well-known deficit and public debt targets for the Eurozone. The SGP consisted of a commitment to a balanced or surplus general government

[2] The possibility that the candidate countries could follow such policies had been pointed out at an early stage by various economists such as Buiter, Corsetti, and Roubini (1993) and Easterly (1999).

[3] Several economists (Dafflon & Rossi, 1998; Easterly, 1999) had predicted the troubles that lay ahead in the absence of coordination in national fiscal and budgetary policies.

[4] Substantial parts in the following paragraphs of this section are based on the previous work of the author, in Papadimitriou (2011) and Papadimitriou and Hadziyiannakis (2012).

budget in the medium-term, a binding 3 % limit for the deficit-to-GDP ratio, and a non-binding 60 % limit for the debt-to-GDP ratio.

Today, after more than a decade of research, a consensus exists that the quantitative targets of the SGP have proved ineffective in restraining the Eurozone member states from running excessive deficits. The SGP became dysfunctional very early, when it became evident that the Council would not impose sanctions and political considerations would prevail. Even from the first years of its implementation, the governments, including those of Germany and France, had started pushing for a reform of the SGP that would allow more 'flexibility'. Quite ironically, Germany, the country that had pushed for tighter fiscal rules in the EMU in the mid-1990s, was the second EMU country to violate the fiscal rules.

Economic theory teaches that a monetary union by itself induces fiscal laxity. According to the Mundell–Fleming model, an expansionary fiscal policy can be effective in increasing output under fixed exchange rates. For many governments, the introduction of the euro was a chance for more active fiscal policies in the context of relaxed fiscal constraints. The ability to borrow with low interest rates, the disappearance of a closed economy crowding out the effects of expansionary fiscal policies, and the removal of the threat of open economy exchange rate crises, created wrong incentives. For some countries, participation in the EMU brought the opportunity of a free ride on the collective creditworthiness of the euro, leading to borrowing at rates that would have been unimaginable with their national currencies. Perverse incentives were also created under the guise of meeting the SGP fiscal deficit target. As we shall see in the following paragraphs, many governments fell into the trap of overlooking the long-term effects while focusing on the short-term benefits.

In the period prior to 1999, when the EMU membership was still not secure, voters in almost all member countries rewarded efforts of fiscal discipline, as the latter would increase the chance of getting into the monetary union. Governments had an incentive to undertake discretionary fiscal contractions even in election years. Once the EMU membership was obtained, the old pattern of political budget cycles re-emerged in many countries. Koen and van den Noord (2005) and von Hagen and Wolff (2004) provided evidence that one-off measures and creative accounting techniques had been used more frequently since the inception of the EMU.

The SGP also produced disincentives in carrying out productive public investments, by treating all expenditures in the same way.[5] In this context, governments often postponed or even cancelled public investment spending, that is, expenditures with the most multiplicative impact on the factors of production and productivity, thus undermining the prospects of future growth rates (Blanchard & Giavazzi, 2004; Coeuré & Pisani-Ferry, 2005; Heller, 2005).

In addition, there have been disposals of public assets with the sole aim of showing a lower budget deficit and lowering public debt. Many of these sales were

[5] The budget deficit criterion did not distinguish between current and capital expenditure.

controversial because, on the one hand, the disposal price of the public assets was often low, and on the other, because most public asset sales were likely to have a negative impact on the net worth of the government concerned (Dafflon & Rossi, 1998; Koen & van den Noord, 2005). Milesi-Ferreti and Moriyama (2004) empirically investigated the dynamics of the EU governments' net worth and they found that many became 'poorer' after the establishment of the SGP. They compared changes in the financial and non-financial assets with changes in financial liabilities and corrected for valuation effects. The research showed a sharp contrast between the periods 1992–1997 and 1997–2002. In the first period, increases in liabilities were matched by changes in assets and the net worth of governments was relatively stable. This was not the case in the second period. The EU governments were worse off in 2002 than they were in 1997. The situation is probably even worse today.

One can easily attribute the above practices to the incentive structure created by the SGP. Many governments ignored sustainability and opted for current consumption and immediate political gains. Short-term considerations overrode long-term perspectives. By emphasising on partial criteria such as deficit and debt, the Pact reinforced the governments' myopia (Coeuré & Pisani-Ferry, 2005) and added to the difficulty of structural reforms, at least for those that implied short-term budgetary cost.

3 The Fundamentals and the Policy Dilemmas

Over the last decade, intra-Eurozone imbalances have grown. Southern Europe has massively lost competitiveness and built-up large current account deficits vis-à-vis its northern counterpart, where industrial activity has gradually concentrated. Public debt has grown to unprecedented levels in almost all Eurozone countries. Private debt—initially very low in the southern Europe compared to the north—has grown impressively, showing that hard times are expected in the process of private deleveraging.

In Fig. 1, the levels of household, non-financial corporate, and government debt are depicted. From the data, it is clear that a large public debt, especially in the southern European countries, coincides with private over-indebtedness. For most countries, the government debt-to-GDP ratio exceeds the 60 % level, which according to Maastricht Treaty represented the upper limit of sustainability. As far as the private debt is concerned, the data from Figs. 2 and 3 show that both non-financial corporate debt and household debt have increased substantially between 1999 and 2009/2010.

At the same time, many Eurozone countries, and especially the southern ones, faced deterioration in competitiveness. Figure 4 shows that there has been a continuous divergence in relative unit labour costs for these economies since 1999. The loss in competitiveness has proceeded along with a significant decline in the share of the manufacturing sector in the total value added. The data in Fig. 5 show that the value added share of manufacturing has fallen by 25 %, highlighting a tendency of de-industrialisation in the euro area 'periphery'.

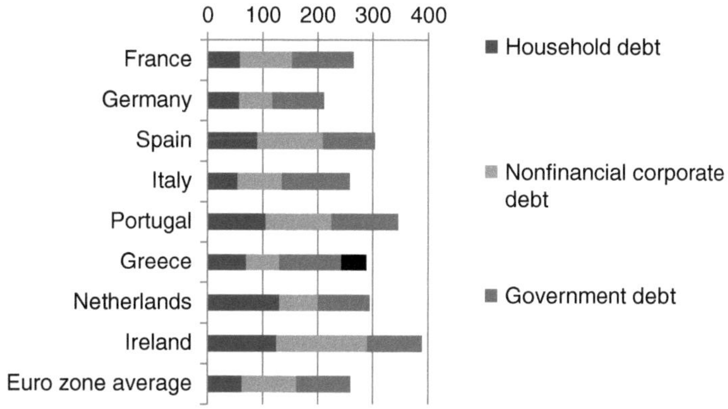

Fig. 1 Household, non-financial corporate, and government debt in Eurozone countries (third quarter 2011). *Source*: Eurostat

Fig. 2 Debt-to-GDP ratio of the non-financial sector (1999–2010). *Source*: Eurostat

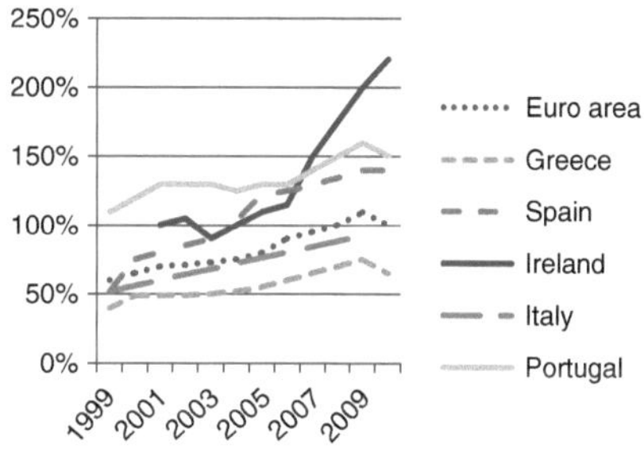

Fig. 3 Household debt as percent of disposable income (1999–2009). *Source*: Eurostat

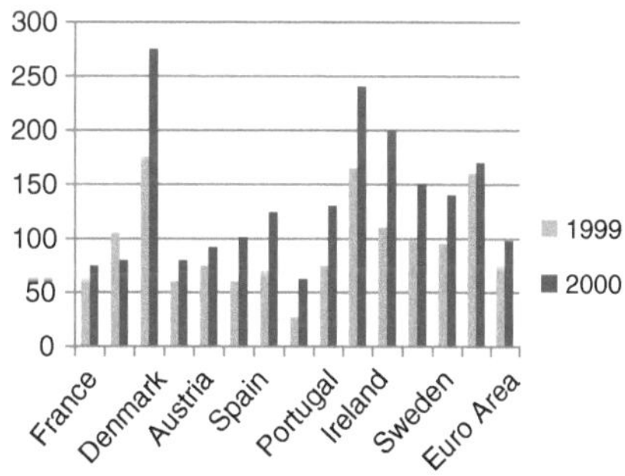

The rise in the debt and the loss of competitiveness in most Eurozone countries can be attributed to, among others, the economic and financial environment that prevailed after the introduction of the euro. The latter coincided with the global credit boom. Furthermore, the convergence of interest rates, because of the

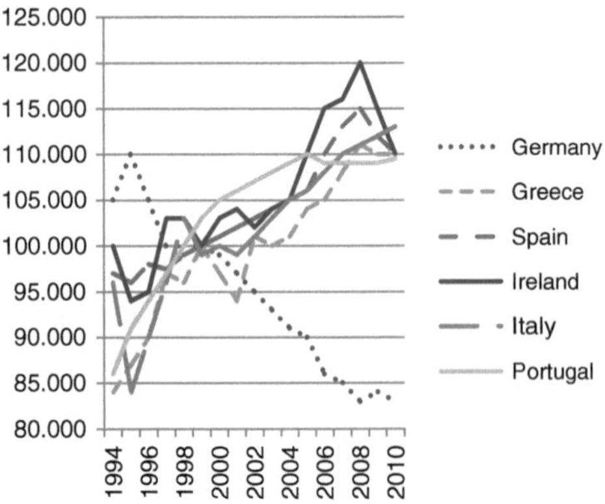

Fig. 4 Competitiveness: ULC indices (1995 = 100). *Source*: Eurostat

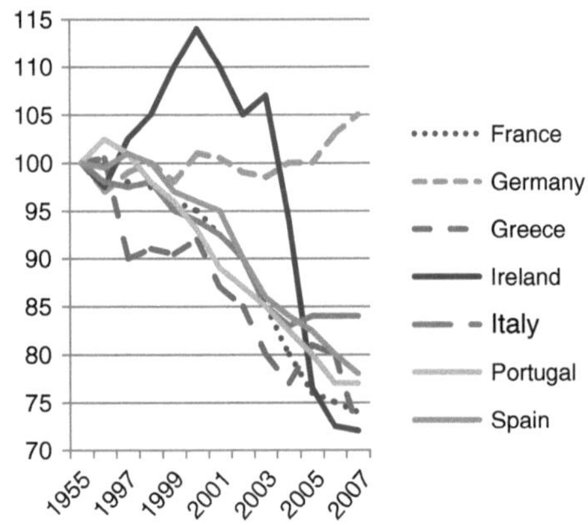

Fig. 5 Manufacturing share of value added (1995 = 100). *Source*: OECD

introduction of the new currency, and the disappearance of the risk spreads, resulted in a surge in cross-border lending to both private and public sectors. This convergence also resulted in a reduction in the pressure for fiscal consolidation, especially in the high-debt countries, and finally in the emergence of huge payments imbalances and divergences in competitiveness. The debt and competitiveness problems have been further aggravated by the financial crisis in 2008, when a 'sudden stop' in lending led to a collapse in private borrowing and spending and to a wave of fiscal crises.

The present situation in the Eurozone creates various policy dilemmas. First, the reduction of the vast debt burden is a difficult task, which, in the case that may occur, takes a lot of time and requires unpopular measures. Second, it is difficult to cope with a debt burden when interest rates on public and private debt are rising, and incomes are falling, due to recession. Increases in taxation, cuts in spending and reduction in consumption, which are usually associated with the implementation of

Table 1 Gross exports as percentage of the GDP

	2007	2011
Ireland	80.5	110
Portugal	32.2	34.6
Italy	29	29.1
Spain	26.9	28.4
Greece	22.7	24

Source: Eurostat

fiscal consolidation programmes, normally result in even lower growth rates and higher unemployment, which, in turn, frustrate the efforts of both the private and public sector to reduce their debt (Eggertsson & Krugman, 2010). Third, the simultaneous effort to restore competitiveness and to repay debt, especially foreign debt, is a difficult task. As Ahearne and Wolff (2012) argue, a decrease in the external debt of countries with sovereign debt problems requires current account surpluses and real exchange rate depreciation, through cuts in prices and wages to boost net exports. However, it usually takes time for improvements in competitiveness to lead to faster export and income growth. Empirical evidence shows that a decline in export prices relative to import prices may, in the short-run, reduce net exports and produce an effect similar to the *J*-curve, which may worsen the trade balance.[6] Under these circumstances, in heavily indebted countries, the required depreciation of the real exchange rate may push up the debt relative to net exports and income in the short term, making debt repayment more difficult.

Another factor that hinders the possibilities of these economies to adjust through growth in exports is the size of the export base in each country. The export sector's contribution to the GDP is quite small in the southern countries (Table 1) indicating that any increase in exports will have less effect on overall economic activity. The unique exception in the case of the over-indebted countries is Ireland, whose exports exceed its GDP.

According to economic theory, the best way to reduce debt-to-GDP ratios is by accelerating growth rates. However, countries have rarely achieved this in the past, and are less likely to do so now. Growth prospects for the developed economies in general and for the Eurozone countries in particular are limited in a world in which growth is gradually shifting to developing countries. Even with substantial structural reforms, the IMF estimates only a 0.5 % additional growth potential for the Eurozone (Allard & Everaert, 2010). Growth will also be hampered by the fact that the European societies are aging,[7] and by the existence of the debt itself, because it reduces the ability and willingness for additional spending and investment.

[6] Backus, Kehoe, and Kydland (1994) note that the negative effects of such deterioration in the terms of trade usually reverse themselves after 2–8 quarters, giving rise to a J-shaped pattern.

[7] By 2020, the workforce in Western Europe is expected to shrink by 2.4 %.

4 The Rebalancing Challenge

The previous section has described the fundamental problems of the Eurozone. The most important problem is, however, that the Eurozone entered this crisis without having an effective way to sustain its banking systems, finance countries in trouble, and secure the adjustments by the creditor and debtor economies. On the contrary, as Martin Wolf (2012) argues, we 'see improvisation instead: the eurozone's aircraft is being redesigned while crashing'.

There is also disagreement on the causes of the crisis and the policies that have to be followed in order to restore symmetry. The dominant German view is that the crisis reflects fiscal indiscipline. Others insist that the core problem is excessive lending, divergent competitiveness, and external imbalances. The European Central Bank (2012) seems to support that southern European countries can become more competitive while Germany can remain unaffected. On the other hand, de Grauwe (2012), drawing on unit labour cost comparisons, found that the adjustment is predominantly achieved by the countries of southern Europe and in contrast, in northern European countries, only a moderate deterioration is observed in relative unit labour costs.

Until recently, the issue of adjustment in the southern European economies was treated as a one-sided process. For most north European countries, budgetary adjustment in southern Europe was regarded as a process that could deliver both fiscal sustainability and a return to competitiveness, without affecting the north heavily. Policy makers seemed to have realised only very recently that 'debt repayments' and the 'restoration of competitiveness' are relative concepts and economic conditions in the north affect the adjustment process in the south. The haircut imposed on private holders of Greek debt in March 2012, the wage agreement in the German metal industry in May 2012 (Wiesmann, 2012), and some recent declarations by the German Finance Minister Wolfgang Schäuble (Bryant, 2012) and by Bundesbank chief economist Jens Ulbrich (Atkins, 2012), are some indications of a new policy direction. However, we are still far from reaching a policy consensus; that is, we are still do not have an accurate perception of the implications of a two-sided approach to rebalancing.

This disagreement, vis-à-vis the causes and the policies of rebalancing, has far reaching repercussions. The adjustment cannot be imposed outright. As Wolf (2012) argues, given the exit option, the adjustment policies have to be negotiated. 'In such a negotiation, creditor nations must understand their role in the crisis. If they wish to preserve their surpluses, they must finance their borrowers. If they wish to be repaid, they must move towards deficit. The two sides—finance and trade—have to be brought into alignment'.

A substantial debt restructuring is a prerequisite for enabling Eurozone countries to return to stable growth. This policy has, however, to be accompanied by a comprehensive plan to restore competitiveness, at least in the periphery countries. An overall rebalancing is vital for the future of the euro. If it does not take place, the existence of the European currency will be ultimately undermined. The principal economic force that now keeps the system together is fear of a break-up. As the

OECD (2011) described, a break-up of the Eurozone in the short run will lead to 'massive wealth destruction, bankruptcies ... and a deep depression in both the existing and remaining euro area countries as well as in the world economy' (6).

However, one cannot rule out the possibility of a breaking up of the euro. Exits from currency unions are not a rare occurrence in history (see Nitsch Volker, 2004) and, in particular, in the second half of the twentieth century. The difference with the Eurozone stems from the size of the currency union and the consequences for the world economy.

Any plan to rebalance will be a very expensive exercise. Without a restructuring of debt and implementation of fundamental reforms, the social and political tensions, and the risk of disorderly exits of countries from the euro zone, increase. The creditor countries have to accept that they will lose money. The existing debt is too large to pay back. Under the present circumstances, creditor countries have the option to choose how they will lose their money, that is, through defaults and economic chaos or though a more organised restructuring and a perception of joint responsibility and solidarity. It goes without saying that such a plan has to include measures for lowering the unit labour cost and introducing more flexibility in labour markets. This effort should also be combined with higher inflation in order to facilitate wage adjustments and to help in real debt reduction. In this context, north European countries have to accept real wage increases and subsequently an increase in total consumption.

5 Concluding Remarks

Any plan for saving the euro must be implemented as soon as possible because a protracted adjustment process is not politically sustainable. Today, the debate has to be focused on learning the lessons of the past and designing realistic plans for the future. However, it is important to understand that, policies and the reforms, similar to those described in the previous section, need a fundamental revision of the EU. Status quo choices will not save the euro and closer fiscal co-ordination, by itself, will not solve the problem. There is need for greater political unification.

In the EU, power still rests with the member states. In the case of the euro, power is concentrated in the hands of Germany, the largest creditor country. This makes the Eurozone function politically like a multi-country arrangement. However, while the Eurozone is not a country, it is much more than a currency union and cannot survive without political legitimacy. Europe's leaders cannot carry out large transfers across countries indefinitely, without a coherent European political framework.

Cutting national sovereignty out of the picture could have many unforeseen consequences and would be a difficult task. However, the interest of the most important member countries to save the euro is huge. The big idea of an integrated Europe, the huge investment of the elite in that project, and the enormous cost that a breaking up of the euro entails are the principal political forces that will eventually save the euro and enhance political unification.

Unless the fundamental structure of the Eurozone changes and a politically unified Europe leads to fiscal transfers and joint liabilities, this crisis will not end. Under the present circumstances, however, the 'most likely outcome, though far from a certainty, is compromise between Germanic ideas and a messy European reality. The support for countries in difficulty will grow. German inflation will rise and its external surpluses fall. Adjustment will occur' (Wolf, 2012).

References

Ahearne, A., & Wolff, G. (2012). *The debt challenge in Europe* (Bruegel Working Paper, 2012/02).

Allard, C., & Everaert, L. (2010, November 22). *Lifting Euro area growth: Priorities for structural reforms and governance* (IMF Staff Position Note, SPN/10/19).

Atkins, R. (2012, May 9). Bundesbank signals softening on inflation. *Financial Times*. http://www.ft.com/intl/cms/s/0/54fa4006-99ed-11e1-accb-00144feabdc0.html#axzz1vaMb6GwR. Accessed 18 May 2012.

Backus, D., Kehoe, P. J., & Kydland, F. E. (1994). Dynamics of the trade balance and the terms of trade: The J-curve? *The American Economic Review, 84*(1), 84–103.

Blanchard, O. J., & Giavazzi, F. (2004). *Improving the SGP through a proper accounting of public investment* (CEPR Discussion Paper, 4220).

Bryant, C. (2012, May 6). Schäuble backs wage rises for Germans. *Financial Times*. http://www.ft.com/intl/cms/s/0/54aa8246-9772-11e1-83f3-00144feabdc0.html#axzz207FrXcr1. Accessed 24 May 2012.

Buiter, W., Corsetti, G., & Roubini, N. (1993). Excessive deficits: Sense and nonsense in the Treaty of Maastricht. *Economic Policy, 16*, 57–101.

Coeuré, B., & Pisani-Ferry, J. (2005). *Fiscal policy in EMU: Towards a sustainability and growth pact*? (Bruegel Working Paper, 2005/01).

Dafflon, B., & Rossi, S. (1998). Public accounting fudges towards EMU: A first empirical survey and some public choice considerations. *Public Choice Journal, 101*(1–2), 59–84.

de Grauwe, P. (2012). *In search of symmetry in the Euro Zone* (Centre for European Policy Studies, Policy Brief, 268).

Easterly, W. (1999). Fiscal illusion: Taking the bite out of budget cuts. *Economic Policy*, 56–76.

Eggertsson, G., & Krugman, P. (2010). *Debt, deleveraging, and the liquidity trap*. Mimeo. http://www.princeton.edu/~pkrugman/debt_deleveraging_ge_pk.pdf. Accessed 12 June 2012.

European Central Bank. (2012, April 4). *Press conference*. Transcrip. http://www.ecb.int/press/pressconf/2012/html/is120404.en.html. Accessed 18 May 2012.

von Hagen, J., & Wolff, G. (2004). *What do deficits tell us about debt? Empirical evidence on creative accounting with fiscal rules in the EU*. Frankfurt: Mimeo.

Heller, P. S. (2005). *Understanding fiscal space* (IMF Policy Discussion Paper, Fiscal Affairs Department, PDP/05/4).

Koen, V., & van den Noord, P. (2005). *Fiscal Gimmickry in Europe: One-off measures and creative accounting* (Economics Department Working Paper, 417). Paris: OECD.

Milesi-Ferreti, G. M., & Moriyama, K. (2004). *Fiscal adjustment in EMU countries: A balance sheet approach* (Working Paper, WP/04/143). Washington: International Monetary Fund.

Nitsch Volker, N. (2004). *Have a break, have a . . . National Currency: When do monetary unions fall apart?* (CESifo Working Paper, 113). Berlin: Germany.

OECD. (2011). *Economic outlook*. Paris: OECD.

Papadimitriou, P. (2008). The competitiveness of European Union in the new international environment. In J. Konstantindis (Ed.), *The European Union in the international context* (pp. 51–67). Thessaloniki: University of Macedonia Press.

Papadimitriou, P. (2011). Fiscal rules in the EU: Time to re-think and start from the basics. In K. Botsiou & A. Klapsis (Eds.), *The Konstantinos Karamanlis Institute for Democracy Yearbook 2011–The global crisis and the case of Greece* (pp. 29–44). Berlin: Springer.

Papadimitriou, P., & Hadziyiannakis, Y. (2012). The importance of fiscal and budgetary discipline, and the crisis in Greece. In A. I. Bitzenis & V. Vlachos (Eds.), *The EU and the Greek budgetary crisis*. Cambridge: Cambridge Scholars.

Wiesmann, G. (2012, May 20). German workers set for 4% pay rise. *Financial Times*. http://www.ft.com/intl/cms/s/0/c9b9090a-a284-11e1-a605-00144feabdc0.html#axzz207FrXcr1. Accessed 22 May 2012.

Wolf, M. (2012, April 17). Why the eurozone may yet survive. *Financial Times*. http://www.ft.com/cms/s/0/782965e6-87b1-11e1-ade2-00144feab49a.html. Accessed 5 June 2012.

Part III

Microeconomic Sectors

Shipping and Sustainable Economic Development: The Case of Greece

Gregory J. Grigoropoulos

1 Introduction

Some 2,500 years ago, waterborne transportation was the dominant mode of trading, at least in the Mediterranean Sea region, which encompassed many highly populated cities along the shoreline. At that time, the most powerful Greek cities established colonies with which they kept close political, economic, cultural, and trading relations. Later, European trade extended into Asia and North Africa based on land routes, travel on which, however, was time consuming, restricted with respect to the bulk of the goods transported, and thereby expensive.

During the Renaissance, new commercial sea routes were established across the world and trade grew enormously. During the nineteenth century, the replacement of wind as the main propulsion source by steam, and later by the internal combustion engine, allowed for the production of faster and more reliable merchant ships. In addition, the introduction of steel as the principal construction material instead of wood enabled the building of large ships capable of transporting huge quantities of cargos.

Nowadays, waterborne transportation remains the prime mode of international trading. Thus, merchant ships transport 90 % of the goods as well as a significant percentage of global passengers. Even in Europe, 30 % of intra-European trade is carried out by sea.

Adam Smith propounded the economic significance of the shipping sector, claiming that it offers a cheap mode of transportation, which in turn helps access larger markets. Indeed, the significance of shipping has not deteriorated despite the relatively long trip times of sailing compared with other modes because the

G.J. Grigoropoulos (✉)
Division of Ship and Marine Hydrodynamics, Department of Naval Architecture and Marine Engineering, National Technical University of Athens, 9 Heroon Polytechneiou, Zografou 15780, Greece
e-mail: gregory@central.ntua.gr

P. Sklias and N. Tzifakis (eds.), *Greece's Horizons*, The Konstantinos Karamanlis Institute for Democracy Series on European and International Affairs,
DOI 10.1007/978-3-642-34534-0_10,

maritime community has enough capacity to feed the markets in a smooth and sufficient way. The huge quantities of goods and large numbers of passengers carried by contemporary ships constitute the other major advantage of sea transport over its land-based and airborne counterparts.

Against the backdrop of the relative strength of shipping and the dominant role that Greek ship owners play in maritime commerce, this chapter thus analyses a pathway of economic development, namely the correlation and interaction between shipping and sustainable economic development, focusing mainly on the Greek case.

The following sections present the advantages of shipping and the opportunities this sector offers for increasing employment and wealth generation. The effect of the relevant EU policies is then shortly discussed. However, as it is demonstrated, the interaction between international shipping companies and national economic activities is not straightforward, and thus a set of attractive measures should be established and maintained in order to offer a convenient and stable business environment to potential investors. The conclusions of this chapter are summed up in the last section.

2 Waterborne Transportation

Further to the strength of shipping as a major commercial activity and its potential for future growth described in the introduction, the environmental effects of sea routes compared with rival transportation modes such as land and air are milder. Indeed, considering the intense interest in environmental pollution, merchant and passenger ships are less polluting than other modes of transportation, being responsible for only 3 % of air pollution.

Furthermore, the operation of ships has been subject to strong antipollution legislation since the establishment of the MARPOL International Convention in 1978.

Nevertheless, the International Maritime Organization (IMO) remains unhappy with the present status of marine pollution by the sea trade, and it recently imposed stronger regulations to reduce further the emissions of marine engines in order to drive the competitiveness of sea transport. This reduction in emissions is directly connected to an analogous decrease in fuel consumption, which will lead to more economically efficient operation of ships.[1] Further, sea routes are located far away from populous regions, which mainly suffer from environmental pollution and are more sensitive to such problems.

The combination of waterborne with airborne and land-based transportation has begun to create new opportunities for efficient transportation; however, this necessitates improvements in airport, road, and rail infrastructure, leading to further development in the country. In light of the foregoing, the perspectives and the

[1] According to the Group of Experts on the Scientific Aspects of Marine Pollution, only 12 % of sea pollution is attributed to the transportation of crude oil, whereas the remainder occurs because of land consumption, the atmosphere, leakages, waste, and oil drilling.

future of shipping seem to be promising, although they still depend heavily on the vicissitudes of international trade, the evolution of political affairs, and the development of domestic economies in conjunction with the available tonnage capacity. The latter will continue to rise over the next 2–3 years, thereby suppressing the fares of standard ship types.

3 EU Influence on the Greek Shipping Community

The Greek shipping community is the largest in the EU, with 3,189 merchant ships (over 1,000 Gross Registered Tons, GRT), which represents 202 million DWT and equates to 14.3 % of the world's transport capacity (Association of Greek Shipowners, 2011). Only 1,200 of them are under the Greek Flag, along with another 900 ships in the 100–1,000 GRT capacity range. In addition, 41.5 % of EU ships are owned by Greeks with Greek Flag being first in EU and fifth worldwide, while Greek ship owners are very active in new buildings with 10 % of the overall orders. Further, the average age of the Greek-owned fleet is 11 years, which is lower than that of the world fleet (13 years) and much lower than it was 10 years ago (17 years). Greek ship owners expect the successful termination of Doha round negotiations to establish a new regulatory arrangement and liberate multilateral trade among World Trade Organization countries. The members of G20 are already actively working towards this outcome, which will open the charter market.

The Greek-owned commercial fleet shows particular characteristics that differentiate it from the fleets of other traditional maritime nations such as Great Britain, Japan and the Netherlands. These characteristics include its specialisation and spatial activities and financial sources. In particular, Greek ships specialise in the bulk transportation of dry and liquid cargos (e.g. crude oil and its by-products, such as coal, grain, and minerals) as well as of traditional general cargos. These ships account for approximately 95 % of the Greek-owned fleet, while the remaining 5 % includes cruisers and commercial and coastal ships (Samiotis, Vlachos, & Tselentis, 2008).

As worldwide leaders in maritime transportation, Greek-owned shipping companies operate on a global scale and serve the transportation needs of countries worldwide. In addition, a number of activities associated with Greek-owned shipping take place abroad (e.g. shipbuilding credits, financing, chartering, marine insurance, shipbuilding, repairs, maintenance, conversions, ship scrapping). Furthermore, even nowadays, Greek-owned shipping is managed within the administrative frameworks of other countries such as the UK, contributing to the development of these important business centres.

It is thus clear that Greek shipping plays a leading role in global development and forms the basis of world trade, such as the charters' international market and the international stock market. It has survived and flourished thanks to the flexibility, knowledge, and adaptability of Greek ship operators and ship owners as regards the international variables that affect the industry and influence business decisions (e.g. flags, specialisation, and markets).

The Greek maritime industry has been influenced both positively and negatively by developments in the EU since Greece became a full member in the early 1980s. Soon after Greece's accession, the EU formulated a European shipping policy, and Greece has played a decisive role in this framework as well as in shipping centres and forums where policy measures are discussed. Furthermore, in matters of commercial shipping, the country often joins forces with other nations in order to support an EU shipping industry based on fair and free competition, without governmental interventions, that will ensure safety and protect the marine environment.

Unfortunately, these endeavours have often been hindered by incidents that threaten the competitiveness of the EU shipping sector, even though they were supported by Greece (Giziakis, Karlis, & Reizis, 2005). The stalemate reached during the negotiations to establish a European registry called EUROS is a case in point. All major maritime countries in the EU support national registries with international activities in order to maintain their competitiveness in the maritime sector. However, these practices have created substantial problems within the EU legal framework. Indeed, Greece has not moved along a similar legal and procedural line despite the losses and lack of competitiveness of its national registry.

Although the EU has not yet adopted a discernible and strong maritime policy, many positive steps have been taken in this direction, especially concerning the impact of shipping on the marine environment and the safety of navigation. Greece, as a member state of the relevant international institutions, has always supported attempts to protect the marine environment (IMO, United Nations Environmental Programme UNEP, etc.) and has developed a modern national institutional framework of its own. Greek shipping has even contributed to international attempts to formulate and adopt relevant policy measures and has always been prompt at harmonising and applying EU legislation within its national boundaries.

Another important agenda item for Greece and the EU over recent years has been the issue of lifting the protection of sea transportation within the territorial waters of member states, known as cabotage. Again, Greece conformed to the pertinent EU legislation, although a series of problems are still to be resolved. Coastal and short sea shipping is vital for Greece, as explained in the next Section.

In general, the establishment of a common maritime policy that combines an integrated cross-sector analysis with effective co-ordination is difficult within an organisation comprising 27 countries, some of which have limited or even no maritime interests, whereas others have vital interests in the framework, range, and consequences of EU policies. Moreover, recent trends in international shipping, especially within EU and OECD countries (OPTIMAR, 2010), have focused on the development of a free and competitive maritime market, in which transport services strive for quality at the lowest possible price.

At the same time, efforts to both ensure vessel and navigational safety and protect the marine environment remain high priorities (MARE-FORUM, 2005). Security has also become a major point of interest, especially following the 9/11 terrorist attacks in New York, thus resulting in a raft of new regulations. These include the International Ship and Port Facility Security (ISPFS) Code, the Code of

Practice on Security in Ports issued jointly by the IMO and the International Labour Organisation (ILO) in 2004, the ILO's Seafarers Identity Documents Convention, and the IMO's Convention for the Suppression of Unlawful Acts against the Safety of Maritime Navigation. These novel approaches to security and safety issues have led to an integrated system of multilateral governance for the maritime industry. However, the above complex of legislation has also imposed additional costs on all parties, including individual countries, shipping firms, ship and port employees, and the international community. Moreover, it does not seem to justify the significantly increased costs and workloads inflicted on the parties involved when the overall status of world security and the industry are taken into account. In general, Greece works positively and constructively towards attaining a high quality level in worldwide shipping.

It is important to note that in 1982 Greek ship owners established a non-governmental organisation in order to promote shipping quality and protect the marine environment. This organisation, known as the Hellenic Marine Environment Protection Association (HELMEPA), has been active both within Greece and in international institutions such as the IMO. In addition, Greece adopted the EU Directive 2008/56/EC of the European Parliament and Council for the protection and management of the sea environment in 2011. Further, initiatives on the port side have led to increased environmental protection and management options. For example, in collaboration with ESPO and the ECOPORTS Foundation, the major ports of Piraeus and Thessaloniki have been certified by the PERS accreditation system for their environmental management systems.

It must be stressed, however, that attaining high quality in the shipping industry is an extremely difficult and painstaking process since it involves international co-operation and it is affected by many factors. Major maritime nations, in particular, face difficulties due to globalisation, while intense and often fierce competition in freight trends competes with quality shipping services. The numerous legal chances open to shipping firms, which allow them to expand their activities into different regions of the world, leads to anonymity and increased difficulties when investigating pollution incidents or the breaching of contractual duties. Further, the ease with which a shipping firm can change registries (e.g. by selecting those that allow increased profits while minimising running and maintenance costs) seems to be one of the most serious problems facing the industry today.

As pointed out earlier, as many other OECD countries, Greece also has many open registries. In addition, many EU countries resort to international as well as parallel registries in order to minimise the losses incurred by their national registries. This situation not only affects the stability and improvement of the maritime sector but also poses a serious threat to maritime safety and the marine environment.

Quality shipping in the modern maritime industry seems to be a difficult objective achievable only through international co-operation between OECD and EU countries. Therefore, it seems reasonable to suggest that the only way forward is to strive for quality shipping throughout the world. This would mean, avoiding the split that exists in the maritime sector between first class shipping (i.e. serving

OECD and EU countries) and second class, comprising lower-standard ships under flags of convenience (mainly owned by firms originating from EU and OECD states), that serve the rest of the world.

4 Interaction of the Shipping Community and National Economy

The leading position of Greek-owned commercial fleets plays an important role in the development of a country that has a small population and territory such as Greece. The positive impact of the Greek shipping industry on the Greek economy and state development is based mainly on the foreign currency entering the country, which is attributed to the fact that the transport sector has enjoyed autonomous development based on its globalised activities.

The data presented herein demonstrate the power of the Greek-owned maritime industry, which in 2010 was ranked second among the foreign currency sources of Greece with €15.5 billion, after exports (€17 billion) and above tourism, which was ranked third (€9.6 billion). According to these statistics provided by the Bank of Greece (Economou, Sambethai, & Symigiannis, 2010), currency from shipping corresponds to 6.7 % of GNP and covers 35.3 % of the deficit in the national balance of payments. Indeed, the overall contribution of shipping in foreign currency income between 2000 and 2010 was €140 billion, which was 3.5 times the size of the EU Cohesion Policy Funds earmarked for the country during the (longer) 2000–2013 period (€46 billion). This influx of currency from shipping, which comprises the amounts transferred by ship owners and mariners, has shown a high degree of consistency over time, thus contributing greatly to improving the national balance of payments, which has been in deficit since the end of World War II.

Unfortunately, half of this currency is re-exported to pay for foreign services that are unavailable in Greece because of the lack of domestic infrastructure (e.g. registries, marine justice, marine equipment). It is interesting to note, however, that Greek ship operators and owners have registered their ships in approximately 40 national registries over recent years. The establishment of Greek providers of these services would thus contribute to sustainable national economic development and rising employment. That said, the Greek state is currently unaffected by the economic, social, and environmental costs associated with these activities.

In addition to the important contribution of imported foreign currency to the national balance of payments, it also improves the national economy and local communities (i.e. the recipients of this foreign currency), creates sea and land employment, and develops activities associated with the industry as well as associated sectors.

Moreover, another sector of shipping that affects the national economy is coastal and short sea shipping. Maritime companies that operate passenger ships and ferries depend on national legislation, and they have long been protected by cabotage, which prevents foreign-owned companies from providing sea transportation within the territorial waters of Greece. This has been an extremely important issue for

Greece, where coastal shipping has developed to the point that it now serves over 3,500 Greek islands, representing approximately 14 % of the total population.

Greece also possesses one of the longest shorelines in the world, amounting to over 15,000 km, thus implying that Greek coastal shipping functions as a critical communication and trade link between the mainland and insular areas. Furthermore, it provides a basic tool for the development and implementation of legal, social, and regional strategies and state policies in this particular island environment. By contrast, however, the Greek government has to fund the provision of transport services to a number of small islands with few inhabitants, especially during winter, because of the lack of business interest in operating private services.

The recent global financial crisis has affected both domestic short sea shipping and the sea connection with Europe via Italy. Traffic has reduced, fuel prices have increased, banks have reduced their funding for maritime companies, and the government's financial support to unprofitable lines has been restricted (Hellenic Chamber of Shipping, 2011). Ship owners have thus requested the state urgently re-examine the operational costs of costal lines, including the depreciation of the capital investment and crew costs that exceed those required by the SOLAS international convention. Consequently, a new ticketing policy is required, island tourism should be supported, and some small islands should be subsumed under Article 167 of the European Constitution to be eligible for governmental funds.

Marine education is a vital interaction between shipping and the national economy. By modernising marine academies, more young people are expected to strive for a maritime career. Importantly, the more Greeks are among crewmembers, the more foreign currency reaches the country. However, marine academies are undergoing further significant improvements in terms of teaching staff (most are currently working on a temporary basis under annual contracts) and equipment. Their upgrading will stimulate higher-level candidates to become marine officers, while lifelong marine and onboard training will provide supplementary knowledge to cope with the up-to-date equipment on board modern merchant ships as well as to manage a diversity of situations using modern fault tree techniques. The two major marine academies in Athens and Thessaloniki could even become famous education institutions of a European and Balkan scope, accepting and educating prospective marine officers from the Balkans and the rest of Europe. Lectures in English should be offered throughout their curricula.

Over recent decades, the European shipbuilding industry has been restricted to high-technology constructions and naval ships because of the excessive labour costs in Europe compared with those in Asia. Even in Eastern European countries, where labour costs are comparable with those of Asian countries, low productivity limits drastically their competitiveness. Large Greek shipyards have thus suffered from low productivity because of a lack of investment and problems with syndicates. After 30 years of operating with deficits, they are now facing the strong possibility of going bankrupt.

By contrast, a number of small and medium-sized companies are active in the shipbuilding and ship-repairing zone located near Piraeus. These companies have always delivered high-quality outcomes at competitive costs and within reasonable delivery times. However, the infrastructural improvements in the area because of the co-operation of the Piraeus Port Authority could improve their ranges of activities, especially among Greek clients, thereby saving currency for the national economy. The growth of port activities and establishment of hubs for container transportation as well as to serve intermodal transportation is a major subject that remains for future research.

5 Effective Management Scheme

In order to enhance the contribution of the shipping industry to the Greek national economy and to support sustainable development, the re-establishment of the Ministry for Shipping seems to be of prime importance. The incorporation of an efficient and effective management and operational scheme within this Ministry would lead to simplified procedures. The organisation chart should be based on contemporary requirements, with Greek coastguard staff supported by suitable civilian employees that have well-defined qualifications and work in specific high-responsibility posts.

The Ministry should also comprise a department for research and technology in order to improve the economic and technical management of ships and fleets and to provide technological support to the maritime industry. Furthermore, another division should prepare, document, and support Greek policy proposals and submissions to European and international organisations as well as assess the proposals put forward by other countries. The opinions of ship owners and mariners should also be taken into account.

In order to attract Greek ship owners to invest into the country, they should be offered incentives, while common advisory councils could be formed to establish a smooth, reliable, and robust setting. The relevant legislation requires urgent and drastic—and permanent—reform, while the opinions of investors should be sought. An essential feature of this initiative is the establishment of mutual confidence between the government and the shipping community.

Under such circumstances, an investment fund could be formed by a dedicated group of ship owners for the privatisation of public-owned companies and the sale of public real estate. Although the procedures for these bids should conform to EU legislation on free markets, Greek candidates that offer foreign currency may be supported, for example, by the right of first refusal. Moreover, Greek ship owners should be encouraged to make social donations and grants to the country by initiating acts of recognition based around famous Greek ship owners (e.g. Onassis and Niarchos). An annual prize could even be awarded by the Greek president to the ship owner who contributed most to national development over the past year. Finally, the re-establishment of marine justice in order to provide a quick response to requests, improve the system of average adjusters, and enhance the support from the Council of Marine Incidents would further assist the maritime community. These initiatives would allow claims and disputes to be resolved efficiently and quickly at a national level.

Conclusions

This chapter has demonstrated the potential of the shipping industry to contribute to sustainable economic development in Greece. To summarise the arguments of this chapter, Greek-owned shipping companies are capable of contributing to sustainable development in the following two ways:

First, by improving the infrastructure of ship management and operations, a greater proportion of the foreign currency imported into Greece by the shipping community would be spent in the country instead of being re-exported and spent on services abroad. The maritime community has moved their headquarters and technical departments to Piraeus from London and other foreign cities, and now more than 1,000 maritime companies are located around Piraeus and Athens, all of which are potential clients to a long list of local service providers. Furthermore, the location of Piraeus and the country in general is convenient, especially for fleets that carry out repairs and maintenance in Europe. Marine education and training is also essential for staffing merchant ships with well-educated and properly trained Greek crews, who will spend their incomes in the country.

Second, attracting Greek investors to invest in domestic enterprises or contribute to productive investments would also help sustainable economic development in Greece. Policy in this arena should be long-term, stable, and reliable and formulated in close co-operation with the maritime community in order to establish a high level of mutual confidence. The relevant legislation should also be efficient and stable, while reforms should be subject to prior negotiations with the maritime community.

References

Association of Greek Shipowners. (2011). *Greek shipping and economy* (Annual Report 2010). Piraeus: Association of Greek Shipowners.

Economou, G., Sambethai, I., & Symigiannis, G. (2010). *Bank of Greece annual report*. Athens: National Balance of Payments and Policy Proposals.

Giziakis, K., Karlis, A., & Reizis, A. (2005). *Investigation and monitoring of the effect of shipping on the Greek economy*. Piraeus: University of Piraeus.

Hellenic Chamber of Shipping. (2011). *Short-sea shipping—Cost and public benefit*. Piraeus: Hellenic Chamber of Shipping.

MARE-FORUM. (2005, November 17). A new European maritime policy, session 2. Maritime Industry Perspective.

OPTIMAR. (2010). *Benchmarking strategic options for European shipping and for the European maritime transport system in the horizon 2008–2018*. HIS Fairplay, 2010 Update.

Samiotis, G., Vlachos, G. P., & Tselentis, B. S. (2008). *The leading role of the Hellenic merchant shipping at the global and the European level*. Greece: University of Piraeus.

The Greek Tourism Industry and the Challenge of the Economic Crisis

George Galanos

1 Introduction

According to the international literature on the subject, tourism has two main effects on the national and global economy: (a) it strengthens the host country's service sector; and (b) it significantly increases the employment in several complementary sectors (Brohman, 1996; Frechtling, 1994; Gibson, 1993). At the same time, numerous studies have focused on the collateral benefits of tourism on the environmental and social level (Balaguer & Cantavella-Jorda, 2002; Dwyer, Forsyth, & Spurr, 2007a, 2007b).

Nowadays, tourism is one of the key sectors of global economic activity with rapid and continuous growth. From 1950 to 2011, the number of international tourist arrivals grew by 6.5 % per year, with the total number of travellers growing from 25 to 925 million. In the same period, the growth in income due to these arrivals was particularly high, reaching 11.2 %. At the same time, these arrivals triggered global economic expansion, rising to 1,030 billion dollars in 2011 (WTO, 2012).

Tourism constitutes one of the most important sectors of the global economy, according to the latest estimates from the World Tourism Organization. According to these estimates, the total contribution of tourism to the global GDP in 2011 was 5 % and its contribution to employment was between 6 % and 7 % (WTO, 2011). These figures strikingly denote the economic and social dynamics of tourism in the new global economic environment (Dwyer, Forsyth, & Dwyer, 2010).

This study initially aims to illustrate the importance of the tourism sector for Greece, and then to record the characteristics of the Greek tourism industry amidst the economic crisis. However, the most important aim of the study is to highlight

G. Galanos (✉)
Department of International Economic Relations and Development,
Democritus University of Thrace, Komotini 69100, Greece
e-mail: galgeorg@webmail.unipi.gr

P. Sklias and N. Tzifakis (eds.), *Greece's Horizons*, The Konstantinos Karamanlis Institute for Democracy Series on European and International Affairs,
DOI 10.1007/978-3-642-34534-0_11,

the ability of the tourism sector to become the bulwark nucleus of a new developmental policy aimed at overcoming the crisis.

2 The Contribution of Tourism Towards the Development of the National Economy and the Growth of Employment

The national economy, as a quantitative concept, stands for the total value of all goods and services produced by the economy of a country in a particular period, and is defined as the Gross Domestic Product (GDP). Its key components are the goods and services produced for consumption and those produced for capital formation or investment.

In order to evaluate the contribution of tourism to the national economy, we can evaluate the impact on the GDP, Following that, tourism industry contributes to every aspect of the GDP. Both the direct and indirect income from tourism flows to the various national and local level companies in the destination country, strengthening the country's infrastructure and investment potential. Tourism, therefore, constitutes an economic activity that contributes directly to national production, because the expenses of tourists generate income for all stakeholders in the tourism circuit. The factors of production are used fruitfully and focused, resulting in the maximisation of utility and efficiency.

Additionally, tourism related receipts are transformed into payments for items (rent, salaries, and profits), increasing the rate of income, profits, and direct and indirect taxes (Sinclair, 1998). The inflow of foreign currency is equivalent to increase in exports and foreign exchange earnings, and leads to improving the balance of payments of the destination country. At the same time, as investments in local tourist destinations are becoming more intensive and co-ordinated, the impact on the national economy and the balance of payments is becoming more tangible, reinforcing economy's competitiveness.

Furthermore, according to the World Travel and Tourism Council (WTTC), tourism's contribution to national economies is described by two basic concepts, the 'tourism industry', and the 'tourism economy'. The first concept is directly associated with tourism activities—such as all kinds of tourist accommodation, catering and entertainment activities, transport, car rental companies, and tourist agency services. The second concept includes capital expenditures through which the public or private sector aid tourism infrastructure and public spending, in order to enhance the national tourism product, for example, museums, advertising campaigns, etc. (Alpha Bank, 2009).

At the same time, it is important to highlight the contribution of tourism to employment. A highly important means of understanding the generation of employment from tourism is investigating the measurement methods. According to the international literature on the subject (Lundberg, Stavenga, & Krishnamoorthy, 1995), the measurement of employment generated by tourism, involves identifying both direct and indirect employment. Direct employment consists of jobs directly catering to tourists, such as that of hotel employees. Indirect employment refers to jobs created in order to provide the businesses directly catering to tourists, for

Table 1 The GDP contribution and employment

	1990	2000	2009	2010	2011
GDP	15.20 %	15.90 %	15.20 %	15.40 %	16.50 %
Direct and indirect employment (% of the total employment)	19.50 %	19.80 %	18.50 %	17.10 %	18.40 %
Direct and Indirect employment ('000)	731.8	781	774.2	754.4	758.3

Source: SETE, WTTC

Table 2 Total incomes (in billion euros) from tourism and tourism's contribution towards reducing the trade deficit

	2000	2008	2009	2010	2011
Incomes	10.1	11.6	10.4	9.6	10.5
Contribution towards reducing the trade deficit	45.90 %	42.30 %	33.70 %	31.10 %	38.60 %

Source: SETE, WTTC

example, workers producing fruits served in the hotels serving tourists. Thus, the very nature of tourism employment makes it difficult to fully detect and measure it, because a complicated, interacting, and long chain of professions is involved, covering a large portion of a country's economic and production activity.

3 The Importance of Tourism for Greece

Tourism for Greece is considered as one of the main pillars of its economy and perhaps the most rapidly developing one. The contribution to the GDP since 1990 exceeds 15.2 %, while the employment in tourism for the same period as a share of total employment has constantly been above 18 %, with more than 750,000 workers employed directly or indirectly. It is noteworthy that, in 2011, amid the economic crisis, tourism has played the role of an extremely effective support for the country; it has shown significant increase both in the share of the GDP and of the total employment (Table 1).

At the same time, the country's total revenues from international tourism have reached a highly respectable figure of 10.5 billion Euros in 2011, while for the entire first decade of this century (2001–2010) it was more than 10 billion Euros, except for the year 2010 (Table 2). The contribution of foreign tourism in making up the trade deficit was as high as 38.6 % for 2011, indicating that it increased by 7.5 % points as compared to 2010.

Another indicative element in the contribution of the tourism industry to the development of national economy is the gross value added to the hotel and restaurants sector in Greece in 2011, which amounted to 8,821.9 million euros and represented the 7.57 % of the total national gross value added. Compared with the past, the size of this share in the total gross value added is constantly growing. It is also important to mention the indirect impact of the tourism industry in other business sectors that are directly connected with tourist activity. These sectors include products consumed by tourists, various supplies to tourism businesses—particularly hotels—transportations of goods and persons, etc. (Horváth & Frechtling, 1999; Paulopoulos & Kouzelis, 1998).

The World Tourism Organization has described this whole process as a 'tourism multiplier', in which the indirect tourism related product is equal to the direct product that the whole tourism industry generates. In fact, there are communicating vessels at the local and national levels, causing diffusion of the revenues originating in tourism to a wide range of activities in the national economy as a whole.

4 The Characteristics of Greek Tourism

The first signs of significant development of tourism activities in our country appeared in the early 1950s. A key feature of the demand for tourism at that time was the standard 'wanderlust' (SETE, 2010a), which refers to travels to new places and the yearning to explore new cultures (Gray, 1970; Mcintosh & Goeldner, 1990). However, from the middle of the 1960s, Greek tourism began adopting the model described as 'the sun lust' (SETE, 2010a), focusing on travel for resting and enjoying the sea and sun (Gray, 1970). From the early 1980s, this tourism product acquired the character of a more specific model—referred to as the '3S' (sea, sex, and sun—SETE, 2010b) or the '4S' (sun, sand, sea, sex) (Butler, 1980). This model has dominated Greek tourism for the last 30 years and has come to determine the character of Greek tourism. This tourism development model based itself on the entire country's comparative advantage as regards sun, sea, and people (Tsartas, 2003). This one-dimensional growth has gradually led to a delicate balance between the environment, economy, and society, a balance that brought extensive changes to the dynamics and structure of this system through multiple direct effects. More explicitly, almost all Greek tourist destinations are characterised by economic monoculture, abandonment or exploitation of the actually deficient natural resources, uncontrolled urban growth, and unforeseen changes in land use, resulting in continuous shrinking of available agricultural land and the spatial-concentration of tourism activity in coastal areas and islands.

One gets an indicative illustration of this overconcentration from resorting to a simple indicator regarding the intensity of traffic and distribution in space (Baum, 1998; Butler, 2004). This shows us that both the population and the concentration of tourists vary greatly across regions, showing the overconcentration in coastal areas, as mentioned above.

From Table 3 and Maps 1, 2, 3, and 4 help us to arrive at the following fundamental conclusions: the Aegean Islands, Crete, the Chalkidiki Peninsula, and the Ionian Islands receive the highest number of tourists. In these regions, the number of overnight halts in comparison to the permanent local population amounts to more than ten thousand overnight halts per resident. The coastal parts of Peloponnese, Central Greece, Macedonia (excepting the Chalkidiki peninsula), and the Epirus experience a more moderate tourist assemblage. The lowest demand,

Table 3 Tourist nights and populations in the counties of Greece

County	Nights	Population 2001	Tourist nights per 1,000 residents
Dodekanisos	15,265,564	190,564	80.11
Zakynthos	2,073,703	38,680	53.61
Corfu	3,605,237	113,479	31.77
Rethymno	2,136,719	81,781	26.13
Lasithi	1,911,060	75,903	25.18
Samos	987,179	43,574	22.66
Heraklion	5,859,801	294,312	19.91
Chalkidiki	2,002,862	107,432	18.64
Chania	2,699,633	149,163	18.10
Kefallinias	626,418	39,579	15.83
Cycle	1,476,704	111,181	13.28
Lefkadas	251,735	22,536	11.17
Lesvos	783,833	108,294	7.24
Argolidas	707,530	105,295	6.72
Kavala	882,675	144,920	6.09
Fokidas	286,779	48,526	5.91
Pierias	757,857	128,950	5.88
Magnisia	1,170,225	207,336	5.64
Preveza	316,136	59,334	5.33
Corinth	708,846	153,941	4.60
Chios	195,783	52,290	3.74
Evritania	112,327	32,026	3.51
Laconia	332,856	99,671	3.34
Evia	686,965	217,278	3.16
Messinia	545,607	172,825	3.16
Ioannina	494,343	170,244	2.90
Evros	426,917	149,023	2.86
Kastoria	145,642	53,054	2.75
Ilea	486,491	192,340	2.53
Achaia	751,010	323,794	2.32
Thesprotia	91,512	45,508	2.01
Trikala	276,297	139,548	1.98
Attica	7,134,006	3,756,607	1.90
Florina	91,707	54,751	1.67
Thessaloniki	1,710,097	1,046,851	1.63
Arkadia	151,579	101,223	1.50
Rodopi	162,735	111,038	1.47
Fthiotida	257,511	178,896	1.44
Aitoloakarnania	294,217	222,984	1.32
Ksanthi	118,533	101,510	1.17
Karditsa	128,118	129,536	0.99
Larisa	243,009	277,973	0.87

(continued)

Table 3 (continued)

County	Nights	Population 2001	Tourist nights per 1,000 residents
Arta	65,129	77,334	0.84
Grevena	31,707	38,481	0.82
Kozani	127,580	156,464	0.82
Serres	149,027	200,561	0.74
Imathia	84,130	144,172	0.58
Viotia	71,679	131,129	0.55
Drama	55,094	103,763	0.53
Pella	68,703	144,340	0.48
Kilkis	24,432	89,611	0.27

Source: EOT/SETE

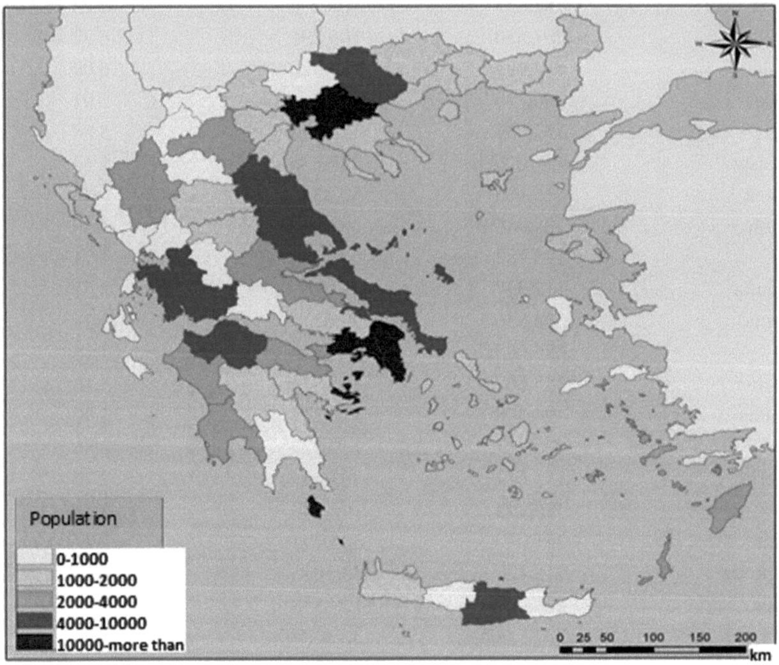

Map 1 Population in the counties of Greece. *Source*: Galanos (2009)

and consequently the lowest attraction and competitiveness, characterise the non-coastal regional departments of Macedonia, Central Greece, and Thessaly, and certain coastal regional departments with less provision for maritime tourism. Consequently, we can conclude that more than 80 % of the country's tourism

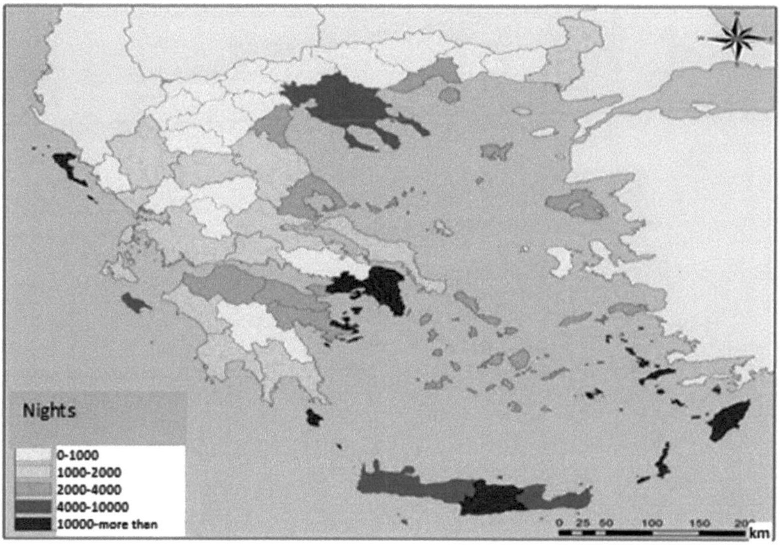

Map 2 Overnight halts in the counties of Greece. *Source*: Galanos (2009)

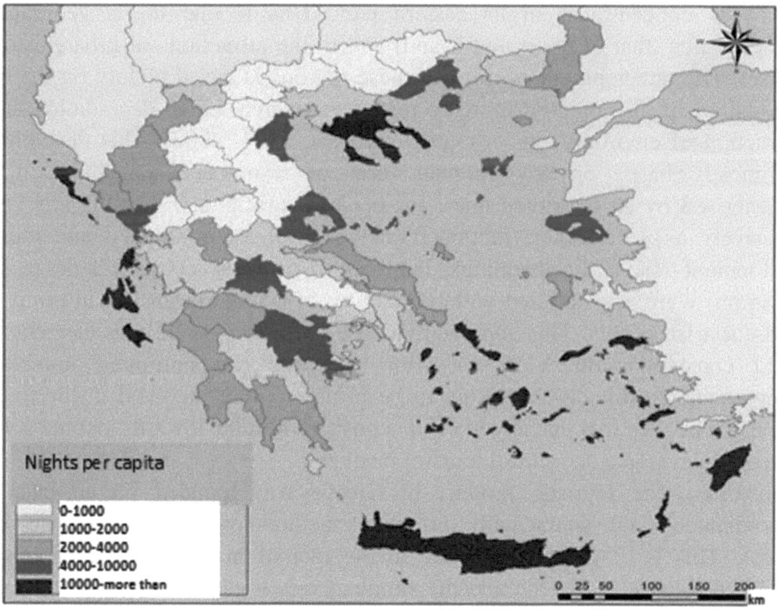

Map 3 Overnights per 1,000 residents in the counties of Greece. *Source*: Galanos (2009)

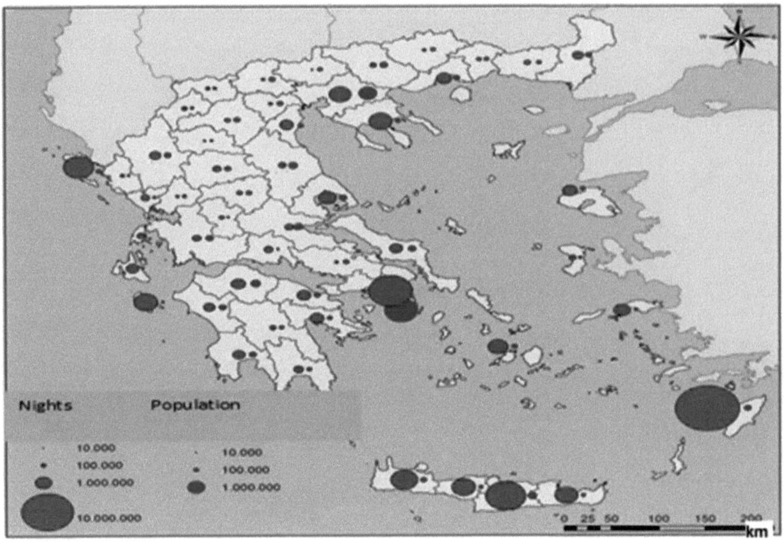

Map 4 Comparative demonstration of the population and overnight halts in the counties of Greece. *Source*: Galanos (2009)

activity is concentrated in its eastern part. This is due to its geographical characteristics (that of coast and island) and to the attractions of urban/historical tourism. The development of most of these regions is based mainly on the over-exploitation of all potential touristic resources, which led to degradation and/or destruction of environmental resources (Kousis, 1994; 2000). This development was mostly based on an irrational form of resource management, mainly characterised by an unbridled quest for personal profits and viewing any visitor exclusively as a customer. In this framework, all environmental and touristic development resources (dwellings, landscapes, beaches, cultural heritage sites, and so on) were appropriated within a culture of economic growth inspired by a blind quest for profits. This approach views all resources merely as elements that would constantly attract incomes for everyone (an unlimited number of entrepreneurs in this case) seeking to be professionally involved in the tourism business. The idea was that anyone with a positive attitude towards income generation could develop a successful tourism business.

Therefore, the touristic product in Greece was founded on an irrational, uncoordinated, and sporadically effective methodology, based on the latest updates. This is of great importance to the fact of heedless waste of valuable touristic resources in Greece and the simultaneous environmental destruction due to development of urban sprawls (Komilis, 1987). The main characteristic of this development methodology is the absence of a centrally designed and applied touristic plan and strategy, resulting in fragmented interventions with limited effectiveness. These occurred from time to time, mainly after the integration of

Greece in the European Union. The absence of a national and central managerial planning in combination with limited control, and resorting to the simplistic 'sun and the sea model', have resulted in touristic oversaturation, which is nowadays noticed in almost every touristic region in the country.

Greece as a tourism destination has arrived at the end of the life cycle of the existing 'product', which, until the present, dominated the development of tourism policies (Formica & Uysal, 1996). The economic crisis has played an important role in this outcome, or at least has accelerated its results, beginning with the 2008 crisis at the international level and from 2009 at the national level.

However, it is unquestionable that the quest for the development of tourism in Greece bears positively on the local economy, financial promotion, and welfare of the country's residents. In any case, each activity undoubtedly generates both positive and negative effects (that are accentuated in case of overdevelopment). Therefore, the questions regarding tourism monoculture are 'how should one tackle the negative effects caused by the excessive growth of the industry in relation to other activities?', and 'what kind of strategies for risk management should one formulate in order to avoid a possible significant decline in tourism activity on a global or local scale?'.

The main issues regarding tourism monoculture are economic, environmental, and social. The social impacts of this development model of mass tourism are significant, due to the seasonality that characterises it. It creates abeyance tourism potential and a great seasonal employment imbalance, while the sharp rise in income leads to the adoption of new consumption patterns by the residents in tourism destinations, as well as a change in the local social and cultural structure. More specifically, the 'abeyance' building stock is deteriorating extremely quickly, leading to its complete disappearance (in 'old' tourism areas). The combination of increased income originating from tourism activities together with high unemployment during the winter season, led to a decrease in importance and in 'obsolescence' of agricultural activity and, as a result, of the income derived from it, resulting in either a partial or a gradual abandonment of rural land.

This model lowers local resistance to potential negative developments in tourism markets on a local and global scale. It also has indirect environmental impacts, since the devaluation and abandonment of agricultural land results in the abandonment of rural environmental practices, such as conserving water resources and protecting rural lands from polluting ingredients and potentially inflammable biomass. All these 'high consumption patterns, accompanied by a corresponding lack of 'culture' (a combination that, most of the time, develops rapidly) is leading to the abandonment social constants and behaviours, leading to the creation, instead of an 'open' sociological space, of an unstable and inconsistently extensive 'urban' sociological space.

Simultaneously, the impacts of mass tourism, both on the natural environment (ecosystems, flora, fauna, landscape, air, seawater) and on the human-made one (built-up environment, quality of life, cultural heritage), are sometimes catastrophic. The water resources are rapidly depleting, aggravated by tourism development practices such as framed lawns and swimming pools. This is resulting in intense disputes regarding which should get priority—using water for agricultural or for tourism purposes.

The local economies of coastal areas receive obvious benefits from the development of tourism, but they are also more vulnerable to its more negative effects. The greater the dependence of the local economy on tourism activities, the greater will be the impact of adverse developments. The demand for tourism services appears to be extremely volatile and the market is largely under the control of tour operators, and, at the same time, global economic conditions and events have a strong impact on tourism activity and demand.

5 The Economic Crisis and the Crisis of the Greek Model of Tourism Development

In recent years, there have been several empirical studies for estimating the impact of the ongoing economic crisis on tourism (Min & McAleer, 2008; Pambudi, McCaughey, & Smyth, 2009; Papatheodorou, Rosselló, & Xiao, 2010; Smeral, 2010; Song & Lin, 2010), and most of them have concluded that a financial crisis largely affects the disposable income for consumption. This, in turn, affects tourism activity and the final choice for tourist destinations. However, the economic crisis in Greece triggered serious questions regarding the Greek model of tourism development.

In particular, if we look carefully at the application of the product cycle theory in the tourism sector (Baum, 1998; Butler, 1980, 1998), and to the 4S model of Greek tourism, we will notice that Greek tourism went through four major phases from 1950 to the present. At first, there was the phase of introduction and development (1950–1970), from which we gradually passed to the stabilisation phase (1971–1980). Subsequently, we moved on to the phase of uncertainty (1981–1990) and, thereafter, to the maturity and saturation phase, in which we are right now (Varvaresos, 2009).

Our country remained wedded to this model of mass tourism from specific countries—mainly those in central and northern Europe—making little effort to enrich its touristic product with novel and innovative tourism components.

Gradually, Greece standardised its tourism product to such an extent, that any economies of scale that were achieved in this process were lost due to increased competition mainly with regard to prices, from its main competitor countries, such as Egypt or Turkey, which emerged as competitors during the last 15 years. These competitors could no longer compete on the field of 4S tourism, especially after Greece joined the euro area. Simultaneously, the insistence in this country on the same target markets in terms of potential customers created a one-dimensional approach to tourism promotions that was stuck for years with the 4S model, which has not significantly changed in relation to the key competitor countries.

It is obvious now that this present model of tourism promotion, which is based mainly on mass tourism and targeted towards a specific type of tourist-consumer, has reached its saturation point and can no longer meet the new demands of the tourism

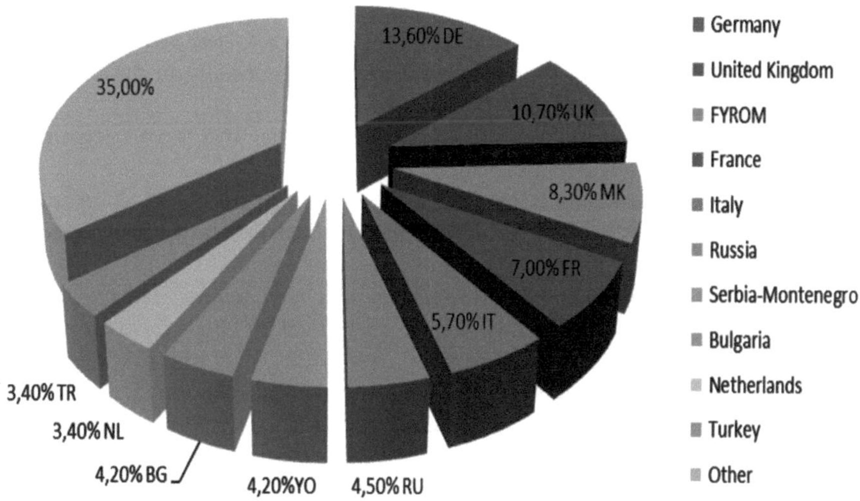

Fig. 1 The main sources of international tourist arrivals, by market share. *Source*: SETE

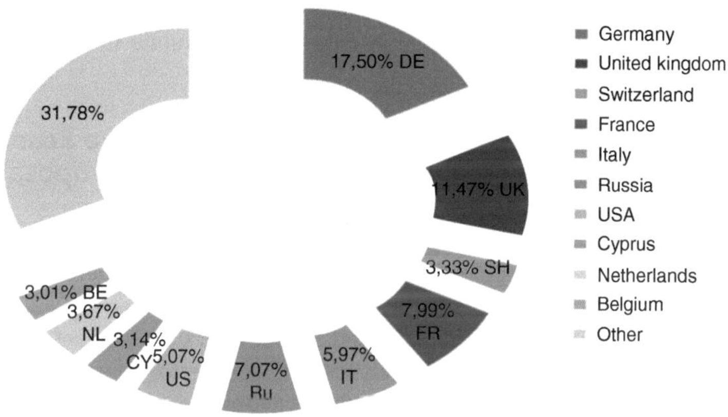

Fig. 2 Income from foreign tourists (travel receipts), by country of origin, 2011. *Source*: SETE

clientele. We can declare that this is a structural crisis of the whole edifice, on which Greek tourism was built (Morucci, 2003; Tsartas, 2010; Varvaresos, 2009). Therefore, the tourism product, based on innovation and the maximisation of satisfaction of the tourists (Hodgson, 1990; Poon, 1993), remained for many years attached to a one-dimensional model, lowering in many cases the standards of quality, because of the cutting of costs that many professionals were trying to achieve.

The result of this procedure for Greece was to apply pressure on the disposable income of potential tourist 'clients' and therefore, reducing the rate of tourist flow from the target countries—Germany, Great Britain, France, and Italy—that continue to be the main source of tourists. These countries, except Germany, appear to suffer from economic recession. Figure 1 demonstrates the share of the 10 most important source markets for international tourist arrivals. Here, we observe that 40.4 % arrivals originate in four countries, which are currently in the middle of economic crisis in the Eurozone.

Figure 2 demonstrates the same fact. Here, we see that 46.8 % of international travel receipts are derived from the same countries.

Today, tourism traffic and bookings for the summer period have, compared to 2011, fallen by 10–15 %, due to the internal political instability that Greece is facing. If this trend continues, 1.5 million fewer tourists are expected to visit the country, while tourism revenue for the first quarter has already been reduced by 15 %. Until the time of writing this chapter, more than 20 hotels have terminated their operation, while jobs fell from 14,000 in May 2011 to 11,000 in May 2012, which accounts for 30 % job cuts. The unprecedented economic crisis that is affecting the country is also asphyxiating the tourism sector. Moreover, the country's constant denigration in the international media and rumours about its exit from the Eurozone has created a negative image in the minds of tourists. It is significant that the reservation rate from Germany appears to be 20–30 % lower than what it was in 2011. This, on the one hand, is due to the fear that German tourists have regarding the so-called 'non-friendly towards Germans' spirit that has supposedly prevailed among Greeks because of the Memorandum. On the other hand, it is due to the uncertainty regarding the country's future in the Eurozone.

6 The Greek Tourism Industry as a Pillar for the Economic and Social Recovery of the Country: Policy Proposals

The saturated model for tourism business that continues to be followed, and which has reached saturation, must be immediately replaced. The new model for developing tourism must establish new and innovative structures aiming at repositioning the Greek tourism product in new markets and trends. The development potential of Greek tourism appears to be much larger than any competitor country in the region and its comparative advantages such as natural environment, historical and cultural heritage, and the diversity of its tourism destinations have not deteriorated significantly. Moreover, the exploitation of its tourism resources appears, at present, to be considerably less than that of its main competitors.

At the same time, tourism is one of the few sectors exhibiting an increase in foreign capital inflow and is one in which major investment groups can show interest. Even today, a substantial portion of the Greek state's property, vast land areas, and tourist facilities remain unexploited, while in the urban centre of Athens, the Elliniko area and the sporting facilities for the Olympic Games can act as a springboard for foreign capital. No doubt, the valuation of the Greek state's real estate 'portfolio' has declined significantly due to the ongoing recession. However, there are alternative ways, like concessions and long-term leases, which could provide the impetus that is now necessary for the national economy and employment, and, at the same time, allow the Greek government to retain its property.

These processes will have a twofold positive effect, by eliminating the need for state subsidies and generating long-term tax benefits and increase in employment rates. It is estimated (McKinsey & Company Report, 2012) that in terms of the annual gross value added, tourism can attract foreign capital to the extent of 18 billion euros in a decade.

It is not easy to find alternatives to monoculture tourism, because intrinsic limitations, such as availability of space, reduced accessibility, and high environmental costs are narrowing the possibilities for developing alternative activities. The strategy being proposed is not linked to policies for reducing tourism activity, but to creating and enhancing alternative sources of income for local economies, in order to increase their resistance to and reduce their interdependence on tourism recession phenomena. At the same time, it will provide the necessary tools for effectively regulating and fine-tuning tourist activity with respect to competing uses of space. The new model will also reduce (if not eliminate) the negative economic, social, and environmental impacts, creating a sustainable tourism product utilising the capacities of existing economic resources, and promote social and environmental uplift, creating new growth opportunities and prospects that will not be necessarily related only to tourism.

In order to enable the country to increase its competitiveness by creating a high quality and upscale tourism product, it should launch a new tourism development model. The proposed tourism policy measures can be divided into three main and interdependent categories: (a) investment measures related to public and private investments in tourism, (b) institutional measures that are more effective and, yet, involve less governmental intervention, and (c) measures for educating and training the human capital employed in tourism. Especially regarding investments, incentives should provide for promoting quality, modernising existing tourism facilities and environmental resources, and attracting capital for general tourism ventures. These investments can include upgradation of superstructures, accommodation facilities, and hotels, and improvement of infrastructures such as roads, port facilities, touristic harbours, berths, and urban and residential remodelling, and improvements in traditional settlements. Special care and study should be undertaken for investing in long-term remodelling of infrastructure for alternative forms of tourism such as diving facilities, theme parks, and medical tourism.

During the last 18 years, 48 different individuals led Greek Tourism, either as general secretaries or ministers and deputy ministers in charge of tourism, with each one usually changing the countries marketing campaign, based mostly on personal choice. In order to change this trend, we need the establishment of an authorised body with the participation of social partners and with non-governmental features and approach, to refashion the country's 'image' abroad in line with the Destination Management Organizations that exist in other countries with highly developed tourism practices. At the same time, organisational and institutional reforms should involve the adoption of a single spatial tourist map that will facilitate investments and long-term programming.

Finally, it needs emphasising that the improvement of the product quality of Greek tourism strongly depends on the level of education of human capital. Therefore, training is of particular importance. The main goal of education should be to upgrade the capabilities and specialisation of the tourism related workforce, with a view towards continuous improvement and modernisation of services. Continuous training and qualification of personnel, in terms of their position capabilities and in the field of information technology, communication, and internet applications and solutions are crucial for the best utilisation of their abilities and their impact on economy and the tourism industry in general.

References

Alpha Bank. (2009). Tourism: Great potential for growth and entrepreneurship. *Economic Bulletin, 110*, 3–19.

Balaguer, J., & Cantavella-Jorda, M. (2002). Tourism as a long-run economic growth factor: The Spanish case. *Applied Economics, 34*(7), 877–84.

Baum, T. (1998). Taking the exit route: Extending the tourism area life cycle model. *Current Issues in Tourism, 1*(2), 167–175.

Brohman, J. (1996). New directions in tourism for third world development. *Annals of Tourism Research, 23*(1), 48–70.

Butler, R. W. (1980). The concept of a tourism area cycle of evolution: Implications for the management of resources. *Canadian Geographer, 24*(1), 5–12.

Butler, R. (1998). *Still pedalling along: The resort cycle two decades on.* Paper presented at Progress in Tourism and Hospitality Research, CAUTHE Conference, Gold Coast, Australia

Butler, R. (2004). The tourism area life cycle in the twenty-first century. In A. Lew, M. Hall, & A. Williams (Eds.), *A companion to tourism* (pp. 159–169). Oxford: Blackwell.

Dwyer, L., Forsyth, P., & Dwyer, W. (2010). *Tourism economics and policy*. Cheltenham: Channel View Publications.

Dwyer, L., Forsyth, P., & Spurr, R. (2007a). Contrasting the uses of TSAs and CGE models: Measuring tourism yield and productivity. *Tourism Economics, 13*(4), 537–551.

Dwyer, L., Forsyth, P., & Spurr, R. (2007b). Productivity & yield measurement in Australia's inbound tourism using tourism satellite accounts & computable general equilibrium models. In J. Tribe & D. Airey (Eds.), *Developments in tourism research* (pp. 77–94). Oxford: Elsevier.

Formica, S., & Uysal, M. (1996). The revitalization of Italy as a tourist destination. *Tourism Management, 17*(5), 323–331.

Frechtling, D. C. (1994). Assessing the economic impacts of travel and tourism—Measuring economic benefits. In J. R. Brent Ritchie & C. R. Goeldner (Eds.), *Travel, tourism and hospitality research* (2nd ed., pp. 91–104). New York: Wiley.

Galanos, G. (2009). *Defining the factors of the European and International Competitiveness of the tourist industry—The case of Greece* (PhD Dissertation). University of Piraeus (in Greek).

Gibson, L. J. (1993). The potential for tourism development in nonmetropolitan areas. In D. L. Barkley (Ed.), *Economic adaptation: Alternatives for nonmetropolitan areas* (pp. 145–164). Boulder: Westview.

Gray, P. (1970). *International travel-international trade*. Lexington: Lexington Books.

Hodgson, P. (1990). New tourism product development: Market research's role. *Tourism Management, 11*(1), 2–5.

Horváth, E., & Frechtling, D. (1999). Estimating the multiplier effects of tourism expenditures on a local economy through a regional input–output model. *Journal of Travel Research, 37*(4), 324–332.

Komilis, P. (1987). *The spatial structure and growth of tourism in relation to the physical planning process: The case of Greece* (PhD thesis). Glasgow: University of Strathclyde.
Kousis, M. (1994). Environment and the state in the EU periphery: The case of Greece. *Regional Politics and Policy, 4*(1), 118–35.
Kousis, M. (2000). Tourism and environment: The local social remonstrance in Crete. In P. Tsartas (Ed.), *Tourism development: Interdisciplinary approaches* (pp. 99–119). Athens: Exantas (in Greek).
Lundberg, D. E., Stavenga, M. H., & Krishnamoorthy, M. (1995). *Tourism economics*. New York: Wiley.
Mcintosh, W. R., & Goeldner, C. R. (1990). *Tourism: Principles, practices, philosophies* (6th ed.). New York: Wiley.
McKinsey & Company Report. (2012). *Greece 10 years ahead*. Athens: McKinsey & Company.
Min, J. C. H., & McAleer, M. (2008). Modelling income effects on long and short haul international travel from Japan. *Tourism Management, 29*(6), 1099–1109.
Morucci, B. (2003). La demande touristique: une approche de son évolution et de ses perspectives. In J. Spindler & H. Durand (Eds.), *Le tourisme au XXI siecle* (pp. 133–155). Paris: L' Harmattan.
Pambudi, D., McCaughey, N., & Smyth, R. (2009). Computable general equilibrium estimates of the impact of the Bali bombing on the Indonesian economy. *Tourism Management, 30*(2), 232–239.
Papatheodorou, A., Rosselló, J., & Xiao, H. (2010). Global economic crisis and tourism: Consequences and perspectives. *Journal of Travel Research, 49*(1), 39–45.
Paulopoulos, A., & Kouzelis, A. (1998). *Regional development of Greece and tourism* (pp. 59–87). Athens: Research Institute for Tourism (ITEP).
Poon, A. (1993). *Tourism, technology and competitive strategies*. Wallingford: CAB International.
SETE. (2010a). *Geek tourism 2020: Proposal for the new development model*. Athens: The Association of Greek Tourism Enterprises.
SETE. (2010b). *The importance of tourism to the Greek economy/society and policy proposals for the tourist development*. Athens: The Association of Greek Tourism Enterprises.
Sinclair, M. T. (1998). Tourism and economic development: A survey. *Journal of Development Studies, 34*(5), 1–51.
Smeral, E. (2010). Impacts of the world recession and economic crisis on tourism: Forecasts and potential risks. *Journal of Travel Research, 49*(1), 31–38.
Song, H., & Lin, S. (2010). Impacts of the financial and economic crisis on tourism in Asia. *Journal of Travel Research, 49*(1), 16–30.
Tsartas, P. (2003). Tourism development in Greek insular and coastal areas: Sociocultural changes and crucial policy issues. *Journal of Sustainable Tourism, 11*(2–3), 116–132.
Tsartas, P. (2010). *Greek tourism development: Evolution, characteristics, potentials*. Athens: Kritiki (in Greek).
Varvaresos, S. (2009). The contribution of alternative and special interest tourism in tourism development activities. In M. Soteriades & J. Farsaris (Eds.), *Alternative and special interest tourism* (pp. 151–171). Athens: Interbooks Editions (in Greek).
WTO. (2011). *UNWTO tourism highlights*. Madrid: UNWTO.
WTO. (2012, May 10). *World tourism barometer*. Madrid: UNWTO, Tourism Trends and Marketing Strategies.

Prospects for Local Development Based on Cultural Assets/Heritage: The Residents' Perspective

Evangelia Georgitsoyanni, Eleni Sardianou, Alexandra Lappa, and Evangelia Mylona

1 Introduction

The development of tourism has been traditionally related to the development of culture. Culture consists not only of performing arts and visits to museums, galleries, archaeological and historic sites, and so on, but also includes the way of life of people living in a certain area, including aspects such as language, beliefs, cuisine, clothing, customs, etc. Cultural tourism is one of the largest and fastest-growing global tourism markets, which also focuses on the protection of the natural and cultural environment, in an effort to solve the problems of mass tourism (i.e. low wages, seasonal employment, and environmental degradation) (Kokkali, Koutsouris, & Chrysochou, 2008; OECD, 2009, 115, Chapter 8; Pavlogeorgatos & Konstantoglou, 2005, 60; Sdrali & Chazapi, 2007, 61). Many locations are now actively developing their tangible and intangible cultural assets as a means of developing comparative advantages in an increasingly competitive tourism marketplace, and of creating local distinctiveness in the face of globalisation. Cultural tourism constitutes an alternative strategy of sustainable local development for improving the quality of life (Bachleitner & Zins, 1999, 201; Besculides, Lee, & McCormick, 2002, 304; Pavlogeorgatos & Konstantoglou, 2005, 40; Sdrali & Chazapi, 2007, 61; Shin, 2010).

The richness and diversity of cultural heritage in Greece is recognised as being vitally important to the county's sustainability. Cultural heritage, both tangible and intangible, and natural heritage constitute the basic elements and the country's most important resources for tourism. Nature and culture are, consequently, valuable assets and the main constituents of the products for attracting tourists. Culture is a fundamental component of sustainable development and a powerful contributor to economic development, social stability, and environmental protection (Harrill, 2004; OECD,

E. Georgitsoyanni (✉) • E. Sardianou • A. Lappa • E. Mylona
Department of Home Economics and Ecology, Harokopio University, 70 El. Venizelou St., Athens 17671, Greece
e-mail: egeorg@hua.gr; esardianou@hua.gr; alappa@hua.gr; ev.mylona@hotmail.com

P. Sklias and N. Tzifakis (eds.), *Greece's Horizons*, The Konstantinos Karamanlis Institute for Democracy Series on European and International Affairs,
DOI 10.1007/978-3-642-34534-0_12,

2009, 115, Chapter 8; Pavlogeorgatos & Konstantoglou, 2005, 59). Communities that are rich in cultural heritage can provide tourists with a wide variety of recreational and cultural opportunities. Museums, historic sites, cultural centres, and other attractions allow tourists to interact with local residents and to learn about and experience the local culture (Besculides et al., 2002, 305). One can classify the benefits under 'personal' (physical and psychological), 'socio-cultural', 'economic', and 'environmental'. These benefits accrue to both the tourists who visit cultural sites and the host communities. The touristic exchange fosters a cross-cultural communication that can promote understanding between the host and the guest. Thus, cultural tourism can contribute to local economic regeneration and prosperity, by generating new employment opportunities for the host population and creating a market for traditional arts, which are promoted and possibly even saved from extinction (Andriotis, 2004, 14; Bachleitner & Zins, 1999, 201; Harrill, 2004; OECD, 2009, 120–122, Chapter 8; Sdrali & Chazapi, 2007, 62; Shin, 2010). According to Bachleitner and Zins (1999), cultural tourism encourages the opening of small and medium-sized family enterprises that offer unique and authentic local products.

The main objective of the current study is to describe the local residents' perception of the cultural benefits of tourism and to gain a better understanding of the residents' evaluation of tourism impacts and of their support for development of tourism in their area. The research was based on a case study, which was conducted at the former Kapodistrian Municipality of Sikyon.

2 Previous Studies

The impact of tourism has tended to become a popular topic in tourism research. Many researchers have studied the attitude of the residents towards tourism and their perceptions of the impacts of tourism development. This is because tourism can have both positive and negative effects and the support of residents is essential for the sustainable growth of tourism. In general, the results of previous studies indicate that the residents tend to have positive perceptions of the impact of tourism. They especially feel that tourism can improve the quality of products and services in their region, increase their pride in the local culture, contribute to the preservation of the natural environment and protection of wildlife, and provide an incentive for the restoration of historic buildings (Andriotis, 2004; Pavlogeorgatos & Konstantoglou, 2005, 59). Previous research has also investigated the relationship between the residents' attitudes and levels of tourism development (Latkova & Vogt, 2012, 54). Respondents who expected tourism to result in personal benefits for them and in positive impacts in general were more likely to support the growth of tourism in their community (McGehee, Andereck, & Vogt, 2002, 3).

Besculides et al. (2002, 310) suggest that benefits considered most important to the residents are greater knowledge of their own culture, the preservation of the traditional way of life, and a stronger sense of ethnic identity and of being part of a community rich in culture and history. The two dominant concerns of the residents appear to be the protection of the cultural and religious sites and greater economic opportunity. With proper planning and management, tourism has been found to improve the quality of life of the residents as well as to strengthen the sense of local identity (Besculides et al., 2002, 306). The respondents also agree that tourism has positive economic impacts, especially in times of economic downturn. They firmly believe that their community should support tourism development and are willing to be personally involved in the future development of alternative types of tourism. Residents consider the positive socio-cultural and environmental impacts of tourism to be as important as the positive economic impacts of tourism. In addition, the findings reveal that when residents perceive that the positive consequences of tourism are likely to be greater than the negative impacts, they are inclined to accept the growth of tourism and support tourism development in their community (Andriotis, 2004, 14; Bachleitner & Zins, 1999, 201; Besculides et al., 2002, 308; OECD, 2009, 122, Chapter 8).

Residents who are engaged in the tourism sector and are economically dependent on tourism seem to have a positive attitude towards cultural tourism, as cultural tourism can be seen as a means of preserving their cultural heritage and enhancing local incomes (Sdrali & Chazapi, 2007, 63; Shin, 2010). As far as economic prosperity is concerned, most residents claim that cultural tourism has generated new employment opportunities, mainly for young adults and women, thus providing a solution to the problem of seasonality of tourism (Andriotis, 2004, 14).

The majority of the residents feel that tourism should have a role in their county equal to, or even greater than that of, other economic sectors. The less the residents benefit from tourism, the more sensitive they are to its negative impacts. Residents who perceive tourism to have positive impacts are more optimistic about their community's future. The results of the study by Andriotis (2004, 14) support the notion that residents who personally benefit from tourism and who recognise tourism as a development strategy are supportive of tourism. On the other hand, Latkova and Vogt (2012) have found that the major apprehension of residents is that tourism would lead to the deterioration of traffic conditions.

Previous research has also identified the residents' attitudes towards tourism as being an important factor in achieving successful and sustainable tourism development. With the aim of mitigating economic difficulties, many rural communities have adopted tourism as a new economic development strategy, which can contribute to revitalisation of communities and enhancement of the residents' quality of life (Andriotis, 2004, 14). The effects of cultural regeneration initiatives are often cumulative, encouraging local investment in improved infrastructure, environmental developments, and better local facilities and services (OECD, 2009, 124, Chapter 8). Culture requires long-term investments in material and technical infrastructure, rendering all sites accessible to everyone, including those with physical handicaps. In order to realise economic and social potential, high-quality services are needed, such as medical services, police vigilance, tourist offices, tour operators, internet services, better intra-city transportation (i.e. taxi, bus, and rail services), restaurants, hotels, and shopping districts. At the same time, most locals agree that it is important to have cultural resources on offer, such as museums and historic sites, as well as events, such as festivals and fairs in their communities (Andriotis, 2004, 1; Besculides et al.,

2002, 316; OECD, 2009, 124, Chapter 8; Pavlogeorgatos & Konstantoglou, 2005, 59; Sdrali & Chazapi, 2007, 62).

To achieve successful and sustainable tourism development, community leaders and developers need to view tourism as a 'community industry' that enables residents to be actively involved in determining and planning future tourism development with the overall goal of improving the residents' quality of life. The involvement and co-operation of local and indigenous community representatives, tourism operators, property owners, and policy makers is necessary in order to achieve a sustainable tourism industry and enhance the protection of heritage resources for future generations (Andriotis, 2004, 17; Latkova & Vogt, 2012, 61). Before a community begins to develop tourism resources, understanding the residents' opinion is crucial for gaining their support for future development (Latkova & Vogt, 2012, 51; McGehee et al., 2002).

3 The Study Area

3.1 General Features

The current research is based on the former Kapodistrian Municipality of Sikyon,[1] an area with a variety of geophysical features, long history, rich cultural resources, and agricultural products. The area was chosen as a case study because of its rich cultural tradition, which is still generally unknown to outsiders, but which could be promoted, to lead to local sustainable development and the improvement of the residents' quality of life. Unfortunately, its coastal areas have suffered the consequences of past tourist practices, because of the unplanned construction of houses by residents of Athens. The relative nearness of the area to Athens, easy access, good climate conditions, and the landscape, which combines the sea with the mountains, makes further development of tourism in this area easier.

The municipality of Sikyon is part of the Peloponnese region, situated between Corinth and Achaea and within the present Corinthia prefecture. Its seat, Kiato, is located 22 km west of Corinth and at a distance of 108 km from Athens. One can easily reach Sikyon by the Corinth–Patras highway or the suburban railway. The census of 2001 gives Sikyon's population as 19,455. Its total land area is approximately 171.1 km^2, of which 60.8 % is mountainous landscape, while the remaining 39.2 % is mostly flat and occasionally hilly. The municipality of Sikyon is crossed by four rivers and has parts of three forests within its area. The altitude in the region ranges from 0 m to 1.171 m, resulting in a significant climatic variation. Intense winters and strong frosts in early spring characterise the mountainous areas, while

[1] The Kapodistrian Municipality of Sikyon was formed in 1997. In 2011, the local government reform 'Kallikrates' lead to the merger of three former Kapodistrian municipalities (Feneos, Sikyon, and Stymfalia).

the climate in the coastal zone is Mediterranean, with mild winters and hot summers (Kokkonakis, 2010; Lagoudaki, Makris, & Pateraki, 2005).

3.2 The Cultural Heritage of Sikyon

During antiquity, Sikyon was one of the major city-states of the Peloponnese. The area was inhabited since the Neolithic Age. Some scholars consider Sikyon to be the oldest organised city-state of Greece. Homer refers to Sikyon as 'eurychoros' (wide-open space), a large area situated on the Corinthian gulf plateau. Between the city and its port was a fertile plain with olive groves and orchards. The city reached the peak of its prosperity about the same time as Corinth—the fifth and sixth centuries BC (Papahatzis, 1977).

According to mythology Sikyon was the gathering place of gods and men for the division of honours, after the Olympian gods had returned victorious from their battle with the Titans. Prometheus, the judge, tricked the gods into choosing the inferior parts of the sacrificial meat. He also stole the fire from them, giving it to humankind. During the classical period, Sikyon became a major artistic centre and commercial city. It was one of the two most significant ports of Corinth, the other being Lechaion. It evolved into a cultural centre where philosophers, poets, and orators gathered, until it was destroyed by two earthquakes and was ravaged in the middle of the second century AD. The treasure of Sikyon in Delphi is an indication of the prosperity and the wealth of the city during the fifth century BC (Lagoudaki et al., 2005, 53; Papahatzis, 1977, 66). Lysippus, one of the greatest sculptors of antiquity and the official statue sculptor of Alexander the Great, was born and worked mainly in ancient Sikyon and greatly influenced the art of sculpture. In addition, according to Aristotle, ancient tragedy was born in the ancient city of Sikyon, in the works of Sikyon's tragic poet Epigenes (ca. 595 BC) (Kaskarelis, 2010, 35 and 54; Kokkonakis, 2010, 9). About this time, Sikyon developed the various industries for which it was noted in antiquity, gaining pre-eminence in woodcarving and bronze work. Moreover, Sikyon's pottery, which resembled Corinthian ware, was exported with the latter as far as Etruria. The art of painting was also supposed to have been invented in Sikyon. In the fifth century BC Sikyon, like Corinth, suffered from the commercial rivalry with Athens in the western seas, and repeatedly faced harassment from Athenian naval squadrons. However, after the Peloponnesian War, Sikyon reached its zenith as a centre of art. Its school of painting gained fame and attracted the great masters Pamphilus and Apelles as students; Lysippus and his pupils elevated Sikyon's sculpture to a level hardly surpassed in Greece. Under the Roman Empire, Sikyon was obscured by the restored cities of Corinth and Patrae and by the time of Pausanias (AD 150) it was almost desolate (Kokkonakis, 2010, 6–8; Lagoudaki et al., 2005, 50).

Habitation continued into the Byzantine period, during which Sikyon remained a small city. It also became a bishop's seat (Kaskarelis, 2010, 88). In 1460, the Ottomans conquered the area, along with the whole Peloponnese. In 1687, the Venetians occupied the Peloponnese, dividing it into four provinces. Sikyon belonged to the province of Naples, with Nafplio as the capital city. In 1700,

'Kiato' is mentioned for the first time in a census, and numbered only 28 inhabitants (Kellaris, 2001, 16). In 1715 the Ottoman Turks re-conquered the Peloponnese. During the period of the Ottoman rule Kiato was a small settlement consisting of 50 small makeshift houses that belonged to Turkish aghas. After the creation of the modern Greek state, and more specifically at the end of the nineteenth century, due to the cultivation, processing, and export of Corinthian currants, the city experienced economic, commercial, and cultural prosperity, its population multiplied, and it gradually obtained its present form (Kaskarelis, 2010, 96 and 107–117).

A great number of ancient and Byzantine monuments are found in this region. This includes the archaeological site in Vassiliko that includes the ancient theatre of Sikyon (which is one of the biggest theatres of ancient Greece and equivalent to that of Epidaurus in terms of acoustics), the restored Roman Baths, which house the archaeological museum, the Gymnasium-Palaestra, the temple of Apollo, the Bouleuterion, the Stoa, and the Stadium. Furthermore, there is the Cave of the Nymphs in Lechova, dated to the sixth century BC, where a number of figurines, associated with the worship of nymphs and Apollo, were found. In the village Titani, an inscription indicates the foundation of the sanctuary of Asklepios. Moreover, the remains of a Basilica of the early Christian era, preserved in Kiato, the so-called Panaghitsa, is regarded as one of the major basilicas built in the Peloponnese during the second half of the fifth century AD (Kaskarelis, 2010, 89; Kokkonakis, 2010, 118–120; Papahatzis, 1977, 67–69). The most significant monastery of the area is the Holy Monastery of the Assumption of Virgin Mary in Lechova, which is dated in the middle-Byzantine period. It has a marvellous marble mosaic floor and its miraculous image of Virgin Mary, dated to the end of the seventeenth century, draws plenty of visitors (Gioulis, 2008, 4; Kokkonakis, 2010, 49 and 85).

A building of architectural interest and worthy of preservation is the neoclassical mansion of Theoharis in Kiato, where the Municipal Gallery will be housed. The German architect Ernst Ziller (1837–1923), who erected many significant neoclassical buildings in various Greek cities during the late 19th and early twentieth century, designed the mansion. In Kiato, he also designed the mansion Zouzoula (1890) and the mansion of the mayor Athanasios Gravas, which were demolished after the earthquake of 1981. The old currant warehouses of ASO (Autonomous Currant Organisation) that flourished in the early twentieth century are also well preserved. Some of them will be used to house the Public Library, the Lysippus Museum, a conference centre, and a theatre hall (Kokkonakis, 2010, 79 and 112).

4 The Economic Development of the Region

Development of the municipality is mainly based on the primary and tertiary sectors. Of the total population, 35.55 % are engaged in agriculture and concerned with the production of items such as the Corinthian currant, sultanina grapes, olives, citrus, and vegetables. On the other hand, the processing of products and the secondary sector in general does not offer any significant prospects for development. The tertiary sector is also important, as it involves 44.02 % of the residents.

Trade, due to the existence of a harbour, plays a major role in the area's economic development. However, the demand for tourist services is characterised by seasonality (summer months) and there is a significant shortage of housing facilities and infrastructure (Kaskarelis, 2010, 718; Lagoudaki et al., 2005, 26).

5 Empirical Analysis

In this section, we employ a cross sectional data set from Sikyon and present the results of statistical and econometric analyses to estimate the profile of residents who are aware of their cultural heritage and are positively inclined towards culture-based local development. In particular, we carried out an extensive survey of 200 residents of Sikyon, from January 2012 to March 2012, using the random stratified sampling method. We distributed 200 questionnaires and conducted the survey using a structured questionnaire and personal interviews. Given the purpose of our study, we interviewed the respondents at their residence. We chose the households at random. The response rate was 80 % and the survey resulted in a data set of 160 respondents.

In the sample of 160 respondents, 51.3 % were women and 48.8 % were men. Most respondents were between the ages of 31 and 50 years (48.2 %); 11.3 % were between 25 and 30 years, 26.8 % between 51 and 70 years, and only 6.2 % above 70 years.[2] As regards the educational level, 53.7 % were university-educated and 28.1 % had graduated from a secondary school. The respondents' average monthly private and non property-related income was between €801 and €1,200, with a small percentage of monthly incomes being above €2,000 (8.7 %). The income of 23.3 % of respondents varied between €1,201 and €1,600 and 15.7 % declared having an income no higher than €400. As to the family income per year, the majority (75.6 %) reported having an income below €30,000 and only 8.2 % had family incomes above €40,000. A total of 28.1 % of the respondents were married.

As shown in Fig. 1, the great majority of respondents claimed that they were mostly aware of the cultural heritage of Sikyon. The average score regarding cultural assets' awareness was five out of nine, and only 4.4 % of the respondents claimed that they were aware of all known cultural assets. In particular, one can see from Fig. 1 that the majority of the respondents (64.4 %) were not aware that the lyric poet Praxilla from Sikyon belonged to the nine lyrical muses of antiquity and was the only known female poet who wrote dithyrambs. In addition, half of the respondents did not know that ancient Sikyon's tragic poet Epigenes is considered to have given birth to ancient tragedy. On the other hand, the majority of the respondents (59.4 %) knew that the Holy Monastery of the Assumption of Virgin Mary in Lechova is one of the oldest monasteries in the Peloponnese.

[2] Age is a quantitative variable and answers have been grouped for better presentation.

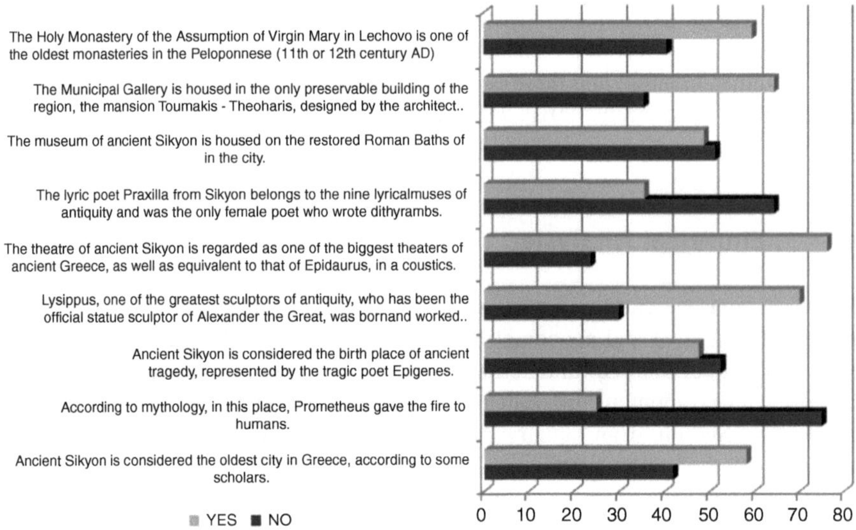

Fig. 1 Responses to 'Which of the following cultural assets of Sikyon are you familiar with?'

In order to discover the factors influencing the respondents' stated awareness of cultural assets, we statistically analysed the impact of specific demographic and economic variables. The empirical results are based on the estimation of multiple regression models. The aim of the following regression analysis was to discover whether a respondent's awareness of cultural assets bore any relationship with his or her socioeconomic profile. For this purpose, the following log linear specification was employed:

$$\text{Know}CA_i = b_o + b_1\text{Gender}_i + b_2\text{Age}_i + b_3\text{University}_i + b_4\text{Income}_i + u_i \quad (1)$$

Here 'KnowCA$_i$' is the dependent variable that indicates the number of cultural assets of Sikyon known per respondent. 'Gender$_i$' is a dummy variable that reads as 1 if the respondent is male and 0 if female. 'Age$_i$' is the respondent's age. 'University$_i$' is a dummy variable that has the value 1 if the respondent has completed undergraduate studies and 0 otherwise. 'Income$_i$' is the respondent's monthly private income in euros; and 'u_i' is an error term. Table 1 reports the empirical results derived from the estimation of Eq. 1.

It is concluded that the gender and age of the respondent are not statistically significant factors in the awareness of cultural assets of Sikyon. Similarly, the respondent's monthly private income does not explain the differences in the awareness level of cultural assets. On the other hand, educational attainment is a statistically significant factor, at a 10 % level of significance, which positively affects the number of cultural assets reported by the respondents. We concluded that those who had completed higher education studies were more informed about

Table 1 Estimated ordinary least square model of residents' awareness of their cultural heritage

	Estimated OLS model
Constant	3.799*** (6.306)
Gender	−0.237 (−0.660)
Age	0.011 (0.898)
University	0.569* (1.851)
Income	0.107 (0.975)
R^2 (adjusted)	0.114

Note: The *t*-statistics are presented in parentheses
*, ***Represent the levels of significance at 10 % and 1 %, respectively

the cultural heritage of their city. It is not surprising that 90.6 % of the residents of Sikyon considered that their city had a significant cultural heritage.

To find out the views of the residents on the possible impact of cultural tourism on local development, we asked them to choose between several possible positive and negative results of the development of tourism in a semi-urban region. Figure 2 presents the respondents' opinion regarding the possible effects of cultural tourism in their region. We find that only 20 % of the residents believed that cultural tourism could increase social problems and criminality in the city. As expected, a great majority of the residents believed that the development of cultural tourism could create job opportunities (98 %) and could encourage business entrepreneurship (90 %). In addition, 79 % considered that the value of their properties would increase because of the development of cultural tourism in the area. Therefore, our sample suggests a strong motive to develop and promote cultural tourism as a means of enhancing economic activity.

The empirical results below follow from an analysis based on probit regression models. Binary probit regression is a popular statistical technique in which the probability of a dichotomous outcome is related to a set of explanatory variables. In our case, according to the binary probit model, the estimated value of the dependent variable is interpreted as the probability of a resident believing that cultural tourism could contribute to the development of the city of Sikyon, as following from the values of the explanatory independent variables. Two subsets of independent variables were used in this analysis, namely: (a) socio-demographic factors and (b) economic variables. Therefore, in the empirical study, we employed the following expanded probit specification for a resident's belief that cultural tourism can benefit local development of the city:

$$\text{EconBenefit}_i = b_o + b_1\text{Gender}_i + b_2\text{Age}_i + b_3\text{University}_i + b_4\text{Income}_i + u_i \quad (2)$$

$$\text{EnterprMotives}_i = b_o + b_1\text{Gender}_i + b_2\text{Age}_i + b_3\text{University}_i + b_4\text{Income}_i + u_i \quad (3)$$

Here, 'EconBenefit_i' is the binary dependent variable indicating whether the respondent *i* considered cultural tourism as having significant economic benefits for local development. The variable takes the value 1 when the respondent's response

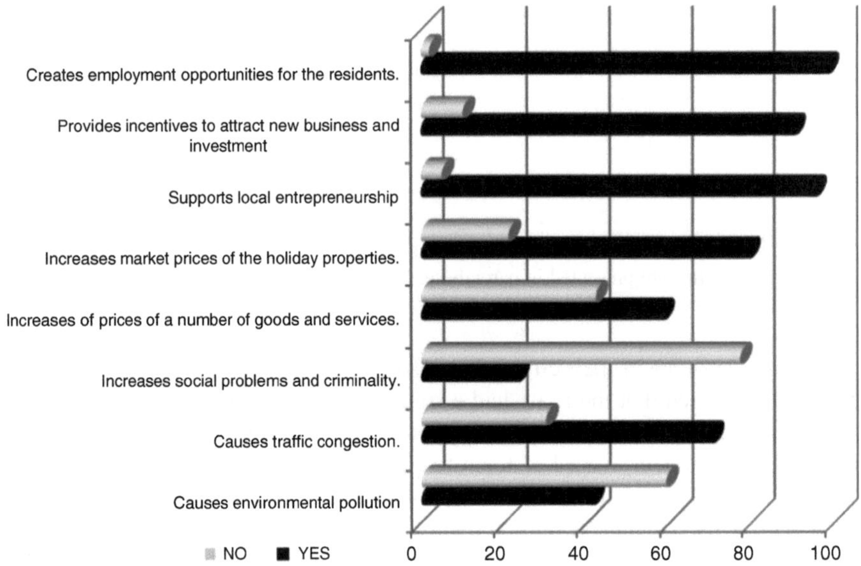

Fig. 2 Which of the following are possible impacts of the development of cultural tourism in the area of the Sikyon?

is positive and 0 otherwise. 'EnterprMotives$_i$' is another binary dependent variable that takes on the value 1 when the respondent *i* believes that cultural tourism can positively affect the development of the entrepreneurship in the area and is 0 otherwise. The independent variables in both equations are the following: 'Gender$_i$' is a dummy variable that reads as 1 when the respondent is male and as 0 when the respondent is female. 'Age$_i$' is the respondent's age. 'University$_i$' is a dummy variable that reads as 1 if the respondent has completed undergraduate studies and as 0 otherwise. 'Income$_i$' is the respondent's monthly private income in euro. Finally, 'u_i' is an error term. Table 2 reports the empirical results derived from Eqs. 2 and 3.

As shown in Table 2 the estimated coefficients for income are positive and statistically significant (Eq. 3). More precisely, this empirical result indicates that as the monthly private income increases, the probability of considering that cultural tourism can contribute to local development also increases, at a 10 % level of significance (Eq. 3). Particularly, those respondents who reported higher monthly incomes were more likely to believe that cultural tourism could lead to the expansion of entrepreneurship in the area of Sikyon. In addition, the results indicate that women were more likely to consider cultural tourism as an opportunity for local development than men were, at a 5 % level of significance (Eq. 2). Finally, the results confirm that age and the educational attainment of the respondents were not statistically significant factors regarding their opinion on the contribution of cultural tourism to local development.

Table 2 Estimated binary probit regressions for the probability of the residents' opinion that cultural tourism can contribute to the local development (yes: 1; no: 0)

Independent variables	EconBenefit (Eq. 2)	EnterprMotives (Eq. 3)
Constant	1.420*** (4.943)	1.560** (3.524)
Age	−0.001 (−0.005)	−0.007 (−0.160)
Gender	−0.697** (−3.205)	−0.700 (−1.612)
University	0.431 (1.227)	0.619 (1.253)
Income	0.102 (0.737)	0.336* (3.143)

Note: Z-statistics are presented in parentheses
*, **, ***Represent levels of significance at 10 %, 5 %, and 1 %, respectively

$$\text{Cultural}Dif_i = b_o + b_1\text{Gender}_i + b_2\text{Age}_i + b_3\text{University}_i + b_4\text{Income}_i + u_i \quad (4)$$

$$\text{ExchangeCult}_i = b_o + b_1\text{Gender}_i + b_2\text{Age}_i + b_3\text{University}_i + b_4\text{Income}_i + u_i \quad (5)$$

Here, 'CulturalDif_i' is the binary dependent variable indicating whether the respondent i thought that cultural tourism offered significant opportunities to the residents of Sikyon to participate in a variety of cultural activities. The variable has the value 1 when the respondent answered in the affirmative and 0 otherwise. 'EchangeCult_i' is another binary dependent variable that has the value 1 where the respondent i believed that cultural tourism enhanced cultural exchanges between residents and the tourists and 0 otherwise. The independent variables in both equations are the following: 'Gender_i' is a dummy variable that has the value 1 if the respondent is male and is 0 if the respondent is female. 'Age_i' is the respondent's age. 'University_i' is a dummy variable that reads as 1 if the respondent has completed undergraduate studies and is 0 otherwise. 'Income_i' is the respondent's monthly private income in euro; and 'u_i' is an error term. Table 3 presents the empirical results from the estimation of Eqs. 4 and 5.

The empirical results presented in Table 3 show that the respondents' private income was not a statistically significant factor regarding their assessment of the cultural impacts of cultural tourism (Eqs. 4 and 5). On the other hand, there is a negative, statistically significant, relation between the respondents' age and the view that cultural tourism could affect the cultural heritage of the city. In particular, this result implies that the probability of considering that tourism might negatively affect the cultural assets increases with age, at a 10 % level of significance (Eq. 4). More important is the impact of the educational level of the residents of Sikyon. In particular, we find that the more educated respondents tended to recognise the importance of cultural tourism for the development of cultural activities in the area (Eq. 4) and for the increase in cultural exchange between tourists and local community (Eq. 5), at a 5 % level of significance.

Finally, the respondents felt that the following practices were strongly effective tools for promoting cultural tourism in Sikyon: (i) media advertising (45.6 %), (ii) video-digitising of cultural assets (33.1 %), and (iii) web-designing for promoting cultural heritage (36.3 %).

Table 3 Estimated binary probit regressions for the probability of residents' perspective that cultural tourism has cultural impacts (yes: 1; no: 0)

Independent variables	CulturalDif (Eq. 4)	ExchangeCult (Eq. 5)
Constant	1.975** (7.123)	1.083 (2.484)
Age	−0.023* (−2.422)	−0.002 (−0.017)
Gender	0.212 (0.225)	0.050 (0.015)
University	0.847** (3.530)	0.922** (4.796)
Income	0.050 (0.123)	0.034 (0.071)

Note: *Z*-statistics are presented in parentheses
*, **, ***Represent levels of significance at 10 %, 5 %, and 1 %, respectively

Conclusions

The study's aim was to examine the impacts of tourism development on the residents' attitudes, when considered in conjunction with a community's total economic activity. It showed that the impacts of cultural tourism could clearly be substantial, especially as one could now consider cultural tourism as a growth industry. Cultural tourism brings benefits to the host communities and provides them with an important motive for caring for and preserving their heritage and cultural practices. It is an alternative tourism strategy with economic, social, cultural, educational, and ecological dimensions, aimed at sustainable local development. In the current economic situation, the preservation of historic cities and the rehabilitation of the heritage offer a major opportunity for the quality of life of Greek citizens, and contributes significantly to the presently endangered social cohesion. At the same time, the society benefits from new jobs generated in process of protecting and rehabilitating cultural heritage. Thus, many urban and rural communities can adopt tourism as a new economic development strategy for mitigating economic difficulties.

This article has focused on discovering which factors significantly influence the residents' views regarding the expansion of cultural tourism, employing cross sectional data from Sikyon, Greece. The results suggest the importance of educational attainment of the residents with regard to culturally based local development. Statistical analysis also confirms the positive influence of economic incentives on the willingness to accept tourism expansion in an area with rich cultural heritage. This study also shows the importance of information dissemination in the promotion of cultural tourism. Finally, the study finds that the economic characteristics of the respondents were not statistically significant factors that affected their possessiveness regarding development based on cultural tourism. Therefore, the results confirm that the residents viewed cultural tourism as an opportunity for enhancing the economic and cultural sustainability of the local community. Additionally, it showed that the positive attitude of the residents was essential for visitor satisfaction and repeat visits. The implication was that determining the local residents' perception of tourism development and its impacts was vital before a community began developing its tourism resources.

Policies aimed at increasing the residents' acceptance of cultural tourism can contribute to the successful adoption of cultural tourism with respect to cultural heritage. In this context, investigating the socioeconomic profile of respondents who were receptive to the adoption of cultural tourism in the area would be useful when one considered targeting specific groups for marketing.

To conclude, because Sikyon's rich history reaches back to antiquity, the area is able to offer a more comprehensive range of cultural products than many of its competitors. Cultural festivals and events can be considered an important component in the marketing of cultural tourism. They offer the tourist additional reasons to visit the place, over and above the regular cultural products offered. The existence of large-scale cultural festivals and events offer Sikyon the opportunity of investing in such events. This is because even if such a festival is a one-off activity, it can have a sustained effect on the quality of the place.

In other words, the Municipality of Sikyon needs to develop a clear strategy regarding the way it wants to develop tourism. This is even more important where cultural tourism is concerned, because it often involves cultural heritage, which is vulnerable and often irreplaceable. Thus, tourism development in Sikyon should base itself on alternative forms of tourism throughout the year and the promotion of the area's cultural resources.

In general, despite the importance of tourism, the attitudes and perceptions of local residents are also vital for its success. When residents perceive that the positive impacts of tourism (regardless of whether they are economic, socio-cultural, or environmental) are likely to be greater than the negative impacts, they are inclined to support tourism development in their community. Consequently, the positive attitude of a local community plays a crucial role in the country's effort to invest in cultural tourism.

References

Andriotis, K. (2004). The perceived impact of tourism development by Cretan residents. *Tourism and Hospitality Planning and Development, 1*(2), 1–22.

Bachleitner, R., & Zins, A. H. (1999). Cultural tourism in rural communities: The residents' perspective. *Journal of Business Research, 44*(3), 199–209.

Besculides, A., Lee, M., & McCormick, P. (2002). Residents' perceptions of the cultural benefits of tourism. *Annals of Tourism Research, 29*(2), 303–319.

Gioulis, A. (2008). *Anthology of Byzantine music from the monasteries and pilgrimage shrines of Corinthia*. Athens: Communication Forms.

Harrill, R. (2004). Resident's attitudes toward tourism development: A literature review with implications for tourism planning. *Journal of Planning Literature, 18*(1), 1–16.

Kaskarelis, G. (2010). *Short chronological history of Sikyon from 5000 BC to 2010 AD*. Athens: Globe Insurance Company (in Greek).

Kellaris, K. (2001). *Journey to the municipality of Sikyon*. Kiato: Self-Publishing (in Greek).

Kokkali, P., Koutsouris, A., & Chrysochou, P. (2008). Pull factors in rural tourism: The case of Lake Plastira, Prefecture of Karditsa. In *10th panhellenic congress ETARGO 'Competitiveness–environment – quality of life and rural development'*, Thessaloniki, 27–30 November (in Greek).

Kokkonakis, S. (2010). *The contemporary municipality of Sikyon*. Kiato: Katagramma (in Greek).

Lagoudaki, A., Makris, A., & Pateraki, A. (2005). *General urban plan of the municipality of Sikyon*. Kiato: Municipality of Sikyon (in Greek).

Latkova, P., & Vogt, C. A. (2012). Residents' attitudes toward existing and future tourism development in rural communities. *Journal of Travel Research, 51*(1), 50–67.

McGehee, N. G., Andereck, K. L., & Vogt C. A. (2002). *An examination of factors influencing resident attitudes toward tourism in twelve Arizona communities*. http://www.ttra.com. Accessed 20 Aug 2012.

OECD. (2009). Temple stay programme, Korea. In OECD (Ed.), *The impact of culture on tourism* (pp. 115–127). Paris: OECD Publishing.

Papahatzis, N. (1977). *Ancient Corinth*. Athens: Ekdotiki Athinon.

Pavlogeorgatos, G., & Konstantoglou, M. (2005). Cultural tourism: The case of Greece. In N. Vernikos, S. Dascalopoulou, P. Badimaroudis, N. Boubaris, & D. Papageorgiou (Eds.), *Cultural industries. Procedures, services, goods* (pp. 59–84). Athens: Kritiki (in Greek).

Sdrali, D., & Chazapi, K. (2007). Cultural tourism in a Greek insular community: The residents' perspective. *Tourismos: An International Multidisciplinary Journal of Tourism, 2*(2), 61–75.

Shin, Y. (2010). Residents' perceptions of the impact of cultural tourism on urban development: The case of Gwangju, Korea. *Asia Pacific Journal of Tourism Research, 15*(4), 405–416.

Education for Economic Development: Can Greece Achieve It?

Anna Saiti

1 Introduction and Aims of the Study

In modern societies, education mainly serves two main aims. These are:

(a) Shaping social beings, that is, improving intellectual levels and abilities in people so that they can better understand the world and make the best possible decisions at every stage of their lives;

(b) Transferring knowledge and skills to younger generations in order to equip them with all the tools necessary for pursuing their aspirations in the workplace and in society (the knowledge and skills that contribute directly to improving the production process depend mainly on the functioning of the education system).

Indeed, any attempt at sustaining economic development and improving the standard of living in a society should be accompanied by an ongoing effort to improve the education process and provide knowledge. Only through the continuous adjustment of the education system to the current needs of the labour market—changes in the technological, economic, and social environment—can human creativity contribute to faster economic development. A low-skilled work force is the result of the education system of a country proving unable to respond to the needs of the economy. One can attribute this mainly to two factors, a bad education system, and inflexible preferences.

Given that economic development is a desirable goal in any country, the road to development clearly demands a stream of trained, skilled, capable, and educated workers (Andere, 2004; De Meulemeester & Rochat, 1995; Glewwe & Jacoby, 2004). This interdependence between education and the economy has prompted many countries to recognise education as a primary concern. Indeed, as Schultz

A. Saiti (✉)
Department of Home Economics and Ecology, Harokopio University, 70 El. Venizelou St., Athens 17671, Greece
e-mail: asaiti@hua.gr

P. Sklias and N. Tzifakis (eds.), *Greece's Horizons*, The Konstantinos Karamanlis Institute for Democracy Series on European and International Affairs,
DOI 10.1007/978-3-642-34534-0_13,

(1961, 3) put it, 'the knowledge and skills are in great part the product of investment and combined with other human investment, predominantly account for the productive superior of the technically advanced countries. To omit them in studying economic growth is like trying to explain Soviet ideology without Marx'.

Therefore, it is evident that high quality human capital accumulation facilitates progress and development, and, through its education system, a country may achieve the following (Altbach & Knight, 2007; Asteriou & Agiomirgianakis, 2001; Blaug, 1987; Bloom, Canning, & Chan, 2006; Bouzakis, 2005; Brown & Lauder, 1996; Daymon & Durkin, 2011; De Meulemeester & Rochat, 1995; Saiti & Mitrosili, 2005):

- Reducing illiteracy and school dropout rates;
- Disseminating knowledge and providing assistance to people for facilitating better decision making (the expansion and improvement of the education system provides leverage for successful economic development);
- Reinforcing the values and beliefs necessary for the functioning of a modern economy. Capable, educated, and skilled human capital can contribute significantly to the qualitative and sustainable development of society
- Promoting technical and vocational education, which helps the country to adjust easily and swiftly to the needs of the socio-economic environment;
- Enabling both the scientific and technical work force by providing new scientific knowledge (through research), the implementation of which significantly and positively affects productivity and the rate of economic growth;
- Determining the long-term prospects for economic growth.

With particular reference to Greece, due to its high public deficit, has faced severe economic problems over the last 2 years, and has been striving to restore economic and fiscal stability and credibility. Moreover, the Greek central government is the main provider of funding for education. Many Greek researchers (Brookes & Saiti, 2003; Kaloutsis, 2007; Karatzia-Stavlioti & Labropoulos, 2006; Karmas, 1995; Psacharopoulos & Papakonstantinou, 2005; Saiti, 2001, 2012; Saitis, 2005; Sassalou, 2011; Spiropoulou, Antonakaki, & Kontaris, 2007; Terzis, 2010; Zervopoulos & Palaskas, 2010) have converged to the conclusion (a) The current financing of education is heavily bureaucratic and, to an extent, ineffective due to a lack of motivation—that is, while the state is able to fund some educational services, it is unable to provide other services effectively, such as funding material substructures (Psacharopoulos, 1999; Saiti, 2001)—and (b) The Greek education system is rather slow in responding to the changes in the technological and economic environment and, therefore, unemployment is growing (Karatzia-Stavlioti & Labropoulos, 2006; Pesmazoglou, 1987; Saiti & Mitrosili, 2005), the main question is whether or not the Greek educational system can respond to the current changes so as to be a useful and effective tool towards economic development.

In this regard, all education systems are dynamic and, no matter how good a system is, if it is to enhance economic development it must undergo continuous improvement and constructive change. The country needs to implement further improvements in the education system in order to avoid any disruption in educational quality, to bring the education system closer to the country's real needs, to minimise any differences and inequalities in the provision of education, and to overcome the lack of financial resources.

Therefore, the purpose of this chapter is to examine and analyse—on the basis of relevant literature—the following: whether Greece is in a position to overcome any weaknesses in its education system, whether the Greek education system deals with the current demands of the labour market, and finally, the degree to which the central government sees education as capable of influencing the economic development of the country.

2 Higher Education and Economic Development: The Greek Case

Higher education is a top priority for investment for any developed nation since it offers a direct return both for individuals and societies and thus contributes significantly to the improvement of society and the economy. Countries that invest substantially in higher education indeed have a competitive advantage (Andere, 2004; Arambewela, Hall, & Zuhair, 2006; Bennell & Pearce, 2003; Petrakis & Stamatakis, 2002). Although development through education can only be achieved at a relatively slow pace (since it takes time to create a well-trained and capable work force), education is a strategic component of any development programme. However, it is only one component. It alone cannot produce the desired results.

The interaction between economy and education is a long-term process because it is based on the continuous advancement of human knowledge and production technology. Contrary to the pre-industrial era (where knowledge and skills were acquired through the family and workplace), modern (industrial) societies can prepare young people and transmit knowledge and skills only through the process of education. This is because modern societies are based on complex organisations and technologies that demand expert knowledge, which cannot be found outside the process of formal education (Petrakis & Stamatakis, 2002; Schultz, 1961). The need of an economy for an expert work force is evident from the impressive development of secondary and higher education in recent decades. The great demand for higher education and training stems from the high wages associated with employment opportunities in the advanced technology market, where access to this type of work is greatly determined by a person's education.

Taking into consideration that the development process is not only influenced by the 'technical knowledge and skills' but also by the moral and spiritual values of people, all levels of education contribute, in one way or another, to the economic and social development of a country. This is because

- The quality of higher education depends heavily on the quality of primary and secondary education provided. Although it seems that the contribution of compulsory education to economic development would follow a downward trend due to the lower demand for an unspecialised work force, primary education remains the basis of all higher levels of education;

- Basic education contributes to the expansion of a knowledge base that helps the individual to make better decisions. The offer of high quality basic education seems to hold particular significance for an economy as it offers the country a competitive advantage;
- Society benefits from a higher educational level of individuals as this has a significantly positive effect on productivity and social change.

In addition, continuous changes in the socio-economic and technological environment, together with the international competition, demand a well-trained and specialised work force capable of adjusting to any working conditions. Higher education prepares young people for entering the labour market, and knowledge and skills are dynamic elements. Therefore, any change in the curriculum of higher education that addresses the needs of an economy can be considered a key strategic element, both for the effective functioning of an education system and enhancing economic development (Altbach & Knight, 2007; De Meulemeester & Rochat, 1995; Glewwe & Jacoby, 2004; Kostoglou & Adamidis, 2009; Kostoglou, Garmpis, Koilias, & Van de Heijden, 2012; Petrakis & Stamatakis, 2002; Saiti & Prokopiadou, 2008; Tsamadias & Prontzas, 2012).

Indeed, any implementation of a large-scale programme of economic development is difficult, especially when the country is not fully equipped with an appropriately well-trained and specialised work force. On the other hand, as Harbison (1973) put it, '. . .a country that does not have the ability to develop the knowledge and the skills of its people and cannot use them efficiently to the national economy it will be incapable to develop anything else'. Of course, this can apply to any country that does not have a modern and effective education system.

Hence, the only way to increase the real income of a country is to increase its productivity and this can be achieved only by increasing high quality human capital accumulation and an improvement in working methods. For this to occur, the countries should adopt a strategic development process. Baran (1957) suggested that a country could achieve development only by attempting to develop both its industry and agriculture. According to this development strategy, the country should first implement improvements in the agricultural sector. Moreover, the efficient management of available resources and an energetic expansion towards new labour markets, new products, and new technologies require people with an open mind, capable of foreseeing situations different from those traditionally inherited. Only when education increases and improves the knowledge, skills, and abilities of the work force of a country (and hence its productivity) can one characterise the education system as efficient. According to Coombs and Hallak (1987), one can classify the efficiency of an education system into two kinds: internal efficiency, and external efficiency. Internal efficiency is the relation between a system, or sub-system, of learning outcomes and the imported resources used to achieve an outcome. This relation is similar to the relation between inputs and outputs of an economic unit with only one difference—the efficiency of an education system is not easy to measure. The cost and the learning outcomes are important since their relation is substantive and significant for assessing the efficiency of the system and comparing it with possible alternative educational approaches with the same learning aims (Tsamadias, 2001; Zervopoulos & Palaskas, 2010).

While there are many ways to improve the internal efficiency of an education system, these improvements depend on the capabilities of educational management and the degree of change needed by the current system. The management of change in education may improve its efficiency, with appropriate change in the quantity, quality, and rate of inputs (or the systematic use of existing inputs), without changes in the foundation of the current structure of the system and technology. Education policy makers can increase the efficiency of the system through changes in the basic planning of the system.

A revolutionary approach to improving system efficiency is a new teaching-learning methodology (Tsamadias, 2001). Indeed, not all changes or innovations can improve efficiency at once, and if these changes are not implemented in the correct way then the opposite might happen.

External efficiency is similar to internal efficiency, although their main differences lie in their direct inputs and final tasks. The external efficiency of a system is the relation between the production cost of learning outcomes (inputs) for a period of time and the benefits (personal, social, economic, and non-economic) that ensues from the learning outcome over a longer duration. An education system may have high internal efficiency and low external efficiency. This is mainly because such an education system spends time and financial resources on teaching what is effectively wrong knowledge ('wrong' in terms of the students' needs).

The same happens when a system produces more than the system needs—relative to employment opportunities and the economy's labour requirements—resulting in a well-trained but under-utilised labour force. In such a situation, although the investment in education has generated a well-trained work force, given the relatively few jobs available, the investment produces relatively low benefits. The same resources devoted to creating a more appropriately specialised work force for that country would have been more productive.

Hence, the flexibility of the education system has a tremendous impact on the final efficiency of a system. Certainly, there are other external determinants of an education system, such as an economy's ability to make efficient use of an effective education system. For instance, well informed farmers are obviously necessary to achieve a green revolution in agriculture. However, if there is a shortage of water, seeds, etc., then educational efforts devoted to creating the human resources necessary for agricultural development could prove to be very expensive (Schultz, 1961).

Compromise on educational quality, to get closer to the needs of the job market, and to reduce educational expenditure, all countries need to implement certain processes and methods adapted to the circumstances and opportunities in their country. In particular, the Greek education system should (more than ever) adjust to the changes of the economic, technological, social, and cultural environment, to serve each student's need and to use all the limited available resources efficiently. However, this need for change requires a long-term strategy on education.

Indeed, in order to confront all the educational issues effectively, Greece needs a total approach that views the education system as a whole, with careful attention to achieving desired outcomes and implementing scientific methods, rather than to political mechanisms or the personal ambitions of individual education ministers. Greece needs a critical assessment of the education framework that focuses mainly on the formal education system in order to identify the signs and weakness of the present education framework and the changes required.

Despite the many attempts made to improve the Greek education system, the decision-making process requires further review if it is to fulfil its purpose. The ineffectiveness of school management in Greece makes it clear that the crisis in the Greek education system persists (Kazamias & Kassotakis, 1995, 15). This crisis can be solved only through constructive reforms with a single aim, the rational planning of education.

Higher education yields both social and economic benefits. According to human capital theory, the duration and the quality of education are the two strategic issues that lead individuals to a greater accumulation of knowledge and skills and hence to greater productive ability. A well-educated individual has the opportunity of finding a job with higher income and improving her quality of life. On the other hand, social benefits are associated with social and political progress—to the reduction of income inequalities and to the designing and implementation of social and economic reforms. Indeed, Bowen (1977) suggested that the positive impact of higher education on society could be increased by allowing individuals with higher education to enter the labour market, thus inducing a positive change in interests, values, beliefs, attitudes, and behaviours.

One should consider the following:

(a) Over the last 2 years, the Greek economy has been facing various problems due to high public deficit and the Greek government has run into debt trying to address it.
(b) If there is a social and productive dimension to the money borrowed, that is, the money is used for investments in human infrastructure (through the funding of education, job training, and health programmes) then the debt will contribute to the development of the economy. If, however, this is not the case, then the high public debt of a country can be a serious hindrance to economic development.
(c) Presently, a large share of governmental spending is not going into productive investment (e.g. education) but only into serving the internal and external financial needs of the country.

Given the above, the only way to overcome the economic crisis and to return to economic growth is to produce competitive products and services. Investment in higher education, particularly in postgraduate studies, is a key strategic variable that enhances research, knowledge capacity, and cultural understanding, and, most importantly, provides direct and long-term benefits to the labour market (Altbach & Knight, 2007; Jepsen & Varhegyi, 2011). Although one might consider that higher education alone cannot provide a radical solution to the problem, the development and improvement of higher (including postgraduate) education, procuring a better position in a competitive environment, and acquiring technological expertise remains a challenge for any nation. Can Greece achieve it? At first sight, it seems that Greece can achieve a change for the better. As Giles and Hargreaves (2006, 153) put it, 'most nations are already signing on to the knowledge. There is no rational reason why *Greeks* cannot do the same' (cited in Saiti, 2012, 130). However, an improvement in the quality of the education process (at any level) requires a reconsideration of the education (and economic) strategy. This requires coherence in Greek education policy, to yield a systematic view of all problems of education. It also requires substantive discussion with all social agents involved in education, in order to ensure that the necessary resources are in place to facilitate an 'easier' implementation of educational change, with a view to the long-term. For this to happen, attitudes need to converge with the aims of education, to assure co-operation among the relevant agents and stability through continuity (Saiti, 2012). But it seems that the Greek educational reforms in recent years have failed not because they did not have the right legislative framework but because of a lack of coherence among social agents (Darra, Ifanti, Prokopiadou, & Saitis, 2010; Fokiali, Vitsilaki, Raptis, & Kouroutsidou, 2009; Karatzia-Stavlioti & Labropoulos, 2006; Saiti, 2012; Saitis, 2008; Terzis, 2010; Toziou, 2012).

In this regard, Greek policy makers should specify their objectives more clearly, while linking policy and action with consistent aims and attitudes (Saiti, 2009). Given that a system cannot be changed immediately, educational reforms should be characterised by continuity, they should not 'be replaced as soon as there is a change in political power' (Saiti, 2009, 399).

A rapid expansion of the Greek education system would lead the country to faster economic development and to the creation of a knowledge-based economy (Daymon & Durkin, 2011). The Greek government, therefore, should see educational development as a long-term project that determines goals and priorities and makes choices that are more sensitive to the needs of the various economic sectors. Planning is the best technical managerial resource that helps countries to confront any problem (Mialaret, 1985). Through strategic planning with regard to the long-term perspective on education (Adams, 1964; Bouzakis, 2005; Daymon & Durkin, 2011; Leithwood, Jantzi, Earl, Watson, Levin, & Fullan, 2004; Levin & Fullan, 2008; Saiti, 2012), government policy can adjust to the changing socio-economical environment, thus ensuring the coherence and continuity of Greek educational policy.

In conclusion, Greek society can benefit immensely from higher levels of production, by upgrading skills and intellectual human capital, by improving living standards, by establishing effective leadership at every level, and by enriching culture through the freedom of human capital to achieve greater creativity and innovation.

Conclusion

Taking into consideration that: (a) every country has limited financial resources, and (b) the efficient use of high-quality human capital is determined by the existence of a certain degree of development, an acknowledgement of the crucial relationship between higher education and economic development is a necessity for increased social capacity, innovation, and creativeness. Due to the rapidly changing environment, countries should move fast if they are to adapt to these changes and find efficient ways of absorbing them. In other words, countries should be prepared to innovate if they are to survive in a competitive environment (Kotter, 1996). Thus, only through cohesion, continuity, and consistency (on the part of all groups involved) and strategic planning for an efficient and sustainable system (both in education and the economy) can Greece achieve greater efficiency in the education system, strengthen the knowledge and skills of human capital, ensure improved working practices, and move towards the development of a healthy economy. Hence, Greece needs measures that are more radical in order to meet the requirements of human development and increased social needs. Greece can achieve it only through innovation, flexibility, coherence, continuity, and the implementation of rational and substantive educational reforms, which, in turn, require capable management of change.

References

Adams, D. (1964). *Educational planning*. New York: Syracuse University.

Altbach, P. G., & Knight, J. (2007). The internationalisation of higher education: Motivations and realities. *Journal of Studies in International Education, 11*(3/4), 290–305.

Andere, G. (2004). The international higher education market: Mexico's case. *Journal of Studies in International Education, 8*(1), 56–85.

Arambewela, R., Hall, J., & Zuhair, S. (2006). Postgraduate international students from Asia: Factors influencing satisfaction. *Journal of Marketing for Higher Education, 15*(2), 105–127.

Asteriou, D., & Agiomirgianakis, G. M. (2001). Human capital and economic growth: Time series evidence from Greece. *Journal of Policy Modeling, 23*, 481–489.

Baran, P. A. (1957). *The political economy of growth*. New York: Monthly Review Press.

Bennell, P., & Pearce, T. (2003). The internationalisation of higher education: Exporting education to developing and transitional economies. *International Journal of Educational Development, 23*(3), 215–232.

Blaug, M. (1987). *The economics of education and the education of an economist*. Aldershot: Edward Elgar.

Bloom, D., Canning, D., & Chan, K. (2006). *Higher education and economic development in Africa*. Harvard University. Human Development Sector. Africa Region. http://siteresources.worldbank.org/EDUCATION/Resources/278200-1099079877269/547664-1099079956815/HigherEd_Econ_Growth_Africa.pdf. Accessed 18 June 2012.

Bouzakis, S. (2005). Globalisation and education: The adjustment of education to the economy of the labour market. In D. N. Gravaris & N. Papadakis (Eds.), *Education and educational policy* (pp. 135–149). Athens: Savvalas Publications (in Greek).

Bowen, H. R. (1977). *Investment in learning: The individual and social value of American higher education*. San Francisco: Jossey-Bass.

Brookes, K., & Saiti, A. (2003). Public expenditure on education: Evidence of the Greek public primary schools. *Journal of Business and Society, 16*(1), 119–138.

Brown, P., & Lauder, H. (1996). Education, globalization and economic development. *Journal of Educational Policy, 11*(1), 1–25.

Coombs, P. H., & Hallak, J. (1987). *Cost analysis in education: A tool for policy and planning*. Baltimore: John Hopkins University Press.

Darra, M., Ifanti, A., Prokopiadou, G., & Saitis, C. (2010). Basic skills, staffing of school units and training of educators. *Nea Paidia, 134*, 44–68 (in Greek).

Daymon, C., & Durkin, K. (2011). The impact of marketization on postgraduate career preparedness in a high skills economy. *Studies in Higher Education*, 1–18i, first article. doi: 10.1080/03075079.2011.590896.

De Meulemeester, J. L., & Rochat, D. (1995). A causality analysis of the link between higher education and economic development. *Economics of Education Review, 14*(4), 351–361.

Fokiali, P., Vitsilaki, C., Raptis, N., & Kouroutsidou, M. (2009). The role of school councils in the functioning of pre-school units. In A. Kontakos & F. Kalavasis (Eds.), *Matters of educational planning: Change and governance of educational systems* (pp. 277–292). Athens: Atrapos Publications (in Greek).

Giles, C., & Hargreaves, A. (2006). The sustainability of innovative schools as learning organisations and professional learning communities during standardized reform. *Educational Administration Quarterly, 42*(1), 124–156.

Glewwe, P., & Jacoby, H. G. (2004). Economic growth and the demand for education: Is there a wealth effect. *Journal of Development Economics, 74*(1), 33–51.

Harbison, F. H. (1973). *Human resources as the wealth of nations*. New York: Oxford University Press.

Jepsen, D. M., & Varhegyi, M. M. (2011). Awareness, knowledge and intentions for post-graduate study. *Journal of Higher Education Policy and Management, 33*(6), 605–617.

Kaloutsis, N. (2007). Budget 2008: Even less educational spending. *Themata Paidias, 30*, 107–110 (in Greek).

Karatzia-Stavlioti, E., & Labropoulos, C. (2006). *Assessment, effectiveness and quality in education*. Athens: Gutenberg (in Greek).

Karmas, K. (1995). *The Greek education in the horizon of 2000*. Athens: KEPE (in Greek).

Kazamias, A., & Kassotakis, M. (1995). Educational manifesto: Thoughts about the reformation and modernization of the Greek education. In A. Kazamias & M. Kassotakis (Eds.), *Prospective of re-organising and modernisation* (pp. 12–39). Athens: Serios Publications (in Greek).

Kostoglou, V., & Adamidis, P. (2009). Analysing the employability of higher education graduates and detecting the effecting factors. *The Cyprus Journal of Sciences, 8*, 73–88.

Kostoglou, V., Garmpis, A., Koilias, C., & Van de Heijden, B. (2012). Predictors of higher technological education graduates labor market entrance success. *European Journal of Higher Education, 1*(2–3), 158–178.

Kotter, J. (1996). *Leading change*. New York: Harvard Business Review Press.

Leithwood, K., Jantzi, D., Earl, L., Watson, N., Levin, B., & Fullan, M. (2004). Strategic leadership for largescale reform: The case of England's national literacy and numeracy strategy. *School Leadership & Management, 24*(1), 57–79.

Levin, B., & Fullan, M. (2008). Learning about system renewal. *Educational Management Administration & Leadership, 36*(2), 289–303.

Mialaret, G. (1985). *Introduction to educational changes*. London: Kingsley Publishing.

Pesmazoglou, S. (1987). *Education and development in Greece 1948–85*. Athens: Themelio (in Greek).

Petrakis, P. E., & Stamatakis, D. (2002). Growth and educational levels: A comparative analysis. *Economics of Education Review, 21*(5), 513–521.

Psacharopoulos, G. (1999). *Economics of education*. Athens: Papazisi Publishing (in Greek).

Psacharopoulos, G., & Papakonstantinou, G. (2005). The real university cost in a "free" higher education country. *Economics of Education Review, 24*(1), 103–108.

Saiti, A. (2001). Management in public education: The case of school financing. *Nea Paidia, 98*(Spring), 92–109 (in Greek).

Saiti, A. (2009). The development and reform of school administration in Greece: A primary school perspective. *Educational Management Administration & Leadership, 37*(3), 378–403.

Saiti, A. (2012). Leadership and quality management: An analysis of three key features of the Greek education system. *Quality Assurance in Education, 20*(2), 110–138.

Saiti, A., & Mitrosili, E. (2005). Parental perception of the education of their adolescent children: Evidence from Greek secondary education. *Journal of Career and Technical Education, 22*(1), 9–30.
Saiti, A., & Prokopiadou, G. (2008). The demand for higher education in Greece. *Journal of Further and Higher Education, 32*(3), 285–296.
Saitis, C. (2005). *Organisation and functioning of school units*. Athens: Saitis Publications (in Greek).
Saitis, C. (2008). *Organisation and functioning of school units*. Athens: Saitis Publications (in Greek).
Sassalou, E. (2011). *Strategic entrepreneurship and organisational change in the public sector* (Master dissertation). Department of Business Administration, Postgraduate Program on Business Administration, University of Patras (in Greek).
Schultz, T. W. (1961). The concept of human capital: Reply. *American Economic Review, 51*(1), 1–17.
Spiropoulou, D., Antonakaki, T., & Kontaris, C. (2007). Economic resources of education. *Epitheorisi Ekpaideutikon thematon, 13*, 152–165 (in Greek).
Terzis, N. (2010). *Educational policy and educational reform: Historical and Social framework and case studies*. Athens: Kyriakides Publication (in Greek).
Toziou, S. (2012). *The contribution of school principal in managing conflicts among primary school educators: The case of prefectures Imathias and Thessaloniki* (Master's degree dissertation). University of the Aegean, School of Humanities, Department of Pre-School Education and Educational Design, Rhodes (in Greek).
Tsamadias, C. (2001). Rate of return to social investment in tertiary technological education by faculty. *Mathimatiki Epitheorisi, 55*, 18–41 (in Greek).
Tsamadias, C., & Prontzas, P. (2012). The effect of education on economic growth in Greece over the 1960–2000 period. *Education Economics, 20*(5), 522–537.
Zervopoulos, P., & Palaskas, T. (2010). Performance–effectiveness – efficiency measurement methods in public sector: international and Greek experience. http://mpra.ub.uni-muenchen.de/30936/1/1/MPRA_paper_30936.pdf. Accessed 18 June 2012 (in Greek).

Energy Resources and Their Use in Greece: Possible Paths to Future Economic Development and Sustainability

Costas Kiparissides

1 Introduction

The present paper assesses the potential, over the next one to two decades, of several new technologies and renewable energy sources to increase sustainability, support long-term economic prosperity, promote energy security, and reduce adverse environmental impact in Greece. Energy has always played a critical role in a country's national security, economic prosperity, and environmental quality. Greece's present dependence on vulnerable sources of imported oil and, in the future, on natural gas is a major concern. The other major concerns are the volatility of energy markets, the increasing worldwide demand for energy, and the expected consequences of climate changes. All these necessitate immediate political actions for securing the country's energy future economic development and sustainability. In the face of the above concerns, Greece must consider how to guarantee sufficient, affordable, and sustainable supplies of energy.

Presently, fossil fuels dominate the country's energy landscape. Thus, necessary changes are urgently required so Greece can move towards a more sustainable energy supply and use that will drastically reduce the environmental cost of burning fossil fuels and the country's dependence on imported fuels. Decisions about future energy options require technology choices that involve a complex mix of scientific, technical, economic, social, and political considerations. This study ascertains that, with a sustained national commitment, Greece could achieve considerable energy efficiency improvements, acquire new sources of energy supply, and effect substantial reductions in greenhouse gas emissions through the accelerated development and deployment of a portfolio of existing and emerging energy-supply and end-use technologies.

C. Kiparissides (✉)
Department of Chemical Engineering, Chemical Process Engineering Research Institute, Aristotle University of Thessaloniki, P.O. Box 472, Thessaloniki 541 24, Greece
e-mail: cypress@cperi.certh.gr

P. Sklias and N. Tzifakis (eds.), *Greece's Horizons*, The Konstantinos Karamanlis Institute for Democracy Series on European and International Affairs,
DOI 10.1007/978-3-642-34534-0_14,

2 Greece's Energy Challenges

In the beginning of the twenty-first century, the global annual growth in primary energy use has been on average almost 3 %. In 2006, the global demand in terms of primary energy was about 490 EJ. Today, over 80 % of the global energy supply is based on fossil energy sources, the most important being oil (35 % of global primary energy supply), coal (26 %) and natural gas (20 %) (IEA, 2008, 2009, 2011).

The ultimate origin of fossil fuels is solar energy that provided the energy needed for the historical accumulation of large amounts of biomass, followed by its transformation through a series of geological processes. Today, the most important renewable energy sources are indirectly (bio-energy, wind and hydro) or directly related to the availability of abundant solar energy. Solar energy has the theoretical potential to cover a large part of the increased energy needs of the entire Mankind. Of the renewable energy sources, geothermal energy has theoretically a great potential as well.

Since the adoption of the Energy 2020 objectives (European Commission, 2010) and Europe's adoption of a long-term strategy towards a low-carbon economy by 2050 (European Commission, 2011), a great deal of efforts have been made to encourage the development and use of energy in a more sustainable manner. Europe needs to be competitive and become less dependent on external energy suppliers. The comprehensive legislative and policy framework on sustainable energy set at the EU level aims at the following specific benefits for the European citizens: clean energy technologies, modern and smart infrastructures, safe and secure energy, hundreds of thousands of jobs, and a better quality of life in the cities. The entire EU is committed to reducing CO_2 emissions and making a radical move towards an almost fully decarbonised energy system by 2050. This means that the share of fossil fuels in the EU will decrease in the coming decades and, whatever are the choices made at the national level, sustainable energy, notably through new and renewable sources or improved energy efficiency, is the direction that we all have to follow.

Greece is highly dependent on imported energy. This is thought to expose the country to crises regarding energy availability and supply and oil and gas prices. Greece's high dependency on oil and gas has resulted in increasing discussions on the need for improvement of the country's energy security. This is considered to be one of the central drivers affecting future energy sector developments. Moreover, in Greece additional problems arise from the ageing energy systems and large greenhouse gas emissions. Thus, environmentally sound energy solutions are required. In fact, revolutionary changes are needed in the energy sector in order to cope with the country's future energy challenges. Principal measures related to meeting the challenges of mitigation and climate change, security of energy supply, as well as economic and environmental concerns, can be divided into two categories, namely, (1) measures enabled by new technology developments and (2) measures enabled by changes in efficient use of energy in industry, in heating/cooling systems of residential and commercial buildings and in transportation.

Renewable energy can supply the world's foreseen energy needs by orders of magnitude. However, with the exception of hydropower, geothermal, and wind, further developments are necessary to make renewable energies cost-competitive. The use of renewable energy is growing rapidly, but it accounts for only about 3 % of the world's primary energy consumption, with only about 1 % from geothermal, wind and solar. In particular, it produces 18 % of the world's electricity, 86 % of it by hydro (Lior, 2008). It should be pointed out that the successful implementation of the various renewable energy sources requires a realistic assessment of their positive and negative aspects. It is well known that renewable energy sources have many clear advantages (i.e. non-depleting and less polluting, limiting the excessive dominance of fossil fuels, etc.). Therefore, they have a strong socio-political appeal that unfortunately sometimes, tends to discount some of the disadvantages of large scale-use of renewable energy. Thus, we must look for renewable energy solutions that are sustainable by definition, i.e. economically, environmentally, and socially. It should be noted that some of the main challenges in massive sustainable implementation of renewable energies are their low energy flux. This necessitates the use of very large areas or/and quantities of materials, with consequence their negative environmental impact, and their time-dependent supply (e.g. with periods of no availability).

Despite all the above, renewable energy sources and new energy efficient technologies can provide distinct benefits to Greece in terms of competitiveness, growth and employment. They can offer an important contribution to security and diversity of energy supply and provide major opportunities in terms of industrial innovation and job creation, including the creation of new industrial sectors. Additionally, the transformation of our energy supply and conversion system will make Greece less dependent on external energy supplies and reduce our external fuels bill. The investments and technological innovation in renewable energy sources and new energy efficient technologies are not only pre-conditions for a low-carbon economy. They can also initiate a green and sustainable knowledge economy. To be successful, these investments must be combined with the development of more cost-competitive technologies that will allow the country to drive down the costs of renewable energy production.

3 Energy Resources and Conversion Technologies

The use of fossil fuels (oil, natural gas and coal) has provided the developed and developing countries with the means to become increasingly more prosperous. This historical model presently faces a number of challenges. The fossil fuels resources are limited and are rapidly being depleted. The present easily exploitable reserves of crude oil and natural gas are estimated to be exhausted in the next 40–100 years. The easily accessible reserves of coal are about twice as large, and probable additional resources would last for centuries at the current energy consumption level. Thus, the world energy supply is predominantly based on fossil fuel reserves and will be for several decades to come (VTT, 2009).

A system for providing energy in a useful form to the end-users primarily consists of an energy source, a transportation (or distribution) network and, in many cases, storage, energy conversion and end-use facilities. Currently, energy is stored in the form of the primary energy source, such as coal, oil, natural gas, etc., and energy production and supply are matched with market demands. Thus, we are mainly concerned with energy supply systems that have an established and widespread infrastructure, for example, electricity and district heat supply systems.

Electricity supply systems include, in addition to power plants, high-voltage power grids and distribution networks. Nowadays, the electrical power network is integrated with telecommunication and tele-control systems in order to ensure safe and reliable operation of the electrical power system. Electrical transmission systems are also expanding rapidly and to much longer distances, yet in most developed countries the core of these systems is antiquated and unreliable, leading not only to large transmission losses but also to severe insecurity of the distribution grid. Unfortunately, both governments and industry have not allotted sufficient funds for the modernisation and improvement of these distribution systems. In the future, the large penetration of distributed generation (i.e. producing energy from small local energy sources), renewable energy sources, demand-side management and energy storages will partially displace energy produced by large conventional plants. Distributed generation will have particular significance, especially in countries, where electricity supply systems are often limited.

Hydrogen is viewed as a possible alternative energy carrier because it is a clean fuel with its only emission being water. However, it has one drawback. In its gaseous form, it has a low density and, therefore, its storage and transportation create some challenges. Like electricity, hydrogen can be produced by a number of technologies using several primary energy sources, many of which are renewable. Carbon-lean technologies (e.g. the electrolysis of water using electricity and/or solar energy, gasification of biomass, etc.) are proposed as the technologies for hydrogen production. The hydrogen economy, including the entire necessary infrastructure, could provide a versatile new energy vector. At present, the use of hydrogen is mainly envisaged as a transport fuel and also as an energy storage medium to balance power production and demand (VTT, 2009).

3.1 Energy Conversion Technologies

The energy conversion technologies discussed in the present paper aim at the reduction of greenhouse gas emissions and the reduced use of depleting fossil resources via the utilisation of renewable energy, near-zero emission technologies, and the development of highly efficient energy conversion processes. For example, large-scale heating requirements, in municipalities and industry, can be accommodated by novel combined heat and power (CHP) conversion technologies. On the other hand, small-scale heating technologies are limited to solar heating, CHP systems based on fuel cells, etc.

The future development steps for carbon capture and storage (CCS) from fossil fuel plants are known as near-zero-emission technologies. The possibilities of CCS in connection with oxygen combustion in fluidised bed boilers, which provides an option for new large CHP and mid-scale (600–800 MW) coal and co-firing plants, as well as retrofits of existing plants, can be the focus of future developments in Greece. Moreover, integrated plant concepts based on fluidised bed pressurised gasification are especially feasible for CCS (VTT, 2009).

Centralised, large-scale bio-energy utilisation is dependent on an efficient procurement system to enable the harvesting, collection, transportation and storage of huge volumes of biomass from fields or forests to the plant. The most efficient and economic concepts of bio-energy utilisation are typically integrated into processes where biomass is primarily utilised as a raw material and its residues or waste are used for energy production. In the future, the production of liquid bio-fuels for transportation can be integrated with upstream industries (e.g. forest-based industry, food manufacturing, waste recycling, etc.) where biomass is used as a raw material.

In principle, carbon capture technologies could be applied to separating the CO_2 originating from biomass, provided the power plant is of sufficient size to justify the cost. Considering the whole life-cycle of biomass, the application of CCS to biomass energy conversion would generate negative atmospheric carbon emissions. Biomass bears certain similarities to fossil fuels, particularly to coal. Therefore, all technological routes for CCS could be applied to biomass energy systems. Biomass could also be co-fired in CCS-equipped coal-fired boilers, which would further reduce the CO_2 emissions from the power plant. The use of biomass is governed by local availability and the biomass cost. It is likely that biomass co-firing would be used predominantly as a means of reducing CO_2 emissions in boilers not equipped with CCS. One can see the potential for bio-CCS in the climate change mitigation scenarios. In the long-term, bio-CCS appears to be a notable option, significantly penetrating into the energy systems beyond 2050 (VTT, 2009).

3.2 Energy Use for Buildings and Transportation

Buildings (residential and commercial) consume about 30–40 % of the world's primary energy. Buildings account for about 45 % of the anthropogenic CO_2 emissions, and are thus an important target for reducing both energy use and CO_2 emissions. The two most important issues closely linked with the efficient use of energy in buildings are: the perennial difficulties of implementing massive improvements in this sector, and the challenging development of 'eco-efficient' or 'living' buildings. It is of fundamental importance to realise that the need for 'eco-efficient' buildings is absolute and not an optional energy conservation issue. Buildings provide comfortable, safe, healthy, and pleasant shelter, while their energy consumption (that also generates the associated CO_2 emissions) is often a major fraction of a building's life-cycle annual cost. It should be noted that technological improvements needed for reducing the energy consumption and

CO_2 emissions of the buildings, are in many cases available with an acceptable cost-benefit ratio based on life-cycle analysis (Lior, 2008).

Transportation accounts for 28 % of the global energy use and 23 % of the global CO_2 emissions. The amount of energy use is obviously affected directly by the fuel efficiency of the vehicle but also importantly by traffic conditions such as the number of vehicle moves (e.g. starting, acceleration, and idling, etc.). Furthermore, the time needed to travel between origin and destination, severely increases due to poor traffic design and control, resulting in significant energy losses and waste of precious time of travellers, but also raises threats to life and health. These consequences of poor traffic design and management can have serious negative economic, environmental and social impacts both individually and nationally. As obvious as all this is, a serious problem is that governments, and even individual vehicle owners, seem to pay much more attention to improving fuel efficiency of vehicles instead of dealing with air pollution and traffic congestion issues that cause enormous losses in terms of health, time, and ultimately economic growth (Lior, 2008).

Today, the transport sector relies on an unbroken and relatively cheap supply of oil for its survival. There is no other sector with such a high level of dependence on one single source of energy. The EU transport sector has an oil dependency of 98 %, the vast majority of which is imported. Transport patterns as well as road, rail, sea faring, and air travelling infrastructures were mainly developed during an era of relatively cheap fossil fuel prices. However, energy intensive pathways are no longer sustainable. In the EU, no other sector exhibits a similar growth rate of greenhouse gas (GHG) emissions as the transport sector. Note that, in the period 1990–2007, the total GHG emissions from transport (excluding international aviation and maritime transport) in the EU-27 increased by 26 % while, during the same period, emissions from non-transport sectors decreased (EREC, 2010).

To meet the Commission's ambition to 'end oil dependence in the transport sector', measures to improve efficiency, expand the use of bio-fuels as well as the promotion of new vehicle technologies (e.g. electric, renewable hydrogen and hybrid cars) are urgently needed. Bio-fuels can play a key role in making the transport sector sustainable. The EU is the world's leading region for both production and consumption of bio-diesel. In 2007, bio-diesel in the EU accounted for 63 % of the world's bio-fuel production. On the other hand, bio-ethanol is the most important bio-fuel at a global level, with the EU accounting for 10 % of its supply. It is estimated that bio-fuels production will increase from 34 Mtoe (million tonnes of oil equivalent) in 2020 to 102 Mtoe in 2050. The Renewable Energy Directive sets a binding target for the share of renewable energy in transport of at least 10 % by 2020, the majority of which will come from bio-fuels (EREC, 2010).

3.3 Energy Conservation

The energy use trends could, and should, of course be reduced by more judicious consumption. Rationally employed conservation is always the first step before other mitigation measures are taken, and is the easiest and cheapest to implement.

In the energy area in general, and in power generation in particular, one could safely say that 'a Joule saved is worth significantly more than a Joule earned' because it takes significantly more than 1 J of energy to generate 1 J of power. This is amplified several fold when one considers the resources and environmental impact associated with the construction and operation of a power plant or even a vehicular engine. It is clear therefore that the first priority in meeting the energy challenges of the twenty-first century is energy conservation. Energy conservation can be significantly improved by the development of highly efficient energy conversion processes, the reduction of blatant waste, the adoption of more modest lifestyles, etc. All these improvements can have a high impact on energy consumption, and importantly, on the associated undesirable emissions and environmental and social consequences (Lior, 2008).

3.4 Renewable Energy Sources

Nature offers a broad range of renewable energy sources, including solar thermal, photo-voltaics, bio-energy, wind, hydropower and geothermal. They all stem in some way or another from the constant flow of solar energy that hits the earth's surface. In fact, the solar energy arriving at the earth's surface in 1 h is about $4.3 \times 1{,}020$ J, which is almost equal to the total energy consumed on the planet in 1 year (U.S. Department of Energy, 2005).

For many centuries, industrialised societies have not been able to exploit this incredibly rich source of energy because of the lack of efficient energy conversion technologies. Today, we have the technologies to largely harvest the various direct or indirect solar energy sources and satisfy a planet hungry for energy. However, when outlining the availability of renewable energy sources, it is important to define their maximum energy utilisation potential (i.e. theoretical, technical and economical). The theoretical potential identifies the upper limit that can be produced from a certain energy resource based on current scientific knowledge. The technical potential takes into account the technical boundary conditions, i.e. the conversion efficiency of technologies, the overall technical limitations, including the land area available for energy generation and the availability of raw materials. The economical potential is the proportion of the technical potential that can be economically realised. Hence, the economic potential takes into account the cost levels which are considered to be competitive.

Thus, the questions to be answered by the renewable energy sector should not only be confined to the desirable centralised or decentralised energy system or to which renewable energy source will dominate in tomorrow's world. The two concepts and all types of energy harnessing technologies must be considered as interdependent if energy supply, climate mitigation and competitiveness are to be secured in a sustainable manner. In the following subsections, a brief outlook of the key renewable energy sources and technologies is presented (Brennan & Owende, 2010; Centi & Perathoner, 2010; Dosch & de Voorde, 2009; EREC, 2008, 2010; European Commission, 2007, 2009a; Martinot, Dienst, Weiliang, & Qimin, 2007;

OECD, 2011; Palz, 2005; The Danish Government, 2011; U.S. Department of Energy, 2008; WBCSD, 2005).

3.5 Hydropower Technology Outlook

The benefits and relevance of hydropower for the renewable energy sector are obvious. Hydropower, in particular, will play a key role in the future through

- The development of hybrid systems combining several technologies to guarantee the maximum energy production in the most efficient way.
- The development of multi-purpose hydro plants with applications in the fields of drinking water supply systems, irrigation channels, flood control and protection, the creation of adjoining environmental areas, waste water treatment plants and recreational purposes.
- The reduction of greenhouse gas emissions. According to a recent study (EREC, 2010), the operation of Small Hydropower Plants (SHP) could annually reduce greenhouse gas emissions such as CO_2 by 29 million tons and sulphur dioxide by 108,000 tons.
- Supporting the development of rural areas via the installation and co-operation of SHP.

3.6 Photo-Voltaics Technology Outlook

It can reasonably be assumed that photo-voltaic electricity will become a mainstream power source in Europe by 2020 and a major power source in 2050. The 'SET for 2020' study (www.SETFOR2020.eu), carried out by the European Photovoltaic Industry Association (EPIA), considered that PV could supply up to 12 % of the electricity demand in Europe by 2020, thus representing 390 GW of installed capacity and 460 TWh of electricity generation. The available land area and buildings in 'zero impact areas' (areas not in competition with food production, natural reserves, housing, industry or other purposes) represent a potential of more than 5,000 TWh of yearly PV electricity production.

All the above estimates are based on present knowledge and technological developments expected in the coming years. With the anticipated improvements in technologies such as concentrated PV and nanotechnologies, one can expect even a higher conversion efficiency and output performance (Dosch & de Voorde, 2009; Parida, Iniyan, & Goic, 2011; PWC, 2009).

3.7 Solar Thermal Electricity Outlook

The installed capacity in Europe is expected to reach 2 GW by 2012, 30 GW by 2020, 60 GW by 2030 and 125 GW by 2050. The technical potential in Europe is estimated at 20 times that figure within reasonable generation costs. For long-term renewable supply in the EU, regional approaches are of paramount importance. By focusing on Solar Thermal Electricity (STE), the EU and its member states should take advantage of the fact that the largest potential of the world is in Southern Europe and the Union's neighbour countries in the Mediterranean region (DESERTEC, 2009; EREC, 2010).

3.8 Solar Thermal Outlook

The importance of the heating and cooling sector in the EU has been clearly recognised, as it currently requires roughly half of the entire energy demand and will continue to be a major player in the total energy consumption. It is anticipated that he overall energy demand for heating and cooling will decline with the implementation of energy efficiency measures for buildings. Therefore, the deployment of renewable heating and cooling technologies must go hand in hand with major energy efficiency improvements in buildings to ensure a widespread take-up of renewable energy systems. Solar thermal has some unique and specific benefits, namely, the direct reduction of primary energy consumption. It is available nearly everywhere, its cost is highly predictable and the systems' lifecycle has a low environmental impact. Last but not least, the use of solar thermal contributes to the security of energy supply and creates local jobs (EREC, 2010; PEW, 2010).

The 2020 goal of the European solar thermal sector, in line with the 'full R&D and policy scenario' developed by the European Solar Thermal Industry Federation (ESTIF), is to have an installed solar thermal capacity of 272 GWh, equivalent to 388 Mio m2 of solar collectors. This corresponds to an estimated 6.3 % of the European Union's 20 % renewable energy target, representing an annual sectoral growth rate of 26 %. Moreover, it will result in an annual reduction of CO_2 emissions by 69 Mt.

3.9 Wind Technology Outlook

The medium term outlook for the wind industry looks strong. In 2009, the European Commission published its communication on 'Investing in the Development of Low Carbon Technologies (SET-Plan)'—COM2009/519, in which it is estimated that Europe needs €6 billion investment in wind energy research over the next 10 years (European Commission, 2009b). According to the European Commission's communication, the return would be fully competitive wind power generation capable of contributing up to 20 % of EU electricity by 2020 and as much as 33 % by 2030. More than 250,000 skilled jobs could be created. The European Wind Energy Association (EWEA) agrees with the European Commission's assessment, highlighting that additional research and significant progress in building grid infrastructure are key to the sector's success. Meeting the European Commission's ambitious plan for wind energy would require 265 GW of wind power capacity, including 55 GW of offshore wind by 2020. The 2030 target of 33 % of EU power from wind energy can be reached by meeting EWEA's 2030 installed capacity target of 400 GW from wind (EWEA, 2009).

3.10 Geothermal Technology Outlook

According to the European Geothermal Energy Consortium (EGEC), geothermal energy can substantially contribute to heating and electricity production, with ca. 20 % of the total EU consumption, or 70 Mtoe for electricity and ca. 30 % of the total EU consumption, or 150 Mtoe for heating and cooling. The availability of the resource, day and night, throughout the year, provides a back-up for the electricity grid anywhere. Thus, the 2020 target is the strengthening of the European geothermal industry by developing hydrothermal resources in Europe and expanding the Enhanced Geothermal System (EGS) concept, as well as by increasing the market penetration of geothermal heat pumps and ensuring a wider spread of geothermal district heating and cooling systems. The 2030 targets are: the decrease in EGS plant costs, the implementation of massive construction programmes, and the transfer of EGS technology outside Europe. Geothermal heat pumps and direct uses will be firmly established and further developed, notably in view of agricultural applications (e.g. heating greenhouses), new applications for pre-heating in industrial processes (high temperature), and new district heating systems for dense urban areas (EREC, 2010).

3.11 Bio-energy Technology Outlook

The leading principles for the further development of bio-energy in future energy systems are sustainability criteria, efficiency and competitiveness. The issues that will drive new developments in the coming years are the integration of bio-energy into supply structures with new conversion technologies, monitoring of bioprocesses, modelling of the whole bioprocess, the development of digestion technologies and training programmes. The technologies that have been already developed and that can have the biggest market potential are the biomass co-firing and combustion in Combined Heat and Power (CHP) plants. Currently, the weakest technology is the bio-hydrogen production, however, it is predicted to have a great market potential in the coming years. Moreover, it is expected that bio-fuels and 'high added' value chemical intermediates will attain a higher market potential with the introduction of second and third generation biomass conversion technologies.

The production of bio-fuels can improve the security of the transportation sector. The first generation of bio-fuels, mainly from Europe, will maintain a significant share of the total liquid fuels consumption. The second generation of bio-fuels from new bioprocesses coming on stream will increase the overall bio-fuels supply. Bio-refineries processing biomass into a spectrum of marketable products will be developed in the coming years and will have an important role in the 2050 strategy (EREC, 2010).

3.12 Renewable Electricity

In 2008, the installed renewable electricity capacity was more than any other conventional source of electricity. In particular, in 2008, the installed renewable electricity capacity made up 57 % of the total 23.8 GW, clearly led by wind, PV and biomass (EREC, 2010).

In order to meet Europe's 2020 climate and energy targets, the EU has to accelerate its ambitious plan of creating a single European power market, based on renewable energy sources electricity (RES-E), an EU Super Grid, and a Smart Grid in order to facilitate an intelligently and efficiently interconnected electricity system of both centralised and decentralised renewable energy installations. From now until 2020, Europe has to invest in new renewable energy production units to replace ageing plants while meeting future electricity demand. Approximately 330 GW of new power capacity needs to be built by 2020, which represents 42 % of the current EU capacity. With an average annual growth rate in renewable electricity capacity of 14 % between 2007 and 2020, the EU will have an installed renewable power capacity of about 520 GW in 2020, which means that an extra 336 GW will be installed in that time.

By 2020, the largest contribution to RES-E will come from wind, hydropower, and biomass. By 2030, this picture changes slightly and wind will be closely followed by PV (556 TWh) and hydropower (398 TWh). Wind and PV continue being the largest contributors up to 2050, but geothermal electricity will see the biggest increase in absolute terms between 2030 and 2050.

4 Greece's Sustainable Path to the Future

4.1 Energy Efficiency and Conservation

Increased adoption of energy efficient technologies is the nearest-term and lowest-cost option for moderating Greece's demand for energy, especially over the next decade. The potential energy savings available from the accelerated deployment of existing energy efficient technologies in buildings, industry, and in transportation sectors could more than offset projected increases in the country's energy consumption through 2030.

Buildings, which account for a high percentage of all energy consumed, have the greatest potential for improvements in energy efficiency. Thus, the use of currently available or emerging energy efficient technologies for buildings could lower energy consumption by 25–30 %, even with the anticipated new energy needs for buildings. These energy savings would eliminate the need of constructing new electric power generating plants except to address regional supply imbalances, replace obsolete generating assets, or substitute more environmentally benign electricity sources. Replacing incandescent lamps with compact fluorescent and new light emitting diode (LED) lamps alone could reduce the electricity use in buildings by 12 %.

Many energy efficient technologies for buildings represent attractive investment opportunities with a payback period of 2–3 years. While lack of information and capital discourages consumers and businesses from using these technologies, setting efficiency standards, incorporating efficiency into building codes, labelling product efficiency, and promoting consumer awareness could dramatically increase adoption of these measures.

The industrial and transportation sectors could also increase their energy efficiency significantly. The industrial sector could expand the use of available systems that both produce electricity and recover waste heat, along with other specific process technology improvements. Using rail for freight shipping could also reduce the transportation sector's fuel use, because it is ten times more efficient in terms of energy use than truck transportation.

4.2 New Supplies of Electricity

Although most electricity is produced conventionally, by burning fossil fuels, several non-traditional sources of electricity have the potential of significantly changing the supply mix during the next two to three decades. They can reduce greenhouse gas emissions substantially but is likely to cost consumers more than the current sources.

Figure 1 depicts the contribution of various energy sources to the total installed electric power in Greece. As can be seen the contribution of the fossil fuels (i.e. oil, gas and coal) is about 76 % of the total.

Coal-fired power plants currently generate most of the electricity consumed in Greece. Domestic coal reserves are sufficient for continued use of coal in power generation, taking into consideration future growth and demand in electricity. However, coal-fired plants produce a significant amount of CO_2, and future restrictions on greenhouse gas emissions may limit their use, unless the CO_2 is captured and stored. Carbon capture and storage (CCS) technology can capture and inject CO_2 into secure rock formations, such as deep saline aquifers, and deep coal beds. This technology has the potential of considerably reducing the amount of CO_2 emissions to the atmosphere from coal-fired plants. Refitting existing coal-fired power plants with CCS could reduce their CO_2 emissions by as much as 50 %, while new plants could eventually produce 90 % less CO_2. The potential exists to replace or refit all coal-fired power plants operating in the country with CCS plants in the future, albeit at considerably increased cost relative to existing plants. However, to demonstrate the reality of this potential at acceptable cost, public and/or private entities need to construct demonstration plants, new and retrofitted, with a variety of fuels (natural gas, biomass, and different types of coal), and carbon capture and storage technologies by 2020. These plants are needed to demonstrate that these technologies can be safely deployed.

Renewable energy sources, such as wind, solar, hydropower, geothermal, and bio-energy have a significant role to play in the future generation of the country's electricity. In 2008, conventional hydropower produced about 5 % (i.e. 3 TWh) of Greece's electricity, but its environmental impact might possibly limit its future

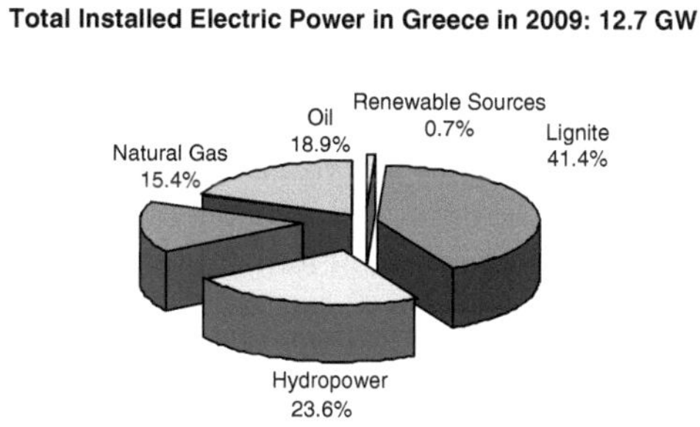

Fig. 1 Contribution of various energy sources to the total installed electric power in Greece. *Source*: Chatziargyriou (2009)

Table 1 Projected contribution of renewable energy resources to the total electric power production

Renewable energy source (RES)	2010 RES power-target (MW)	Percentage to total electric power production
Wind	3,648	10.7 %
Small hydropower plants	364	1.5 %
Biomass	103	1.1 %
Photo-voltaics	200	0.3 %
Geothermal	12	0.1 %
Large hydropower plants	3,325	6.4 %
Total	7,652	20.1 %

Source: Panagos (2009)

expansion. In 2008, non-hydropower renewable sources contributed less than 5 % of electricity. However, the use of both wind and solar power has grown dramatically in the last years. Table 1 shows the projected contribution of RES to the total installed electric power in Greece in 2010.

Overall, wind power has the highest potential in Greece, followed by solar. Apart from higher costs relative to traditional energy alternatives, neither has any technical constraints on expansion. According to the figures of Table 1, RES-E could realistically provide 20 % of the country's needs by 2020. To achieve this potential, however, Greece needs to help the price of renewable energy sources compare favourably with conventional ones. Moreover, because renewable energy sources are intermittent and geographically distributed, their large-scale use will require an expansion of and investment in the transmission and distribution of electric power. Fast-responding back-up electricity generation will be needed as well. If RES-E production increases over 20 % of the total generation, advanced electricity storage technologies will also be necessary.

4.3 The Electric Grid

The country's electric power transmission and distribution network urgently needs upgrading to improve reliability, increase security, and expand the use of energy efficient technologies. Much of the technologies to modernise the grid are available now and can help consumers to save energy, operators to be better informed, renewable energy to be incorporated, etc. The grid could be completely modernised and expanded in 20 years and the benefits, it is estimated, will significantly outweigh the costs. Carrying out modernisation and expansion simultaneously has the additional benefit of further lowering costs and implementing modifications at a faster pace.

4.4 Alternative Liquid Transportation Fuels

Petroleum is an indispensable transportation fuel today and will continue to be so for many decades. Improving vehicle efficiency is the best near-term option for reducing petroleum use. However, some fuel substitutes may become available after 2020. To reduce the country's dependence on imported petroleum, converting biomass into liquid fuels could provide, to an extent, domestic sources for transportation fuels. Cellulosic (non-food biomass) bio-fuel is another major non-petroleum option, although conversion of cellulosic energy crops has not been demonstrated on a commercial scale. Although biomass is renewable, limited availability of land and water resources would restrict its annual output. Conversion of cellulose to liquid fuels would require government incentives to farmers to sustainably grow cellulosic energy crops.

In principle, one can view all photosynthetic organisms as sunlight-driven cell factories that convert CO_2 into organic molecules with bio-fuel potential. It has been estimated that on an area basis, the productivity of photosynthetic microbes (PMs, i.e. microalgae comprising prokaryotic cyanobacteria and eukaryotic 'true' algae) is higher than that of terrestrial plants by at least one order of magnitude. However, there is huge variation among species regarding the lipid content they can attain under specific conditions. Oil contents between 20 % and 70 % of dry biomass weight have been reported and rather conservative calculations foresee yields starting at 60,000 litres/hectare. These figures illustrate the enormous potential of PMs. However, technologies that provide practical solutions, including cultivation and processing for the mass production of PMs on the scale required, are still insufficiently developed (Brennan & Owende, 2010).

The bio-refinery concept fully integrates chemicals and energy chains. The remaining biomass, after lipid extraction, can be utilised in different ways, such as in microbial conversion to methane, hydrogen, ethanol, lipids, or electricity. Additionally, chemical compounds can be extracted as valuable by-products, further benefiting the overall economics of the process. In addition to selecting suitable species as mentioned above, the genetic engineering of PMs could substantially help achieving the economical production of bio-fuel. Photosynthetic efficiency, growth, and yield are obvious traits for optimisation. At present, however, researchers have sequenced and annotated only a few algal genomes. Thus, only more research can generate a solid knowledge base on algae and lead to development of the molecular tools of genetic modification.

4.5 Future Obstacles and Policies

New emerging energy production and supply technologies have to overcome significant barriers before their widespread adoption. These barriers vary across technologies. These include the slow turnover of infrastructure, limited resources, potentially higher costs, concerns about performance, and uncertainty about restrictions on greenhouse gas emissions. As noted earlier, new energy-supply options will be more expensive than conventional fuels. In many cases, significant capital investments will be needed. Investor uncertainty about future energy prices may inhibit investments in new technologies. Policies, such as those that set efficiency standards, support renewable energy, and encourage demonstrations of CCS, solar, wind, and bio-fuels technologies, can help overcome these obstacles.

References

Brennan, L., & Owende, P. (2010). Biofuels from microalgae—A review of technologies for production, processing, and extractions of biofuels and co-products. *Renewable and Sustainable Energy Reviews, 14*(2), 557–577.

Centi, G., & Perathoner, S. (2010). Towards solar fuels form water and CO_2. *Chemistry & Sustainability, Energy & Materials, 3*(2), 195–208.

Chatziargyriou, N. (2009). *Future development of Greek electric production system*. In Workshop on green energy, International Hellenic University, Thessaloniki.

DESERTEC Foundation. (2009). *Red paper: An overview of the Desertec concept*. http://www.desertec.org/fileadmin/downloads/desertec-foundation_redpaper_3rd-edition_english.pdf. Accessed 20 Aug 2012.

Dosch, H., & de Voorde, M. H. V. (Eds.). (2009). *GENNESYS: White paper*. Stuttgart: Max-Planck-Institut für Metallforschung.

EREC. (2008, November). *Renewable energy technology roadmap: 20 % by 2020*. European Renewable Energy Council. http://www.erec.org/fileadmin/erec_docs/Documents/Publications/Renewable_Energy_Technology_Roadmap.pdf. Accessed 20 Aug 2012.

EREC. (2010, April). *RE-thinking 2050: A 100 % renewable energy vision for the European Union*. European Renewable Energy Council. http://www.rethinking2050.eu/fileadmin/documents/ReThinking2050_full_version_final.pdf. Accessed 20 Aug 2012.

European Commission. (2007, January 10). *Renewable energy roadmap. Renewable energies in the 21st century: Building a more sustainable future*. COM(2006) 848 final. Brussels.

European Commission. (2009a, April 24). *The renewable energy progress report*. COM(2009) 192 final. Brussels.

European Commission. (2009b, October 7). *Investing in the Development of Low Carbon Technologies (SET-Plan)*. COM(2009) 519. Brussels.

European Commission. (2010, November 10). *Energy 2020 – A strategy for competitive, sustainable and secure energy*. COM(2010) 639 final. Brussels.

European Commission. (2011, December 15). *Energy roadmap 2050*. COM(2011) 885 final. Brussels.

EWEA. (2009, November). *Pure power: Wind energy targets for 2020 and 2030*. European Wind Energy Association. http://www.ewea.org/fileadmin/ewea_documents/documents/publications/reports/Pure_Power_Full_Report.pdf. Accessed 20 Aug 2012.

IEA. (2008). *Energy technology perspectives: Scenarios and strategies to 2050*. Paris: International Energy Agency.

IEA. (2009). *World energy outlook*. Paris: International Energy Agency.

IEA. (2011). *World energy outlook*. Paris: International Energy Agency.
Lior, N. (2008). Energy resource and use: The present situation and possible paths to the future. *Energy, 33*(6), 842–857.
Martinot, E., Dienst, C., Weiliang, L., & Qimin, C. (2007). Renewable energy futures: Targets, scenarios and pathways. *Annual Review of Environment and Resources, 32*(1), 205–239.
OECD. (2011). *Towards green growth: A summary for policy makers*. Paris: Organisation for Economic Co-operation and Development.
Palz, W. (2005). *A PV roadmap for Europe*. Bonn: World Council for Renewable Energy. http://www.wcre.de/en/images/downloads/wrea_palz_pv_roadmap_europe.pdf. Accessed 20 Aug 2012.
Panagos, T. (2009). *Green energy perspectives*. In Workshop on green energy, International Hellenic University, Thessaloniki.
Parida, B., Iniyan, S., & Goic, R. (2011). A review of solar photovoltaic technologies. *Renewable and Sustainable Energy Reviews, 15*(3), 1625–1636.
PriceWaterHouseCoopers (PWC). (2009, September). *Delivering of earth's solar potential: Concentrating solar thermal power as a solution to the world's energy challenges*. http://www.pwc.com/gx/en/sustainability/assets/earths-solar-potential.pdf. Accessed 20 Aug 2012.
The Danish Government. (2011, February). *Energy strategy 2050 – From coal, oil and gas to green energy*. Copenhagen: The Danish Ministry of Climate and Energy. http://www.ens.dk/Documents/Netboghandel%20-%20publikationer/2011/Energy_Strategy_2050.pdf. Accessed 20 Aug 2012.
The PEW Charitable Trusts. (2010). *Who's winning the clean energy race: Growth, competition and opportunity in the world's largest economies*. Washington, DC. http://www.pewtrusts.org/uploadedFiles/wwwpewtrustsorg/Reports/Global_warming/G-20%20Report.pdf. Accessed 20 Aug 2012.
U.S. Department of Energy. (2005, April 18–21). *Basic research needs for solar energy utilization*. Report of the basic energy sciences workshop on solar energy utilization. Office of Science. http://science.energy.gov/~/media/bes/pdf/reports/files/seu_rpt.pdf. Accessed 20 Aug 2012.
U.S. Department of Energy. (2008, December). *New science for a secure and sustainable energy future*. A report from the basic energy sciences advisory committee. http://science.energy.gov/~/media/bes/pdf/reports/files/nsssef_rpt.pdf. Accessed 20 Aug 2012.
VTT. (2009). *Energy Visions 2050*. VTT technical research centre of Finland. http://www.vtt.fi/files/publications/EnergyVisions_2050.pdf. Accessed 20 Aug 2012.
WBCSD. (2005). *Pathways to 2050, energy and climate change*. Conches-Geneva, World business council for sustainable development, facts and trends series. http://www.wbcsd.org/web/publications/pathways.pdf. Accessed 20 Aug 2012.

The Burgas–Alexandroupolis Pipeline: Macroeconomic Impact for Greece

Periklis Gogas and Theophilos Papadimitriou

1 Introduction

The proposed investment plan for the construction of the Burgas–Alexandroupolis Pipeline (BAP) is a significant energy transportation project for South East Europe and for the concerned local economies in Greece and Bulgaria. The BAP is designed to serve as a channel supplementing the maritime route of crude oil transportation from the Black Sea and the Caspian Sea to the international markets. The construction and operation of the pipeline is expected to have a significant impact, direct and indirect, on the national and local economies in terms of increased demand for goods and services, government revenue, and employment. We examine the financial viability of the BAP in comparison with all alternative scenarios, as this is a prerequisite for assessing the macroeconomic effects on the national and local economy. We also explore the project's financial viability using the Cash Flow analysis, the Internal Rate of Return (IRR), the Net Present Value (NPV), and the Break-Even Point (BEP) analysis. Finally, after establishing the viability of the investment plan, we investigate its macroeconomic impact on local and national unemployment, the GDP, and local government revenue. The impact appears to be significant, especially at the local government level.

2 Energy, Pipelines, and Development

The construction and operation of a large-scale pipeline is expected to have a significant positive impact on the host economies (Afrodad, 2007; Chase & Leistritz, 1982). In the construction phase, the initial investment in the

P. Gogas (✉) • T. Papadimitriou
Department of International Economic Relations and Development, Democritus University of Thrace, Komotini 69100, Greece
e-mail: perrygogas@gmail.com; papadimi@ierd.duth.gr

P. Sklias and N. Tzifakis (eds.), *Greece's Horizons*, The Konstantinos Karamanlis Institute for Democracy Series on European and International Affairs,
DOI 10.1007/978-3-642-34534-0_15,

infrastructure, the main pipeline, and the peripheral facilities is significant. Depending on the host country's level of economic growth and the total scale of the particular project, such investments have been found to have large positive effects on the GDP. For example, Azerbaijan saw a 35 % growth in its GDP in the year following the construction and initial operation of the Baku–Tbilisi–Ceyhan (BTC) pipeline. However, even countries that are merely hosts of the pipeline, and not the producers of the transported fuel like Azerbaijan, enjoy substantial transit fees. In the case of the BTC pipeline, Georgia and Turkey are expected to receive an average of $62.5 and $290 million for each year of the 40 years of operation. Moreover, the macroeconomic multiplicative effects of these inflows are even greater. For example, in the case of Georgia, they are estimated to be 1.2 % of its annual GDP.

3 The Burgas–Alexandroupolis Pipeline

The proposed project for the construction of the Burgas–Alexandroupolis pipeline (BAP) is one of the largest investment plans ever designed for Greece. The project is of great importance not only because of the amount of investment involved, but, more significantly, for the income that is expected to be generated from the BAP's operation. The project's importance for Greece resides not merely in the revenue generated by the Implementing Organisation (IO) and the corresponding taxes and fees, but in the offset transit fee payments proposed by the IO to the local governments. Thus, the BAP is expected to have a significant effect on the Greek macroeconomic environment, in terms of the impact of a foreign direct investment and the corresponding multiplicative consequences for the national economy. However, in addition to the general macroeconomic effects, the BAP's impact on the regional economy of the Evros prefecture is expected to be vastly greater. We analyse all expected national and regional effects of the project in the following sections.

The proposed investment plan was at the epicentre of heated discussions and political procedures for the last couple of decades in both Greece and Bulgaria. It was the object of controversy and public discussions, particularly in the Evros prefecture in northeast Greece, where the pipeline is scheduled to be constructed. The proposed pipeline will transport crude oil produced in the area of the North Caspian Sea and the Russian Federation for final destination in Europe and elsewhere. Currently, the crude oil produced in the above region is transported via tankers through the Straits of the Dardanelles or via the BTC (Baku–Tbilisi–Ceyhan) pipeline and the Mediterranean Sea. It is expected that future global economic growth will lead to an inevitable surge in the demand for energy in general and thus also for crude oil. As a result, the production, export, and transportation of oil from the North Caspian Sea and the Russian Federation are expected to increase rapidly. The BAP, therefore, aims to supplement the maritime transport of crude oil through the Straits of the Dardanelles. The latter involves tankers, which are subject to a physically limited capacity for maritime safety reasons.[1] It is important to note here that the BAP is not designed to replace sea transportation through the Straits, but rather to serve as a competing cost effective alternative and additional route. According to plan, the pipeline will be part of an integrated combined transportation scheme that incorporates both sea and land transportation. Tankers will transport crude oil from Black Sea ports to the port-city of Burgas in Bulgaria. From there the crude oil will pass through the pipeline to a sea platform off the port of Alexandroupolis in Greece, for transhipment to tankers and delivery to the final international destination. The pipeline is scheduled to be completed in 2 years. It will operate at a maximum 70 % capacity or 35 MTA (million tons per annum) for the first 3 years and after that at its full capacity of 50 MTA. The pipeline is designed for a total service life of 30 years. The total length is 259 km and the diameter is 42 in.

4 Economic Viability of the Burgas–Alexandroupolis Pipeline

In order for the proposed BAP to have any macroeconomic or regional impact, it must be a financially viable project at the microeconomic level of the Implementing Organization (IO). Financial viability is measured in terms of profitability and liquidity resulting from the pipeline's operation. In this section, we perform a detailed cash-flow analysis using a large number of alternative scenarios and a dynamic analysis of the sensitivity of the results to a wide range of significant parameters. This sensitivity analysis is necessary in order to examine the degree of the dependence of a scenario's results to its basic assumptions. The alternative scenarios for the study have been created by changing the four fundamental variables that significantly affect the financial returns of the project's IO—the traffic volume (M), the amount of crude oil transported through the BAP, the transportation fee (T) in US dollars per ton of crude oil transported, the USD/EUR exchange rate (I), and the total estimated construction cost (K) of the project.

4.1 Transportation Fee Scenarios

In the basic scenario, the transportation fee (T) is set on the basis of international standards regarding similar projects in the pipeline industry, adjusting for the BAP's total length and transportation capacity. In this scenario, we use a transportation fee of $10 for a ton of crude oil from Burgas to Alexandroupolis. In the optimistic scenario, the fee is set to $12 per ton of crude oil, while in the pessimistic scenario it is set to $8.

[1] For a discussion on the issue of safety in the straits, see Ozturk (2002).

Table 1 Initial scenarios: alternative parameter values

	Basic scenario	Optimistic scenario	Pessimistic scenario
Traffic volume(tons)	35,000,000	50,000,000	25,000,000
Transportation fee ($/ton)	11.00	13.00	9.00
Exchange rate ($/€)	1.25	1.10	1.40
Construction cost (€)	1,250,000,000	1,000,000,000	1,500,000,000

4.2 Exchange Rate Scenarios

The USD/EUR exchange rate affects the expected net cash flows for the IO operating the BAP. This is because while the company's revenues from the operation of the pipeline are measured in US dollars, the overheads and most other expenses and costs are paid in euros. This creates an exchange rate risk for the IO. At this point, we need to emphasise that the main cost variable for the IO is the annual offset payments to the local governments in exchange for the right of passage of the pipeline. These offset payments are set at $1 per ton and thus they do not add to the exchange rate risk. In the basic scenario, the USD/EUR exchange rate is set at $1.25 per euro and in the optimistic and pessimistic scenarios at $1.10 and $1.40 respectively.

4.3 Construction Cost Scenarios

The IO has estimated that the total construction cost (K) will be between €1 billion and €1.5 billion. Thus, we use the dollar value of €1.25 for the basic scenario and €1 and €1.5 billion for the optimistic and pessimistic scenarios respectively. In Table 1, we summarise the range of values that are used in our three initial scenarios.

5 Cash Flow Results

Based on the values for the three scenarios,[2] total revenues range from €308,000,000 in the basic scenario to €590,909,091 and €160,714,286 in the optimistic and pessimistic scenarios respectively. Total operating costs range from €61,908,000 in the basic scenario to €96,817,091 and €41,622,286 in the optimistic and pessimistic scenarios. These results translate to a net profit, after tax deductions, of €153,319,000, €345,569,000, and €51,819,000 for the basic, optimistic, and pessimistic scenarios respectively. The Internal rate of Return (IRR) for the three scenarios is 15.37 % for the basic, 37.88 % for the optimistic, and 5.35 % for the pessimistic scenario. The Net Present Value of the investment,

[2] Detailed results were omitted due to space limitations and are available upon request.

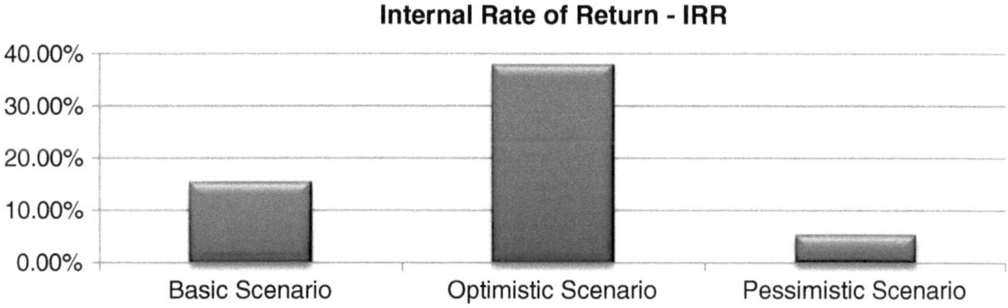

Fig. 1 Estimated IRRs for the initial scenarios

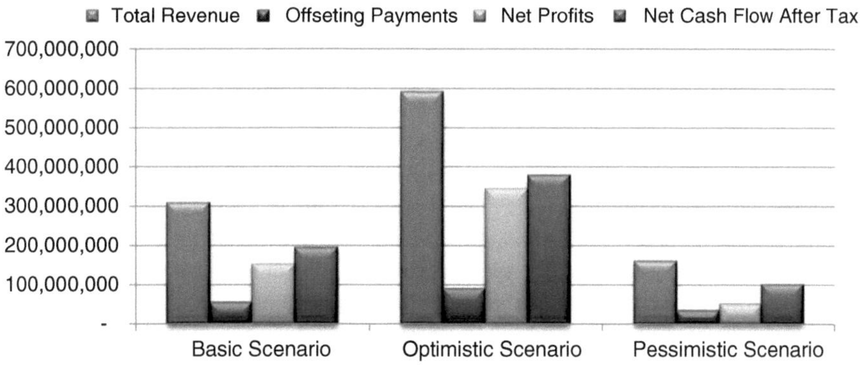

Fig. 2 Basic cash flow results for the initial scenarios

with a discount rate of 5 %, is €1,659,650,404.33 in the basic scenario, €4,590,364,643.72 in the optimistic scenario, and €57,555,146.54 in the pessimistic scenario. From the above results, we conclude that in all cases, with the possible exception of the IRR for the pessimistic scenario, the proposed investment plan appears economically viable with high IRRs and with significantly positive NPVs, justifying the implementation of the project. Figures 1, 2, and 3 summarise these results.

6 Sensitivity Analysis of the Initial Scenarios

The next step is to investigate the sensitivity of the above results to asymmetric changes in the four fundamental variables. These variables are, the traffic volume (M), the transportation fee (T), the exchange rate between the euro and the US dollar (I), and the total cost of the investment (K). In this case, for each of the three initial scenarios, basic (1), optimistic (2) and pessimistic (3), we create eight different sub-scenarios, by allowing one fundamental variable at a time to take the two values from the other scenarios. For example, we start with the basic scenario (1) and create two more sub-scenarios, by letting the fundamental variable for the traffic volume (denoted as M1 in

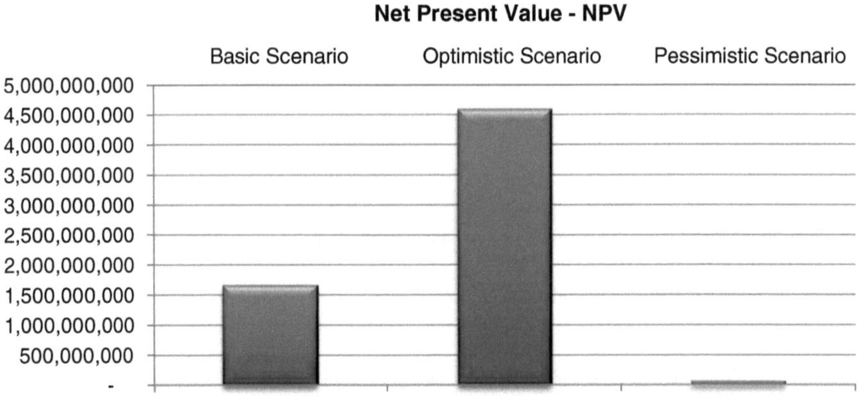

Fig. 3 NPV results for the initial scenarios

the basic scenario) first to take the value from the optimistic scenario (denoted as M2) and then the value from the pessimistic scenario (denoted as M3). Thus, for each one of the three initial scenarios we create eight more, resulting in twenty-four new scenarios for the sensitivity analysis. By doing this, we are able to evaluate the sensitivity of the initial scenarios to changes in a specific variable. We omit the detailed sensitivity results due to space limitations (these results are available on request). From the above analysis of the sensitivity of the initial scenarios to the asymmetric changes in the four fundamental variables of the cash flow analysis, we conclude the following:

6.1 Basic Scenario

Changes in the traffic volume from 25 MTA to 50 MTA have the most significant impact on the projected figures of the Cash Flow of the project. The change in net profit ranges from −35.22 % to +52.83 %. These translate into €99,319,000 net profit for the pessimistic M3 to €234,319,000 for the optimistic M2 traffic volume, compared to the basic scenario's €153,319,000 net profits in the case of no asymmetric changes. The IRR, as expected, is very sensitive to changes in the traffic volume, the transportation fee, and the construction cost, with minimum and maximum values of −4.64 % for M3 and 6.64 % for M2. For the NPV we observe high sensitivity to the traffic volume and to a lesser degree to the transportation fee, with values ranging from −47.64 % for M3 to 71.45 % for M2.

6.2 Optimistic Scenario

Changes in the traffic volume produce the greatest changes in absolute and percentage terms in the project's financial results, followed by the transportation fee and the exchange rate. The construction cost has only marginal influence on the results, with the exception of the IRR, which in the case of K1 and K3 (basic and pessimistic construction cost), is reduced by 7.42 and 12.38 percentage points respectively. Net profit reduction ranges, in all asymmetric changes, from −1.81 % to −54.26 %, in the case of K1 and M3 respectively. The figures in all the alternative scenarios are, as expected, lower, with the exception of the Net Cash Flow after tax deductions (which shows an increase from 0.55 % to 1.10 % for K1 and K3 respectively). This is because of the increased depreciation due to the higher construction costs K1 and K3, which are subtracted from the project's taxable income.

6.3 Pessimistic Scenario

In this scenario, the traffic volume is again the most important factor in the BAP's cash flows. Net profits are significantly increased by 72.37 % in the pessimistic scenario for traffic volume M1, and by 180.92 % for traffic volume M2. The second most important factor affecting the project's Net Profits is the transportation fee with percentage changes 51.69 % and 103.38 % for T1 and T2 respectively. The exchange rate and the construction cost have a smaller impact on Net Profits. The IRR increases most for M2, T2, and K2 (7.31, 4.35, and 3.66 respectively). The same three variables, and with the same order of significance, affect the NPV as well. The NPV appears to be by far the most sensitive financial variable in the pessimistic scenario. It is dramatically increased by the asymmetric changes ranging from 286.17 % in case of I1 to 2,384.74 % in case of M2.

7 Break-Even Point (BEP) Analysis

The BEP is the volume or amount of sales for which a company's total revenue equals its total cost. From this analysis, a firm can estimate the minimum level of sales that make it profitable. Underlying this significant threshold is the factor of cost. The project's total cost is divided into fixed and variable cost. Fixed cost is independent of the volume of production and sales. Variable cost is a function of the units of production. An increase in sales implies a proportional increase in variable cost. Next, for each one of our initial scenarios (basic, optimistic, and pessimistic) we estimate the BEP for the project and we calculate the relative elasticities of the BEP with respect to the fundamental variables: traffic volume (M), transportation fee (T), and construction cost (K).

7.1 Break-Even Point with Respect to the Traffic Volume

In the basic scenario, the traffic volume is 35,000,000 tons and the BEP is calculated at 6,607,593 tons. At this level of crude oil transportation through the BAP, the project has neither profit nor loss. This implies an elasticity of units of sale with

Table 2 Break-Even Point with respect to the traffic volume (tons)

Scenario	BEP	Traffic volume	Elasticity (%)
Basic	6,607,593	35,000,000	81.12
Optimistic	3,924,133	50,000,000	92.15
Pessimistic	11,181,600	25,000,000	55.27

Table 3 Break-Even Point with respect to the transportation fee

Scenario	BEP	Transportation fee	Elasticity (%)
Basic	3.70	11.00	66.36
Optimistic	2.86	13.00	78.00
Pessimistic	5.13	9.00	43.00

respect to the BEP equal to 81.12 %. Thus, the traffic volume will have to fall by 81.12 % before the implementing organisation experiences any losses.[3]

7.2 Break-Even Point with Respect to the Transportation Fee

Next, we estimate the BEP for the project with respect to the transportation fee in US dollars. It is presented in Table 3. In the Basic Scenario, this fee is set to $11 and the BEP is at $3.70. At this price for the transportation of crude oil through the BAP, the project has neither profit nor loss. This implies an elasticity of the transportation fee with respect to the BEP equal to 66.36 %. Thus, the price will have to fall by 66.36 % before the implementing organisation experiences any losses.

7.3 Break-Even Point (BEP) with Respect to the Construction Cost

Finally, we estimate the BEP for the project with respect to the construction cost of the Burgas–Alexandroupolis pipeline. The results are presented in Table 4. For the basic scenario, the construction cost is €1,250,000,000 and the BEP is at €7,382,760,000. At this level of construction cost, the project has neither profit nor loss. This implies an elasticity of 490.62 % with respect to the BEP. Thus, the construction cost will have to increase by 490.62 % before the implementing organisation experiences any losses. Tables 2, 3, and 4 summarise the above results.

[3] Full tables with the detailed results of the Break-Even Point Analysis can be obtained from the authors.

Table 4 Break-Even Point with respect to the construction cost

Scenario	BEP	Construction cost	Elasticity (%)
Basic	7,382,760,000	1,250,000,000	−490.62
Optimistic	14,822,760,000	1,000,000,000	−1,382.28
Pessimistic	3,572,760,000	1,500,000,000	−138.18

8 The Macroeconomic Impact of the Burgas–Alexandroupolis Pipeline

According to the microeconomic viability analysis in the previous section, the BAP will be profitable. We can now investigate the expected macroeconomic effects of the project to the national and local economy. First, we investigate the impact of the initial investment to the total demand in both the local and national economies, taking into account the macroeconomic multipliers for income and employment. Second, we estimate the impact of the offsetting payments to the local government revenue for the period of operation of the pipeline.

9 The Investment Multiplier

The total macroeconomic impact resulting from the implementation of the proposed investment for the BAP includes the direct increase in demand (equal to the construction cost and all related expenses in the construction phase of the pipeline) and the indirect increase in total demand from the multiplicative effects to the economy of the initial demand stimulus. Employment is affected in a similar way, first, by the people directly employed in the construction phase and the subsequent operation of the pipeline and, second, by the multiplicative effects of these positions to the employment in related sectors such as housing, food and beverages, etc. In macroeconomics, an investment as an autonomous variable (a variable that does not depend on income) has multiplicative effects on the total demand and total income in the economy. The investment multiplier is represented as $\prod_I = 1/1(1 - mpc)$ where mpc is the marginal propensity to consume and it is the first derivative of the consumption function with respect to the income. We know that $mpc = \partial c/\partial y$. Here y is the income and C is the consumption. The final change in total income as a result of a change in the investment is represented as $\Delta y = \Pi_I \times \Delta I$. Here, Δy is the final change in income and ΔI represents the initial change in investment.

10 Multiplicative Effects on the National Economy

It is estimated that the final cost of investment for the BAP project will be approximately 1, 1.25, and 1.5 billion euros in the optimistic, basic, and pessimistic scenarios respectively. According to plans, 48 % of the project will be carried out in the Greek side of the pipeline, in the prefecture of Evros. This implies that the total investment expenditure on the Greek side will be between 480 and 720 million euros. The marginal propensity to consume for Greece is estimated to be 0.8, which implies an investment multiplier equal to 5. This multiplier takes into account the total cash flows generated in the economy from an initial investment. Thus, for the total actual investment scheduled to be made in the Evros prefecture we estimate a multiplicative final increase in total demand equal to 2.4, 3.0, and 3.6 billion euros, for the pessimistic, basic, and optimistic scenarios respectively. These multiplicative effects correspond to 0.96 %, 1.20 %, and 1.44 % respectively of the GDP of Greece in 2010.

11 Multiplicative Effects on the Local Economy

Based on the above investment multiplier, calculated to be equal to 5 on the basis of various studies, and assuming that of the total investment made in each of the three initial scenarios, 20 % will be spent directly within the Evros prefecture, we estimate the total multiplicative effects on the local economy. The following estimates take into account the recent fiscal crisis in Greece and its impact on the rates of growth. The implementation of the BAP project will entail a direct investment expenditure of €96,000,000, €120,000,000, and €144,000,000 in the three initial scenarios. Thus, the multiplicative effects on the local economy will be €480,000,000, €600,000,000, and €720,000,000 respectively. Based on the projected cash flows of the project and the projected GDP,[4] the percentage increase in the GDP will range from 19.2 % to 31.68 % per year.[5]

World Bank (2003) and other similar studies[6] show that the creation of one job position in similar projects leads to an indirect increase of 5 or 10 new jobs in businesses that support the operation of such projects. It is expected that the project will employ, on the Greek side, 140 persons. Therefore, the number of jobs indirectly created, for the construction and operation of the pipeline, will be between 700 and 1,400. The total work force of the prefecture is 59,000 for 2011 and the unemployment rate is 21 % for the same year. The implementation of the project can reduce the number of unemployed by 1,400–11,100 persons, resulting in a reduced unemployment rate of 18.6 %.

[4] GDP and unemployment figures are from the National Statistical Service of Greece accounts.

[5] Full results are available upon request.

[6] See for example Sadler (1970), Murdock, Leistritz, Hamm, & Hwang (1984), Lynn (2004), and Dinc (2002).

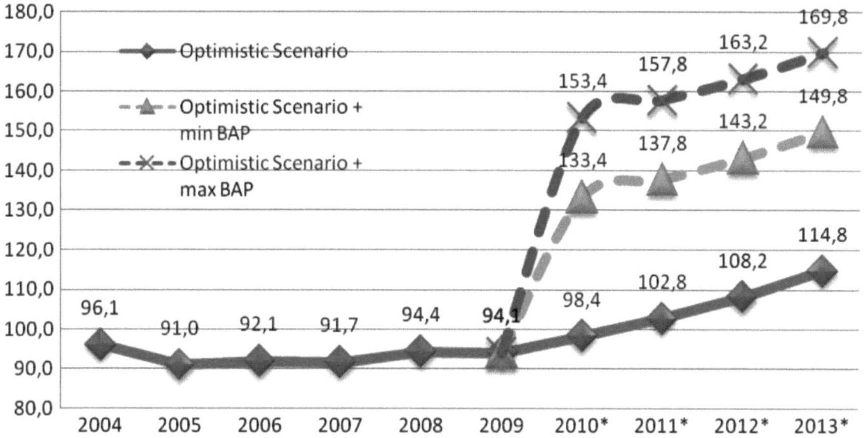

Fig. 4 Total local government revenue: Optimistic scenario with and without the BAP (constant prices 2005 million €)

12 Fiscal Impact on the Local Government

The implementation of the BAP project will bring significant revenues to the local government. Offset payments from the implementing organisation, at the rate of $1 per ton of transported crude oil, will constitute direct benefits. This will provide a total revenue of $35,000,000–55,000,000 for the Evros prefecture, depending on the scenario we consider. These amounts would have significant impact on the fiscal resources of the prefecture and could finance important public investments in developing local infrastructure, both social and educational. Such development projects can provide significant advantages to the local economy compared to those of other neighbouring Greek localities. Indirectly, the operation of the pipeline will generate considerable revenue for the local government through various local taxes and fees. This revenue will be generated both from the direct operation of the BAP and from the secondary increase in total demand and expenditure of the prefecture. Figure 4 depicts the sensitivity of the optimistic scenario for the total local government revenue to the minimum and maximum operation of the BAP. The projected revenue without the implementation of the BAP is 114.8 million euros for the year 2013. This number increases to 149.8 in the case of minimum offsetting inflows from the operation of the pipeline, and to 169.8 in the case of maximum operational capacity. In Fig. 5, we show that in the case of the pessimistic scenario, local government revenues are estimated at 92.4 million euros for 2013. This increases to 127.4 and 147.4 million euros respectively, in the minimum and maximum offsetting inflow scenarios from the BAP.

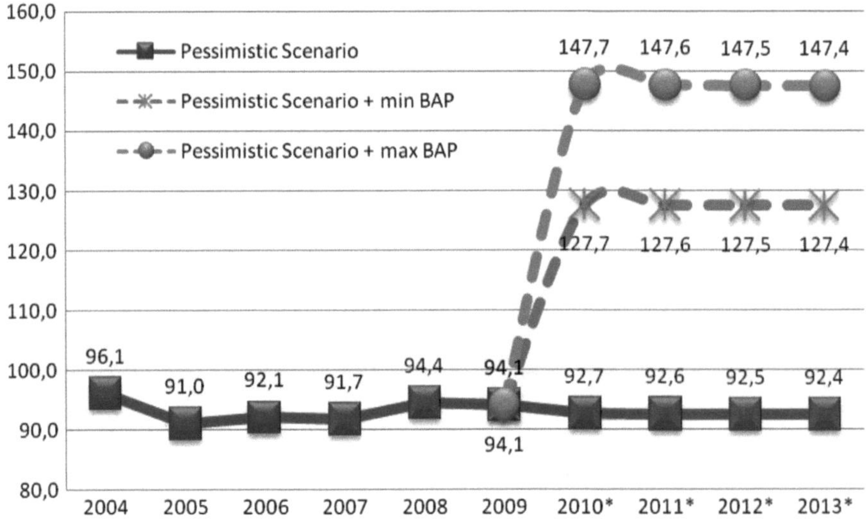

Fig. 5 Total local government revenue: pessimistic scenario with and without the BAP (constant prices 2005 million €)

Finally, Fig. 6 depicts the above optimistic and pessimistic scenarios for the local government revenue and minimum and maximum offsetting payments from the BAP in the same graph, to provide a better view of the sensitivity of the total revenue in all possible outcomes.

Conclusion

The proposed Burgas–Alexandroupolis Pipeline (BAP) appears to be an important investment for Greece, particularly for the Evros prefecture. We constructed three initial scenarios for the fundamental variables that have substantial influence on the project's success, namely, the traffic volume, the transportation fee, the exchange rate, and the construction cost to obtain the basic, the optimistic and the pessimistic scenarios. For each of these initial scenarios, and in order to measure the sensitivity of our results to the fundamental variable values, we constructed eight more scenarios by altering the value of one fundamental variable at a time to get 24 additional scenarios. According to these results and on the basis of the corresponding Internal Rate of Return (IRR) and Net Present Value (NPV) for each scenario, the proposed project appears to be viable in most alternative scenarios, exhibiting high IRR and NPV values. Only in the case of the pessimistic scenario is the IRR as low as 5.35 % and the NPV €57,555,146.54. The Break-Even Point analysis provides additional evidence in support of the viability of the project, as both the BEPs calculated are low enough to guarantee the profitability of the BAP given the range of transportation capacities expected in all scenarios.

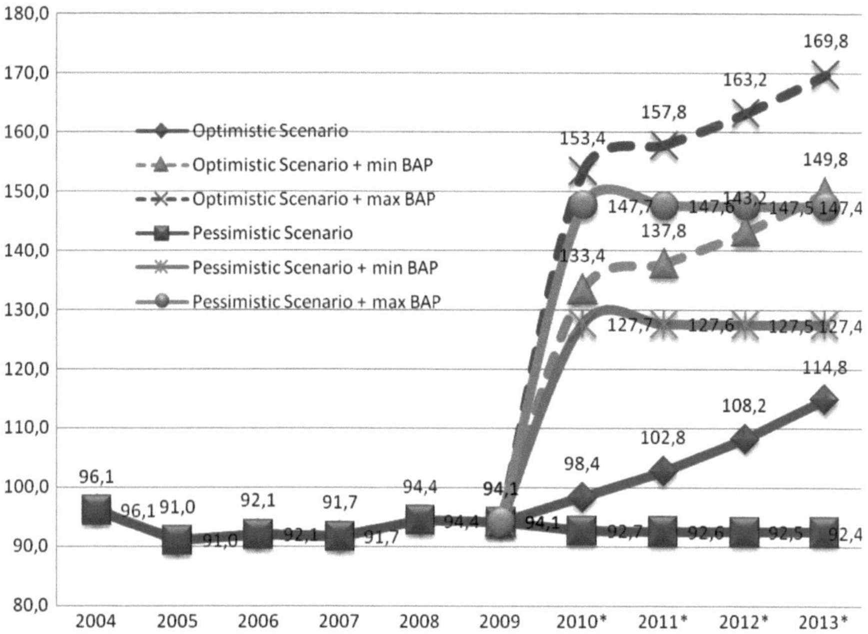

Fig. 6 Total local government revenue: optimistic and pessimistic scenarios (no BAP, min BAP, max BAP, constant prices 2005 million €)

Moreover, the elasticities of the profits are sufficiently high, providing considerable buffer for adverse market situations.

As the above analysis seemed to indicate that the proposed investment project was profitable, we examined the macroeconomic impact of the Burgas–Alexandroupolis Pipeline on the local and national economies. We estimated a significant direct and indirect increase of total demand equal to 2.4, 3.0, and 3.6 billion euros for the pessimistic, basic, and optimistic scenarios respectively. This translates into a sizeable total increase in national GDP, measuring 0.96 %, 1.20 %, and 1.44 % respectively for the three scenarios. At the same time, the implementation of the BAP is expected to create between 700 and 1,400 direct and indirect jobs in the local economy. This effect can reduce the local economy's unemployment rate by 2.4 percentage points. Probably the most important impact of the BAP to the local and national economy stems from the offset payments promised by the implementing organisation to the local government, at the rate of $1 per ton of crude oil transported. This translates into estimated total revenue for the local government ranging from €35,000,000 to €55,000,000 per year, depending on the scenario that we are considering. Adding these offsetting payments to the local government's revenue for all plausible operational capacities of the pipeline, we find that in the pessimistic scenario, the total revenue will increase from 92.4 million euros (without the BAP) to €127.4 and €147.4 million euros (in situations of minimum and maximum offsetting inflows, respectively, from the BAP). In the optimistic scenario for local government revenues, without the BAP the total local government receipts are €114.8 million and this significantly increases to €149.8 million for minimum offsetting payments and to €169.8 for maximum offsetting payments. It is clear from the above that the implementation of the Burgas–Alexandroupolis Pipeline will be a viable and profitable business venture, with important macroeconomic impact in terms of GDP, employment, and fiscal gains, for the national economy and much more significantly for the local economy and government.

Should these revenues be utilised in a manner that they enhanced the local economy's infrastructure and work force, creating significant economies of scale, industrial specialisation, and increase in human capital value (utilising the expected spillover effects), they could render the region a model of peripheral economic development. After the severe recession that hit the Greek economy because of the austerity measures following the fiscal crisis, income and employment are at the lowest levels in decades. The economy desperately needs stabilisation and growth. Large foreign direct investment in the energy sector can provide, as discussed above, the necessary funds and cash inflow to become a new pillar of development, employment, and government revenue. It can be the spark igniting the flame of growth, reviving the economic spirit and reversing the recession.

References

Afrodad. (2007). *The Chad–Cameroon oil pipeline project: An analysis of the socioeconomic and environmental impact*. Zimbabwe: Afrodad Publications.

Chase, R. A., & Leistritz, F. L. (1982). Socioeconomic impact assessment of onshore petroleum activity. In *Second international conference on oil and environment*. Halifax: Nova Scotia.

Dinc, M. (2002). *Regional and local economic analysis tools*. Washington: The World Bank. http://info.worldbank.org/etools/docs/library/128789/Dinc%202001.pdf. Accessed 17 March 2012.

Lynn, K. T. (2004). Oil-led development: Social, political, and economic consequences. In Cleveland, Cutler J (Eds.) *Encyclopedia of energy*, Vol. IV (pp. 661–672). New York: Elsevier.

Murdock, S.H., Leistritz, F.L., Hamm, R.R. & Hwang, S.S. (1984). An assessment of the accuracy and the utility of socioeconomic impact assessments. In C.M. Mckel, D.G. Browne, E.C. Cruze, W.R. Freudenburg, R.L. Perrine & F. Roach, (Eds.), *Paradoxes of western energy development: How can we maintain the land and the people if we develop?* (pp. 265–296). Boulder: Westview.

Ozturk, A. (2002). From oil pipelines to oil straits: The Caspian pipeline politics and environmental protection of the Istanbul and the Canakkalle Straits. *Journal of Balkan and Near Eastern Studies, 4*(1), 57–74.

Sadler, P. (1970). Regional multipliers and input–output analysis. Economic Research Paper, Bangor.

World Bank. (2003). *Social analysis sourcebook: Incorporating social dimensions into bank-supported projects*. Washington: World Bank Publications.

Transportation as a Driver of Growth in Greece: Policy-Making Issues

John C. Mourmouris

1 Introduction

The Greek authorities consider investment in transportation as a driver of growth. However, this remains an unproven assumption. Even if transportation were a key factor in economic growth, there is a crucial question about the optimum amount of transportation, in both urban and non-urban areas, for a given country at a particular stage of development. The present challenges—that of climate change and of environment in general, economic recession, energy issues, and substitution technologies such as telecommunication—show that transportation is not necessarily compatible with or a prerequisite for sustainable development. Thus, there is no unanimity regarding determination of desirable capacities.

The transport sector is one of the basic structures of modern society depending on

- Geographic and demographic factors;
- Economic, political, and social factors;
- Technological factors.

Planning, programming, and implementing transport investments are difficult tasks, whether they are integral parts of a comprehensive process, or they are used as more traditional means of sub-optimising in an individual sector. The above becomes more crucial for the Greek economy where planning and programming are not systematic but are rather random and seemingly chaotic. Therefore, the impact of transportation on the Greek economy is more difficult to discern. In the following sections I will try to analyse policy making issues by defining the objectives of transportation investment, evaluating some transportation projects, and discussing the issues that need to be addressed when transportation is associated with growth and development.

J.C. Mourmouris (✉)
Department of International Economic Relations and Development, Democritus University of Thrace, Komotini 69100, Greece
e-mail: jomour@eexi.gr

P. Sklias and N. Tzifakis (eds.), *Greece's Horizons*, The Konstantinos Karamanlis Institute for Democracy Series on European and International Affairs,
DOI 10.1007/978-3-642-34534-0_16,

2 Problem Definition: Objectives of Transportation

In order to determine the impact of transportation investment on the Greek economy one needs to define the objectives of transportation and the rationale for such an investment. This is the first step towards a comprehensive policy.

So, a national transportation system or the formulation of a national transportation policy must begin with the most difficult question: 'Which are the national purposes that the transportation system is intended to serve'? (Heymann, 1965). Unfortunately, one hardly ever asks this question with regard to the Greek economy. If one were to ask this question, one would immediately become aware of the painful fact that large parts of the society are in conflict with national objectives. These are well-known conflicts, between regional interests and national interest, and even more between departments with different degrees of development. Therefore, the traditional question 'which infrastructure and where' is not adequate.

Transportation is a means to serve other aims, and therefore, it needs to be carefully considered in connection with a national plan and its objectives. Some of these objectives are economic—to increase industrial or agricultural production, to exploit natural resources, to restart the regional economy, etc. The other objectives are non-economic—to strengthen the country's cohesion and defence, preserve the environment, etc. (Heymann, 1965). Economic and non-economic objectives are not always in the same direction and major conflicts might occur. Moreover, notorious examples of expensive transportation infrastructure that have never been used (e.g. the second luxurious airport of Valence in Spain constructed for the Olympic Games) make such decisions quite dangerous during a period of recession and capital scarcity.

The fact that transportation objectives are competing, conflicting, incommensurate, and often incompatible with one another, poses a set of serious problems for the economist trying to optimise the transportation needs and system.

The emphasis of the objectives is on *economic efficiency*, in the broad sense of the term. Therefore, economic analysis plays a predominant role.

However, let us try to examine the role and limitations of economic analysis with regard to such problems. Economics deal primarily with the logic of the allocation process, which instructs us how to choose, and not what to choose (Heymann, 1965). An economist is at his best in finding the most efficient or the least costly method of achieving a simple and well-defined objective.

The transportation economist must recognise that the choice among alternative national transport systems fundamentally affects and in part determines the nation's path of development and its strategy for growth. This is not an economic efficiency problem but a high-level policy decision, for which no single criterion is appropriate. Decisions aiming at 'maximizing national growth' are bound to be somewhat intuitive and based on the faith that some objectives are much more important than other objectives (Heymann, 1965), making the choice faces numerous problems, such as quantitative versus qualitative data, conflicting objectives, uncertain information, conflict between locality and nation, optimisation issues, and reckoning with political orientations.

In a planned economy, one can make transportation and location choices much more deliberately and consistently. As regards the location of an economic activity (Heymann, 1965), we can emphasise three main objectives:

- To redress the 'unevenness' of economic activity;
- To increase the proportion of output coming from the formerly neglected regions of the country;
- To reconcile the principle of comparative advantage with that of simultaneous and similar levels of development in an open society.

Minimising transportation demand by using substitution technologies provides an interesting task for planners.

The location of industrial plants and the location of workers' housing near industrial plants are often motivated by the desire to economise on transportation rather than by broader economic and social considerations.

The people providing land transportation by building railways are merely responding to the economic opportunity, admittedly enhanced by the government's land grant policies (Heymann, 1965), to which transportation creates or supports new activities will surely depend upon the existence of other conditions affecting the economy—the existence of industrial infrastructure and raw materials, the quality of administration, peace and order, the education system, the nature of legal and property relationships, and other aspects of a nation's 'will to grow'.

3 The Economic Evaluation of Transportation Projects

The economic evaluation of a transportation project measures the impact of the transportation investment on a particular economy.

The investment in transportation is not made for its own sake but as a means for achieving broader aims, and it acts as a catalyst for development.

It is a common assumption that a broad availability of transportation is an essential precondition for economic development in most low-income societies. Yet, this is far from being true for developed countries, including Greece. Therefore, the evaluation of transportation investments in Greece would depend on the nature and purpose of such investment. Moreover, as no serious feasibility or viability study is required in Greece, political arguments usually prevail over economic ones.

Since it is difficult to assess objectively how much investment in transportation infrastructure is really needed in any given situation, there is a tendency to overestimate. This leads to wastage. Examples of Pharaonic transportation infrastructure are common the world over.

Undoubtedly, transportation strongly affects the course of economic development (Litman, 2010). However, whether it is able to trigger other economic activities is doubtful at best. Therefore, the fact that there is a significant impact on economic development during the construction period of a transportation infrastructure, but rather little during its life, very often misguides the investment decision if development is the main criterion.

Reducing the demand for transportation may mean better land-use planning, efforts to reduce peak loads, and attempts to introduce efficient substitutions (e.g. transmission of electric power eliminating the need for coal transportation). Such measures could result in important economies, if an overall efficiency calculus justified them (Heymann, 1965).

The economic art of evaluating transport projects in less developed countries is still primitive, given the absence of basic statistics and the influence of narrow political interests. In the transportation field, the evaluation of railway projects and to some extent of shipping and port projects was usually limited to a financial analysis in order to determine whether future revenues would cover costs (Adler, 1965).

Before one can evaluate a specific transport project, two preliminary steps are essential (Adler, 1965). The first step consists of a general economic survey of the country with two aims:

> The first aim is to identify the country's overall transportation needs and the second aim is to provide a basis for appraising the transportation needs in comparison with the requirements in other sectors of the economy.
>
> The second step is undertaking a detailed transportation survey of the country in order to determine the priorities within this sector.

In evaluating a project, one should undertake separate economic analyses for each sub-project; otherwise, it is possible that the extra-large benefits of one subproject will conceal the insufficient benefits of another (Adler, 1965).

Limitations on competition, emerging as monopolistic or oligopolistic market phenomena, blur the direct relationship between prices and costs. Moreover, problems arise from the direct and indirect subsidisation by governments of many transportation services.

Measuring the economic costs of a project is substantially easier than measuring its economic benefits. The subjective overestimation of social and indirect benefits of a project is a common weapon in political arguments.

Shadow prices, social costs and benefits, and external costs are useful tools, concepts, and techniques for the economic evaluation of transportation projects.

Cost–benefit analysis, and in general financial analysis, focuses on the ability of a project to meet all operating costs continuously (that is to satisfy the liquidity requirements) and to earn an adequate return on the funds invested.

One can use three different methods for evaluating a project in monetary terms: the rate of return on investment, the cost–benefit ratio, and the payback period.

The traditional cost–benefit analysis, discounting benefits and costs by the opportunity costs of capital, is theoretically the best way of comparing different projects. The most important disadvantage of this approach is that one must choose a particular interest rate for discounting. In practice, the interest rate selected is frequently the one being paid, which may not be related to the opportunity cost of capital in a country (Adler, 1965). Unfortunately, the opportunity cost of capital is frequently not known, or can only be estimated with a considerable margin of error.

This is crucial since the discount rate chosen is one of the major determinants of the cost–benefit approach.

Combined approaches, sensitivity analysis, and multi-criteria methods provide more secure results.

It is also important to consider the diffusion of the consequences of such an infrastructure in the regional and national economy by a Leontief-type input–output analysis (Leontief, 1986) or methods such as PROPAGE (1980), of the French national institute of statistics (INSEE).

Therefore, if we want to consider transportation investment as a driver of growth in the Greek economy, it is imperative to devise a method of evaluation appropriate to the specific investment. Else, we risk wasting our capital and effort. The error in such cases is discovered many years later. The negative consequences consist mainly of the capital that was withheld from other more productive investments, the human resources wasted, and the disorientation of the economy.

4 Transportation and Economic Growth

It is frequently assumed that all transportation improvements stimulate economic growth. The truth is that some do, while others do not (Leuning, 2011), and that even those that do might not be economically justified in the sense that there might have been better investment opportunities in other sectors.

Economic development implies both growth of national income and the resulting benefits leading to improvements in the standard of living of low-income groups. Consequently, economic growth means not only income growth but also income distribution (Lefeber, 1965).

Regional economic growth has been analysed in the context of a labour surplus economy, with an emphasis on the criteria for efficiency. Efficiency is not a goal in itself, it is a necessary companion for the highest attainable rate at which a national economy can grow and reduce unemployment. Competitive pricing and investment policies will lead, if conditions are favourable, to efficient patterns of national and regional growth (Lefeber, 1965).

Promoting economic development without planning is like attempting to reach a port that is unknown or nonexistent.

Maintenance versus new construction is always a necessary question to be examined before any decision on investment is made.

Continuity and lumpiness of the transportation projects are significant characteristics for any evaluation. They should complement investment requirements to ensure that a project becomes functional and effective.

There is already dialogue and considerable international experience on the following concerns:

- How much transportation is necessary or desirable for development?
- Which modes of transportation should be expanded?
- How should new industrial capacity be regionally distributed?

- What are the conflicts of economic growth with industrial and transportation dispersion?
- What is the appropriate new infrastructure under a recession environment?

The Greek authorities do not consider the above concerns and experiences. Therefore, it is difficult to expect that transportation will be the driving force of development in this country.

A significant amount of transportation infrastructure, highways, railways, ports, and airports, of acceptable quality have been constructed and/or improved over the last two decades, with European Union co-funding, but we have a very vague idea of their real impact on the economy. There are not any ex-ante and ex-post empirical studies to compare the improvements over a period. There are many examples in Greece where an old infrastructure is replaced by a new one that works perfectly and is technologically exceptional. However, the old one could continue to operate, like the Hellenicon airport (the old Athens airport). Alternatively, it competes with the new construction, like the ferries of Rion–Antirrion after the construction of the new bridge. In both cases, the real impact on the economy is not known and only qualitative arguments are advanced.

Another very important element in evaluating transportation investments and infrastructures is the 'external cost', for the assessment of which we consider:

- Pollution.
- Accidents.
- Noise.
- Congestion.

The effect of these factors, with regard to transportation, on development or their negative effects on the Greek economy are completely unknown.

One of the major unsolved transportation issues is whether an investment in infrastructure promotes economic growth at a regional or national level and its impact in terms of global land use (Banister & Berechman, 2000; Leong, Lichtman, & Russell, 2002; Quinet, 1992; Rietveld & Nijkamp, 1993; Wilson, Stevens, & Holyoke, 1982).

The transportation sector participates on a scale of 4–5 % in the GDP (Tsekeris & Tsouma, 2010), which is rather small when the public investment is mainly transportation infrastructure. It is interesting to note that the revenues from international shipping is also around 4 % of the GDP, but since this sector makes substantial payments abroad makes this figure relatively less significant for the national economy.

It is worthwhile to underline that the transportation investment in Greece has not followed a specific regional development plan but is rather a patchwork of local demands and political decisions. Thus, the transportation sector on its own cannot be the driving force of development, for national planning with regard to this sector continues to be as vague as it has always been. The problem has become more critical under recession; therefore, one needs to undertake specific studies before making any transportation investments. This would be the only way to avoid wasting the scarce capital resources of the Greek economy.

Conclusions

In order to transform the transportation investment into a driver of development for Greece, it is necessary to take into account all the above issues and elaborate a specific evaluation method for development policy purposes. A synthesis of the previous approaches could lead to rational decisions.

The international experience highlights that planning has not proved to be the magic key to optimum solutions. Transportation in a society serves a variety of conflicting and incommensurable objectives. The selection of a national transportation system implies a choice among these goals. Without a comprehensive global development plan for the economy, transportation infrastructures are public works with no future.

The transportation economist and planner can best contribute to this policy decision by offering his transportation plans as a range of feasible and viable transportation alternatives and predicting some of their foreseeable social implications. In this way, he may help the community to broaden its own understanding of its goals and values (Heymann, 1965).

Thus, the widely held belief that transportation stimulates new productive activity is questionable. When a country is deficient in the factors conducive to growth and development, no amount of transport investment will create the economic dynamism that is so ardently desired (Heymann, 1965).

Finally, it is necessary to adapt the Greek national investment plan for transportation infrastructure to the needs of national growth and development.

References

Adler, A. H. (1965). Economic evaluation of transport projects. In G. Fromm (Ed.), *Transport investment and economic development* (pp. 170–194). Washington: The Brookings Institution.

Banister, D., & Berechman, Y. (2000, November). *The economic development effects of transport investments*. Paper presentation at the TRANS-TALK Workshop. Brussels.

Heymann, H. (1965). The objectives of transportation. In G. Fromm (Ed.), *Transport investment and economic development* (pp. 18–33). Washington: The Brookings Institution.

Lefeber, L. (1965). Economic development and regional growth. In G. Fromm (Ed.), *Transport investment and economic development* (pp. 108–122). Washington: The Brookings Institution.

Leong, D., Lichtman, L., & Russell, R. (2002). *Transportation investment, economic development, and land use goals in Wisconsin* (Technical Report SPR-0092-45-97). Madison: Wisconsin Department of Transportation-Bureau of Planning, Economic Planning and Development Section.

Leontief, W. (1986). *Input–output economics* (2nd ed.). New York: Oxford University Press.

Leuning, T. (2011, April). *Cart or horse: Transport and economic growth* (Discussion paper 2011-4). Brussels: OECD/ITF, International Transport Forum.

Litman, T. (2010). *Evaluating transportation economic development impacts: Understanding how transport policy and planning decisions affect employment, incomes, productivity, competitiveness, property values and tax revenues*. Victoria Transport Policy Institute. Victoria, BC, Canada.

PROPAGE. (1980). Modèle détaillé de projections à moyen terme. *Economie et statistique, 121*(121), 61–74.

Quinet, E. (1992). *Infrastructures de transport et croissance*. Paris: Economica.

Rietveld, P., & Nijkamp, P. (1993). Transport and regional development. In J. Polak & A. Heertje (Eds.), *European transport economics* (pp. 130–151). Blackwell: CEMT-ECMT.

Tsekeris, T., & Tsouma, A. (2010). *Transport and economy: Contribution, trends and prospects in Greece with emphasis on surface transport* (Report 63). Athens: Centre of Planning and Economic Research (KEPE) (in Greek).

Wilson, F., Stevens, A., & Holyoke, T. (1982). Impact of transportation on regional development. *Transportation Research Record, 851*, 13–16.

The Role of Greece as a Transport Node in the South Eastern Europe

Dimitrios A. Tsamboulas

1 Introduction

Within the general framework of globalisation and market liberalisation, trade growth in Europe is currently recovering from the impact of the recent financial crisis. This is mostly due to the emerging economies of countries such as China, the Russian Federation, India, and the countries in the Far East, the increase of purchasing power of the Black Sea countries, the emergence—albeit at a slower pace—of the southern Mediterranean countries, and the development of new strong poles of attraction within the Single European Market. To this end, as the industry works hard to mitigate the effects of the challenging economic climate, there is increased attention on how to shape the European transport sector for recovery and growth, given that it is the pillar for trade facilitation, economic recovery, and regional social cohesion.

Significant targets been accomplished since the European Union first issued its 2001 White Paper on Transport, mostly dealing with opening markets in aviation, road transport, and, to a certain extent, rail transport. Most importantly, Trans-European Transport Networks (TEN-T) promoted the construction of high-speed railway lines and contributed to territorial cohesion, and strengthening of international relations and co-operation. In addition, the accession of eastern European countries and liberalisation of their economics, have re-oriented EU's policies towards central European countries, eastern European countries, western Balkans, and southern Mediterranean countries.

D.A. Tsamboulas (✉)
Department of Transportation Planning and Engineering, National Technical University of Athens, 5 Iroon Polytexneiou Str, Zografou 15773, Greece
e-mail: dtsamb@central.ntua.gr

P. Sklias and N. Tzifakis (eds.), *Greece's Horizons*, The Konstantinos Karamanlis Institute for Democracy Series on European and International Affairs,
DOI 10.1007/978-3-642-34534-0_17,

At the same time, the volume of international trade with Asia has been growing sharply in recent years, driven by the development of new economies of the Asian countries, particularly that of China and India. According to figures of the World Trade Organization, the Asian trade accounts for the largest share after Europe in the global trade. This continuous trade growth has brought about a wider spatial dissemination of trade flows, not just between the extremities of the two continents, but also among major centres and hubs within the interior of Europe and Asia.

Indeed, the new Europe becomes progressively the origin and destination of growing intra-European flows, mainly those with South Eastern Europe, including Turkey. This will generate flows with origin and destination in the neighbouring regions of the European Union, particularly in the East—the Russian Federation, Ukraine and other Caucasian economies, and Asian countries, such as China, Kazakhstan, India, etc. These trade volumes are nowadays expected to consolidate in favour of Asia and South America, and to a lesser degree Africa (something evident in part even before the 2008 recession erupted), given the structural difference in the development rates that characterise the post-recession recovery period.

Geography and history have placed Greece at the crossroads of East and West, and North and South, in an area of high geopolitical importance, connecting three continents, Europe, Asia, and Africa. It constitutes both a destination and a nodal point of the Trans-European Networks (TEN-T) and that of the Mediterranean Sea maritime network, serving a large number of converging global maritime connections.

The developments described in the above have opened up new perspectives and opportunities of trans-regional, trans-European, and Euro-Asian co-operation for Greece. Therefore, the country must exploit its unique advantage of a strategic location connecting South Eastern Europe, the Black Sea basin and the Mediterranean Sea, to strengthen its position and become a key transport node and player in the region.

In light of the above, the present chapter seeks to analyse the role of Greece as an important transport node of South Eastern Europe, within the new environment for transportation that is now emerging. The chapter begins with an analysis of the country's trade flows and routes transiting the area, identifying its transport links with neighbouring regions. The sections that follow provide an outline of the current initiatives and actions taking place with regard to the European transport networks, their planned extensions, and the establishment of Euro-Asian links, exploring the ways that these affect Greece's transportation system and economy. The chapter also highlights the role of Greek ports. Further, it discusses the current actions to address the challenge of upgrading the country's role to that of an important transport node in the Mediterranean Sea. Finally, it provides recommendations on the possible strategies to achieve these vital objectives.

Table 1 EU27 external trade flows (in million tons)

	EU27 and east–west[a]		EU27 and south–north[b]	
Year	Export	Import	Export	Import
1999	76	512	50	232
2000	87	557	53	237
2001	80	580	49	240
2002	91	593	50	246
2003	101	645	50	251
2004	105	715	52	253
2005	122	754	60	257
2006	129	763	62	258
2007	135	781	60	247
2008	149	756	70	240
2009	143	669	73	207
2010	157	724	82	204
2011	174	758	77	154

Source: Eurostat

[a]China, India, Japan, United Arab Emirates, Afghanistan, Armenia, Azerbaijan, Bangladesh, Bahrain, Georgia Iraq, Islamic Republic of Iran, Kyrgyzstan, Kuwait, Kazakhstan, Oman, Pakistan, Qatar, Russian Federation (Russia), Saudi Arabia, Tajikistan, Turkmenistan, Turkey, Ukraine, Uzbekistan, and Yemen

[b]Central African Republic, Congo, Algeria, Egypt, Eritrea, Ethiopia, Israel, Jordan, Kenya, Lebanon, Libya, Morocco, Madagascar, Mozambique, Seychelles, Sudan, Syria, Chad, Tunisia, Uganda, South Africa Zambia, and Zimbabwe

2 Greece and Its Neighbouring Region: Trade Flows and Routes

According to figures released by the World Trade Organisation for the year 2010, the European Union was both the origin and destination of more than half of Greece's imports and exports of goods (E-27), with percentage shares of 62.6 % and 51.3 %, respectively.[1] Turkey is the second largest destination of the country's total exports (receiving 5 % of its exports), while the Russian Federation and China are the second and third largest sources of the country's total imports, 9.8 % and 6.0 %, respectively. Although the import and export flows of Greece are not significant, the opposite is true for the flows transiting through the wider geographical area of Greece. Table 1 presents the main trade flows of the EU-27 along the East–west corridor and North–south corridor for the years 1999–2011. It is evident that EU imports along the East–west corridor prevail over all other trade flows.

The predominance of the Greece-EU trade creates the need for physical routes connecting the country to the rest of Europe. These are—besides the aviation links—the maritime ones through the Adriatic Sea and the land routes through

[1] See World Trade Organization, http://wto.org, accessed on 3 May 2012.

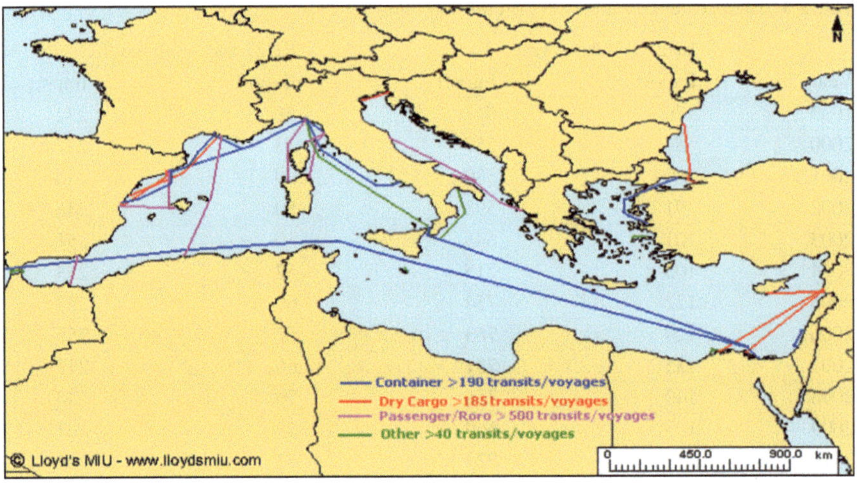

Map 1 Major non-tanker routes in the Mediterranean Sea. *Source*: Lloyd's Marine Intelligence Unit (2008, 18)

the Balkan countries. Greece's links to the East are currently limited to maritime links to the Black Sea and Middle East and land routes through Turkey.

Greece is located in the Mediterranean Sea, whose transport significance spans several levels. It is one of the world's major trade routes, through which nearly a third of world trade passes—from the Suez Canal to the Straits of Gibraltar and Bosporus, and from the Atlantic to the Black Sea. Transport flows between the two ends of the Mediterranean are very dense, and the EU is the main maritime and aviation partner of a large number of Mediterranean countries (MEDA countries). Although transit transport is intensive, the level of integration is low, particularly with regard to South–South trade.

Prior to the economic crisis, intra-Mediterranean traffic represented only 24 % of the total non-bulk traffic. Of this, EU-Mediterranean flows constituted 16 %, south-eastern Mediterranean-EU flows constituted 7 % (mainly north to south), and south eastern Mediterranean flows only 1 %. Regarding extra-Mediterranean traffic, Asia dominated at 29 %, out of which 26 % were EU-Asia flows, while the remaining 3 % were south-eastern Mediterranean-Asia flows and some Asia-sub-Saharan Africa flows (Zallio, 2011, 1).

With regard to oil tanker flows, the dominating maritime routes include crude oil shipments from Novorossiysk in the Black Sea to Mediterranean destinations, from Sidi Kerir/Alexandria to both Mediterranean destinations and the west of Gibraltar, and exports from the Persian Gulf through Mediterranean via Suez. Nevertheless, the routes of non-tanker vessels in the Mediterranean are fragmented, as depicted in Map 1 (EU, SAFEMED, 2008, 18).

Based on the above, container throughputs of major Greek ports are related to feeder services from ships calling at Gioia Tauro, Taranto, Port Said, and Malta for the trade routes between the western Mediterranean and the Black Sea countries (such as Romania, Bulgaria, Ukraine, Russian Federation, and Turkey), and North American and Asian countries, Australia, and South Africa. Only Piraeus has direct container lines, especially when COSCO S.A. with the subsidiary company Piraeus Container Terminal S.A. became the operator of the container terminal at Ikonion.

3 Greece and the European Transport Networks

Transport is a key factor in the European economy and there is an increasing demand for efficient transport systems within Europe, particularly following the accession of the ten new Member States. The development of the Trans-European Transport Network (TEN-T) lies at the heart of the European initiative for mobility and transport. However, there are several other initiatives that aim at extending the TEN-T network beyond the geographical constraints of the European Union and connecting it with neighbouring countries, such as the Motorways of the Sea, the Trans-Mediterranean Transport Network, the Black Sea Cooperation, Northern Dimension Partnership, the Central Axis, etc. The majority of such networks and related initiatives are affecting Greece to a varying degree, owing to the nodal position of the country in the eastern Mediterranean.

4 TEN-T

Establishing an efficient trans-European transport network (TEN-T) has been a key element in the re-launched Lisbon Strategy for competitiveness and employment in Europe, and will play an equally vital role in the attainment of the objectives of the Europe 2020 Strategy. The TEN-T program consisted of thirty Priority Projects (or axes) identified according to their European value added, and their contribution to the sustainable development of transport. Greece's participation in the above projects, whose completion is planned for 2020, relates to both the road and rail sector, as per the following projects:

- Priority Project 7: Motorway axis Igoumenitsa/Patras–Athens–Sofia–Budapest
- Priority Project 22: Railway axis Athens–Sofia–Budapest–Vienna–Prague–Nuremberg/Dresden
- Priority Project 29: Railway axis of the Ionian/Adriatic intermodal corridor

In 2010, the European Parliament and the Council issued a recast of the TEN-T Guidelines on TEN-T policy and infrastructure planning (European Commission, 2010), aiming at developing the network through a dual-layered approach—developing a core network and a comprehensive network. The comprehensive network constitutes the layer of the TEN-T, aimed to be in place by December 2050. The core network is part of the comprehensive network and comprises its strategically most important sections that according to plans will be in place by December 2030.

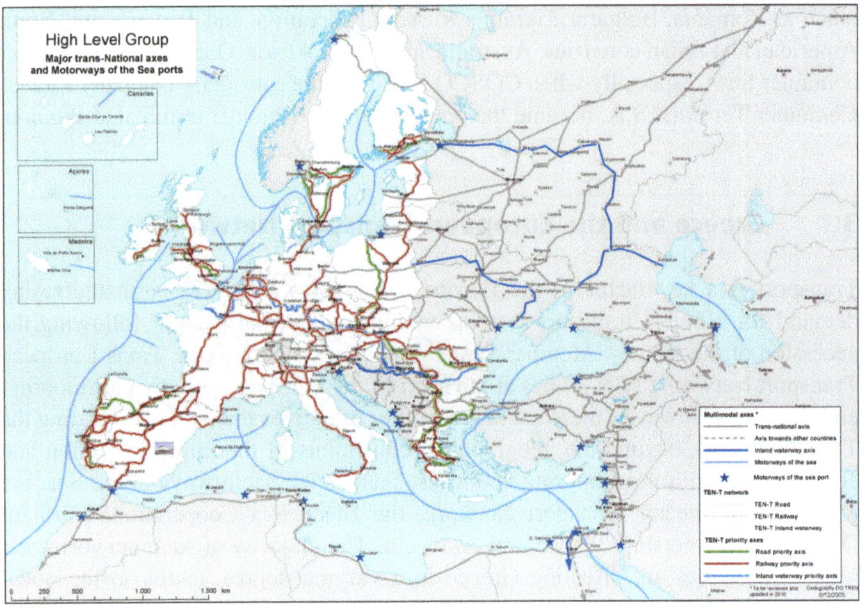

Map 2 High level group major transnational axes and European 'motorways of the sea' ports. *Source*: High Level Group (2005, 30)

5 TEN-T Extension Outside the EU

In 2005, the European Union appointed a High Level Group, chaired by Ms. Loyola de Palacio, to revise the TEN-T policy and the network's extension to the neighbouring countries and regions. The group identified five major transnational axes, extending and complementing the major axes of the Trans-European transport network. The main reference to land transport in the Mediterranean region affecting Greece appeared within the 'South Western Axis'. Greece's maritime connections were included in the two identified 'Motorways of the Sea' (MoS), more specifically, the extension of the motorways of the Mediterranean Sea towards North Africa and Middle East, including the Red Sea and beyond, and the extension of the MoS of the Mediterranean to the Black Sea. These are depicted in Map 2.

5.1 Motorways of the Sea

The term 'Motorways of the Sea' was mentioned for the first time in the European Commission's White Paper on European Transport Policy in 2001, and represented an EU initiative aimed at providing improved intermodal freight transport options, relying on integrating short sea shipping with the respective hinterland connections of the ports serving the supply chain.

Table 2 Overview of East Mediterranean potential MoS corridors

MoS potential corridors (indicative link)	Cluster-to-cluster	Type of service
Igoumenitsa–Taranto	South Adriatic-Italian ports and Ionian Sea/ West Greece ports	RO-PAX
Kavala–Limassol	EMR-Middle East ports and North Aegean ports	LO-LO
Igoumenitsa–Koper	Ionian Sea/west Greece ports and the eastern segment of the North Adriatic ports cluster	RO-RO
Venice–(Igoumenitsa)–Patras–(Corinth)	North Adriatic ports–Ionian Sea/West Greece ports	RO-RO
Igoumenitsa–Ancona–Koper	The eastern segment of the North Adriatic ports cluster and the western segment of the North Adriatic ports cluster	RO-RO
Limassol–Pireaυs	EMR–Middle East ports and Central/South Aegean ports	RO-PAX
Patras–Catania	Ionian Sea/West Greece ports and the Italian ports of the Central Mediterranean ports cluster	RO-PAX

Source: European Commission (2009, 2–31)

As per plan, the MoS will include improvement of the quality of transport services, facilities, and procedures concerning at least two ports in two different Member States, including their hinterland connections, safety and security aspects, logistics technology and supply chain management systems, and simplification and harmonisation of administrative and custom procedures. Greece was one of the countries that elaborated the 'Master Plan for the East Mediterranean Motorways of the Sea', which resulted in the identification of ten potential MoS corridors and the infrastructure investments required for each. Table 2 presents an overview of the potential MoS corridors, in which Greece participates through three of its key ports, namely Igoumenitsa, Patras, and Piraeus.

In addition, Map 3 presents the proposed MoS corridors together with the estimated trade flows in 1,000 tonnes for the 2015 time horizon. The establishment and operation of MoS in the south eastern Mediterranean region is of exceptional importance for the countries that it serves. It is also a unique opportunity for Greece, since it can enhance the growth of its maritime and port sector, attracting significant investments.

5.2 Trans-Mediterranean Transport Network

The definition of the Trans-Mediterranean Transport Network (TMN-T), presented in Map 4, is the result of a long process of co-operation between the EU and its

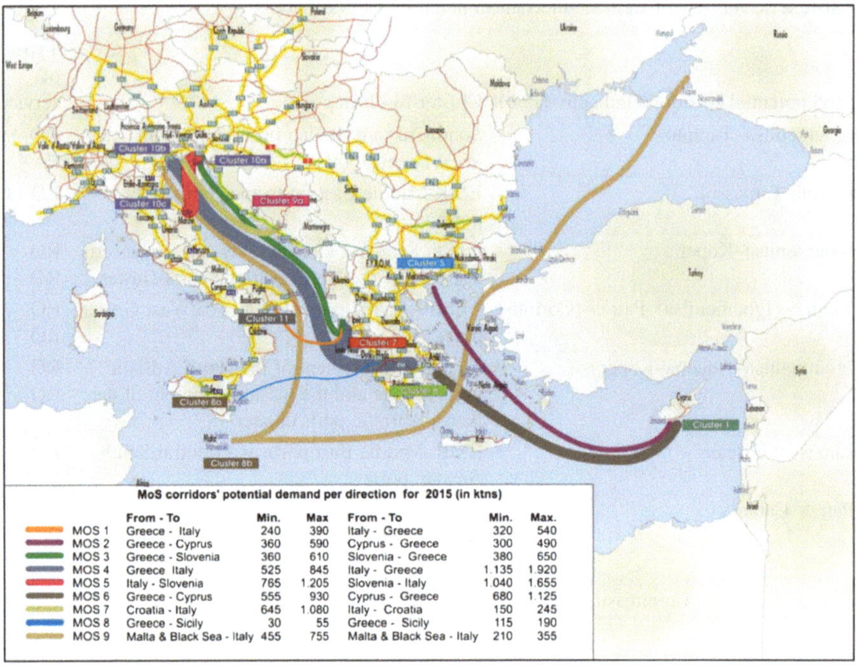

MoS corridors' potential demand per direction for 2015 (in ktns)

	From - To	Min.	Max	From - To	Min.	Max.
MOS 1	Greece - Italy	240	390	Italy - Greece	320	540
MOS 2	Greece - Cyprus	360	590	Cyprus - Greece	300	490
MOS 3	Greece - Slovenia	360	610	Slovenia - Greece	380	650
MOS 4	Greece Italy	525	845	Italy - Greece	1.135	1.920
MOS 5	Italy - Slovenia	765	1.205	Slovenia - Italy	1.040	1.655
MOS 6	Greece - Cyprus	555	930	Cyprus - Greece	680	1.125
MOS 7	Croatia - Italy	645	1.080	Italy - Croatia	150	245
MOS 8	Greece - Sicily	30	55	Greece - Sicily	115	190
MOS 9	Malta & Black Sea - Italy	455	755	Malta & Black Sea - Italy	210	355

Map 3 East Mediterranean MoS potential flows. *Source*: European Commission (2009, 33)

southern Mediterranean partners.[2] The methodology for building the TMN-T network consists of developing a strategic network of transport infrastructure for the entire Mediterranean basin, using unified criteria, taking as reference the exercises previously made, the TEN-T guidelines, and the current status of the Mediterranean region.

As part of the network definition, an infrastructure project prioritisation exercise is included in the work done by the Working Group on Infrastructures and Regulatory issues on land transport (WG Infra), which forms part of the Euromed Transport Forum. The criteria employed were grouped in six categories (general, technical, social, policy-based, economic, and environmental), according to which projects have been selected in Algeria, Israel, Jordan, Lebanon, Morocco, Palestinian Authority, Syria, Tunisia, and Turkey. An additional key criterion has been employed, aimed at contributing to the South–South connection and the South–north connection, which would effectively benefit the majority of Greek ports.

[2] For more details, see Euromed Trasport Project, http://euromedtransport.org, accessed on 5 May 2012.

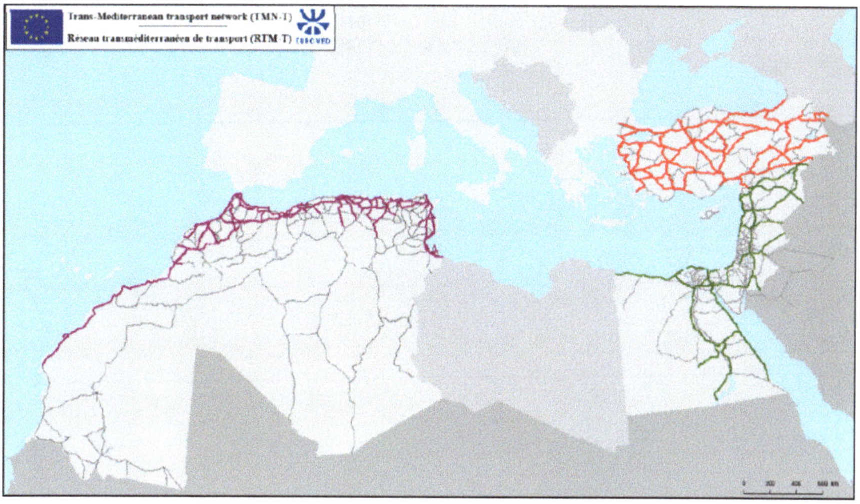

Map 4 Trans-Mediterranean transport network. *Source*: Euromed Transport Project

5.3 Black Sea Cooperation

Greece is one of the three EU Member States (the others being Bulgaria and Romania) taking part in the Black Sea Economic Cooperation (BSEC). The following three main transport initiatives have been launched within the BSEC framework (these are likely to have strong influence in the near future on traffic flows both for passenger and freight for Greece):

1. Black Sea Ring Highway
2. Motorway of the Seas
3. Facilitation of Road transport

In 2007, the Ministers of Foreign Affairs of the member states of the Organization of the Black Sea Economic Cooperation (BSEC) signed a Memorandum of Understanding (MoU) for the construction of the Black Sea Ring Highway. The Greek State has assumed a significant role, since 'EGNATIA ODOS S.A' was assigned the responsibility of the Joint Permanent Technical Secretariat (JPTS) for the realisation of the project. According to the MoU, the BSEC member states initially decided that the Ring Highway would pass through the Greek cities of Komotini and Alexandroupolis. In addition, the development and elaboration of the Master Plan for the MoS in the Black Sea area through Bulgaria and Romania, interconnecting with the MoS of eastern Mediterranean, is presently being studied.

6 The Euro-Asian Links

Today, maritime transport dominates the transport of goods from Asia to Europe. In addition, maritime transport rates are often incorrectly compared with the rates for inland transport modes. At the same time, pressure of competition reduces the

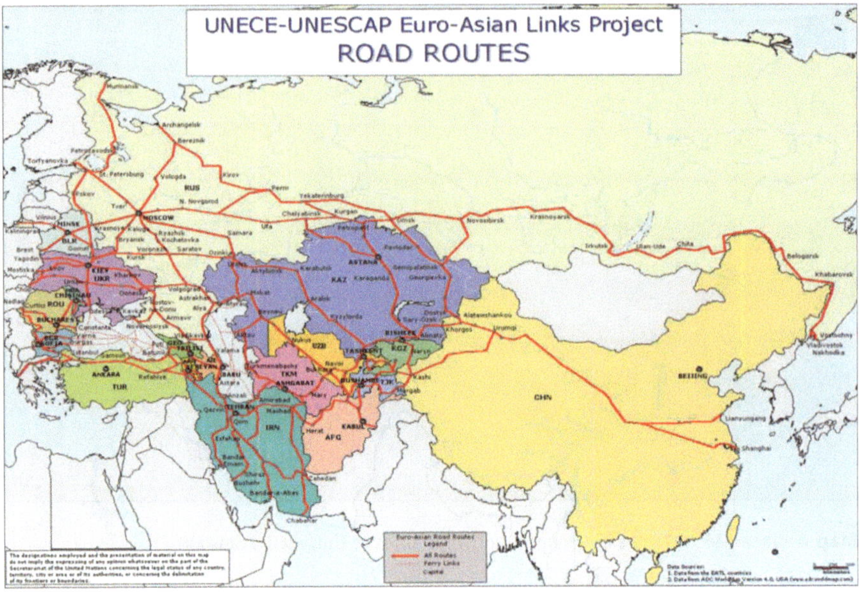

Map 5 EATL road routes

number of maritime ports, while these are rapidly approaching full capacity. There is also growing concern for congestion and saturation of land access to ports, as well as safety and security issues arising from maritime traffic concentrating at certain points along the defined routes between hubs. Ports continue to serve limited hinterland, considering the vast distances involved in trade transits across the entire Eurasia region. An additional challenge for international transportation operators is trade imbalance, with a large number of empty containers being transported in Asia.

The above issues necessitate the diversification of existing routes and the opening up of alternative ones between the two continents, or, in some cases, the revival of old trade routes, such as the Silk Road and the Trans-Siberian route.

With the above challenges in view, the United Nations Economic Commission for Europe (UNECE) and the United Nations Economic and Social Commission for Asia and the Pacific (UNESCAP) worked closely with governments of the Euro-Asian region during 2003–2007 on the 'Joint Study on Developing Euro-Asia Transport Linkages' (EATL), as part of a global United Nations Development Account Capacity-building Project. In 2004, Greece, during its chairmanship-in-office of the BSEC, expressed the wish to be associated with the activities of the project and joined the study. The study identified priority Euro-Asian routes, presented in Maps 5 and 6 (United Nations, 2008), and an investment plan for priority transport infrastructure projects (ongoing or planned) along the designated routes. UNECE and UNESCAP elaborated a joint proposal for Phase II of the study, which was finalised within 2012.

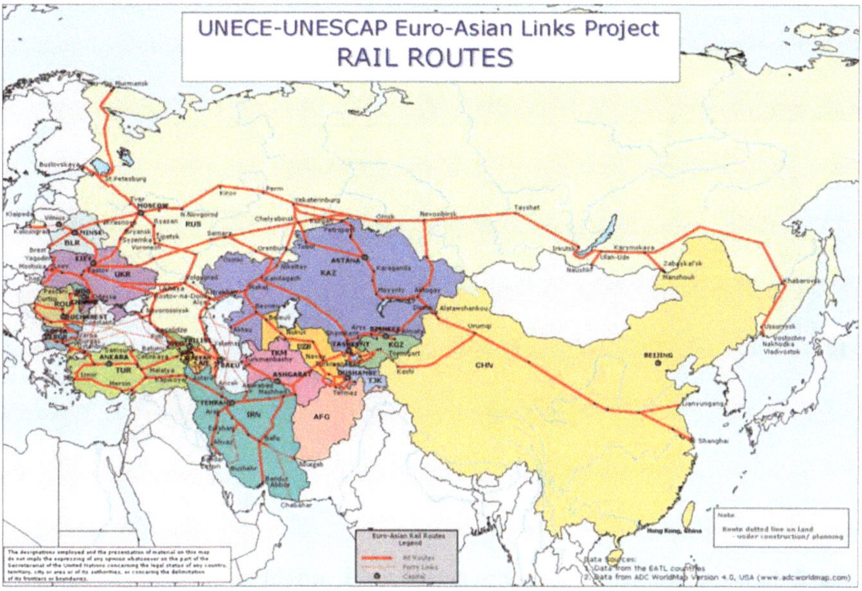

Map 6 EATL rail routes. *Source* for both maps: United Nations (2008, 70 and 72)

Furthermore, the transport sector of the Economic Cooperation Organization (ECO) is currently performing Corridor Management Studies for (among others) identifying priority routes and related infrastructure investment projects, similar to the EATL ones, to connect its members. The routes identified extend from Greece's borders with Turkey to Pakistan and Kazakhstan.

Other significant programmes and initiatives promoting the linkage of the two continents are the Trans-European North–South Motorway (TEM) and the Trans-European Railway (TER) Projects, and the European Union Transport Corridor Europe-Caucasus-Asia (TRACECA) Programme. The Central Asia Regional Economic Cooperation (CAREC), the Organization of the Black Sea Economic Cooperation (BSEC), and the Eurasian Economic Community (EurAsEC) are also active in the region. Finally, the development of Euro-Asian transport linkages has also attracted the interest of several banks investing in development of infrastructure, such as the European Bank for Reconstruction and Development (EBRD), Asian Development Bank (ADB), Islamic Development Bank (IDB) and the World Bank.

Greece has participated in the EATL study and TEM and TER studies. Given its strategic geopolitical location, it should exploit every opportunity to harvest the benefits of these initiatives, for eventually expanding its trade with Asian countries. In addition, due to its position, it can become an energy hub for the transit of oil and gas from the Caspian Basin and western Asia to consumers in Europe.

An indicative example of the role of Greece constitutes the intermodal road and railway connection of Igoumenitsa with the port of Shanghai in China within the framework of the EATL, as depicted in Map 7. This connection ensures the access

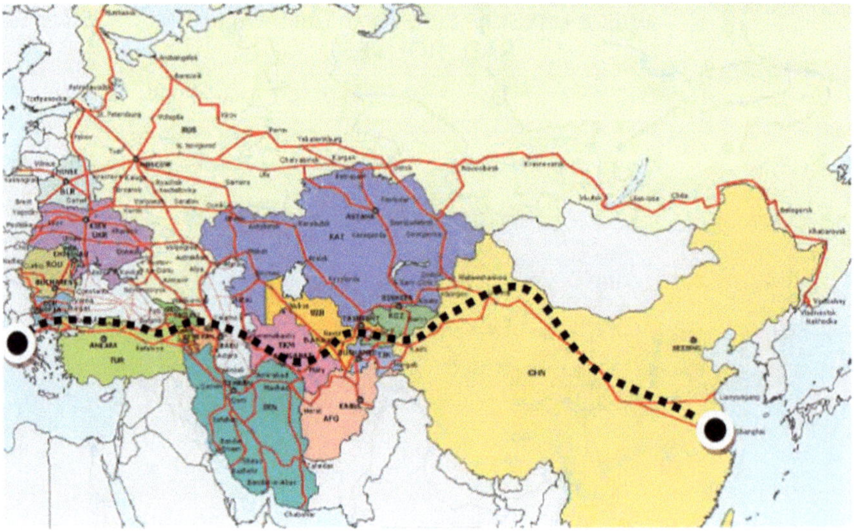

Map 7 Igoumenitsa–Shanghai connection through EATL network

of freight flows originating in the port of Igoumenitsa to the markets of not only China, but also of other Asian countries such as those bordering the Caspian Sea (Azerbaijan, Turkmenistan, Iran, and Kazakhstan), Uzbekistan, Kyrgyzstan, and Tajikistan. Once established, the supply chain along the Igoumenitsa–Shanghai corridor could contribute considerably to the economic growth of Greece, strengthening its trade relations with the Asian continent.

Another example of a connection with Asia is the proposed development of an international intermodal freight transportation corridor that will connect the Northern Greek ports of Thessaloniki or Alexandroupoli with one of the two Russian Federation ports, Novorossisk or Kafkas. This connection will involve intermodal transport (maritime-railway) with the Bulgarian ports of Varna and Burgas and connection with Russian railways, and bypassing highly congested Bosporus Straits (Greek Railway Organization, 2007).

The proposed axis, depicted in Map 8, will traverse three countries (Russia, Bulgaria, and Greece), opening up new prospects of growth for Greece, increasing its accessibility to the countries in the region, and establishing international networks of co-operation in merchandise trade and other business between Europe and Asia. It is also expected to have important impacts on regional growth, particularly in the Greek town/port of Alexandroupoli, which will be developed as a modern transhipment centre of regional, national, and international significance.

Finally, Turkey is also using the concept of bypassing the congested Bosporus Strait in its ambitious project of building a canal connecting the Black Sea and Sea of Marmara, namely the Istanbul Canal, which, if realised, would also connect directly with Greece.

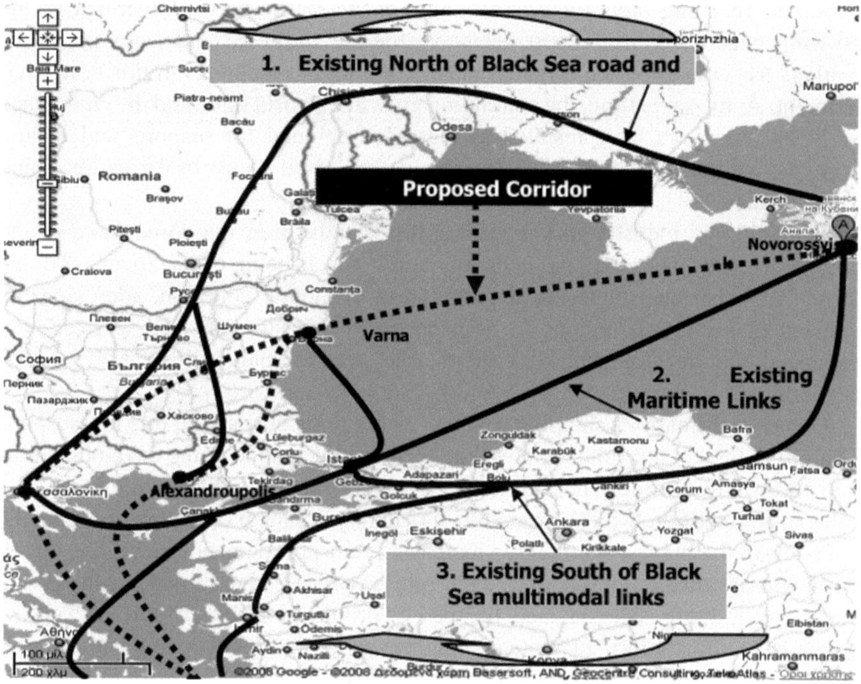

Map 8 Proposed corridor Russian Federation–Bulgaria–Greece

7 Trans African Network

The latest development policy, which was officially launched in 2007, aimed at increasing the role of EU and African partnership on transport, with two main areas highlighted for future actions: the financing of the construction of high quality transport infrastructure, and systems integration and sharing of knowledge and best practices between partners. The EU and the African Union have recently launched the Programme for Infrastructure Development in Africa (PIDA).

Apart from Northern Africa, which is already included in the Euro Mediterranean links, Greece can consider participating in the project of connecting the Trans African Network with the Trans European Networks, which entails the development of links between the Sub Saharan corridor and the Trans Mediterranean Networks, and the connection of the Motorways of the Sea corridors to key African seaports.

8 The Role of Greek Ports

Until recently, the principal North Sea ports continued to operate as gateways for the whole of Europe, even serving the flow of goods to and from the Far East, despite the fact that ships would travel from Suez across the Mediterranean Sea to

Gibraltar, reaching their final destinations in the Baltic ports. Nevertheless, the growing need to optimise port gateways for the traffic to and from the Asian markets has converted the Mediterranean ports into key players in this new environment. At the same time, the continuing growth of world trade and the emergence of global operators have resulted in increased demand for seaports and related services, while these are divided into competing nodal points in the entire global logistic chain.

The shipping industry in Greece has historically been the cornerstone of the competitiveness of its national economy and the well-being of its citizens. To this day, it has also contributed to territorial and economic cohesion, addressed the demand of peripheral regions for transportation infrastructure and services, and enhanced the development of tourism, the second main pillar of the Greek economy.

Greece is primarily a shipping country, where ports play a vital role in transport. Therefore, the country must address the increased demand for the development of hub ports in the Mediterranean. Greece can achieve this only by abiding to the new rules of competition, which dictate the prevalence of global operators of terminals, who absorb the biggest share of the increasing transport demand. Therefore, Greek ports are in direct competition with other ports in the region, such as the Haydarpasa, Izmir, Mersin, and the newly promoted Candarli port in Turkey, which have already formed strategic alliances with big global operators.

9 The Challenge to Upgrade the Role of Greece

Greece is located at the converging point of the key initiatives and programmes described above, as depicted in Map 9. Nevertheless, the transport infrastructure is not developing at a fast rate, with lack of funding securitisation being the main hindering factor.

Moreover, Greek policy makers will function, at least for some time, in the shadow of the country's economic recession. This will drastically affect their capacity to undertake new projects or even implement existing transport investment plans. A balanced strategy is therefore required to attract opportunities for value added services to Greece, summarised in what follows.

9.1 Transport Infrastructure Development and Funding

It is of the utmost importance to complete the priority infrastructure projects that come under the Trans-European networks and link the country with the TEN-T network of motorways and railways, while taking into account the existing sub-regional, regional, and interregional agreements on infrastructure. The large-scale investments that have been made in the past years must also be maintained and enhanced through coherent development of the internal transport network.

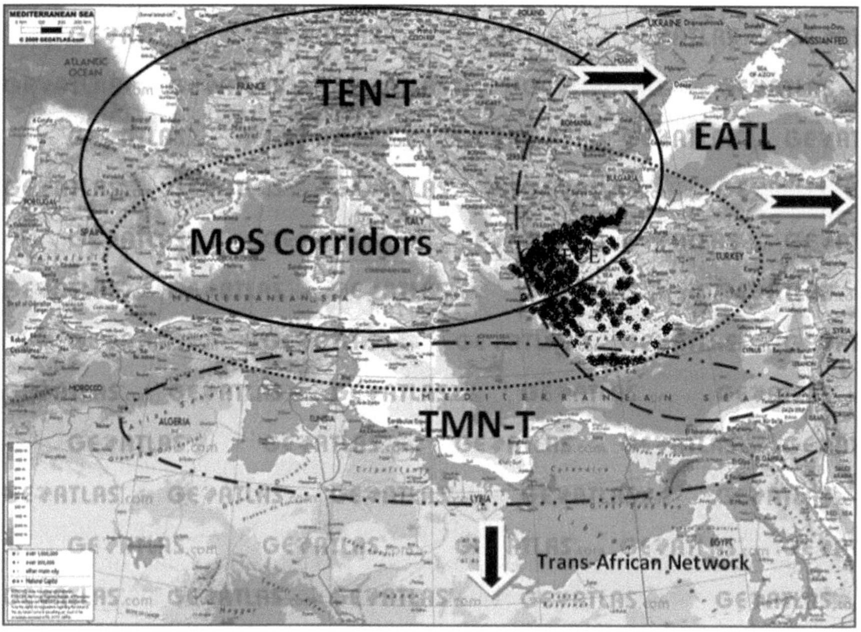

Map 9 Key initiatives in the South East Mediterranean

The share of the GDP devoted to transport infrastructure is limited, and hence, strong political persuasion is necessary for providing adequate funds for infrastructure development. In addition, it is necessary to explore potential non-public sources of funding, such as dedicated funds collected from users in the forms of fares, tolls, and taxes, bank loans from sources such as the European Investment Bank (EIB) and private banks, and Public–Private Partnership (PPP) schemes.

9.2 Integration to Existing and Planned International Transport Networks

The governmental agencies and organisations must work towards the active participation of Greece in the development of the Trans-European, Trans-Mediterranean, and Euro-Asian transport links and concentrate efforts in integrating its national transport network with each programme's identified routes and corridors.

9.3 Maritime Transport and Ports

Enhancing the maritime transport sector ought to be the most prominent common objective towards safeguarding Greece's role as an important node in the

Mediterranean, particularly along selected corridors (MoS of the Eastern Mediterranean, links with the Black Sea, Middle East, etc.). The general goal is to improve the maritime transport network—restoring or modernising existing facilities and developing suitable port infrastructure to cater to the demand of both passenger and freight transport, and improving Greece's services in container transport.

Investments should be targeted at increasing the capacity and improving services of the Greek seaports to avoid congestion and to promote the shift from land transport to intermodal transport, promoting—where available—railway connections. This would, however, necessitate improving the accessibility of selected Greek ports to the hinterland, with connections to the road and rail network, particularly those ports that can become part of Motorways of the Sea corridors with non-EU countries. Maximising shipping routes and minimising those by land, will also contribute to reducing energy costs, CO_2 emissions, and their impacts.

Another issue concerns creating a competitive environment for and liberalisation of maritime and port services, which could result in increasing the efficiency of resource allocation. The attraction of private capital to the port industry for investments in infrastructure and superstructure and the collaboration of the public and private sectors are a priority that requires long-term planning and policies.

The Greek state has several plans regarding port privatisation. The ports portfolio includes as assets 12 ports in the form of 'Societe Anonyme', namely the ports of Piraeus, Thessaloniki, Volos, Rafina, Igoumenitsa, Patras, Alexandroupoli, Iraklion, Elefsina, Lavrio, Corfu, and Kavala, and several other small ports and marinas.

The forthcoming liberalisation of the port market in Greece is expected to increase significantly the opportunities for the involvement of the private sector and attract private funds for port investments. Granting access to the port market services to private providers will enhance competition and affect the quality of port services in a positive way. In accordance with international best practice, a key priority is the separation of regulatory and commercial functions through the creation of 'landlord port' systems, particularly in large ports. This implies a three-tier institutional structure—the government remains in charge of sector policy and planning, autonomous port authorities manage and regulate ports, while private companies provide commercial services.

9.4 Operation and Logistic Services

With supply chains becoming increasingly long and international, efficient supply chain management and logistics are prerequisites for the competitiveness of a country in the international transport and trade arena. Greece is lagging behind in this particular sector, while there are neighbouring countries that have significantly developed their logistic services, thus making Greek transport uncompetitive.

Consequently, the efficiency and sustainability of the emerging Greek transport network lies to a significant extent in the quality and effectiveness of its logistic services and the transhipment capabilities of its transport terminals (both maritime and inland, that is, the ports and the freight villages, respectively). Therefore, what is imperative is a special focus on the need for efficient logistic services, and investments in the creation of intermodal 'interfaces', such as freight villages, logistic centres, multi functional maritime ports, and dry ports/inland container terminals. Port services should be developed accordingly. Finally, technological evolution and development of Intelligent Transport Systems (ITS) is mandatory and presents opportunities for significant growth advantages.

Conclusions

Currently, Europe–Asia and Europe–Mediterranean relations are progressively prevailing over the transatlantic ones. This is a consequence of the fact that Asia is becoming the biggest world market, while at the same time a progressive shift of the EU economy towards its new member countries in the East is evident. In this context, the European Union, through a multitude of policies, initiatives, and programmes (past and ongoing) promotes the interconnection and interoperability of EU national networks and their extension to the neighbouring countries and regions. Similar initiatives are emerging in eastern and central Asian countries, the Middle East, even in Africa. In addition, the rapid development of Euro-Asian trade will trigger the expansion of container shipping activity within the Mediterranean, with an increasing use of Mediterranean ports for freight to/from EU Member States.

All the above clearly demonstrate that an appropriate transportation infrastructure system and related services are currently in place in a number of Greece's neighbouring countries. However, since the demand will increase considerably, Greece could seize the opportunities offered and become a key transportation node in the region, particularly in the maritime sector. The attraction of trade flows will have immediate and tangible effects in terms of enabling new trade relations with other economic regions, providing access to a wider market, increasing the country's accessibility, enhancing productivity and exports, reducing unemployment, etc., thus contributing significantly to its economic growth and the social well-being of its citizens at a challenging time.

To this end, it is imperative to take immediate steps towards establishing real competition in transport services, dissociating the state from transport operations and commercial activities. The private sector is well accustomed to reacting to such challenges and exploiting the opportunities offered. The state is here to guarantee fair competition, adherence to the laws, and protection to the public.

References

Euromed Transport Project. http://euromedtransport.org. Accessed 5 May 2012.

European Commission. (2009, December). *Elaboration of the east Mediterranean motorways of the sea master plan*. DG TREN, East Mediterranean Master Plan of the Motorways of the Sea, Deliverable 5.2. http://ec.europa.eu/transport/maritime/studies/doc/mos/east_med_deliverable5.pdf. Accessed 3 May 2012.

European Commission. (2010, August 5). Decision No 661/2010/EU of the European Parliament and of the Council of 7 July 2010 on Union Guidelines for the development of the trans-European transport network (recast). *Official Journal L, 204*, 1.

European Union. (2008). *Study of maritime traffic flows in the Mediterranean Sea* (p. 18). Final Report, Euromed cooperation on maritime safety and prevention of pollution from ships (SAFEMED), MEDA Regional Project MED 2005/109.

Eurostat. http://epp.eurostat.ec.europa.eu/portal/page/portal/eurostat/home. Accessed 5 May 2012.

Greek Railway Organization. (2007). *Feasibility study for the creation of an intermodal (rail-maritime) connection for freight transport between Russian Federation-Bulgaria-Greece*. National Technical University of Athens.

High Level Group. (2005, November). *Networks for peace and development: Extension of the major trans-European transport axes to the neighbouring countries and regions*. European Commission. http://ec.europa.eu/ten/transport/external_dimension/doc/2005_12_07_ten_t_final_report_en.pdf. Accessed 3 May 2012.

Lloyd's Marine Intelligence Unit. (2008, July). *Study of maritime traffic flows in the Mediterranean Sea*. Regional Marine Pollution Emergency Response Centre for the Mediterranean Sea (REMPEC) and Euro-Mediterranean Partnership, EU-Funded MEDA Regional Project MED 2005/109-573, Final Report - Unrestricted Version. http://80.33.141.76/esatdor/attachments/article/69/Maritime_Traffic_Flows.pdf. Accessed 3 May 2012.

United Nations. (2008). *Joint study on developing Euro-Asian transport linkages*. Prepared under the United Nations Development Account Project on 'Capacity building through cooperation in developing land and land-sea interregional transport linkages'. New York and Geneva: Economic Commission for Europe and Economic and Social Commission for Asia and the Pacific.

World Trade Organization. http://wto.org. Accessed 3 May 2012.

Zallio, F. (2011). *Maritime transport and regional cooperation in the Mediterranean basin* (p. 1). Policy Brief, Mediterranean policy program—Series on the region and the economic crisis, The German Marshall Fund of the United States.

The Greek Agro-Food Industry: Regional Competitiveness in a Globalised Market

Maria Tsampra

1 Introduction

The present analysis focuses on regional agglomerations of agricultural tradition in Greece as a case of regional sustainability and competitiveness in the globalised agro-food industry. The following presentation emphasises the developmental potential of traditional economic activities rooted in lagging areas, when these are fine-tuned within a trajectory of smart regional specialisation. The concentration of development resources in the most promising areas of comparative advantage (e.g. clusters, existing sectors, high value-added markets, etc.) is the most effective strategy for regional sustainability. In this way, even less developed regions can have an opportunity to capitalise on their intangible (production tradition, the amount and quality of knowledge) and tangible assets by investing in those economic fields where they can be competitive.

Such potential has emerged for the Greek rural regions since the 1990s, due to the shift of demand towards traditional food products of high safety, quality, and diversity. This turn in consumption has generated new market opportunities for local agro-food agglomerations of small specialised firms, despite the predominance of powerful multinational corporations (MNCs) in the agro-food value chain. As a consequence, agro-food industries (i.e. of dairy and meat products, processed fruit and vegetables, etc.) operating in peripheral regions demonstrate significant competitiveness in high value-added niche-markets on the national and the international level. Peripherality itself constitutes a solid basis for regional advantage, as it has preserved the products' 'purity', high quality, and diversity.

M. Tsampra (✉)
Department of Business Administration of Food and Agricultural Enterprises,
University of Western Greece, 2 G. Seferi St, Agrinio 30100, Greece
e-mail: mtsampra@cc.uoi.gr

P. Sklias and N. Tzifakis (eds.), *Greece's Horizons*, The Konstantinos Karamanlis Institute for Democracy Series on European and International Affairs,
DOI 10.1007/978-3-642-34534-0_18,

On this ground, small family-owned or co-operative enterprises form competitive local agglomerations in most Greek rural regions, based on comparative advantages such as traditional specialisation, control over raw inputs, local expertise, etc. Such regional economies embed traded and non-traded assets, which attribute market competitiveness to the local agro-food systems. The Greek agro-food manufacturing industry has grown in tight connection with the country's agricultural tradition and specialisation, in local business milieux 'secured' from the forces of global competition. Several successful agro-food enterprises have therefore emerged, taking advantage of both traditional and dynamic territorialised factors in order to penetrate the markets with their 'unique' and 'specialty' produce.

Nevertheless, organisational and technological inadequacies, along with the increasing global competition in the regional, national, and international market, form the main impediments to the viability of the respective regional economies. Thoroughly addressing the factors that define regional production structures, inter-firm and intra-firm relations, divisions of labour, regulations, and institutions will enable the better understanding and formation of effective policies supporting the efficiency and competitiveness of the Greek agro-food industry.

2 The Re-Emergence of the Region: Local Agro-Food Systems

The increasing globalisation of economic activities during the last decades implied a new international division of labour—a change in the geographical pattern of production specialisation on the global scale. Whereas many kinds of commodity chains are spread out across the globe, many of the most rapidly growing industries are at the same time strongly associated with particular regional agglomerations. In those, intermediate goods, sub-assemblies and other kinds of inputs and outputs are produced within local industrial networks and are then passed on to other locations and agglomerations. In other words, in many industries today, the concentration of key-activities coexists with the dispersal of other elements of the commodity chain. The 'roundaboutness' of the division of labour is both functional and spatial (Scott & Storper, 1992).

Globalisation has reinforced the importance of regional agglomerations by fostering the integration of their most dynamic sectors within international networks (Castells, 1996; Cooke, 1995). Regional economic competitiveness rests on the successful interlinking of local networks with global networks of production and innovation (De Vet, 1993; OECD, 1993). Regional specialisation is enhanced as local clusters mobilise their assets to establish competitive advantages in the global market. The selective re-emergence of successful regional economies in the early 1980s as world-scale 'industrial districts', manifests 'regionalisation' rather, than global integration (Shan, Walker, & Kogut, 1994).

Mainstream theory cannot adequately explain the persistence of regional diversity and growth by the traditional concepts of transaction costs and agglomeration externalities. The socio-economic reality and its spatial outcome are strongly defined by non-purely economic factors, as well. Although untraded interdependencies cannot be easily measured, they nevertheless form region-specific determinants of industrial competitiveness. Localised synergies play a decisive role in the formation of relational assets, which are critical for regional economic viability in contemporary globalised capitalism (Storper, 1997). Such processes differentiate regional resilience and adjustability to external competition (Martin & Sunley, 1996).

Thus, despite the prevalence of MNCs, which account for the lion's share of the markets, flexibly specialised small, fast-paced firms have managed to compete successfully with their bigger rivals. The agro-food industry is a characteristic example of global convergence ensuing from marketing and technical progress, coexisting with regional divergence—based on locally differentiated production, learning and marketing structures, resulting from region-specific assets and territorialised synergies of relations and codes of practice (Storper, 1997). The strong tradition of self-employment and small-scale entrepreneurship in the regions concerned has sustained the proliferation of independently owned firms in the context of a self-contained regional economy. The organisation of regional agro-food systems of production, processing, retailing, and consumption on a local basis has allowed for geographical distinctiveness and recognition (Tsampra, 2000).

Small agro-food producers and processors take advantage of niche market opportunities for high-quality artisanal products of distinct originality (Protected Designation of Origin, or Protected Geographical Indication), of short supply chains, and more direct relationships with consumers (Sonnino & Marsden, 2006). These types of products are contrasted to the 'placeless' and standardised foods marketed through mass retail outlets (Kneafsey, 2010). Local initiatives highly depend on 'territorial' development in the sense of the existing supportive environments, consisting of the place-specific human and social capital, the institutional context, and the external agglomeration economies enhanced by spatial proximity. These are the necessary factors for initiatives striving to exploit the advantages which are embedded in the territory.

Human capital (i.e. education, skills and experience), along with social capital (i.e. networking, co-operation culture, trust relations, principles and attitudes) are built gradually through time and they are rooted in places' history, tradition, and socio-economic structure. In this sense, their place-specific nature defines the particular local conditions affecting production and business activities in a certain way. Tangible and intangible territorial resources, valuable to the consumer and difficult to replicate, define the basis of sustainable competitive advantages and successful economic performance. In this way, the locality becomes increasingly important in adding value to traditional/conventional agricultural products (Dimara, Petrou, & Skuras, 2003).

Innovation and marketing are essential tools for the formation of a sustainable strategy for both firms and territories. The place-specific quality of agro-food products is a key-feature in the development of niche-market strategies. By adopting a niche-market strategy, small firms avoid direct confrontation with large competitors as they specialise along market, customer, product, or marketing-mix lines (Kotler, 2000; Porter, 1986). Niche-market strategy implies

Table 1 EU-27 country-members with highest contribution in food and beverages industry

	Value added (millions €)		Employment (thousands)		Number of firms (%)		Revenue (%)		Value added (%)		Employment (%)	
1	Germany	33,299	Germany	822	France	26.5	Cyprus	29.7	Cyprus	23.8	Cyprus	28.7
2	UK	30,691	France	625	Belgium	20.8	Latvia	24.9	Latvia	21.1	Latvia	21.5
3	France	29,038	Italy	457	Luxemburg	19.5	Greece	20.1	Greece	20.8	Greece	21.4
4	Spain	18,897	Poland	448	Bulgaria	19.2	Poland	19.2	Lithuania	20.3	Lithuania	19.2
5	Italy	18,422	UK	441	Romania	17.9	Lithuania	19.0	Poland	16.5	Poland	17.3

Source: Eurostat, CIAA: data and trends of the EU food and drink industry 2006

niche-marketing techniques based on: (1) the identification of consumer groups (willing to spend more for quality products) and (2) innovation—technological and organisational—to attract demanding consumers.

3 The Case Study: Regional Agro-Food Agglomerations in Greece

According to Eurostat 2006 data on the food and drink industry (Table 1), Germany, the UK, France, Spain, and Italy produce the highest value added in EU-27. But on the national level, the industry's highest contribution—in terms of share in revenue, value added, and employment—is identified in Cyprus, Latvia, Greece, Lithuania and Poland (FEIR, 2009). The industry's importance is further substantiated when explored in terms of regional specialisation. Drawing on the 2011 data from a study by the Center for Strategy and Competitiveness (CSC, 2011) on the production specialisation of all EU-27 regions, we identify (at a 3-digit level of analysis) the production sectors in which Greek regions have the highest specialisation.

Focusing on the farming, agriculture, and agro-food sectors, we observe that all Greek regions—with the exception of metropolitan Attiki and the low representation of the tourism-oriented South Aegean—are highly specialised in growing of crops—market gardening—horticulture, farming of animals, fishing and fish farming, manufacture of dairy products—other food products beverages, processing and preserving of fruit and vegetables, manufacture of vegetable and animal oils and fats, grain mill products, starches and starch products.

Drawing on data of the same source (CSC, 2011), we also identify the most specialised regions in EU-27 in the aforementioned sectors. In the following table (Table 2), regional industrial specialisation is defined by a minimum degree of 1.5, meaning that the region is at least 50 % 'overrepresented' in the industry; whilst the industries included are those of at least 500 employees in the region.

We can see above that the majority of the Greek regions—Epirus, Thessaly, Peloponnese, Central Macedonia, Eastern Macedonia and Thrace, Central Greece, Western Greece, South Aegean, North Aegean, and Crete—are highly specialised in the agro-food and related industries, with significant contribution in the EU-27. All these areas host local agro-food industrial agglomerations that function as major

Table 2 Specialisation ranking in the agro-food sectors of EU-27 of the different regions of Greece

Rank in EU-27	Greek region	Degree of specialisation	Number of employees
Growing of crops; market gardening; horticulture			
4	Peloponnese	19.18	69,562
7	Eastern Macedonia and Thrace	12.71	41,861
8	Thessaly	12.68	52,425
9	Crete	10.95	39,638
10	Western Greece	10.85	42,122
11	Central Greece	9.12	28,946
12	Western Macedonia	9.09	13,696
13	North Aegean	9.00	8,983
15	Ionian Islands	7.76	9,476
17	Central Macedonia	5.98	64,559
18	Epirus	5.51	10,234
Farming of animals			
3	Epirus	9.66	5,923
5	Eastern Macedonia and Thrace	8.68	9,428
7	Western Macedonia	5.27	2,621
8	Thessaly	5.23	7,132
11	Central Greece	4.25	4,453
16	Western Greece	3.23	4,144
17	Ionian Islands	2.98	1,201
18	Peloponnese	2.96	3,538
19	Crete	2.79	3,336
Growing of crops combined with farming of animals (mixed farming)			
8	Epirus	3.79	8,278
9	Western Greece	2.47	11,251
11	Peloponnese	2.04	8,701
12	Crete	1.84	7,849
14	Eastern Macedonia and Thrace	1.51	5,842
Fishing, fish farming, and related service activities			
1	South Aegean	44.50	2,621
3	North Aegean	36.79	1,327
6	Ionian Islands	22.16	978
7	Central Greece	17.60	2,019
9	Eastern Macedonia and Thrace	11.79	1,403
10	Peloponnese	10.70	1,403
14	Central Macedonia	7.17	2,797
16	Western Greece	7.06	991
Processing and preserving of fruit and vegetables			
8	Peloponnese	5.01	1,766
14	Thessaly	4.54	1,825
18	Central Macedonia	3.99	4,180

(continued)

Table 2 (continued)

Rank in EU-27	Greek region	Degree of specialisation	Number of employees
Manufacture of vegetable and animal oils and fats			
1	Central Greece	13.88	882
Manufacture of dairy products			
7	Epirus	4.55	1,303
19	Thessaly	2.98	1,895
Manufacture of grain mill products, starches, and starch products			
4	Central Greece	6.67	1,493
Manufacture of other food products			
4	Central Macedonia	2.14	18,671
9	Central Greece	2.01	5,171
19	North Aegean	1.73	1,395

regional employers and income sources. Even in the less developed region of Epirus, the fruit, meat, and dairy products industries contribute significantly to the regional GDP, income, and employment. The region hosts some of the most successful Greek agro-food industries that also lead in exports, for example, IPEIROS, PINDOS, and DODONI.

Empirical findings of primary research concerning the local business structures, ties with suppliers and distributors, use of labour resources, market specialisation, learning and innovation practices, indicate a variety of visible and invisible entrepreneurial networks rooted in the locale (Tsampra, 2000). The competitiveness of the local agro-food industrial systems in Greek rural regions is traced in: (1) the socio-economic embeddedness of agro-food production, (2) the territorialisation of supply, distribution, and consumption, and (3) niche-marketing through supra-local links/channels. The outcome is measured by the firms' economic performance and the successful integration of the regional agro-food systems in the global supply chain. Three types of enterprises are identified in the country's specialised regional agro-food agglomerations:

1. Small and very small firms, which constitute the majority of local business; they provide mainly for the domestic market, and they have a limited impact on the local economy
2. Dynamic small and medium-size enterprises (SMEs); they produce for the regional and national market and often for highly specialised niche-markets abroad, achieving significant benefits for the local economy
3. Large firms, which often operate as MNC subsidiaries, benefiting from the 'local product' label; they have weak ties with the local economy in terms of supplies, but they employ the local work force and produce for the national and the international market.

In order to strengthen their potential, small/very small and small/medium sized firms often collaborate or establish strategic alliances with larger domestic or foreign rivals. For example, in dairy products manufacture the dynamic enterprise IPEIROS collaborates with the wholesale retailer (and importer) OPTIMA for products distribution. Likewise, the local DELFI (an SME operating in Western Greece) has established an alliance with the Dutch FRIESLAND-CAMPINA for the production of the international label cheese 'white' Milner and the international label milk 'NOYNOY Family'. As FRIESLAND-CAMPINA consolidates her place in the dairy products industry, the position of Greek dairy manufactures in South East Europe improves.

Intra-industry competition increases on the national level, especially among firms of brand name products reaching consumers through supermarkets. In the domestic dairy products industry, the competing firms include: FAGE, MEVGAL, KOLIOS, TYRAS (which recently acquired OLYMPOS and RODOPI), MINERVA and many more others. The competition from imported agro-food products is also intense, especially as large international enterprises strengthen their position through purchases (e.g. Campina purchased by Friesland). Moreover, major super-market chains provide price-competitive 'private label' agro-food products in the domestic market, by subcontracting small local producers. Small/very small firms, operating with lower market shares, are self-contained and have several technical and organisational weaknesses, which prevent full development of their potential. However, they maintain their share in the local/regional market and they manage to survive competition by investing in quality, tradition, and face-to-face contact with customers and local suppliers.

Inter-personal relations and collaborations embedded in the locale have strongly enhanced local business initiatives in the agro-food industry. The tradition of self-employment and the size and level of the local market supports the development of personal-type small-scale enterprises operating efficiently with just a small number of low-cost skilled employees. These enterprises focus on batch production of low standardisation—a general feature of the Greek agro-food sector. Local agro-food firms in such regional agglomerations establish long-term ties with suppliers meeting primarily the criterion of quality, and secondarily the criterion of cost. Spatial proximity is also very important for smaller firms, while larger firms develop a more geographically dispersed network in order to satisfy larger demand and attain lower prices.

Loyalty and trust are the primary criteria when it comes to personnel, but satisfactory labour expertise is also an essential priority which all firms seek and accomplish in the local market. The broad diversity of products provided by the versatile and small-scale regional agro-food systems is a comparative advantage of local firms that their non-local rivals cannot compete. Local agro-food firms avoid inter-firm collaboration, in order to prevent leakage of knowledge. They keep their resources centralised on the development of their most skill-intensive and profitable tasks. At the same time, know-how 'spillovers' create place-specific dense intangible relations, which counteract at some degree the lack of systematic innovation support.

Agro-food products sales cover the local/regional market, but in many cases, local firms find ways to reach the national, the European, and other international markets with impressive results. Nevertheless, institutional support to local firms is severely inadequate for developing exporting activities in isolated regional agglomerations. Moreover, local firms rely mainly on self-funding as business financing is very problematic due to the country's rigid banking system. Whilst EU funds do not provide efficient financial support either, due to rigidities in allocation processes. All aforementioned weaknesses leave space for improvements and better performance of the Greek agro-food industry.

4 Concluding Remarks

The main theoretical account adopted in this paper is that regional specialisation is a necessary source of economic viability and hence, of the developmental dynamism of contemporary capitalism itself. In this context, the adaptability and competitiveness of the Greek agro-food industry was discussed. Fragmented entrepreneurship, strong self-employment based on small-scale production of independently owned units or co-operatives, strong rural and territorial embeddedness are the main characteristics of agro-food manufacturing in Greece.

From one point of view, the competitiveness of the country's regional agro-food agglomerations can be explained by the increased consumers' interest for 'authentic', 'healthy', 'traceable', and 'wholesome' foods (Tsakiridou, 2012). The social dimension of this shift in food-products demand is associated with trust in quality and confidence in safety pursued by consumers in short agro-food supply chains, where they can practically know the producers of their food. The economic benefits for local agro-food systems consist of the sustainability of rural areas, new business and job opportunities, and new sources of income. From another point of view, local/regional competitiveness is the outcome of territorialised expertise and specialisation, production modes which embed traded and untraded relations and practices formed by tradition and place history, local physical and socio-economic assets.

The Greek regional agro-food agglomerations are structured around local diversified production and consumption norms, imposed by local demand. Product specialisation is related to the structures of agriculture, which is characterised by low standardisation and certain territorial production and consumption patterns. The comparative advantages which consolidate the place of the Greek local agro-food firms in the domestic market and give them impetus in the international market are based not just on quality but also on versatility. The efficiency of the local agro-food production systems rest strongly on local expertise and highly skilled labour resources; the latter, form the critical region-specific asset attracting large foreign investment as well. Human and social capital is sustained by untraded interdependencies, informal linkages, and networks of contacts embedded in the local rural economies. Moreover, face-to-face contact of the producers with suppliers and customers is the most valuable element for learning and innovation.

As the indigenous agro-food industry serves mainly local demand requirements, its territorialisation is further enhanced. Nevertheless, as previously argued its strong territorialisation enhances its competitiveness and allows for a successful performance when direct relations are established between local firms and international customers. The viability condition for Greek regional agro-food agglomerations is the recognition and exploitation of new market opportunities for niche or specialty produce. In other words, the main issue is the internationalisation of such highly territorialised agro-food systems and the establishment of channels marketing their products abroad. Inter-firm collaboration, sense of common purpose, social consensus, extensive institutional support, skills upgrading, and circulation of ideas are critical factors for competitiveness in the contemporary globalised economy (Storper, 1997).

However, such elements are weak in most regional agro-food agglomerations the lack of institutional support restricts the development of the regional knowledge base and entrepreneurial capacity to adopt organisational innovations and access international markets; the lack of financial and marketing expertise, the inadequate funding and the poor business services also form severe obstacles to economic viability and competitiveness. Nevertheless, research has identified forms of localised production—oriented to local specialised tastes—which successfully respond to global competition challenges. Loose coupling and rivalry among local firms allow for new forms of production and organisation, new customer and supplier links; whilst, they further sustain firms' experience and innovativeness in their operating environments.

The crucial regulatory problem is to balance co-operation and competition among local manufacturing firms, within a solid institutional and regulatory context. This is the most essential requirement for the majority of local agro-food firms in all regional agglomerations, to overcome serious obstacles in developing demand beyond the regional or national borders and to fully explore their potential for further development.

References

Castells, M. (1996). *The rise of network society*. Oxford: Blackwell.

Center for Strategy and Competitiveness. (2011, April). *Smart specialisation in Europe: European specialisation data by region*. Stockholm School of Economics, European Cluster Observatory. http://www.clusterobservatory.eu/common/galleries/downloads/Smart_Specialisation_Analysis_Region_Report.pdf. Accessed 10 May 2012.

CIAA. (2008). *Data and trends of the European food and drink industry*. Brussels: Confederation of the food and drink industries of the EU. http://www.fooddrinkeurope.eu/. Accessed 10 May 2012.

Cooke, P. (1995). *Innovative regional clusters: The automotive and electronics industries in Wales* (Regional Industrial Research Report, 19). Cardiff: Cardiff University, Centre for Advanced Studies (CASS).

De Vet, J. (1993). Globalization and local and regional competitiveness. *STI Review, 13*, 89–121.

Dimara, E., Petrou, A., & Skuras, D. (2003). The socio-economics of niche market creation: A social ecology paradigm for the adoption of organic cultivation in Greece. *International Journal of Social Economics, 30*(3), 219–235.

Foundation of Economic and Industrial Research. (2009). The Greek industry of Food and Beverages: Annual Report for 2008.

Kneafsey, M. (2010). The region in food—Important or irrelevant? *Cambridge Journal of Regions Economy and Society, 3*(2), 177–190.

Kotler, P. (2000). *Marketing management. The millennium edition*. Upper Saddle River: Prentice Hall.

Martin, R., & Sunley, P. (1996). Paul Krugman's geographical economics and its implications for regional development theory: A critical assessment. *Economic Geography, 72*(3), 259–92.

OECD. (1993). *Territorial development and structural change: A new perspective on adjustment and reform.* Paris: Organisation for Economic Co-operation and Development.

Porter, M. (Ed.). (1986). *Competition in global industries.* Boston: Harvard Business School Press.

Scott, A. J., & Storper, M. (Eds.). (1992). *Pathways to industrialization and regional development.* London: Routledge.

Shan, W., Walker, G., & Kogut, B. (1994). Interfirm cooperation and startup innovation in the biotechnology industry. *Strategic Management Journal, 15*(5), 387–394.

Sonnino, R., & Marsden, T. K. (2006). Beyond the divide: Rethinking relations between alternative and conventional food networks in Europe. *Journal of Economic Geography, 6*(2), 181–199.

Storper, M. (1997). *The regional world: Territorial development in a global economy.* London: The Guilford.

Tsakiridou, E. (2012). *The importance of local food products in a consumers' oriented market.* In 1st Meeting of the Mediterranean Macro-regional NRN Cluster, Thessaloniki.

Tsampra, M. (2000). *A study of regional diversity in a global sector: The case of the Greek IT industry* (PhD thesis). London: University of London: King's College.

Key Conditions for the Effectiveness of Special Economic Zones in Regional Development: Opportunities and Challenges for the Thrace Region

Konstantinos J. Hazakis

1 Introduction

Since the 1980s, the influence of special economic zones (SEZs) has grown steadily throughout the world. Despite the lack of aggregate annual statistical data, it has been estimated that the number of SEZs grew from 25 in 1975 to 176 in 1986 (Aggarwal, 2006, 4533) and 3,000 in 2003 to more than 3,500 in 2007 (Boyenge, 2007). Furthermore, $850 billion of goods and services are exported through SEZs in developing countries on an annual basis (which equates to almost 20 % of their exports), while the relative contributions of SEZs to exports in these nations is approximately 40 times greater than its influence on direct employment (FIAS, 2008, 34). As a result of this rising trend, SEZs now employ over 68 million workers directly and another 65 million indirectly (FIAS, 2008).

SEZs can be differentiated in terms of their ownership structures, spatial locations, forms of economic activity, preferential policies, and degrees of global integration. Modern types of SEZs range from classical industrial SEZs (such as the Shannon SEZ in Ireland founded in 1958) to Mexican *Maquiladoras* and *sui generis* Chinese coastal zones. Moreover, the average number of zones per state has also increased manifold over time illustrating the liberalisation of the global macroeconomic environment.

Additionally, the way in which SEZs are owned, regulated, and governed is changing rapidly. Specifically, there has been a shift from publicly operated SEZs (FATF-OECD, 2010, 13) to privately developed and operated SEZs. It is estimated that 62 % of the 2,301 SEZs in transition and developing economies are private sector operated, mostly located in the Asia-Pacific region. Consequently, the majority of states prefer to divest project development to private firms, thereby changing zone authorities into promotional and regulatory bodies. Parallel to this shift, public–private

K.J. Hazakis (✉)
Department of International Economic Relations and Development, Democritus University of Thrace, Komotini 69100, Greece
e-mail: kmhazaki@otenet.gr

P. Sklias and N. Tzifakis (eds.), *Greece's Horizons*, The Konstantinos Karamanlis Institute for Democracy Series on European and International Affairs,
DOI 10.1007/978-3-642-34534-0_19,

partnerships in governing/operating SEZs are continuously gaining ground. Further, a new geographical concentration of zones is in place; although most SEZs were clustered in Western Europe in the 1970s, the preferred locations had switched to the Asia-Pacific (991 SEZs), central and Eastern Europe (443 SEZs), and the Middle East and Africa (213 SEZs) regions by the 1990s (Palit, 2009, 137; Wei, 1999).

The above-described shift should be examined within the context of recent globalisation (between 1983 and 2008 trade grew 85 % above the rate of GDP) and the subsequent rising impact of global value chains. Indeed, SEZs are beginning to claim greater shares of global production and trade through the attraction of commercial/industrial outsourcing based around competitive costs and the internalisation of SEZ firms in multinational value chains. Nevertheless, the majority of SEZs remain focused on labour-intensive and assembly-based operations such as the production of garments, textiles, and electrical equipment (Madani, 1999). Finally, the purpose of SEZs is considerably influenced by trade liberalisation, resulting in a mixture of incentives being offered to foreign investors. Although the bulk of SEZs still target low-skilled jobs, there is a steady but growing preference for medium-level technology sectors, resulting in generous financial and infrastructural incentives being made available to transnational firms.

This chapter examines the case study of the Thrace SEZ in South East Europe in order to shed light on the key success factors for SEZs. It principally draws out the lessons and policy implications that will enable a well-organised and efficient zone to be designed and implemented in the Thrace region. Although the creation of an SEZ is not necessarily compatible with the functioning of the EU internal market, European practice allows deviations from EU provisions under two broad conditions, namely that SEZs are temporary and that they should cause the least possible disturbance to the functioning of the EU internal market (Article 27, Para. 2, Treaty on the Functioning of the EU). By taking into consideration the provisions of articles 27 and 174 of the Treaty (based on the strengthening of economic–social–territorial cohesion) as well as the current structural, debt and economic problems of the Greek economy, a deviation could be granted for the establishment of an SEZ in Thrace. However, it must be emphasised from the outset that before any SEZ initiative can begin, there should be official application from the Greek government to the EU Commission, which would subsequently need to be approved by the relevant EU authorities (e.g. the Directorate of the Internal Market and Services and the Directorate of Taxation and Customs Union).

The remainder of this chapter is divided into three sections. The first section explores the fundamental traits of an SEZ. The chapter then analyses the incentives and prerequisites for establishing a successful SEZ in the Thrace region. Finally, the last section concludes by emphasising the key policy implications for the success of SEZs.

2 Definition of SEZs

Although many authors have tried to clarify the status of SEZs, no consensus has been achieved in defining the term (Schweinberger, 2003, 620). In the academic literature, customs-free zones, export-processing zones, and SEZs are too rarely distinguished and classified (Farole & Kweka, 2011, 1). According to Farole (2011, 24), the multiplicity of names for economic zones is the outcome of several factors, including the need to differentiate among types of zones that display very real differences in terms and function, differences in economic terminology among states, the need to differentiate new zones from already existing competitors, and the repercussions of various translations. These definitions do not usually clarify how 'special' a free zone's regulatory framework should be before it can be categorised as an SEZ. The definitional effort becomes even more difficult because the SEZ model has evolved considerably in terms of policies, governance, ownership structures, and spatial locations (MENA-OECD, 2005, 7–10).

According to FIAS (2008, 9), the features that characterise the concept of a zone include a geographically delimited area (which is usually physically secured), single management, the eligibility of advantages based upon physical location within an SEZ, a separate customs area, and streamlined procedures. Ahrens and Meyer-Baudeck (1995, 88) argue that SEZs are geographically or functionally limited parts of an economy in which rules and other institutions concerning the production and distribution of goods and services differ from those in the rest of the economy. Farole (2011) further proposes that any definition of an SEZ should comprise both structural and policy features. Regarding the former, he underlines the following three traits:

- Zones are primarily delimited portions of the national territory and are defined by a specific regulatory regime.
- The administration of the regime demands a dedicated governance mechanism.
- Zones are provided with a physical infrastructure that supports the activities of the economic agents that operate within them.

FIAS (2008, 8) adds another three structural characteristics, namely single management/administration, eligibility for benefits, and separate customs area procedures. On the issue of policy features, Farole (2011), Madani (1999), and Cling and Letilly (2001) all distinguish between the following four motives behind the establishment of an SEZ:

- To attract foreign direct investment (FDI) inflows.
- To serve as pressure valves to address high unemployment rates.
- To support national reform strategy.
- To serve as experimental laboratories for the application of new economic policies.

The present article suggests a fifth policy feature, namely the enforcement of regional competitiveness by embedding productive regional networks within global economic/commercial networks. Further, any attempt to comprehensively define SEZs should be broad enough to incorporate the typology of past and present zones and yet sufficiently precise to avoid all structural/policy traits that do not constitute a clear SEZ. Following this approach, the chapter underlines the necessity to expand future definitions of the informal institutional characteristics and cognitive traits of SEZs as well as include a social capital dimension. Such a broader SEZ definition should include the regulative, normative, and cognitive features that stress that SEZs are shaped and transformed through a complex interweaving of economic, political, social, and institutional factors.

3 Analysing the Fundamental Pillars of SEZ Success

Tracing the necessary success factors in the Thrace SEZ requires understanding its main targets in the current global macroeconomic framework. First, the macroeconomic environment in which the Thrace SEZ operates is qualitatively different from that experienced by the zones created in East Asia and Latin America in the 1970s and 1980s. For instance, the level and nature of competition for traditional manufacturing in SEZs makes unreliable the growth potential in the same sectors in the Thrace region. Taking account of the absence of comparative advantage in unskilled labour-intensive assembly-based production, focusing on traditional export-processing activities would be futile and would deliver poor economic results. Equally importantly, the intense competition of neighbouring states based on their low labour costs and social dumping would render unproductive a strategy based on unskilled labour factor intensity.

Likewise, if SEZs in Greece are based dogmatically on lower wages, such a policy somewhat treats the symptom rather than the disease. This oversight avoids addressing the true problems of competitiveness, namely the lack of cluster productivity, the absence of profound production base restructuring, bureaucratic complexity (Koutsoukis & Roukanas, 2011; Sklias, 2011), and isolation from global production and commerce networks. Moving beyond the enclave perception and retaining a sustainable competitive position means dynamic upgrading towards medium-level technology activities. Although this approach does not preclude the existence of manufacturing activities with labour intensity (basically as outsourcing partners in a cluster), it underlines the fact that SEZ success in Thrace is in doubt if based primarily on the traditional assembly of imported semi-finished products.

Second, a critical foundation for SEZ success is the rigorous assessment of the potential for regional competitiveness in various sectors. A 'build it and they will come' approach is both inefficient and costly. There is thus little doubt that industrial clusters in the Thrace SEZ should focus on those activities aligned with actual/potential regional comparative advantages, including developing clear sources of differentiation in sectors such as food and beverages, agro-processing, and alternative energy resources. Likewise, SEZ authorities should have a targeted positioning strategy that focuses on specific product combinations within clusters. Attracting reliable investors is crucial for forming the initial base of the SEZ in order to positively signal its potential. As the global experience clearly manifests, second-level investors who aim to take advantage of sustainable SEZ benefits are concerned with accessing sources of robust externalities. Consequently, the existence of leading-edge firms offers opportunities for learning, creative routines, and knowledge spillovers.

Third, it is worth noting that location contributes to agglomeration effects. Therefore, positive results are more easily achieved if SEZs are established in areas that already have a basic infrastructure. One favourable site for an SEZ is suggested to be the wider area of the city of Alexandropoulis. Having clarified the basic success factors of Thrace, the incentives (e.g. regulative, fiscal, financial, infrastructural) that determine firm performance in the zone should also be examined in detail.

Although various shortcomings can contribute to the failure of an SEZ strategy, they are most often traced back to the planning phase and they result from an inefficient institutional and regulatory framework. Regulatory incentives are thus fundamental to attracting long-term and high-quality investors as well as building transparency and predictability, two crucial rules of the game in SEZs. Legal prescriptions and routines/practices should also be comprehensive, thereby guiding the site selection, investment, development, licensing, and operation of FDI projects in the Thrace SEZ. This means avoiding overlapping investment regimes/rules, accountabilities, and responsibilities, which reduces investor uncertainty, creates transaction costs, and diminishes business network trust.

Equally important to the successful performance of SEZs is a political environment that favours zone development by targeting regional structural shifts, while the planning and operation of SEZs is fundamental to their success. Further, the SEZ authority and all involved regional/national leaders should have a clear vision of the development path and specific role of the Thrace SEZ in economic growth. Their commitment should go beyond words and promises to ensuring the successful daily implementation of the SEZ's strategy. This commitment would promote export-oriented and medium-level technology activities, thus shifting Thrace away from its previous inward-looking growth paradigm. However, establishing a clear regulatory framework and reaching a strong cognitive consensus on an SEZ's strategy are necessary but not sufficient conditions for success and thus the practical regulative aspects of the smooth implementation of the zone's principles must be considered.

This chapter suggests a single SEZ authority based on a public–private partnership that acts as a 'one-stop shop' in the Thrace SEZ. Significant private sector representation on the board of directors (up to 49 %) would also give a voice to investors in terms of affecting the daily operations of the SEZ. Private sector participation on the board should include the association of zone companies and other private sector representatives elected among SEZ investors. All remaining board members (seven out of 12) would then be selected and appointed by the Minister of Finance for 4-year fixed terms irrespective of the usual electoral cycle. The new SEZ authority governed by this board of directors (and controlled at 51 % by the Greek state) would thus help investors obtain business licenses, export/import licenses, work permits and safety certificates, environmental clearances, and all other relevant authorisations. Similarly, the SEZ authority would handle environment impact reports and immigration/construction permits, thereby mitigating the usual bureaucratic constraints on entrepreneurship. More precisely, the SEZ authority in Thrace would be responsible for the planning, promotion, and daily operations of the zone, including the following responsibilities:

- Put in place a land-use plan and prepare the SEZ territory accordingly (preconstruction activities).
- Guarantee efficient infrastructure provision within the SEZ.
- Prepare cost planning and lease/rental agreements with firms and provide follow-up services.

- In combination with the 'Invest in Greece' agency (based on a memorandum of co-operation), formulate an international marketing strategy to build the SEZ brand name and to differentiate it from actual/potential SEZ competitors (the President of the SEZ board could act as a non-voting member on the 'Invest in Greece' board). Close co-operation with regional promotion agencies is also critical in the field of investor after-care in order to avoid overlapping marketing actions. The SEZ authorities should target high-profile investors at the outset of the SEZ program because they usually bring with them a regional or even global network of competent suppliers.
- Facilitate/approve licensing in all areas of firm operation in the SEZ. Thus, automaticity according to transparent rules would be applied to avoid bureaucratic corruption and red tape.
- Monitor firm compliance with the labour force and environmental standards and requirements of the SEZ and enforce penalties where necessary based on the approval of the Greek Ministry of Finance.
- Train the labour force in close co-operation with the Democritus University in Thrace. This means close co-operation with SEZ investors with the objective of identifying the skills required for cluster growth and implementing programs to address them through a skills development centre operated within the SEZ.
- Ensure the availability of the appropriate resources for SEZ funding through lease/rental fees. In order to avoid excessive administrative charges, which could deter foreign investors, all proposed changes would be under the approval of the Greek Ministry of Finance.
- Monitor and evaluate performance based on the systematic collection of all necessary data for the relevant benchmarking indicators. Hence, the SEZ authority should take serious account of SEZ performance in the following five areas:
  - Length and cost of business start-up (i.e. receiving a firm name, registering firms, getting licenses, registering for municipal/national taxes).
  - Customs clearance duration and cost, the reported clearance time inside/outside the SEZ (as well as among SEZ customs authorities in different locations in Greece), and the quality of on-site customs clearance services.
  - Duration and cost of approval for immigration licenses (i.e. residence permits, visas).
  - Duration and cost of granting labour permits.
  - Cost efficiency of the on-site infrastructure (i.e. monthly downturn caused by electricity and water outages).
- Ensure that labour regimes within the SEZ are consistent with Greek and EU norms including International Labour Office standards and rules.

Based on the foregoing, the SEZ authority should aim to publish an annual report that states the shortcomings in its practices and proposes ways to overcome them. It should again be recognised that worldwide best practice is in favour of automatic authorisations if approval periods are violated. An online connection between all departments of the SEZ authority and the Greek Ministry of Finance could thus permit real-time information sharing in order to avoid bureaucratic delays and hurdles.

On the issue of controlling SEZ operations, this chapter therefore proposes that such a complex task should be under the jurisdiction of a single ministry (i.e. the Greek Ministry of Finance), reporting directly to Prime Minister. Acting as the second regulative pillar, it would thus play a crucial role in avoiding co-ordination failures by the semi-independent SEZ authority. The SEZ responsibilities of the ministry would include the following:

- Selecting SEZ sites in close co-operation with regional political authorities based on detailed feasibility studies.
- Selecting seven (out of 12) members to sit on the SEZ board every 4 years.
- Guaranteeing the off-site infrastructure in SEZs (e.g. high-speed telecommunications and incubator facilities) in order to develop agglomeration prerequisites. Equally importantly, ensuring that the authorities responsible for services delivery (e.g. electricity companies, municipal water authorities) meet their obligations and that they are capable of maintaining good standards of supply. This means establishing an infrastructure/planning utility within the Ministry of Finance to ensure off-site provision is adequately supported.
- Controlling the implementation of legal prescriptions for SEZ operations.
- Enforcing a memorandum of understanding across public agencies on the deployment of staff and on the delineation of SEZ authority.
- Determining the annual share of fees/taxes selected within the zone, which would be attributed to the annual budget of the SEZ authority based on multiyear SEZ budget programming and needs.
- Establishing tax and customs authorities within the SEZ that are sufficiently equipped to offer reliable customs clearance in order to avoid red tape and cross-institutional conflict over the control of SEZ operations.

The preceding two-pillar institutional framework not only provides organisational efficiency and functional interdependence for the Thrace SEZ but also guarantees national economic interests through the effective involvement of the Greek Ministry of Finance. Indeed, such ministry involvement in SEZ operations avoids any confusion of responsibilities across ministries, departments, agencies, and local authorities and reduces transaction costs and uncertainty for foreign investors. Overall, the two fundamental regulative pillars (SEZ board and Ministry of Finance), acting within a coherent cognitive framework, would eliminate gaps between the initial concept/design of the Thrace SEZ and its efficient implementation.

Finally, we are in favour of a seven-member review committee (appointed by the Ministry of Finance) composed of three academics from economic departments at the Democritus University in Thrace, one technocrat from the Ministry of Finance, a representative of the Internal Markets Directorate of the EU, and two representatives from local/regional municipalities). This committee could provide the necessary expertise to improve SEZ capacity and performance.

Further, fiscal incentives can also play a role in attracting FDI in the short-term but these motives do not have a strong positive effect on the long-term performances of SEZs. Consequently, applying such incentives as the fundamental tool for SEZ development distorts investor behaviour and expectations

(Warr, 1989), promotes a 'race to the bottom' situation with neighbouring states, and fails to address the structural inefficiencies of local production chains. Previous research has insisted that the major shortcomings of the Greek economic environment are the country's poor administrative capacity, complex bureaucratic procedures, and inadequate supporting infrastructure. Thus, SEZ policy should be devoted to delivering high-quality services to foreign investors in order to ensure that the business environment is as competitive as possible.

Based on the abovementioned principles, we argue in favour of fiscal incentives during the initial (establishment) phase and a reduced tax rate (subject to specific employment and export criteria) thereafter. Nevertheless, all incentives should be granted automatically based on transparent and simple rules rather than being subject to administrative discretion for three main reasons. First, budget costs in the form of sunk revenue for the long-term implementation of tax holidays could be detrimental to Greece's current financial plight as well as incompatible with the provisions of the stability program agreed with the troika (IMF, EU, and ECB). Second, incentives tend to be more successful when linked with the actual process of capital formation in the medium- to long-term. General incentive schemes in the form of beneficial tax holidays often encourage tax planning rather than productive investments among investors in SEZs. Finally, complex administrative procedures for the approval of tax incentives favour red tape and corruption. Moreover, it is considered to be crucial to offer a 1-year tax holiday in order to permit initial greenfield investment and allow the full development of operations from SEZ investors. In light of the foregoing, the present research proposes the following tax incentives:

- Complete exemption from corporate/property tax for 1 year after the beginning of the implementation of each investment project. A reduced rate of 10 % would then be applied indefinitely thereafter. Obviously, the issue of tax rates on reinvested profits should be examined thoroughly through a feasibility study undertaken before SEZ operations begin.
- Total exemption from ad hoc and unscheduled taxation imposed by national, regional, and local authorities on corporate operations. Such common practices in Greek tax administrative structures work against tax predictability and stability and distort the capacity of investor planning.
- Exemption from all taxes and duties on machinery, input goods, the spare parts required for the production process, and the capital goods necessary for the investment. However, full taxation on motor vehicles unconnected with investment projects should still be applied in SEZs.
- No tax exemption on the incomes, salaries, wages, or bonuses of all employees in SEZs. Regarding social security contributions, a reduction of 50 % could be applied indefinitely following the completion of two criteria: (a) at least 70 % of the labour force in an SEZ firm holds Greek nationality and (b) at least 70 % of firm output is exported to third-party countries.
- Complete wavering of initial permit and registration fees.
- Depreciation rates identical to those of non-SEZ firms.
- The tax exemption of SEZ firms financing directed towards the R&D activities of local and regional technological and academic research centres.

Ultimately, however, the investment into any SEZ project should total at least 100,000 euros and all aforementioned incentives should be applied only in the case of the full application of the export/employment criteria stated in the fourth point above.

We are against the application of financial incentives in the Thrace SEZ for two reasons. First, based on the well-known limits of the Greek budget, it is infeasible to crowd out scarce local capital in favour of SEZ firms. Second, financial incentives could drive a wedge between SEZ and non-SEZ firms, forcing corporations to relocate to SEZ territories. Such migration might result in the further contraction of industrial activities in Macedonia-Thrace, with negative repercussions on balanced growth, employment opportunities, and resource allocation. Nevertheless, it is suggested that if the two fundamental criteria (exports/employment) hold for an SEZ firm, preferential energy rates (including those for natural gas, electricity, and water) as well as preferential rental/leasing rates could be applied.

Global experience also highlights that one of the fundamental advantages of an SEZ could be its ability to overcome land and infrastructural constraints, thereby making land plots and infrastructure available to SEZ investors. Further, SEZs should be linked with wider trade gateways as well as with the main sources of human and social capital in the region. The closer the Thrace SEZ moves to the main gateways (i.e. airport/ports) the more likely it is to offer an effective logistics and transport environment for SEZ firms. Moreover, the establishment of warehousing facilities to create trade-related infrastructure and to facilitate the imports and exports of goods could render Thrace a reliable regional trading centre in the medium-term. Lastly, our research is against a build-own-operate method of off-site infrastructure and facilities, which may place new burdens on non-users of the Thrace SEZ.

4 Conclusions and Policy Implications for a Successful SEZ in Thrace

This chapter underlined the rationale for an SEZ in Thrace and identified the key hurdles for its successful implementation. It also set out guidelines to maximise the spillovers of SEZ strategy, demonstrating that an SEZ can act as a catalyst of structural shift in the region as long as it emphasises integration into the global networks of production and trade.

The policy implications of this analysis are fourfold. First, SEZs are not a panacea for learning and neither are they a *deus ex machina* in light of the current Greek economic depression. However, they could fundamentally signal a national competitive shift and induce positive spillovers, but only if an adequate economic/institutional framework leads to structural transformation in both the SEZs and the rest of the country. Institutions and sustainable business networks are the links between the perception of SEZs as a tool for regional economic rescheduling and the perception of SEZs as a tool for the maximisation of firm performance. To achieve this target, the institutional setting is a decisive trait that shapes the learning performances of SEZ firms, stabilises the expectations and patterns of economic behaviour, promotes network linkages, and favours co-ordination and co-operation between public and private agents. However, the role of clusters is vital and SEZs should be perceived as an ensemble of competencies derived from linkages among business networks. The greater the interaction between different networks in SEZs (i.e. firms, research centres, academic departments, local institutions), the more dynamic the SEZ will be.

Second, delivering a favourable investment climate and a high-quality infrastructure in SEZs will be more influential in the long-term than simply delivering unconditional tax and financial incentives. Third, learning is a process of collective action within SEZ clusters and concerns not only outsourcing common productive routines but also co-ordinating knowledge production strategies. This in turn presupposes that the SEZ authority ensures synergies between all the actors and institutions involved in economic activity within the SEZ territory. Fourth, to unleash the potential of the Thrace SEZ, efficient co-ordination between all the institutions involved in establishing SEZ operations is a prerequisite.

Overall, SEZ policy in Thrace should be designed in a sophisticated manner that fully takes account of the nature of market imperfections in the region and that implements efficient enforcement mechanisms in order to overcome market and/or policy failures. Although such an SEZ may be difficult to operate, this approach is not impossible, as the experiences of other developed countries in the EU show. However, without an institutionalist approach (Hazakis, 2011) that acknowledges the imperfections of both states and markets, Thrace SEZ developers will be unable to formulate realistic policy on the issue of sustainable, well-balanced, and export-oriented economic development in the region.

References

Aggarwal, A. (2006). Special economic zones: Revisiting the policy debate. *Economic and Political Weekly, 41*(43/44), 4533–4536.

Ahrens, J., & Meyer-Baudeck, A. (1995). Special economic zones: Shortcut or roundabout way towards capitalism? *Intereconomics, 30*(2), 87–95.

Boyenge, J. (2007). *ILO database on export processing zones, revised*. Geneva: International Labor Organization.

Cling, J., & Letilly, G. (2001). *Export processing zones: A threatened instrument for global economic insertion*? Document de travail DT/2001/17 November, DIAL/Unite de recherche CIPRE.

Farole, T. (2011). *Special economic zones in Africa: Comparing performance and learning from global experience* (Paper 60059). Washington, DC, The World Bank.

Farole, T., & Kweka, J. (2011). *Institutional best practices for special economic zones: An application to Tanzania*. Washington: The World Bank.

FATF-OECD. (2010). *Money laundering vulnerabilities of free trade zones*. Paris: OECD Publications, Financial Action Task Force.

FIAS. (2008). *Special economic zones: Performance, lessons learned and implications for zone development*. Washington: International Finance Corporation.

Hazakis, K. (2011). Rethinking the interaction between FDI and competitiveness in West Balkans: An institutionalist approach. *International Journal of Economic Policy in Emerging Markets, 4*(2), 177–196.

Koutsoukis, N., & Roukanas, S. (2011). The Greek crisis that should have been avoided. *Scientific Bulletin (Faculty of Economic Sciences, University of Pitesti), 10*(1), 20–27.

Madani, D. (1999). *A review of the role and impact of export processing zones* (Research paper 2238). Washington: The World Bank.

MENA-OECD. (2005). *Incentives and free zones in the MENA region: A preliminary stocktaking*. Working Group 2. Paris: OECD Publications.

Palit, A. (2009). Growth of special economic zones in India: Issues and perspectives. *Journal of Infrastructure Development, 1*(2), 133–152.

Schweinberger, A. (2003). Special economic zones in developing and/or transition economies: A policy proposal. *Review of International Economics, 11*(4), 619–629.

Sklias, P. (2011). The political economy of the Greek crisis in the framework of the European Monetary Union. In K. E. Botsiou & A. Klapsis (Eds.), *The Konstantinos Karamanlis institute for democracy yearbook 2011. The global economic crisis and the case of Greece* (pp. 67–76). Heidelberg: Springer.

Warr, P. (1989). Export processing zones: The economics of enclave manufacturing. *World Bank Research Observer, 4*(1), 65–88.

Wei, G. (1999). Special economic zones and the opening of the Chinese economy: Some lessons for economic liberalization. *World Development, 27*(7), 1267–1285.

Greece's Outward FDI: A Window for Growth?

Aristidis P. Bitzenis and Vasileios A. Vlachos

1 Introduction

After the introduction of the euro in 2002, the Greek economy grew annually, displaying its highest GDP growth in 2006 (7.5 %).[1] The peak of 2006 was explained at that time by financial market liberalisation coupled with membership of the European monetary union, which led to a substantial reduction in borrowing costs, buoyant activity in export markets in South East Europe (SEE), and the fiscal stimulus and focal point given by the Olympic Games in 2004 (see OECD, 2007). However, recent evidence indicates that the growth of the Greek economy until the eruption of the global financial crisis was on account of the internal demand fostered by the chronic phenomena of clientelism and rent-seeking behaviour (see Katsimi & Moutos, 2010) rather than that resulting from economic reforms that aimed to enhance competitiveness. Greece suffers from high levels of political and economic corruption, which has contributed greatly to the size of the country's shadow economy[2] and its low global competitiveness compared with other eurozone member states.

The bailouts granted to the Greek economy in order for it to service its sovereign debt (indeed, to keep it sustainable) have not yet managed to meet the country's optimistic expectations for recovery. The difficulty of fulfilling the goals of the economic adjustment programme i.e. via fiscal austerity, internal devaluation,

[1] Based on the authors' calculations from Eurostat data on GDP in purchasing power standards. Available at http://epp.eurostat.ec.europa.eu/portal/page/portal/statistics/search_database (accessed 20 August 2012).

[2] See Schneider, Buehn, and Montenegro (2010) for relative figures on the size and determinants of the shadow economy.

A.P. Bitzenis (✉) • V.A. Vlachos
Department of International and European Studies, University of Macedonia, 156 Egnatia St, Thessaloniki 54006, Greece
e-mail: bitzenis@yahoo.com; vlachosuk@hotmail.com

P. Sklias and N. Tzifakis (eds.), *Greece's Horizons*, The Konstantinos Karamanlis Institute for Democracy Series on European and International Affairs,
DOI 10.1007/978-3-642-34534-0_20,

economic reforms—indicates the significance of attracting the necessary private investment flows (as a substitute for public investment) in order to end the economic depression.

The importance of foreign direct investment (FDI) to Greece's current predicament can be easily comprehended by the significance of inward FDI as a substitute for public investment. However, the depth and nature of the Greek recession suggest that levels of inward FDI will be primarily influenced by privatisations in the short- to medium-term. Hence, the importance of Greece's outward FDI in stimulating domestic levels of employment and growth should not be overlooked. From a theoretical perspective, the positive externalities from outward FDI to the home country depend on whether the scale effects dominate the substitution effects. The characteristics of Greece's outward FDI, particularly the expansion of Greek multinational enterprises (MNEs) into SEE, namely the Balkans,[3] Turkey, and Cyprus, seem to generate such externalities.

The remainder of this chapter is organised as follows. The first section provides an overview of Greece's outward FDI. The next section discusses the theoretical context on which the prospective benefits of outward FDI to the home country are rooted and analyses the potential for these benefits to be realised in Greece. Finally, the last section makes some concluding remarks.

2 Greece's Outward FDI

The sizeable growth of Greece's outward FDI stock over the past decade (see Table 1) can be broadly explained by its accession to the eurozone, since it has been generally indicated that the euro has promoted intra-eurozone trade and FDI (see Baldwin, DiNino, Fontagne, De Santis, & Taglioni, 2008). Nevertheless, Greece's outward FDI stock amounted to just 14 % of GDP in 2010, which ranked the country second last (ahead of Slovakia) among eurozone member states.[4] Despite this relative paucity of outward FDI, Greece presents specific spatial characteristics that demand further analysis, because Greek MNEs have directed substantial amounts of outward FDI towards SEE and managed to accumulate considerable market shares in this region.

The all-encompassing study of Bitzenis and Vlachos (2011) provides an excellent guide to the development, determinants, policies, and current situation of Greece's outward FDI. Specifically, it describes how the fall of centrally planned economies in the Balkans and the subsequent gradual openness and liberalisation of these countries along with the Europeanisation process of Turkey contributed to Greece's outward

[3] The Balkans include Albania, Bosnia and Herzegovina, Bulgaria, Croatia, the FYR of Macedonia, Moldova, Montenegro, Romania, Serbia, and Slovenia.

[4] This ranking is based on the authors' calculations from Eurostat data on outward FDI stock and GDP. http://epp.eurostat.ec.europa.eu/portal/page/portal/statistics/search_database (accessed 20 August 2012).

Table 1 Key hosts of Greece's outward FDI (percentage of total)

	2001	2002	2003	2004	2005	2006	2007	2008	2009	2010	2011
Albania (%)	1.40	1.60	2.20	1.70	–	2.30	1.90	1.80	1.20	1.30	2.40
Armenia (%)	*0.90*	1.30	1.30	1.40	*0.00*	*0.90*	*0.70*	*0.00*	*0.00*	*0.00*	–
Austria (%)	*0.10*	*0.10*	2.10	2.10	2.10	1.40	1.00	0.90	1.30	1.00	*−0.40*
Bermuda (%)	*0.10*	1.50	1.40	*0.00*	*0.00*	*0.00*	*0.00*	*0.00*	*0.00*	*0.00*	–
Bulgaria (%)	7.00	5.10	5.30	5.60	6.50	5.40	5.00	5.00	5.10	6.50	5.90
Cayman Islands (%)	*0.00*	*0.00*	*0.00*	*0.00*	*0.00*	*0.00*	1.70	3.50	3.70	3.50	–
Cyprus (%)	41.10	32.50	33.00	31.30	31.20	30.80	30.60	28.50	28.50	27.70	11.20
Egypt (%)	*0.10*	*0.10*	*0.10*	*0.10*	*0.80*	*0.50*	*0.60*	*0.60*	1.30	2.00	*0.00*
France (%)	1.00	*0.80*	*0.70*	*0.70*	*0.70*	*0.30*	*0.20*	*0.20*	*0.10*	*0.10*	*0.40*
Germany (%)	1.90	3.10	2.50	2.70	2.90	2.00	1.60	1.50	1.30	1.20	2.40
Hong Kong (%)	*0.60*	*0.70*	*0.80*	1.00	*0.90*	*0.60*	1.10	1.20	1.30	1.50	–
Jersey (%)	*0.90*	*1.40*	*1.30*	*1.20*	*0.00*	*0.70*	*0.50*	*0.80*	1.20	1.20	–
Liberia (%)	3.20	2.50	2.30	2.10	*0.00*	1.30	*0.00*	*0.00*	*0.00*	*0.00*	–
Luxembourg (%)	5.00	10.70	10.10	9.20	5.70	3.60	2.40	3.80	*0.40*	*0.50*	*−0.60*
FYROM (%)	2.00	2.30	2.90	3.70	*0.00*	2.20	1.80	1.60	1.20	1.20	1.10
Netherlands (%)	1.50	1.90	1.90	1.60	1.10	1.60	3.10	8.60	14.90	7.70	*−7.00*
Poland (%)	*0.30*	*0.40*	*0.30*	*0.30*	*0.40*	*0.30*	*0.20*	*−0.30*	*0.20*	*0.20*	35.50
Romania (%)	8.30	8.80	12.00	11.50	17.70	14.40	17.10	12.10	11.30	11.80	*−1.70*
Serbia (%)	2.60	2.90	3.60	3.70	–	7.80	7.10	6.50	6.30	6.60	*0.00*
Spain (%)	*0.70*	1.50	1.70	1.80	1.20	*0.80*	*0.60*	*0.70*	*0.60*	*0.60*	1.20
Turkey (%)	*0.20*	*0.20*	*0.50*	*0.70*	*0.50*	13.20	16.50	12.50	13.70	14.10	*−0.40*
Ukraine (%)	*0.30*	*0.30*	*0.30*	*0.20*	*0.00*	*0.10*	*0.50*	1.00	*0.90*	1.60	–
United Kingdom (%)	2.90	4.30	4.90	4.20	*0.80*	*0.10*	*−1.50*	*0.50*	*−2.90*	*−1.10*	48.40

(continued)

Table 1 (continued)

	2001	2002	2003	2004	2005	2006	2007	2008	2009	2010	2011
United States (%)	13.60	12.00	9.40	8.10	9.00	6.30	4.90	3.60	4.40	6.60	4.90
Virgin Islands (British) (%)	*0.00*	*0.00*	*0.00*	*0.00*	*0.00*	*0.00*	*0.00*	2.50	1.00	1.60	–
Sum of outward FDI in key hosts (%)	**91.50**	**92.00**	**96.80**	**91.90**	**77.30**	**92.20**	**95.90**	**94.70**	**97.60**	**97.10**	**113.00**
Outward FDI (€ billion)	7.97	8.75	9.84	10.07	11.37	17.02	23.09	26.92	29.76	32	1.29

Notes:
(1) The figures for 2001–2010 represent outward FDI stock, while the figures for 2011 represent net outward FDI flows
(2) The figures for 2001–2010 are the authors' calculations based on OECD data (http://stats.oecd.org/). A key host accumulates 1 % or more of Greece's outward FDI stock. Figures less than 1 % are in *italics*
(3) The figures for 2011 are the authors' calculations based on Bank of Greece data (http://www.bankofgreece.gr/BoGDocuments/FDI_WEB1_K_ANA_ΧΩΡΑ.XLS). A key host accumulates 1 % or more of Greece's net outward FDI flows. Figures less than 1 % are in *italics*
(4) Bold values are the sums of outward FDI accumulated by key hosts (i.e, values in italics are not included)

FDI growth and the gradual rise of FDI from Greece into SEE. The rise of Greek MNEs as major corporate players in SEE has also been influenced by their search for new markets, acquisition of strategic resources, the host countries' low labour costs, geographical and cultural proximity, and the absence of decisive western investment. Policy developments, such as the Greek Balkan policy and the upgrading of the Athens Stock Exchange, have further played an important role in promoting Greece's position as a key investor in SEE. However, the liquidity constraints imposed on Greek MNEs in the wake of the sovereign debt crisis have threatened their leading role in SEE.[5] The foregoing discussion is supported by the figures presented in Table 1. This Table shows that Greece's outward FDI stock increased from €7.97 billion in 2001 to €32 billion in 2010, with over two-thirds (67.2 %) of this amount directed towards SEE in 2010.[6] Moreover, the top three key hosts in 2010 were countries in SEE, namely Cyprus, Turkey, and Romania, which together comprised more than 50 % of Greece's outward FDI stock.[7]

With regard to industry allocation, Table 2 indicates that the majority (80–90 %) of Greece's outward FDI over the past decade has been targeted towards services, notably financial intermediation, which comprised 71.7 % of outward FDI in 2010, and post and telecommunications, which accounted for over 20 % during the early to mid-2000s but decreased to 9.6 % in 2010. Even though the overseas expansion of Greek MNEs in the post and telecommunications sector dates back to the 1990s (see UNCTAD, 2001, 32), outward FDI in that industry in the 2000s never reached the magnitude of financial intermediation, which comprises Greece's commercial banks. Despite the fact that these commercial banks operate in a relatively small and increasingly saturated domestic market, they have expanded rapidly into SEE over the past decade by acquiring existing enterprises and establishing new branches. Indeed, despite stiff competition from much larger European banks, they enjoy considerable market shares in SEE on the back of this expansion strategy (see UNCTAD, 2010, 54).

As suggested from the foregoing, MNEs from Greece typically expand their overseas activities in relatively small, open, developing, and emerging markets, and this expansion is generally encouraged by their geographical and cultural proximity and the absence of decisive western interest. The benefits of this expansion approach are (a) turnover growth, which is realised through access to new and

---

[5] The leading role of Greek MNEs in SEE is put forward by Bitzenis and Vlachos (2011), who indicate that Greece accounts for a considerable share of the inward FDI stocks of several countries in SEE.

[6] See Eurostat database theme 'EU direct investment positions, breakdown by country and economic activity'. http://epp.eurostat.ec.europa.eu/portal/page/portal/statistics/search_database (accessed 20 August 2012).

[7] Table 1 indicates that a considerable sum of net outward FDI flows in 2011 was destined to Poland and the UK. While Poland's recent FDI attractiveness is indicated by its very high global rankings according to FDI Intelligence (see http://en.poland.gov.pl/FDI,Intelligence,highly,of,Polish,investment,capacity,13463.html, accessed 20 August 2012), the UK has been regarded by Greek direct investors as an alternative to the sovereign debt crisis.

Table 2 Greece's outward FDI by industry (percentage of total)

	2001	2002	2003	2004	2005	2006	2007	2008	2009	2010	2011
Manufacturing (%)	***15.70***	***15.80***	***14.70***	***16.70***	***17.90***	***12.80***	***10.10***	***8.30***	***8.40***	***10.90***	***−6.90***
Food products (%)	1.50	2.20	2.10	2.10	2.20	1.70	1.40	2.50	2.30	1.90	−10.50
Chemical products (%)	1.30	0.70	0.80	0.60	0.60	0.10	0.10	0.10	0.10	0.00	0.10
Metal products (%)	2.40	3.80	3.90	5.30	4.90	3.60	2.30	2.10	1.90	1.90	2.20
Total services (%)	***83.20***	***82.20***	***83.40***	***81.40***	***80.80***	***86.20***	***89.20***	***91.80***	***91.10***	***88.50***	***102.00***
Trade and repairs (%)	2.80	3.00	5.00	5.40	6.60	6.50	5.70	5.60	5.40	4.90	10.80
Water transport (%)	3.20	2.50	2.30	2.20	0.80	1.30	0.00	0.00	0.00	0.00	0.50
Post and telecommunications (%)	20.30	17.50	23.70	22.30	24.00	19.10	19.20	11.20	9.70	9.60	6.50
Financial intermediation (%)	55.70	58.30	51.60	50.80	48.10	58.40	63.30	73.40	74.50	71.70	80.60
Sum of outward FDI in key industries (%)	**98.90**	**98.10**	**98.00**	**98.10**	**98.70**	**99.00**	**99.30**	**100.10**	**99.50**	**99.40**	**95.10**

Notes:
(1) The figures for 2001–2010 represent outward FDI stock, while the figures for 2011 represent net outward FDI flows
(2) The figures for 2001–2010 are the authors' calculations based on OECD Statistics data (http://stats.oecd.org/)
(3) The figures for 2011 are authors' calculation based on Bank of Greece data (http://www.bankofgreece.gr/BoGDocuments/FDI_WEB1_K_ANA_ΚΛΑΔΟ.XLS)
(4) Bold italics are sum categories of rows beneath them, i.e, "manufacturing" include food, chemical and metal products. Bold values are sum of bold italics.

growing markets, (b) diversification, which is regarded as highly important during periods of economic turmoil, and (c) the generation of ownership advantages through internationalisation.[8]

3 Can Greek MNEs Contribute in Greece's Effort to Exit the Crisis?

This section assesses whether Greek MNEs can assist in Greece's effort to reignite the engine of economic growth through the international operations described in the previous section. The first subsection discusses the theoretical context on which the prospective benefits of outward FDI to the home country are rooted, while the second subsection describes the potential for these benefits to be realised.

3.1 Outward FDI and the Home Country's Economic Welfare

FDI generates both costs and benefits to the home country (see Bitzenis & Vlachos, 2012). In addition to tax losses, the disadvantages to the home country concern the balance of payments and level of employment. The balance of payments is negatively affected by the capital outflows required to finance FDI, and the current account suffers when FDI is a substitute for direct exports, or aims to supply the home market with imports. Moreover, employment levels decline in the home country when FDI replaces exports. However, the capital account is credited from inward FDI by the repatriation of profits and the current account is credited if the affiliate imports from the parent enterprise. These imports also have positive externalities on employment levels. Finally, exposure to foreign markets generates further skills and knowledge development (i.e. ownership advantages).

However, the critical question regards the degree to which the international activities of Greek MNEs can assist Greece to recover economic growth and exit the crisis. The answer to this query lies within the economic interests of nation states (and their subsequent fulfilment) in becoming home countries to MNEs.

While the 'eclectic paradigm' (see Dunning, 2001) specifies the conditions that have to be met for FDI to take place, namely the possession of ownership advantage (s) by the MNE, possession of location advantage(s) by the host country, and internalisation advantage(s) as a result of successful cross-border investment, the role of the home country is rather determined by the 'distance premium penalty', which constitutes a barrier to international trade and FDI (Hirsch, 2005, 2012). The distance premium penalty is defined as the sum of the costs incurred in the process

[8] A number of reports for several industries about the motives for and barriers to internationalisation—undertaken by the Federation of Industries of Northern Greece in 2008 (titles in Greek are available online at: http://www.sbbe.gr/m2/m2_3.asp, accessed 20 August 2012)—indicate that Greek enterprises with internationalised activities are more competitive and have a competitive advantage over Greek enterprises that do not engage in international business.

of overcoming the negative effects of multiple legal, cultural, financial, and institutional factors when engaging in value-adding cross-border activities.[9] These value-adding activities related to the home country are those resulting from senior management (i.e. strategy formulation) and thus they require higher-quality skills compared with those related to host countries (which do not involve decision making). Consequently, being a home country to MNEs entails positive externalities on economic welfare.

Hirsch (2012) argues that MNEs lower the barriers that separate countries from foreign sources of supply and international markets, thereby enabling home countries to increase the benefits they derive from the international division of labour and exploit economies of scale and ownership advantages. As a result, global expansion through cross-border value-adding activities is likely to compensate for the tax loss and diminution of sovereignty implied by outward FDI.

3.2 Greek MNEs Can Encourage Competitiveness and Growth

As mentioned in the previous subsection, outward FDI is not always detrimental to the employment level and economic growth of the home country. Several studies have investigated how FDI influences a home country's economic development and have indicated that under specific circumstances outward FDI does not cause negative externalities due to the relocation process, namely where outward FDI replaces domestic employment through the replacement of the home country's production and exports. A survey by Kokko (2006) on the effects of outward FDI on the developed home countries of MNEs concludes that although outward FDI is beneficial to the investing enterprise, the effects on the home country vary depending on the characteristics of the investment project and the business environment in the home and host countries. The same survey also indicates that negative externalities on the employment level of the home country primarily occur because of a shift in production structure, whereby labour-intensive activities are outsourced to host countries that have lower wage levels, while more advanced operations are kept at home.[10]

Evidence of the positive relationship between outward FDI and domestic output and between outward FDI and total factor productivity has been put forward by recent studies. The simplistic idea that outward FDI represents a diversion of domestic economic activity is contradicted by the observation that increased output and productivity are both a consequence and a cause of increased outward FDI

[9] The reader should refer to the value chain framework for an overview of both primary and supporting value-adding activities (see Porter, 1985, 11–15).

[10] In line with the allocation of labour-intensive activities to low-wage countries, the larger volumes of employment in affiliates located in less developed countries are associated with lower labour intensity at home (Mariotti, Mutinelli, & Piscitello, 2003).

(Herzer, 2012).[11] Recent studies have also indicated that employment growth in local areas that invest abroad is stronger compared with the industry average, especially in capital-intensive sectors. Further, it has been shown that the amount of outward FDI does not negatively affect the employment levels of local enterprises that do not engage in international business (see Federico & Minerva, 2008).

Understanding the conditions that shape the externalities of the international expansion of MNEs to their home countries requires analysing the form and direction of Greece's outward FDI. Since no empirical studies have thus far examined how the international activities of Greek MNEs influence Greece, an analysis of the intrinsic characteristics of (a) the Greek expansion into SEE, (b) the role of services FDI (primarily financial intermediation), and (c) the competitiveness gains of MNEs over domestic rivals that do not internationalise their activities will indicate the kinds of externalities caused by Greece's outward FDI.

Horizontal MNEs seek to exploit their existing advantages by replicating most of their activities abroad. Greek horizontal FDI is represented by the intention of Greek financial intermediaries to reap the benefits of foreign market opportunities and economies of scale. Since the majority of Greece's outward FDI is in the non-tradable sector (services), there cannot be a substitution between foreign and home employment, as there is no relocation process. In addition, this type of substitution cannot occur because the majority of Greece's outward FDI is directed towards less developed economies.[12] This type of substitution thus occurs between countries that have comparable factor endowments. In other words, low-wage host countries are better employment substitutes for one another than for a higher-income home country (see Slaughter, 2000; Braconier & Ekholm, 2001).

Furthermore, the complementary effect from a foreign affiliate's activities expands the activities of the parent enterprise and generates positive externalities on the employment levels of the home country. An expansion of the value chain requires an expansion of support activities. For example, the expansion of Greek financial intermediaries abroad requires the expansion of strategic decision-making units of the parent enterprise. Moreover, with regard to Greece's services-oriented outward FDI, investing in a low-cost host country can increase competitiveness, generate economies of scale, and improve cost effectiveness, which in turn lead to increased turnover and a competitive advantage over Greek enterprises that do not engage in international business. As a result, the specificities of the Greek case seem to generate an outcome where scale effects dominate substitution effects, thus leading to an increase in domestic employment following foreign expansion.

Finally, the importance of outward FDI during the ongoing sovereign debt crisis was highlighted by Moon, Cheng, Kim, and Kim (2011), who assert that such

[11] In another relatively recent study, the unidirectional relationship between GDP and outward FDI was shown to be true only in the long run (Lee, 2010).

[12] A certain amount of Greece's outward FDI in Cyprus is actually transferred to the Balkans (Bitzenis & Vlachos, 2011).

investment stabilises a country's economic growth during periods of financial crisis. These authors also imply that the rising levels of outward FDI in Greece have still not managed to place the country back on the growth track, because countries that had higher levels of FDI prior to the crisis have experienced milder recessions and more gradual recoveries.

Conclusion

The difficulty of the Greek economy exiting recession amidst the sovereign debt crisis—which in turn has reduced public investment expenditure—highlights the importance of FDI flows. Further, despite the straightforward significance of inward FDI, the positive externalities of the international operations of Greek MNEs should not be overlooked. No study has thus far empirically examined the externalities caused by the overseas expansion of Greek MNEs, and while the present article does not provide empirical findings, it does describe the theoretical background behind the positive externalities to home countries based on the characteristics of Greece's outward FDI.

Although Greece's outward FDI stock in 2010 is very low among eurozone members, Greek MNEs have directed substantial amounts of outward FDI towards SEE and have managed to accumulate considerable market shares in that region. The majority of Greece's outward FDI comprises services and it is directed to countries that have lower labour costs, a combination of characteristics that generates scale effects that dominate substitution effects. As a result, it can be assumed that the expansion of Greek MNEs increases their competitiveness, generates economies of scale, and improves cost effectiveness, which in turn leads to increased turnover and competitive advantage over Greek enterprises that do not engage in international business. These positive externalities point towards the significance of outward FDI in the efforts of the Greek economy to reignite the engine of economic growth.

The reader must keep in mind that these conclusions are based on the suppositions constructed according to the existing theoretical framework that categorises the characteristics of Greece's outward FDI. Although the authors do not expect these suppositions to be altered by future empirical research, further study is necessary in order to generate solid conclusions.

References

Baldwin, R., DiNino, V., Fontagne, L., De Santis, R. A., & Taglioni, D. (2008). *Study on the impact of the euro on trade and foreign direct investment* (European Economy Economic Papers, 321). Brussels: European Commission, Directorate-General for Economic and Financial Affairs.

Bitzenis, A., & Vlachos, V. A. (2011). *Columbia FDI profiles: Outward FDI from Greece and its policy context*. New York: Vale Columbia Center on Sustainable International Investment. http://www.vcc.columbia.edu/files/vale/documents/Greece_OFDI_16_Jan_12.pdf. Accessed 20 Aug 2012.

Bitzenis, A., & Vlachos, V. A. (2012). The impact of foreign direct investment. In A. Bitzenis, V. A. Vlachos, & P. Papadimitriou (Eds.), *Mergers and acquisitions as the pillar of foreign direct investment* (pp. 67–80). New York: Palgrave Macmillan.

Braconier, H., & Ekholm, K. (2001). *Foreign direct investment in central and eastern Europe: Employment effects in the EU* (CEPR Working Paper, 3052). London: Centre for Economic Policy Research.

Dunning, J. H. (2001). The eclectic (OLI) paradigm of international production: Past, present and future. *International Journal of the Economics of Business, 8*(2), 173–190.

Federico, S., & Minerva, G. A. (2008). Outward FDI and local employment growth in Italy. *Review of World Economics, 114*(2), 295–324.

Herzer, D. (2012). Outward FDI, total factor productivity and domestic output: Evidence from Germany. *International Economic Journal, 26*(1), 155–174.

Hirsch, S. (2005). Internationalization, distance barriers and home country size: Lessons from the world investment report 2005. *Academy of International Business (AIB) Insights, 5*(4), 8–12.

Hirsch, S. (2012). Nation states and nationality of MNEs. In *Columbia FDI Perspectives* (p. 57). New York: Vale Columbia Center on Sustainable International Investment. http://www.vcc.columbia.edu/content/nation-states-and-nationality-mnes. Accessed 20 Aug 2012.

Katsimi, M., & Moutos, T. (2010). EMU and the Greek crisis: The political-economy perspective. *European Journal of Political Economy, 26*(4), 568–576.

Kokko, A. (2006). *The home country effects of FDI in developed countries* (EIJS Working Paper Series, 225). Stockholm: European Institute of Japanese Studies.

Lee, C. G. (2010). Outward foreign direct investment and economic growth: Evidence from Japan. *Global Economic Review, 39*(3), 317–326.

Mariotti, S., Mutinelli, M., & Piscitello, L. (2003). Home country employment and foreign direct investment: Evidence from the Italian case. *Cambridge Journal of Economics, 27*(3), 419–431.

Moon, H. C., Cheng, J. L. C., Kim, M. Y., & Kim, J. U. (2011). FDI, economic decline and recovery: Lessons from the Asian financial crisis. *Multinational Business Review, 19*(2), 120–132.

OECD. (2007). *OECD economic surveys: Greece 2007*. Paris: Organization for Economic Cooperation and Development.

Porter, M. E. (1985). *Competitive advantage*. New York: Free.

Schneider, F., Buehn, A., & Montenegro, C. (2010). *Shadow economies all over the world: New estimates for 162 countries from 1999 to 2007* (p. 5356). Washington: The World Bank, Policy Research Working Papers Series.

Slaughter, M. (2000). Production transfer within multinational enterprises and American wages. *Journal of International Economics, 50*(2), 449–472.

UNCTAD. (2001). *World investment report 2001: Promoting linkages*. New York: United Nations, United Nations Conference on Trade and Development.

UNCTAD. (2010). *World investment report 2010: Investing in a low-carbon economy*. New York: United Nations, United Nations Conference on Trade and Development.

About the Authors

Andreas Antoniades teaches European and international political economy at the Panteion University (Athens) and the University of Sussex and is the Head of the Athens Centre for International Political Economy at the Institute of International Relations in Athens (IDIS). He has taught at the University of Essex and The London School of Economics and has been the Director of the Centre for Global Political Economy at Sussex. His publications include the monograph, *Producing Globalisation* (Manchester University Press, 2010) and articles in the *Cambridge Review of International Affairs, The British Journal of Politics and International Relations, Review of International Political Economy*, and *Global Society*.

Aristidis P. Bitzenis is an associate professor at the Department of International and European Studies, University of Macedonia, Thessaloniki (Greece). His main research field includes FDI, entrepreneurship, privatisation, globalisation, European business environment, and corporate restructuring in South East Europe. He has published extensively and participated in various conferences in his research field. His research record and forthcoming publications are 7 books (4 of them are in the Greek language), 16 book chapters, 15 entries in encyclopaedias, 36 refereed journal articles, 9 refereed papers in conference proceedings, and participation in 15 research grants. His latest book is an edited volume titled *Mergers and Acquisitions as the Pillar of Foreign Direct Investment*, published by Palgrave Macmillan in August 2012. He has been supervising graduate and PhD students on issues around international business, transition economics, European Union, and FDI.

George Galanos is lecturer in international economic relations at the Department of International Economic Relations and Development of the Democritus University of Thrace. He holds a PhD in international economics and tourism competitiveness from the University of Piraeus, an MBA in tourism management and a BSc degree in economics. During 2002–2009, he worked as a researcher and head of the European Programmes Department, at the Research Centre of the Evaluation of Development Policies and Programmes of the University of Thessaly. He has also acted as a consultant to Greek enterprises. He has published in academic journals and books, such as the *World Economy*, *Intereconomics*, *International Research Journal of Finance and Economics*, *Research Journal of International Studies*, and

P. Sklias and N. Tzifakis (eds.), *Greece's Horizons*, The Konstantinos Karamanlis Institute for Democracy Series on European and International Affairs,
DOI 10.1007/978-3-642-34534-0,

International Bulletin of Business Administration and has participated in international conferences.

Evangelia Georgitsoyanni is associate professor in history of art and civilization at the Department of Home Economics and Ecology of the Harokopio University, Athens. She is also the vice-rector of Academic Affairs and Personnel at the same university. She has a bachelor's degree in history and archaeology from the National and Kapodistrian University of Athens and a master's degree (DEA) and a PhD (Doctorat de Nouveau Regime) from the Faculty of History of the University of Paris I (Panthéon-Sorbonne). She has also been vice-president of the General Archives of the Greek State (2007–2010).

Periklis Gogas is assistant professor of economic analysis and international economics at the Democritus University of Thrace and was recently a Visiting Scholar at the Ross School of Business of the University of Michigan. He is an EABCN fellow, serves on the editorial board of several journals, and edits the journal *Economics and Finance Notes*. He publishes in journals such as the *Journal of Banking and Finance*, *Open Economies Review*, and the *Journal of Economics and Finance*. He received his PhD from the University of Calgary, his master's degree from the University of Saskatchewan, and his bachelor's degree from the University of Macedonia. His research interests include macroeconomics, financial economics, chaotic and non-linear dynamics, and machine learning applied to macroeconomics and finance. He has also served as the financial director of a large Greek multinational company.

Gregory Grigoropoulos is professor of ship and marine hydrodynamics at the National Technical University of Athens (NTUA) since 2007. He qualified as naval architect and marine engineer (1981), as mechanical engineer (1986), and as doctor of naval architecture and marine engineering (1989), all from NTUA. He is fluent in English and German. After serving Kavala Shipyards Ltd as Managing Director (1988–1991), he joined NTUA as academic staff and manager of the experimental facility in 1992. He specialises in ship hydrodynamics, experimental techniques, computer-aided ship design, with a focus on high-speed fishing and sailing vessels, and development of decision support systems for shipping. He is a fellow of SNAME and member of many professional societies and international committees. He is the author of 60 publications, 220 technical reports, and 7 lecture notes and he has participated in 50 research projects.

Konstantinos J. Hazakis is assistant professor at Democritus University of Thrace, (Greece), where he teaches economic development and international political economy. He received his BSc from University of Athens, his MSc from London School of Economics, and his PhD from Panteion University of Athens (with distinction). His research interests include FDI and privatisation in transition economies, international economic development, and international and European economic policy co-ordination.

Costas Kiparissides is professor and chairman of Chemical Engineering Department at Aristotle University of Thessaloniki. In 1978, he received his PhD from McMaster University (Canada). During 1978–1983, he taught as an assistant and associate professor at the University of Alberta (Canada). He had also been a visiting professor of University of Newcastle (UK) and Queen's University (Canada). During 2001–2006, he was director of Chemical Process Engineering Research Institute (CPERI) at CERTH and from 2005 to 2010, director of the Centre for Research & Technology Hellas (CERTH). He is member of the Expert Advisory Group (EAG) of the NMP programme, member of the Mirror Group of the European Technology Platform for Sustainable Chemistry, member of the Ad-hoc Advisory Group on Industrial Nanotechnologies, vice-chair of the working group on Nanopharmaceutics of the European Nanomedicine Technology Platform, etc. He has supervised more than 50 PhD theses and 160 diploma theses and has presented more than 300 invited seminars and lectures at international scientific conferences, industrial research centres, institutes, and universities in Europe and North America. In addition, he has published more than 200 scientific papers in refereed journals, 350 conference papers, and 6 books.

Angelos Kotios is professor of international and European economic and development relations at the University of Piraeus, where he has been working since 2009. During 1995–2008, he was professor at the University of Thessaly. He received a diploma in economics from the University of Thessaloniki in 1979 and his PhD in Economics from the University of Tübingen (Germany) in 1986. From 1987 to 1990, he worked at the University of Tübingen as research fellow. From 1991 to 1993, he was a special adviser at the Greek Ministry of Foreign Affairs. His research interests are economic crisis, international trade policy, international monetary policy, European integration, and development policy. He is the author of many books and papers on international and European economy.

Stella Ladi is a lecturer of Europeanisation and Public Policy at Panteion University. She previously worked as a lecturer at the University of Sheffield and the University of Exeter. She has also been a research fellow at the Barcelona Institute of International Studies (IBEI). She has acted as a public policy expert at the Ministry of the Interior and the Ministry of the Aegean, Greece. In July 2002, she completed her doctoral thesis at the University of York. Her research interests include public policy and public administration reforms, Europeanisation, and the role of experts in public policy. Some of her latest publications are *Public Policy Analysis* (with V. Dalakou, Athens: Papazisis, 2010, in Greek); Policy Change and Soft Europeanization: The Transfer of the Ombudsman Institution to Greece, Cyprus, and Malta (*Public Administration*, 89:4, 2011); and Rival Hypotheses of Europeanization: Comparing the Roles of the EU and BSEC in Good Governance Reforms (in Th. Exadaktylos and C. Radaelli, Eds, *Research Design in European Studies*, Palgrave, 2012).

Alexandra Lappa is a PhD candidate at Harokopio University in the field of protection of cultural heritage. She has a bachelor's degree in archaeology and history of art from the National and Kapodistrian University of Athens and a master's degree in protection of monuments from the National Technical University of Athens. She has worked at the Hellenic Ministry of Culture and Tourism and at Harokopio University (Department of Home Economics and Ecology), assisting in the preparation of educational material for undergraduate and master's programmes. She has participated in seminars and conferences related to the protection of monuments, cultural heritage management, and environmental archaeology.

Kostas A. Lavdas is professor of European Politics and Head of the Department of Political Science at the University of Crete. Born in Athens in 1964, he was educated in Greece, the UK (LSE, University of Manchester), and the USA (MIT). He is the author of *The Europeanization of Greece: Interest Politics and the Crises of Integration* (London: Macmillan, 1997), *Politics, Subsidies and Competition: The New Politics of State Intervention in the European Union* (with M. Mendrinou, Cheltenham: Edward Elgar, 1999), *A Republic of Europeans: Civic Potential in a Liberal Milieu* (with D. Chryssochoou, Cheltenham: Edward Elgar, 2011) and has numerous contributions in edited volumes and international journals (including the *European Journal of Political Research, West European Politics, Journal of Political and Military Sociology,* and *Politics*).

Panagiotis Liargovas received his BA degree from the University of Athens and his MA and PhD from Clark University, USA. He has been a Fulbright Scholar, a Bakalas Foundation Scholar, a Teaching Assistant Scholar, and a European Commission trainee, Brussels. He has taught in many universities including Clark University, Bologna University, the Universities of Athens, Patras, and Crete, and the Athens University of Economics and Business. He is presently professor at the Department of Economics of the University of Peloponnese. He is also the chair of the department and the director of two post-graduate programmes, economic analysis, and public management. He has published various articles in areas such as open economy macroeconomics and European economics.

Maria M. Mendrinou is associate professor of European Political Economy and European Integration at the University of Piraeus. She holds degrees from the University of Athens and Brandeis University (USA) and a PhD in Government from the University of Manchester (UK). She has participated in international conferences in Europe and the USA and in numerous research projects. She has published extensively in Greek and English. Her English publications include the book *Politics, Subsidies and Competition: The New Politics of State Intervention in the European Union* (with K. Lavdas, Cheltenham: Edward Elgar, 1999), and articles in international journals such as the *European Journal of Political Research* and the *Journal of European Public Policy*. She also has numerous contributions in edited volumes.

John C. Mourmouris is professor of management and transportation economics at the Democritus University of Thrace. During 1983–1987, he worked as a Researcher at the INRETS (National Institute of Transportation Research and

Security) of France and at the LAMSADE (Laboratory of Systems analysis and Decision Making) of the University of Paris-Dauphine. He has held several top managerial positions, that of vice president, Citibank Shipping Bank S.A. of the Citicorp Group, and of CEO, Hellenic Railways Organisation S.A. He has been involved in several projects and consultancies in the following areas of interest: investment and development strategy, privatisation, transportation restructuring, location and evaluation of waste disposal facilities, operations research, and multi-criteria decision making.

Evangelia Mylona was born in Kiato, Corinth. She has obtained a bachelor's degree from the Department of Economics of the University of Piraeus in 2007 and a bachelor's degree from the Department of Home Economics and Ecology of Harokopio University in 2012. During her studies, she has attended several seminars and conferences related to sustainable development, corporate governance, health education, nutrition, and quality of life.

Pyrros Papadimitriou is a lawyer, an economist, and associate professor in international economic relations at the University of Peloponnese. He holds a degree in political science and public administration from the University of Athens (1985), a law degree from Athens Law School (1989), a post-graduate diploma in economics from Sussex University (1987), and a master's degree in economics (1988) and a PhD in economics (1992), both from Kent University. In the past, he worked in managerial positions in the Foundation for Economic and Industrial Research in Athens (1994–1995), in the ALPHA Bank (1995–1996), in ICAP S.A. (1999–2000), and in the HEADWAY Economic Consultants Ltd. In 2007, as president and CEO of Olympic Airlines S.A. and Olympic Airways–Services S.A., he undertook the privatisation of Greece's flag carrier, the Olympic Group of Companies. He has led several major restructuring projects of private and public companies in Greece and he is involved as an expert in international projects.

Theophilos Papadimitriou holds a degree in mathematics from the Aristotle University of Thessaloniki, Greece, the DEAARAVIS (Automatique, Robotique, Algorithmique, Vision, Image, and Signale) degree from the University of Nice-Sophia Antipolis, France, and the PhD degree in electrical engineering from the Aristotle University of Thessaloniki. In 2001, he joined the Department of International Economic Relations and Development of the Democritus University of Thrace, Komotini, Greece, where he served as a lecturer (2002–2008) and is presently an assistant professor. He has served as a reviewer for various publications and as a scientific committee member for many conferences and workshops. His current research interests include blind source separation, data analysis, and machine learning and their application on macroeconomic and financial data series. He is an IEEE member.

Manos G. Papazoglou is lecturer in political systems at the Department of Politics and International Relations of the University of the Peloponnese. He studied political science at the University of Athens, received an MA degree in political philosophy from the University of York, and completed his PhD on *Citizenship and*

Democratic Legitimacy in the European Union: Euro-Republicanism and the Concept of Responsive Citizenship at the University of Essex. He has taught at the University of London (Goldsmiths College), the London Metropolitan University, the University of Essex, and Athens University of Economics and Business (MBA International). His main research interests include political theory, Greek politics, and European integration. He has published in international academic journals and has edited volumes on the EU and higher education. He is the author of the monographs *Modern Political Leadership: Crisis and New Foundations of Governance* (Athens, 2012); *The Challenges of Europeanization and Deliberation in the Greek Political System: Euro-Republicanism and the Democratic Management of Consent and Contestation* (Athens, 2009).

Spyridon Repousis received his BA degree in economics from Athens University of Economics and Business in 1994, his MSc degree in banking and finance from University of Stirling, Scotland, UK, in 1995, and his PhD in economics from University of Peloponnese in 2012. He has taught at the Technological Educational Institute of Patras and works in a private bank. He is a certified fraud examiner and long-life adult trainee and has written books about banking and finance in Greek. He has contributed to books in the English language as well. He has written scientific articles published in English journals, in areas such as banking, finance, fraud, and money laundering and has participated in two international conferences.

Spyridon Roukanas is an elected lecturer at the Department of International and European Studies of the University of Piraeus. He graduated (2003) from the Department of International Economic Relations and Development of Democritus University of Thrace. He was awarded his MA in International Political Economy (2004) from the University of Leeds (UK). He received his PhD (2008) from the Democritus University of Thrace. The title of his PhD thesis is 'Economic Theory and Development under the prism of International Political Economy'. He has taught at the Department of International Economic Relations and Development (2008–2010) and at the Department of Financial and Management Engineering (2008–2012) of University of the Aegean. His main research interests are in international political economy, international economic relations, and international economic development.

Anna Saiti is an associate professor at the Department of Home Economics and Ecology in Harokopio University, Athens, Greece. She received her bachelor's degree in organization and business administration from the University of Piraeus, Athens, Greece, her MA in banking and finance from the University of North Wales, UK, and her PhD in administration and economics of education from the University of Hull, UK. Her research interests focus on management and economics of education. She has participated in several international conferences and has published several articles on management and the economics of education in international journals.

Eleni Sardianou is a lecturer of environmental economics at the Department of Home Economics and Ecology of Harokopio University, Athens. She is also a research assistant at the Laboratory of Social and Economic Analysis for Family and Consumer Science, at the same department. She has a master's degree with honours in sustainable development and consumer behaviour and a PhD in environmental economics from Harokopio University. Her research emphasises the impact of consumer behaviour on the environmental assets of Greece. Her research fields include econometrics and microeconomic theory.

Dimitrios Tsamboulas is professor at the Department of Transportation Planning and Engineering, Faculty of Civil Engineering, at the National Technical University of Athens (NTUA). He has more than 39 years of professional experience and has been involved in more than 200 research and consultancy projects. He is also the co-author of three books. He has contributed articles in 16 international books in the field of transport and more than 250 papers in scientific journals and conferences, with more than 500 citations. He has wide knowledge of all modes of transport (road, air, rail, maritime and, intermodal), for both passenger and freight. In addition, he has carried out extensive work on the development of Euro-Asian transport linkages, a UNECE initiative, and on the development of transport in the Mediterranean region through several EC financed projects.

Maria Tsampra is lecturer in the University of Western Greece and teaching associate in the Hellenic Open University. She was previously lecturing in the University of the Aegean. She has a PhD degree in geography from Kings' College, University of London. She has collaborated in research mainly with the Department of Economic and Regional Development and the Regional Development Institute of Panteion University and the Foundation for Economic and Industrial Research, Athens. Her research focus is on issues of: local/regional development and competitiveness, entrepreneurship, clusters and niche-production in rural regions, and the economic geography of innovation and technical change. Her work is published in international journals (*Regional Studies, Environment and Planning A*, etc.) and in books by Routledge, Edward Elgar, Academy of Athens, IOVE, etc.

Aristotle Tziampiris is associate professor of international relations at the Department of International and European Studies of the University of Piraeus and Director of the Centre for International and European Affairs at the University of Piraeus. Dr Tziampiris was visiting scholar at Columbia University (The Harriman Institute) during 2009. He is a former member of the Scientific Board of the Institute of Defence Analyses (IAA-Athens, Greece, 2004–2009) and IAA's Board of Directors (September 2005–June 2006). He is the author of *Faith and Reason of State: Lessons from Early Modern Europe and Cardinal Richelieu* (New York: Nova Science, 2009); *Kosovo's Endgame: Sovereignty and Stability in the Western Balkans* (Athens: IAA, 2006); *International Relations and the Macedonian Question* (Athens: ELIAMEP, 2003, in Greek); and *Greece, European Political Cooperation and the Macedonian Question* (Aldershot: Ashgate Press, 2000). Dr Tziampiris has also published a series of essays primarily on international relations and Greek foreign policy in the Balkans. He holds a PhD from the London School of Economics and Political Science and is a graduate of Middlebury College.

Vasileios A. Vlachos is a PhD candidate at the Department of International and European Studies of the University of Macedonia in Thessaloniki, Greece. His main research interests and publications focus on the association between direct investment, international transactions, and economic growth. He is also interested in the shadow economy and micro-issues of unemployment.

Index

P. Sklias and N. Tzifakis (eds.), *Greece's Horizons*, The Konstantinos Karamanlis Institute for Democracy Series on European and International Affairs,
DOI 10.1007/978-3-642-34534-0,

FSC
www.fsc.org
MIX
Papier aus verantwortungsvollen Quellen
Paper from responsible sources
FSC® C105338

If you have any concerns about our products,
you can contact us on
ProductSafety@springernature.com

In case Publisher is established outside the EU,
the EU authorized representative is:
Springer Nature Customer Service Center GmbH
Europaplatz 3, 69115 Heidelberg, Germany

Printed by Libri Plureos GmbH
in Hamburg, Germany